Contents

PENGUIN ACADEMICS

READINGS FOR TODAY

FIRST EDITION

Gary Goshgarian
Northeastern University

New York Boston San Francisco
London Toronto Sydney Tokyo Singapore Madrid
Mexico City Munich Paris Cape Town Hong Kong Montreal

Senior Sponsoring Editor: Virginia L. Blanford
Development Editor: Katharine Glynn
Senior Marketing Manager: Sandra McGuire
Production Manager: Stacey Kulig
Project Coordination, Text Design, and
Electronic Page Makeup: Pre-Press PMG
Senior Cover Designer Manager: Nancy Danahy
Cover Image: "Terra," Charles Heppner, 2007, 3" × 3" Watercolor and Ink on paper.
Photo Researcher: Jody Potter
Senior Manufacturing Buyer: Alfred C. Dorsey
Printer and Binder: Courier/Westford
Cover Printer: Coral Graphics Services

For more information about the Penguin Academics series, please contact us by mail at Longman Publishers, attn. Marketing Department, 51 Madison Avenue, 29th Floor, New York, NY 10010, or by e-mail at www.ablongman.com.

For permission to use copyrighted material, grateful acknowledgment is made to the copyright holders on pp. 367–372, which are hereby made part of this copyright page.

Library of Congress Cataloging-in-Publication Data

Readings for today / [edited by] Gary Goshgarian.— 1st ed.
p. cm.
Includes index.
ISBN 0-205-56856-4
1. College readers. 2. English language—Rhetoric—Problems, exercises, etc. 3. Report writing—Problems, exercises, etc. 4. Critical thinking—Problems, exercises, etc. I. Goshgarian, Gary.

PE1417.R425 2007
808'.0427—dc22 2007041366

Please visit us at www.ablongman.com

ISBN 13: 978-0-205-56856-7

ISBN 10: 0-205-56856-4

1 2 3 4 5 6 7 8 9 10—CRW—10 09 08 07

Douglas Rushkoff

Which One of These Sneakers Is Me? 65
"I was in one of those sports 'superstores' the other day, hoping to find a pair of trainers for myself. As I faced the giant wall of shoes, I noticed a young boy standing next to me, maybe 13 years old, in even greater awe of the towering selection of footwear. His jaw was dropped and his eyes were glazed over—a psycho-physical response to the overwhelming sensory data in a self-contained consumer environment."

James B. Twitchell

Lux Populi 71
"Call them yuppies, yippies, bobos, nobrows, or whatever, the consumers of the new luxury have a sense of entitlement that transcends social class, a conviction that the finest things are their birthright. Never mind that they may have been born into a family whose ancestral estate is a tract house in the suburbs, near the mall, not paid for, and whose family crest was downloaded from the Internet."

VIEWPONTS

William Lutz

With These Words, I Can Sell You Anything 77
"Advertisers use weasel words to appear to be making a claim for a product when in fact they are making no claim at all."

Charles A. O'Neill

The Language of Advertising 89
"At best, we view advertising as distracting. At worst, we view it as dangerous to our health and a pernicious threat to our social values."

CHAPTER 3 The American Family in Flux 102

Betty G. Farrell

Family: Idea, Institution, and Controversy 103
"Fundamental changes in the expectations, meanings, and practices defining American family life have characterized much of the twentieth century. Consequently, concern about the family has moved to the center of the political arena."

James Q. Wilson

The Decline of Marriage 112
"To explain the staggering increase in unmarried mothers, we must turn to culture. In this context, what I mean by culture is simply that being an unmarried mother and living on welfare has lost its stigma."

Stephanie Coontz

For Better, For Worse 119
"Although some people hope to turn back the tide by promoting traditional values, making divorce harder or outlawing gay marriage, they are having to confront a startling irony: The very factors that have made marriage more satisfying in modern times have also made it more optional."

rhetorical contents

Process Analysis

Explanation of How Something Operates

Comparison and Contrast

Explaining Similarities

Division and Classification

Sorting Things Out

Cause and Effect

Telling Why

preface

The purpose of any composition "reader" is to provide students with essays that inspire thought, stimulate class discussion, and serve as writing models. But a reader will fail to achieve any of these goals unless its essays fulfill one crucial task—they must interest the student.

Yes, many essay collections for college students contain fine prose pieces that exceed the scope and purpose of composition courses. Some writings are simply too advanced and require sophisticated literary and philosophical explication beyond the purview of most beginning writing students. Other pieces are historically important but fail to speak to today's college student. And then there are those essays with important subject matter but deadly prose.

There are several things that distinguish *Readings for Today* from other college composition anthologies. First is its emphasis on the contemporary. All of the selections in this book were chosen because they are about current experiences and issues to which today's college students can relate. And most were written within the last three years of the publication of this book. Second, the pieces are student-friendly. That is, they are interesting to read and accessible while being well-written and thought-provoking. These essays span a wide variety of cultural and social topics that we think will greatly appeal to students of composition. Thirdly, these essays that will stimulate classroom discussion, critical thinking, and writing. Finally, the book is perfect for one-semester courses, but it could also accompany a rhetoric text in longer courses—or simply provide a more focused set of readings for any composition course.

The nearly sixty selections in this collection have been organized around nine different thematic units representing a large range of topics that students can identify with—self-image, consumerism, the effects of television on viewers, global warming, racism, sexual politics, education, family, and immigration. Most importantly, the debates in each chapter capture the conflicts and paradoxes that make our culture unique. Ours is a society in constant conflict. We are a people who crave the modern, yet long for what's gone by. We are as much a society steeped in traditional values and identities as we are a people who redefine ourselves in response to trends and subcultures. With each chapter focusing on a theme of contemporary importance, students are encouraged to enter into the debates and develop their own points of view. Likewise, instructors are encouraged to connect the themes to current events and trends in popular culture, adding a dynamic dimension to their teaching approaches.

Similarly, the essays reflect a wide range of writing styles and genres, including academic essays (e.g., Betty G. Farrell), dialogues by noted columnists (e.g., Robert J. Samuelson, Ellen Goodman), debates from experienced journalists (Gregory Rodriguez, Niranjana Iyer and Tomás R. Jiménez), a press release (American Academy of Pediatrics), and heated arguments including one from former Vice President Al Gore. Students have a variety of models of good writing.

Toward that end, we have included rhetorical apparatus that has been fashioned to help students improve their writing and that reflects the latest and most effective rhetorical theories and practice. The Introduction contains strategies on critical thinking and critical writing—strategies that are based on the premise that effective writing grows out of effective thinking, and effective thinking grows out of thoughtful reading. Preceding each reading is a headnote that helps orient the student to the topic and the reading. The "Questions for Thinking and Writing" that follow each essay aid students in processing the text, encourage the flow of ideas, and promote class discussion. The writing assignments, likewise, encourage students to explore topics on their own and in collaboration with other students both inside and outside the classroom, with special emphasis on community-oriented writing. In "Viewpoints" articles, a feature appearing at the end of each chapter, authors explore different aspects of the same controversial issue. The intent here is to help students understand both that issues can have many sides, and that there are many ways to present opposing arguments effectively. There are also suggestions for further research and group work following these pieces. Finally, we have included visuals in every chapter—including ads, cartoons, graphs, charts and photos—to help students develop critical visual literacy skills.

Acknowledgments

Many people behind the scenes deserve much acknowledgment and gratitude. It would be impossible to thank all of them, but there are some for whose help I am particularly grateful. I would like to thank the people at Pearson Longman/Allyn & Bacon for supporting this project, in particular Lynn Huddon who first conceptualized the book and my editor Virginia Blanford and developmental editor Katharine Glynn who helped see it through. I'm also grateful to editorial assistant, Rebecca Gilpin, and production liaison, Katy Bastille. I would also like to thank Amy Trumbull for her help in securing permissions for the readings. Finally, I want to thank Kathryn Goodfellow for her invaluable assistance in compiling this volume. This book could not have been done without her.

Gary Goshgarian

Introduction

How to Read and Write Critically

What Is Critical Thinking?

Whenever you read a magazine article, newspaper editorial, or a piece of advertising and find yourself questioning the author's claims, you are exercising the basics of critical reading. You are looking beneath the surface of words and thinking about their meaning and significance. And, subconsciously, you are asking the authors some of the following questions:

- What did you mean by that?
- Can you back up that statement?
- How do you define that term?
- How did you draw that conclusion?
- Do all the experts agree?
- Is this evidence dated?
- What is your point?
- Why do I need to know this?
- Where did you get your data?

You are also making some internal statements:

- That is not true.
- You are contradicting yourself.
- I see your point, but I do not agree.

- That's a poor choice of words.
- You are jumping to conclusions.
- Good point. I never thought of that.
- That was nicely stated.
- This is an extreme view.

Whether conscious or unconscious, such responses indicate that you are thinking critically about what you read. You are weighing claims, asking for definitions, evaluating information, looking for proof, questioning assumptions, and making judgments. In short, you are processing another person's words, rather than just accepting them at face value.

Why Read Critically?

When you read critically, you think critically. Instead of blindly accepting what is written on a page, you begin to separate yourself from the text and decide for yourself what is or is not important, logical, or right. And you do so because you bring to your reading your own perspective, experience, education, and personal values, as well as your own powers of comprehension and analysis.

Critical reading is an active process of discovery. You discover an author's view on a subject, you enter into a dialogue with the author, you discover the strengths and weaknesses of the author's thesis or argument, and you decide if you agree or disagree with the author's views. The result is that you have a better understanding of the issue and the author. By questioning and analyzing what the author says with respect to other experiences or views on the issue, including your own, you actively enter into a dialogue or a debate and seek the truth on your own.

In reality, we understand truth and meaning through interplay. Experience teaches us that knowledge and truth are not static entities but the by-products of struggle and dialogue—of asking tough questions. We witness this phenomenon all the time, recreated in the media through dialogue and conflict. And we recognize it as a force of social change. Consider, for example, how our culture has changed its attitudes concerning race and its concepts of success, kinship, social groups, and class since the 1950s. Perhaps the most obvious example regards gender: Were it not for the fact that rigid, old conventions have been questioned, most women would still be bound to the laundry and the kitchen stove.

The point is that critical reading is an active and reactive process that sharpens your focus on a subject and your ability to absorb information and ideas; at the same time, it encourages you to question accepted norms, views, and myths. And that is both healthy and laudable, for it is the basis of social evolution.

Critical reading also helps you become a better writer, because critical reading is the first step to critical writing. Good writers look at one another's writing the way architects look at a house: They study the fine details and how those details connect and create the whole. Likewise, they consider the particular slants and strategies of appeal. Good writers always have a clear sense of their audience: their reader's racial makeup, gender, and educational background; their political or religious persuasions; their values, prejudices, and assumptions about life; and so forth. Knowing your audience helps you to determine nearly every aspect of the writing process: the kind of language to use; the writing style, whether casual or formal, humorous or serious, technical or philosophical; the particular slant to take, appealing to the reader's reason, emotions, ethics, or a combination of these; what emphasis to give the essay; the type of evidence to offer; and the kinds of authorities to cite.

The better you become at analyzing and reacting to another's written work, the better you will analyze and react to your own. You will ask yourself questions such as the following: Is it logical? Do my points come across clearly? Are my examples solid enough? Is this the best wording? Is my conclusion persuasive? Do I have a clear sense of my audience? What strategy did I take: an appeal to logic, emotions, or ethics? In short, critical reading will help you to evaluate your own writing, thereby making you both a better reader and a better writer. Although you may already employ many strategies of critical reading, the following text presents some techniques to make you an even better critical reader.

How to Read Critically

To help you improve your critical reading, use these six proven, basic steps:

- Keep a journal on what you read.
- Annotate what you read.

- Outline what you read.
- Summarize what you read.
- Question what you read.
- Analyze what you read.

Keep a Journal on What You Read

Unlike writing an essay or a paper, journal writing is a personal exploration in which you develop your own ideas without set rules. It is a process of recording impressions and exploring feelings and ideas. Journal writing is a freewriting exercise in which you express yourself without restrictions and without judgment. You do not have to worry about breaking any rules, because in a journal, anything goes.

Reserve a special notebook just for your journal—not one you use for class notes or homework. Also, date your entries and include the titles of the articles to which you are responding. Eventually, by the end of the semester, you should have a substantial number of pages to review, enabling you to see how your ideas and writing style have developed over time.

What do you include in your journal? Although it may serve as a means to understand an essay, you are not required to write only about the essay itself. Perhaps an article reminds you of a personal experience. Maybe it triggers an opinion you did not know you had. Or perhaps you wish to explore a particular phrase or idea presented by the author.

Some students may find keeping a journal difficult, because it is so personal. They may feel as if they are exposing their feelings too much. Or they may feel uncomfortable thinking that someone else, perhaps a teacher or another student, may read their writing. Do not let such apprehensions prevent you from exploring your impressions and feelings. If you must turn in your journal to your teacher, do not include anything you do not want others to read. Consider keeping a more private journal for your own benefit.

Annotate What You Read

It is a good idea to underline or highlight key passages and to make margin notes when reading an essay. If you do not own the publication in which the essay appears, or choose not to mark it up, make a photocopy of the piece and annotate that. You should annotate on the second or third reading, once you have an understanding of the essay's general ideas.

There are no specific guidelines for annotation. Use whatever technique suits you best, but keep in mind that in annotating a piece of writing, you are engaging in a dialogue with the author. As in any meaningful dialogue, you hear things you may not have known: things that may be interesting and exciting to you, things with which you may agree or disagree, or things that give you cause to ponder. The other side of the dialogue, of course, is your response. In annotating a piece of writing, that response takes the form of underlining or highlighting key passages and jotting down comments in the margin. Such comments can take the form of full sentences or some shorthand codes. Sometimes "Why?" or "True" or "NO!" will be enough to help you respond to a writer's position or claim. If you come across a word or reference that is unfamiliar to you, underline or circle it. Once you have located the main thesis statement or claim, highlight or underline it and jot down "claim" or "thesis" in the margin.

Outline What You Read

Briefly outlining an essay is a good way to see how writers structure their ideas. When you physically diagram the thesis statement, claims, and supporting evidence, you can better assess the quality of the writing and decide how convincing it is. You may already be familiar with detailed, formal essay outlines in which structure is broken down into main ideas and subsections. However, for our purposes, a brief and concise breakdown of an essay's components will suffice. This is done by simply jotting down a one-sentence summary of each paragraph. Sometimes brief paragraphs elaborating the same point can be lumped together:

- Point 1
- Point 2
- Point 3
- Point 4
- Point 5, and so on.

Such outlines may seem rather primitive, but they demonstrate how the various parts of an essay are connected—that is, the organization and sequence of ideas.

Summarize What You Read

Summarizing is perhaps the most important technique to develop for understanding and evaluating what you read. This means reducing the essay to its main points. In your journal or notebook, try to write a brief synopsis (about 100 words) of the reading in your own words. Note the claim or thesis of the discussion or argument and the chief supporting points. It is important to write these points down, rather than passively highlighting them with a pen or pencil, because the act of jotting down a summary helps you absorb the argument.

Question What You Read

Although we break down critical reading into discrete steps, these steps will naturally overlap in the actual process of reading and writing critically. As you read an essay, you simultaneously summarize and evaluate the author's points, perhaps adding your own ideas or even arguing with the author in your mind. If something strikes you as particularly interesting or insightful, make a mental note of it. For beginning writers, a good strategy is to convert that automatic mental response into actual note taking. Write your thoughts down in the margins or in a notebook for future reference. Likewise, if something strikes you the wrong way, argue back, making a note in your book so you can go back and think about it more deeply later.

In your journal or in the margins of the text, practice this technique of questioning and challenging the writer. Jot down any points in the essay that do not measure up to your expectations or personal views. Note anything about which you are skeptical. Write down any questions you have about the claims, views, or evidence. If some point or conclusion seems forced or unfounded, record it and briefly explain why. The more skeptical and questioning you are, the better reader you are. Likewise, note what features of the essay impressed you: outstanding points, interesting wording, clever or amusing phrases or allusions, particular references, the general structure of the piece. Record what you learned from the reading and the aspects of the issue you would like to explore.

Of course, you may not feel qualified to pass judgment on an author's views, particularly if the author is a professional writer or expert on a particular subject. Sometimes the issue discussed might be too technical, or you may not feel informed enough to make critical evaluations.

Sometimes a personal narrative may focus on experiences completely alien to you. Nonetheless, you are an intelligent person with the instincts to determine if the writing impresses you or if an argument is sound, logical, and convincing. What you can do in such instances, and another good habit to get into, is to think of other views on the issue. If you have read or heard of experiences different from those of the author, or arguments with opposing views, jot them down. Similarly, if you agree with the author's view, highlight the parts of the essay with which you particularly identify.

Analyze What You Read

To analyze something means to break it down into its components, examine those components closely to evaluate their significance, and determine how they relate as a whole. In part, you already did this by briefly outlining the essay. However, there is more. Analyzing what you read involves interpreting and evaluating the points of a discussion or argument as well as its presentation—that is, its language and structure. Ultimately, analyzing an essay after establishing its key points will help you understand what may not be evident at first. A close examination of the author's words takes you beneath the surface and sharpens your understanding of the issues at hand.

Although there is no set procedure for analyzing a piece of prose, there are some specific questions you should raise when reading an essay, particularly one that is trying to sway you to its view.

- What kind of audience is the author addressing?
- What are the author's assumptions?
- What are the author's purposes and intentions?
- How well does the author accomplish those purposes?
- How convincing is the evidence presented? Is it sufficient and specific? Is it relevant and reliable, or dated and slanted?
- What types of sources were used: personal experience, outside authorities, factual references, or statistical data?
- Did the author address opposing views on the issue?
- Is the perspective of the author persuasive?

What Kind of Audience Is the Author Addressing?

Before the first word is written, a good writer considers his or her audience—that is, their age group, gender, ethnic and racial makeup, educational background, and socioeconomic status. Writers also take into account the values, prejudices, and assumptions of their readers, as well as their readers' political and religious persuasions. Some writers, including several in this book, write for a target audience of readers who share the same interests, opinions, and prejudices. Other authors write for a general audience. Although general audiences consist of very different people with diversified backgrounds, expectations, and standards, think of them as the people who read *Time*, *Newsweek*, and your local newspaper. You can assume general audiences are relatively well informed about what is going on in the country, that they have a good comprehension of language and a sense of humor, and that they are willing to listen to new ideas.

What Are the Author's Assumptions?

Having a sense of the audience leads writers to certain assumptions. If a writer is addressing a general audience, then he or she can assume certain levels of awareness about language and current events, certain values about education and morality, and certain nuances of an argument.

What Are the Author's Purposes and Intentions?

A writer has a purpose in writing that goes beyond wanting to show up in print. Sometimes it is simply the expression of how the writer feels about something; sometimes the intent is to convince others to see things in a different light; sometimes the purpose is to persuade readers to change their views or behavior.

How Well Does the Author Accomplish Those Purposes?

Determining how well an author accomplishes such purposes may seem subjective, but in reality it comes down to how well the case is presented. Is the thesis clear? Is it organized and well presented? Are the examples sharp and convincing? Is the author's conclusion a logical result of what came before?

How Convincing Is the Evidence Presented? Is It Sufficient and Specific? Is It Relevant and Reliable, or Dated and Slanted?

Convincing writing depends on convincing evidence; that is, it depends on sufficient and relevant facts along with proper interpretations of facts. Facts—such as statistics, examples, personal experience, expert testimony, and historical details—are pieces of information that can be verified. A proper interpretation of the facts must be logical and supported by relevant data. For instance, it is a fact that SAT verbal scores went up in 2003, and that students from Massachusetts had the highest national scores. One reason might be that students are spending more time reading and less time watching TV than in the past, or that Massachusetts has many colleges and universities available, prompting students to study harder for the test in that state. But without hard statistics that document the viewing habits of a sample of students, such interpretations are shaky: the result of a writer jumping to conclusions.

Is the Evidence Sufficient and Specific?

Writers routinely use evidence, but sometimes it may not be sufficient. Sometimes the conclusions reached have too little evidence to be justified. Sometimes writers make hasty generalizations based solely on personal experience as evidence. How much evidence is enough? It is hard to say, but the more specific the details, the more convincing the argument. Instead of generalizations, good writers cite figures, dates, and facts. Instead of paraphrasing information, they quote the experts verbatim.

Is the Evidence Relevant?

Good writers select evidence based on how well it supports their thesis, not on how interesting, novel, or humorous it is. For instance, if you are claiming that Barry Bonds is the greatest living baseball player, you should not mention that he was born in California, had a father who played for the San Francisco Giants, or that his godfather is Willie Mays. Those are facts, and they are very interesting, but they have nothing to do with Bonds' athletic abilities. Irrelevant evidence distracts readers and weakens an argument.

Is the Evidence Reliable and Current?

Evidence should not be so dated or vague that it fails to support your claim. For instance, it is not accurate to say that candidate Jones fails to support the American worker, because 15 years ago, she purchased a foreign car. Her current actions are more important. Readers expect the information writers provide to be current and specific enough to be verifiable. A writer supporting animal rights may cite cases of rabbits blinded in drug research, but such tests have been outlawed in the United States for many years. Another may point to medical research that appears to abuse human subjects, while it fails to name the researchers, the place, or the year of such testing. Because readers may have no way of verifying the evidence, the claims become suspicious and will weaken your points.

Is the Evidence Slanted?

Sometimes writers select evidence that supports their case and ignore evidence that does not. Often referred to as "stacking the deck," this practice is unfair and potentially self-defeating for a writer. Although some evidence presented may have merit, an argument will be dismissed if readers discover that evidence was slanted or suppressed. For example, suppose you heard a classmate state that he would never take a course with Professor Sanchez because she gives surprise quizzes, assigns 50 pages of reading a night, and does not grade on a curve. Even if these statements are true, that may not be the whole truth. You might discover that Professor Sanchez is a dynamic and talented teacher whose classes are stimulating. Withholding that information may make an argument suspect. A better strategy is to acknowledge counterevidence and to confront it; that is, to strive for a balanced presentation by raising views and evidence that may not be supportive of your own.

What Types of Sources Were Used: Personal Experience, Outside Authorities, Factual References, or Statistical Data?

Writers enlist four basic kinds of evidence to support their views or arguments: *personal experience* (theirs and others'), *outside authorities, factual references and examples,* and *statistics.* In your own writing, you should aim to use combinations of these.

Personal testimony cannot be underestimated. Think of the books you have read, or movies you have seen, based on word-of-mouth recommendations. (Maybe you learned of the school you are attending through word of mouth.) Personal testimony, which provides eyewitness accounts not available to you or to other readers, is sometimes the most persuasive kind of evidence. Suppose you are writing about the abuse of alcohol rising on college campuses. In addition to statistics and hard facts, quoting the experience of a first-year student who nearly died from alcohol poisoning would add dramatic impact. Although personal observations are useful and valuable, writers must not draw hasty conclusions based only on such evidence. The fact that you and a few friends are in favor of replacing letter grades with a pass-fail system does not provide support for the claim that the student body at your school is in favor of the conversion.

Outside authorities are people recognized as experts in a given field. Appealing to such authorities is a powerful tool in writing, particularly for writers wanting to persuade readers of their views. We hear it all the time: "Scientists have found . . . ." "Scholars inform us that . . . ." "According to his biographer, Abraham Lincoln . . . ." Although experts try to be objective and fair-minded, their testimony may be biased. You would not expect scientists working for tobacco companies to provide unbiased opinions on lung cancer. And remember to cite who the authorities behind the statements are. It is not enough to simply state "scientists conducted a study"; you must say who they were and where the study was conducted and even who paid for it.

Factual references and examples do as much to inform as to persuade. If somebody wants to sell you something, they will pour on the details. Think of the television commercials that show a sports utility vehicle climbing rocky mountain roads as a narrator lists all its great standard features: four-wheel drive, alloy wheels, second-generation airbags, power brakes, cruise control, and so on. Consider cereal "infomercials" in which manufacturers explain that new Yummy-Os have 15 percent more fiber to help prevent cancer. Although readers may not have the expertise to determine which data are useful, they are often convinced by the sheer weight of the evidence—like courtroom juries judging a case.

Statistics impress people. Saying that 77 percent of your school's student body approves of women in military combat roles is much more persuasive than saying "a lot of people" do. Why? Because statistics have a no-nonsense authority. Batting averages, polling results, economic indicators, medical and FBI statistics, and demographic percentages are all reported in numbers. If accurate, they are persuasive, although they can be used to mislead. The claim that 139 people on campus protested the appearance of a certain controversial speaker may be accurate; however, it would be a distortion of the truth not to mention that another 1,500 people attended the talk and gave the speaker a standing ovation. Likewise, the manufacturer who claims that its potato chips are fried in 100 percent cholesterol-free vegetable oil misleads the public, because vegetable oil does not contain cholesterol, which is found only in animal fats. That is known as the "bandwagon" use of statistics, appealing to what people want to hear.

Did the Author Address Opposing Views on the Issue?

Many of the essays in this book will, in varying degrees, try to persuade you to agree with the author's position. But any slant on a topic can have multiple points of view. In developing their ideas, good writers will anticipate different and opposing views. They will cite alternative opinions and maybe even evidence that does not support their own position. By treating alternative points of view fairly, writers strengthen their own position. Failing to present or admit other views could leave their perspective open to scrutiny, as well as to claims of naïveté and ignorance. This is particularly damaging when discussing a controversial issue.

Is the Perspective of the Author Persuasive?

Style and content make for persuasive writing. Important points are how well a paper is composed—the organization, the logic, the quality of thought, the presentation of evidence, the use of language, the tone of discussion—and the details and evidence.

By now you should have a fairly clear idea of how critical reading can improve your comprehension of a work and make you a better writer in the process. Make critical reading part of your daily life, not just something you do in the classroom or while studying. As you wait for the bus, look at some billboards and consider how they try to hook their audience. While watching TV, think about the techniques advertisers use to convince you to buy their products. And try to apply some of the elements of critical reading while perusing the articles and editorials in your favorite magazine or newspaper. The more you approach writing with a critical eye, the more natural it will become, and the better writer you will be.

What Is Critical Writing?

Critical writing is a systematic process. When following a recipe, you would not begin mixing ingredients together haphazardly. Instead, you would first gather your ingredients and equipment, and then combine the ingredients according to the recipe outlined. Similarly, in writing, you could not plan, write, edit, and proofread all at the same time. Rather, writing occurs one thoughtful step at a time.

Some writing assignments may require more steps than others. An in-class freewriting exercise may allow for only one or two steps: light planning and writing. An essay question on a midterm examination may permit enough time for only three steps: planning, writing, and proofreading. A simple plan for such an assignment need answer only two questions: "What am I going to say?" and "How am I going to develop my idea convincingly?"

A longer, out-of-class paper allows you to plan and organize your material and to develop more than one draft. In this extended version of the writing process, you will need to do the following to create a strong, critical paper:

- Develop your ideas into a focused thesis that is appropriate for your audience.
- Research pertinent sources.
- Organize your material and draft your paper.
- Proofread your paper thoroughly.

Those are the general steps that every writer goes through when writing a paper. In the following sections, the use of these strategies will be discussed so that you can write most effectively.

Developing Ideas

Even the most experienced writers sometimes have trouble getting started. Common problems you may encounter include focusing your ideas, knowing where to begin, having too much or too little to say, and determining your position on an issue. There are developmental strategies that can help promote the free expression of your ideas and make you more comfortable with writing.

Although your finished product should be a tightly focused and well-written essay, you can begin the writing process by being free and sloppy. This approach allows your ideas to develop and flow unblocked onto your paper. Writing techniques such as brainstorming, freewriting, and ballooning can help you through the development process. As with all writing strategies, you should try all of them at first to discover which ones work best for you.

Brainstorming

The goal of brainstorming is to generate and focus ideas. Brainstorming can be a personal exercise or a group project. You begin with a blank sheet of paper or a blackboard and—without paying attention to spelling, order, or grammar—simply list ideas about the topic as they come to you. You should spend at least 10 minutes brainstorming, building on the ideas you write down. There are no dumb ideas in brainstorming: the smallest detail may turn into a great essay.

Freewriting

Like brainstorming, freewriting is a free expression of ideas. It helps you jump-start the writing process and get things flowing on paper. Freewriting is unencumbered by rules—you can write about your impressions, ideas, and reactions to the article or essay. You should devote about 10 minutes to freewriting, keeping in mind that the goal is to write about the topic as ideas occur to you. If you are writing on a particular topic or idea, you may wish to note it at the top of your paper as a visual reminder of your focus. Structure, grammar, and spelling are not important—just focus on the free flow of ideas. And above all, do not stop writing, even if you feel that what you are writing is silly or irrelevant. Any one idea or a combination of ideas expressed can be developed into a thoughtful essay.

Ballooning

There are many names for ballooning, including *mind mapping, clustering,* or *grouping.* These techniques all provide a more graphic presentation of ideas, allowing writers to visualize ideas and connections stemming from these ideas. Ballooning is particularly effective if you already have a fairly clear idea about your topic and wish to develop it more fully.

Write your main topic in the center of a large sheet of paper or a blackboard and circle it. Using the circled idea as your focus, think of subtopics and place them in circles around the center circle, connecting them to each other with radiating lines. Remember to keep the subtopics short. Continue doing this until you feel you have developed all the subtopics more fully. When you have finished this exercise, you should be able to visualize the connections between your main topic and its subpoints, which will provide a starting point for your essay.

Narrowing the Topic

Although brainstorming, freewriting, and ballooning help list and develop general ideas, you still need to narrow one idea down to something more manageable. Narrowing a topic can be quite a challenge: you might like more than one idea, or you may be afraid of limiting yourself to only one concept. Nevertheless, you must identify one idea and focus on developing it into an essay. Choose an idea that will interest you and your audience. Remember that if you do not like the way one idea begins to develop, you can always go back and develop another one instead. Once you identify your topic, you are ready to develop the thesis statement for your essay.

Based on the freewriting exercise described earlier, and additional idea development using ballooning techniques, we will follow a student who has decided to write his paper on the idea that language sensitivity is a good idea and that it helps more students than it harms. The idea stems from a response to Leo's essay, but it will develop into a thesis that uniquely belongs to the student.

Identifying Your Audience

Identifying your audience is one of the most important steps in organizing your essay. Knowing what your audience needs and expects from your essay will help you compose a convincing, effective paper. The following questions can help you identify the expectations of your audience:

- Who is my audience?
- What do they already know about my topic?
- What questions do they have about my topic?
- What do they need to know to understand my point?
- What is the best order in which to present information?
- How do they feel about this topic?
- Why would they want to read my essay?

Developing a Thesis

The *thesis* is a form of contract between the writer and reader. It makes a claim or declaration and tells your audience exactly what you are going to discuss. It should be stated in the opening paragraph with the rest of the paper developing and supporting it.

As you write and develop your paper, your thesis should guide you as clearer and more precise thoughts evolve. Do not be constrained by your first thesis: If your paper is changing as you write, your thesis may change. Remember to go back and revise the thesis so that it matches the points made in your essay.

Before determining how to research or organize your paper, consider what you are trying to achieve by writing it. Your objective may be to inform, to describe, or to persuade. To define your purpose, you should first determine your objective, and then identify what you need to do to accomplish this objective. This helps you determine what you need to put into the body of your paper.

Writing to inform involves anticipating the questions your audience may have regarding the topic and how much background they will need to understand it. Once you have developed a list of questions, you can determine what order will best present the information that will answer these questions.

Writing to describe also involves answering some questions. First, you must identify what is important or relevant about the topic you intend to describe. Then you should determine what information is vital to conveying this importance. List these elements and order them in a way that presents a clear view of the experience to the reader.

Writing to persuade presents a perspective on an issue and attempts to convince readers to agree with it. You must provide reasons and supporting evidence to persuade your audience that your perspective makes sense. Although you might not sway all readers to your point of view, you should make enough of a case to allow them to understand your argument, even if they might not agree with it.

The first step in persuasive writing is to determine your position and to identify the objections others might have to it. Remember that there are many different reasons readers may not agree with you. By identifying the arguments against your position, you are better able to address them and thus support your own argument in the process. Three primary kinds of arguments are used in persuasive writing:

- *Arguments based on disputed facts or consequences,* such as the claim that the building of a gambling casino generated revenue for a bankrupt town, created jobs, and improved the quality of life there.
- *Arguments that advocate change,* such as arguing for a lower drinking age or changing how the penal system punishes juvenile offenders.

Arguments based on evaluative personal claims, as right or wrong, ethical or immoral, or favoring one thing or idea over another—such as arguing that physician-assisted suicide is wrong, or that supermodels contribute to the development of eating disorders in young women. The key to effective persuasive writing is to support your perspective with statistics, factual data, and examples. Although your opinions drive the essay, your supporting evidence is what convinces your audience of the validity of your main point.

Researching

Research can involve a few or many steps, depending on the type and length of the paper you are writing. In many cases, simply reviewing the article and applying the steps of critical reading will be the final step you take before organizing your paper. For longer research papers that require outside sources, you will probably need to tap into library resources or look for information online.

Selecting Sources for Your Paper

The best place to start is the library, either physically or online. Most libraries have their holdings archived on electronic cataloging systems that let you look up books by author, title, and subject. Although books are a rich source of information, they can be dated and are sometimes inappropriate for essays addressing contemporary issues. For such papers, journals and periodicals are better. With all the different ways of researching, gathering useful and appropriate information can be overwhelming. Do not be afraid to ask the librarian for help.

For many people, the Internet has become the first avenue of research on a topic, and it can be an extremely useful way to locate information on contemporary issues. In addition to Web sites, newsgroups and bulletin boards can aid your research process. Remember that the Internet is largely unregulated, so you should surf the Web with the careful eye of a critic. Simply because something is posted online does not mean it is accurate or truthful. Whenever possible, take steps to verify your sources. When you do find a good source, write it down immediately. Many students lament the loss of a valuable resource, because they forgot to write down the title of the book or Internet address. A good technique is to write down your sources on 3 by 5 cards, which allow you to add sources and arrange them alphabetically without having to rewrite, as you would have to with a list. You can write down quotes for your paper on these cards for quick retrieval and use them to help write the Works Cited section at the end of your essay.

Documenting Sources

Sources help support your ideas and emphasize your points. It is very important to cite these sources when you use them in your essay. Whether you quote, paraphrase, or use an idea from another source, you must identify the source of information. Documenting sources gives credit to the person who did the work, and it helps locate information on your topic. Even if you rewrite information in your own words, you must still document the source, because it is borrowed information. Failure to document your sources is called *plagiarism,* which is presenting someone else's work as your own, and it is considered a form of theft by most academic institutions. The following checklist should help you determine when documenting is appropriate. Always document your sources when

- using someone's exact words
- presenting someone else's opinion
- paraphrasing or summarizing someone else's ideas
- using information gathered from a study
- citing statistics or reporting the results of research that is not yours

It is not necessary to cite dates, facts, or ideas considered common knowledge.

Organizing Your Paper

There are many ways to organize your paper. Some students prefer to use the standard outline technique, complete with Roman numerals and indented subpoints. Other students prefer more flexible flowcharts. The key to organizing is to define your focus and plan how to support your thesis statement from point to point in a logical order.

Drafting Your Essay

When writing your essay, think of your draft as a work in progress. Your objective should be to present your ideas in a logical order. You can address spelling, grammar, and sentence structure later. If you get stuck writing one paragraph or section, go on and work on another.

Depending on how you write, you may choose to write your draft sequentially; or you may choose to move from your thesis to your body paragraphs, leaving your introduction and conclusion for last. Feel free to leave gaps or to write notes to yourself in brackets to indicate areas to develop later when revising. Do not make the mistake of thinking that your first draft has to be your final draft. Remember that writing is a process of refinement: you can always go back and fix things later.

Writing Your Introduction

For many students, the hardest part of writing an essay is drafting the first paragraph. Humorist James Thurber once said "Don't get it right, get it written." What Thurber means is just start writing, even if you do not think it sounds very good. Use your thesis statement as a starting point and build around it. Explain what your essay will do, or provide interesting background information that serves to frame your points for your audience. After you have written the first paragraph, take a break before you revise it. Return to it later with a fresh outlook. Likewise, review your first paragraph as you develop the other sections of your essay to make sure that you are meeting your objectives.

Developing Paragraphs and Making Transitions

A paragraph is a group of sentences that supports and develops a central idea. The central idea serves as the core point of the paragraph, and the surrounding sentences support it.

There are three primary types of sentences that comprise a paragraph: the *topic sentence, supporting sentences,* and *transitional sentences.*

The core point, or the *topic sentence,* is usually the first or second sentence in the paragraph. It is the controlling idea of the paragraph. Placing the topic sentence first lets the reader immediately know what the paragraph is about. However, sometimes a transition sentence or some supporting material needs to precede the topic sentence, in which case the topic sentence may appear as the second or third sentence in the paragraph. Think of the topic sentence as a mini thesis statement; it should connect logically to the topic sentences in the paragraphs before and after it.

Supporting sentences do just that: they support the topic sentence. This support may be from outside sources, in the form of quotes or paraphrased material, or it may be from your own ideas. Think of the supporting sentences as proving the validity of your topic sentence.

Transitional sentences link paragraphs together, making the paper a cohesive unit and promoting its readability. Transitional sentences are usually the first and last sentences of the paragraph. When they appear at the end of the paragraph, they foreshadow the topic to come. Words such as *in addition, yet, moreover, furthermore, meanwhile, likewise, also, since, before, hence, on the other hand, as well,* and *thus* are often used in transitional sentences. These words can also be used within the body of the paragraph to clarify and smooth the progression from idea to idea. For example, the last sentence in our student's introductory paragraph sets up the reader's expectation that the paragraphs that follow will explain why language sensitivity in educational materials is a good idea. It forecasts what will come next.

Paragraphs have no required length. Remember, however, that an essay comprised of long, detailed paragraphs might prove tiresome and confusing to the reader. Likewise, short, choppy paragraphs may sacrifice clarity and leave the reader with unanswered questions. Remember that a paragraph presents a single, unified idea. It should be just long enough to effectively support its subject. Begin a new paragraph when your subject changes.

Use this list to help keep your paragraphs organized and coherent:

Organize material logically and present your core idea early in the paragraph.

- Include a topic sentence that expresses the core point of the paragraph.
- Support and explain the core point.
- Use transitional sentences to indicate where you are going and where you have been.

Concluding Well

Your conclusion should bring together the points made in your paper and reiterate your final point. You may also use your conclusion as an opportunity to provoke a final thought you wish your audience to consider. Try to frame your conclusion to mirror your introduction—in other words, be consistent in your style. You may wish to repeat the point of the paper, revisit its key points, and then leave your reader with a final idea or thought on your topic.

Conclusions are your opportunity to explain to your reader how all your material adds up. In a short essay of about three to four pages, your conclusion should begin around the penultimate paragraph, winding down the discussion. Avoid the temptation to simply summarize your material; try to give your conclusions a little punch. However, it is equally important not to be overly dramatic, because you can undercut your essay. Rather, conclusions should sound confident and reflective.

Editing and Revising

Once you have drafted a paper and, if possible, spent several hours or even a day away from it, you should begin editing and revising it. To edit your paper, read it closely, marking the words, phrases, and sections you want to change. Have a grammar handbook nearby to quickly reference any grammatical questions that may arise. Look for things that seem out of place or sound awkward, passages that lack adequate support and detail, and sentences that seem wordy or unclear. Many students find that reading the essay aloud helps them recognize awkward sentences and ambiguous wording. This technique may also reveal missing words.

As you read, you should always ask if what you have written refers back to your thesis. Keep the following questions in mind:

- Does this paragraph support my thesis?
- What does my reader need to know?
- Do my paragraphs flow in a logical order?
- Have I deviated from my point?

As you revise your paper, think about the voice and style you are using to present your material. Is your style smooth and confident? How much of yourself is in the essay, and is this level appropriate for the type of paper you are writing? Some writers, for example, overuse the pronoun *I*. If you find that this is the case, try to rework your sentences to decrease the use of this pronoun.

Using Active Voice

Although grammatically correct, the use of the passive voice can slow down the flow of a paper or distance the reader from your material. Many students are befuddled by the active versus the passive voice, confusing it with past, present, and future tense. The active voice can be used in any tense, and, in most situations, it is the better choice. In the active voice, you make your agent actively perform, rather than having an action done to them, as evidenced by some form of the verb *to be.*

Grammar and Punctuation

You probably already have a grammar handbook; most first-year composition courses require students to purchase these invaluable little books. If you do not have a grammar handbook, get one. You will use it throughout college and probably throughout your professional career. Grammar handbooks can help you identify problems with phrases and clauses, parallel structure, verb-tense agreement, and the various forms of punctuation. Most have useful sections on common usage mistakes, such as when to use *further* and *farther* and *effect* and *affect.* Try not to rely on grammar-checking software available on most word-processing programs. You are the best grammar checker for your essay.

Proofreading Effectively

The final step in preparing a paper is proofreading, or reading your paper to correct errors. You will probably be more successful if you wait until you are fresh to do it: Proofreading a paper at 3:00 AM immediately after finishing it is not a good idea. With the use of word-processing programs, proofreading usually involves three steps: *spell checking, reading,* and *correcting.*

If you are writing your paper using a word-processing system, you probably have been using the spell checker throughout the composition process. Most word-processing systems highlight misspelled words as you type them into the computer. Remember to run the spell checker every time you change or revise your paper. Many students make last minute changes to their papers and neglect to run the spell checker one last time before printing it, only to discover a misspelled word as they turn in their paper, or when it is returned to them. Keep in mind that spell checkers can fix only words that are misspelled, not words that are mistyped that are still real words. Common typing errors in which letters are transposed—such as *from* and *form* and *won* and *own*—will not be caught by a spell checker, because they all are real words. Other common errors not caught by spell checkers include words incompletely typed, such as when the *t* in *the* or the *e* in *here* are left off. Reading your paper carefully will catch these errors.

To proofread correctly, you must read slowly and critically. Try to distance yourself from the material. One careful, slow, attentive proofreading is better than six careless reads. Look for and mark the following: errors in spelling and usage, sentence fragments and comma splices, inconsistencies in number between nouns and pronouns and between subjects and verbs, faulty parallelism, other grammar errors, unintentional repetitions, and omissions.

After you have proofread and identified the errors, go back and correct them. When you have finished, proofread the paper again to make sure you caught everything. As you proofread for grammar and style, ask yourself the questions listed above and make corrections on your paper. Be prepared to read your essay through multiple times. Having only one or two small grammatical corrections is a good indication that you are done revising.

If your schedule permits, you might want to show your paper to a friend or instructor for review. Obtaining feedback from your audience is another way you can test the effectiveness of your paper. An outside reviewer will probably think of questions you have not thought of, and if you revise to answer those questions, you will make your paper stronger.

In the chapters that follow, you will discover dozens of current pieces, both written and visual, that range widely across contemporary matters; we hope you will find them exciting and thought provoking. Arranged thematically into nine chapters, the writings represent widely diverse topics—from the ways we construct beauty, to what makes us want to buy something, to race and inequality, to global warming and issues connected to immigration and what it means to be an American today. Some of the topics will be familiar, others you may be encountering for the first time. Regardless of how these language issues touch your experience, critical thinking, critical reading, and critical writing will open you up to a deeper understanding of our culture.

1 CHAPTER

Identity and the Images We Project

PICK UP A MAGAZINE. TURN ON THE TELEVISION. VIEW A film. Every day we are bombarded with images and messages telling us that slim is sexy, buff bodies are the best, and beauty means happiness. The right labels mean success and respect. The right look means acceptance. And overwhelmingly, our culture buys into these messages.

We live in a society caught up in images of itself—a society seemingly more driven by the cultivation of the body and how we clothe it than in personal achievement. In fact, so powerful is the influence of image that other terms of self-definition are difficult to identify. In this chapter, writers grapple with questions raised by our cultural preoccupation with flesh and fashion. Some essays in this chapter recount people at war with their bodies due to cultural pressure. Other essays are accounts of people rising above the din of fashion's dictates to create a sense of self that is authentic and rooted in personal happiness. Are we our bodies? Can our inner selves transcend the flesh? Do the clothes we wear express the self we want to be? Where does all this body-consciousness pressure come from?

JOHN CLOUD

Never Too Buff

We tend to assume that most men simply do not care about their appearance the way women do. But psychiatrists Harrison Pope and Katharine Phillips, and psychologist Roberto Olivardia, report in The Adonis Complex *(2000) on a disturbing trend: just as many young women aspire to be supermodel thin, an increasing number of young men yearn for the steroid-boosted and buff bodies typical of today's action heroes and weightlifters. John Cloud reports on this groundbreaking research and what it might mean for boys and men in the years ahead. This essay first appeared in the April 24, 2000 issue of* TIME *magazine.*

Pop quiz: Who is more likely to be dissatisfied with the appearance of their chests, men or women? Who is more likely to be concerned about acne, your teenage son or his sister? And who is more likely to binge eat, your nephew or your niece?

If you chose the women and girls in your life, you are right only for the last question—and even then, not by the margin you might expect. About 40 percent of Americans who go on compulsive-eating sprees are men. Thirty-eight percent of men want bigger pecs, while only 34 percent of women want bigger breasts. And more boys have fretted about zits than girls, going all the way back to a 1972 study.

A groundbreaking new book declares that these numbers, along with hundreds of other statistics and interviews the authors have compiled, mean something awful has happened to American men over the past few decades. They have become obsessed with their bodies. Authors Harrison Pope and Katharine Phillips, professors of psychiatry at Harvard and Brown, respectively, and Roberto Olivardia, a clinical psychologist at McLean Hospital in Belmont, Massachusetts, have a catchy name to describe this obsession, a term that will soon be doing many reps on chat shows: the Adonis Complex.

The name, which refers to the gorgeous half man, half god of mythology, may be a little too ready for Oprah, but the theory behind it will start a wonderful debate. Based on original research involving more than 1,000 men over the past 15 years, the book argues that many men desperately want to look like Adonis, because they constantly see the "ideal," steroid-boosted bodies of actors and models, and because their muscles are all they have over women today. In an age when women fly combat missions, the authors ask, "What can a modern boy or man do to distinguish himself as being 'masculine'?"

For years, of course, some men—ice skaters, bodybuilders, George Hamilton—have fretted over aspects of their appearance. But the numbers suggest that body-image concerns have gone mainstream: nearly half of men don't like their overall appearance, in contrast to just one in six in 1972. True, men typically are fatter now, but another study found that 46 percent of men of normal weight think about their appearance "all the time" or "frequently." And some men—probably hundreds of thousands, if you extrapolate from small surveys—say they have passed up job and even romantic opportunities because they refuse to disrupt workouts or dine on restaurant food. In other words, an increasing number of men would rather look brawny for their girlfriends than have sex with them.

Consider what they're spending: Last year American men forked over $2 billion for gym memberships—and another $2 billion for home exercise equipment. *Men's Health* ("Rock-hard abs in six weeks!" it screams every other issue) had 250,000 subscribers in 1990; now it has 1.6 million. In 1996 alone, men underwent some 700,000 cosmetic procedures.

At least those profits are legal. Anabolic steroids—the common name for synthetic testosterone—have led to the most dramatic changes in the male form in modern history, and more and more average men want those changes for themselves. Since steroids became widely available on the black market in the 1960s, perhaps 3 million American men have swallowed or injected them—mostly in the past 15 years. A 1993 survey found that one Georgia high school boy in every 15 admitted to having used steroids without a prescription. And the Drug Enforcement Administration reports that the percentage of all high school students who have used steroids has increased nearly 50 percent in the past four years, from 1.8 percent to 2.8 percent. The abuse of steroids has so alarmed the National Institute on Drug Abuse that . . . it launched a campaign in gyms, malls, bookstores, clubs, and on the Internet to warn teenagers about the dangers. Meanwhile, teenagers in even larger numbers are buying legal but lightly regulated food supplements, some with dangerous side effects, that purport to make you bigger or leaner or stronger.

As they infiltrated the bodybuilding world in the seventies and Hollywood a decade later, steroids created bodies for mass consumption that the world had literally never seen before. Pope likes to chart the changes by looking at Mr. America winners, which he called up on the Internet in his office last week. "Look at this guy," Pope exclaims when he clicks on the 1943 winner, Jules Bacon. "He couldn't even win a county bodybuilding contest today." Indeed, there are 16-year-olds working out at your gym who are as big as Bacon. Does that necessarily mean that today's bodybuilders—including those 16-year-olds—are 'roided? Pope is careful. "The possibility exists that rare or exceptional people, those with an unusual genetic makeup or a hormonal imbalance" could achieve the muscularity and leanness of today's big bodybuilders, he says.

But it's not likely. And Pope isn't lobbing dumbbells from an ivory tower: the professor lifts weights six days a week, from 11 AM to 1 PM. (He can even mark historical occasions by his workouts: "I remember when the Challenger went down; I was doing a set of squats.") "We are being assaulted by images virtually impossible to attain without the use of drugs," says Pope. "So what happens when you change a million-year-old equilibrium of nature?"

A historical loop forms: steroids beget pro wrestlers—Hulk Hogan, for one, has admitted taking steroids—who inspire boys to be just like them. Steroids have changed even boys' toys. Feminists have long derided Barbie for her tiny waist and big bosom. The authors of *The Adonis Complex* see a similar problem for boys in the growth of G.I. Joe. The grunt of 1982 looks scrawny compared with G.I. Joe Extreme, introduced in the mid 1990s. The latter would have a 55-inch chest and 27-inch biceps, if he were real, which simply can't be replicated in nature. Pope also points out a stunning little feature of the three-year-old video game *Duke Nukem: Total Meltdown,* developed by GT Interactive Software. When Duke gets tired, he can find a bottle of steroids to get him going. "Steroids give Duke a super adrenaline rush," the game manual notes.

To bolster their argument, the *Adonis* authors developed a computerized test that allows subjects to "add" muscle to a typical male body. They estimate their own size and then pick the size they would like to be and the size they think women want. Pope and his colleagues gave the test to college students and found that on average, the men wanted 28 pounds more muscle—and thought women wanted them to have 30 pounds more. In fact, the women who took the test picked an ideal man only slightly more muscular than average. Which goes a long way toward explaining why Leonardo DiCaprio can be a megastar in a nation that also idealizes "Stone Cold" Steve Austin.

But when younger boys took Pope's test, they revealed an even deeper sense of inadequacy about their bodies. More than half of boys ages 11 to 17 chose as their physical ideal an image possible to attain only by using steroids. So they do. Boys are a big part of the clientele at Muscle Mania (not its real name), a weight-lifting store that *TIME* visited last week at a strip mall in a Boston suburb. A couple of teenagers came in to ask about Tribulus, one of the many over-the-counter drugs and bodybuilding supplements the store sells, all legally.

"A friend of mine," one boy begins, fooling no one, "just came off a cycle of juice, and he heard that Tribulus can help you produce testosterone naturally." Patrick, 28, who runs the store and who stopped using steroids four years ago because of chest pain, tells the kid, "The s__ shuts off your nuts," meaning steroids can reduce sperm production, shrink the testicles, and cause impotence. Tribulus, Patrick says, can help restart natural testosterone production. The teen hands over $12 for 100 Tribulus Fuel pills. (Every day, Muscle Mania does $4,000 in sales of such products, with protein supplements and so-called fat burners leading the pack.)

Patrick says many of his teen customers, because they're short on cash, won't pay for a gym membership "until they've saved up for a cycle [of steroids]. They don't see the point without them." The saddest customers, he says, are the little boys, 12 and 13, brought in by young fathers. "The dad will say, 'How do we put some weight on this kid?' with the boy just staring at the floor. Dad is going to turn him into Hulk Hogan, even if it's against his will."

What would motivate someone to take steroids? Pope, Phillips, and Olivardia say the Adonis Complex works in different ways for different men. "Michael," 32, one of their research subjects, told *TIME* he had always been a short kid who got picked on. He started working out at about 14, and he bought muscle magazines for advice. The pictures taunted him: he sweated, but he wasn't getting as big as the men in the pictures. Other men in his gym also made him feel bad. When he found out they were on steroids, he did two cycles himself, even though he knew they could be dangerous.

But not all men with body-image problems take steroids. Jim Davis, 29, a human-services manager, told *TIME* he never took them, even when training for bodybuilding competitions. But Davis says he developed a form of obsessive-compulsive disorder around his workouts. He lifted weights six days a week for at least six years. He worked out even when injured. He adhered to a rigid regimen for every session, and if he changed it, he felt anxious all day. He began to be worried about clothes, and eventually could wear only three shirts, ones that made him look big. He still felt small. "I would sit in class at college with a coat on," he says. You may have heard of this condition, called *bigorexia*—thinking your muscles are puny when they aren't. Pope and his colleagues call it *muscle dysmorphia* and estimate that hundreds of thousands of men suffer from it.

Even though most boys and men never approach the compulsion of Jim Davis or Michael (both eventually conquered it), they undoubtedly face more pressure now than in the past to conform to an impossible ideal. Ripped male bodies are used today to advertise everything that shapely female bodies advertise: not just fitness products but also dessert liqueurs, microwave ovens, and luxury hotels. The authors of *The Adonis Complex* want guys to rebel against those images or to at least see them for what they are: a goal unattainable without drug use.

Feminists raised these issues for women years ago, and more recent books, such as *The Beauty Myth*, were part of a backlash against the hourglass ideal. Now, says Phillips, "I actually think it may be harder for men than women to talk about these problems, because it's not considered masculine to worry about such things." But maybe there is a masculine alternative: Next time WWE comes on, guys, throw the TV out the window. And order a large pizza.

QUESTIONS: For Thinking and Writing

1. Pope, Phillips, and Olivardia report that, in general, men would like to add 28 pounds more muscle to their frames but believe women would prefer even more—at least 30 pounds more muscle. What, in your opinion, accounts for this perception? Does it seem reasonable?
2. According to the author, what cultural messages tell children that steroid use is okay? Describe some of the ways children receive these messages.
3. Write a detailed description of your ideal male image (what you desire in a male or what you would most want to look like as a male). How does your description compare with the conclusions drawn by the psychiatrists and psychologist in the article? Did outside cultural influences direct your description? Explain.
4. Evaluate the comment made by Pope, Phillips, and Olivardia, that young men are increasingly obsessed with body image, because they

feel that muscle is all men "have over women today." Do you agree or disagree with this statement? Explain.

5. Looking back at your experience in high school, think about the males who were considered the most "buff." What qualities made these particular males more desirable and more enviable than their peers? How much of their appeal was based on their physical appearance? How much of it was based on something else?

GARANCE FRANKE-RUTA

The Natural Beauty Myth

Critics of the beauty industry argue that it is attacking women's self-esteem as it raises the beauty bar impossibly high. But journalist Garance Franke-Ruta argues that the fashion industry doesn't oppress women: It makes beauty accessible to all. Because the truth is that there is no such thing as "natural beauty." Is what we have come to recognize as "natural beauty" really the result of chemicals, surgery, and a whole lot of suffering in the name of fashion? This essay was published in The Wall Street Journal *on December 15, 2006.*

Last week, Italy's government and some of its fashion moguls announced plans to crack down on the use of ultrathin models on the catwalk. This decision follows in the wake of Madrid's recently instituted ban on underweight models at its annual fashion show. Let's not rush to celebrate.

Pictures of beautiful but undernourished-looking women have led, in recent months, to a round of fashion-industry bashing in the press. One anonymous wit even mocked up satirical pictures of women who looked like concentration camp victims—except that they had masses of glossy hair and wore slinky clothes. As often happens when satire meets a mass audience, lots of people thought that the doctored pictures were real—which is how, one day in November, they wound up in my inbox, courtesy of a women and media list-serv.

A predictable discussion followed. Curvy women were praised for their healthy-seeming fuller figures. "Self-acceptance" was praised, too. It was argued that the evil images presented to women by the fashion industry were part of the broader plan of beauty magazines to make women feel bad about themselves and thus buy products for self-improvement.

Such a critique, which we hear over and over today, is based on a conceptual error. The beauty industry is not the problem; it is a part of the solution. American women today are the victims of a more insidious idea, an idea that underlies the American obsession with self-esteem: the tyrannical ideal of "natural beauty."

Few Americans today live a "natural" life, whatever that may be. The more educated and well-to-do among us may eat organic foods and avoid chemicals as best they can, but such efforts hardly make us "natural." Our society is too complex for that. Indeed, all societies involve such a thick layering of culture over our malleable essence that it is virtually impossible to say what we might be like in a natural state.

What is clear is that, over the past century, American women have changed their shape. Most noticeably, they have gained so much poundage that, today, more than half are overweight and a third are clinically obese. The sharpest spike in obesity has come since the late 1970s. There are all sorts of reasons, of course—from the rise of corn syrup as a sweetener to the increased portion sizes of our daily meals and our increasingly sedentary styles of life. And yet the doctrine of "natural beauty," so favored by the self-esteem brigades of the 1970s and still confusing women today, asks women to accept themselves as this unnatural environment has made them.

What the critics of the beauty industry further fail to recognize is that the doctrine of "natural beauty," and the desire it breeds in women to be accepted as they are or to be seen as beautiful without any effort, is a ruthless and antiegalitarian ideal. It is far more punishing than the one that says any woman can be beautiful if she merely treats beauty as a form of discipline.

Only in America do we think that beauty is a purely natural attribute, rather than a type of artistry requiring effort. Look at the French: They are no more beautiful as a people than we Americans, but they understand that every woman can be attractive—if not beautiful—if she chooses to be. Yes, we are given forms by nature, but how we choose to present them is a matter of our own discretion. Few people are blessed by nature and circumstance with the Golden Mean proportions that seem to be universally appreciated. Thus, in the end, it is more democratic to think of beauty or attractiveness as an attribute that one can acquire, like speaking a foreign language or cooking well. To see beauty as a capacity like any other—the product of educated taste and daily discipline—is to see it as something chosen: to be possessed or left aside, according to one's preference.

The same goes, relatedly, for maintaining a certain size. In contemporary America, becoming thin is a choice that for most people requires rigorous and sometimes painful self-discipline. But so does becoming a lawyer or a concert pianist. The celebrity press is wrongly decried for giving women false ideals. In fact, it has demystified the relationship between effort and beauty, between discipline and weight. It opens up a path for noncelebrities.

One celebrity glossy recently estimated that, in a single year, actress Jennifer Aniston spends close to the average woman's annual salary on trainers and other aspects of a high-level workout. Former tween-queen Britney Spears told Oprah Winfrey that she used to do between 500 and 1,000 crunches a day to perfect her on-display abs. Actress Kate Hudson told one interviewer that, to lose postpregnancy "baby weight," she worked out three hours a day until she lost her 70 pounds: It was so hard that she used to sit on the exercise cycle and cry. Entertainment figures and models are like athletes; it takes a lot of discipline and social support to look like them. Money helps, too.

The celebrity magazines also specialize in a genre of stories best understood as tutorials in beauty as artifice: celebrities without their makeup. Makeover shows like *What Not to Wear* and *The Biggest Loser*—even *Queer Eye for the Straight Guy*—show beauty as something created, a condition to which anyone can have access with the right education and effort. This is a meritocratic ideal, not an insistent, elitist one. The makeover shows also help to make it clear that a life of artifice is not for everyone. Once we see the effort and hours that go into making a body more appealing, we may decide not to attempt a labor-intensive presentation of the self. We may decide that other things are more important.

Take, for example, U.S. Navy Commander Sunita L. Williams, an astronaut who recently joined the staff of the International Space Station for 6 months. Since entering orbit, she has announced plans to cut her long, chestnut tresses and donate them to charity, because all that hair was uncomfortable and hard to manage in a zero-gravity environment. Most of us live in a less exotic environment, but the essence of our choice is the same. Just as it would be difficult for anyone to be a concert pianist and a nuclear scientist at the same time, it can be a pointless distraction for women to strive to maintain the time-consuming artifices of beauty while pursuing their other goals.

Ms. Williams spent her time in other ways and today has access to the most majestic natural beauty of all: the vision of our globe from space. But it took a half-century of human effort and discipline to put her there.

QUESTIONS: For Thinking and Writing

1. Evaluate the author's tone in this editorial. Identify phrases and words in which the author's tone attempts to influence her readers' reception of her point of view.
2. Is the fashion industry exerting pressure on women to be thin? Consider the women featured on the covers of popular magazines for men and women, including *Marie Claire, Cosmopolitan, Vogue, Maxim,* and *Vibe*. Do you think such magazine covers influence how we define beauty and desirability?
3. What does "natural beauty" mean to you? Why does the author claim that it is a false concept? Do you agree?
4. Write about your own feelings about your self-image. What factors do you think shaped your feelings? What elements of our culture, if any, influenced your development of body consciousness? Explain.
5. This essay appeared as an editorial in *The Wall Street Journal*. Imagine that you are a newspaper editorialist. Write a response to Franke-Ruta's essay, focusing on how effective you find her argument. Support your critique with examples from your personal observation and external research if necessary.

NIRANJANA IYER

Weight of the World

Beauty is a cultural construct. In some areas of the world, such as the Pacific Islands and India, a more plump shape is considered healthy and, thus, beautiful. In the next essay, writer Niranjana Iyer explores the definitions of beauty in two cultures and the challenges she faces as a "slimmigrant." And as western media permeates even the most remote corners of the world, the battle of the bulge has gone global. This narrative appeared in the August 2006 issue of Smithsonian Magazine.

Like several million people on this planet, I weigh 15 pounds more than I'd like. But my 15 pounds appeared overnight, after an airplane ride from my home in India to Boston.

As a child in Chennai, I was considered worryingly thin. My mother sluiced an appetite stimulant down my throat at dinnertime and force-fed me cod-liver oil once a week—to no avail. As I grew into a slim teen, Ma would point to my collarbones as evidence that I was wasting away, but I was unmoved. If my figure didn't quite match the voluptuous Bollywood heroine standard, well, my salwar kameezes (flowing tunics worn over drawstring pants) fit me fine. Rare was the woman who wore pants in Chennai, which was far too hot for anything but the lightest and loosest of clothing.

Then I moved to New Hampshire for graduate school and began a life in denim.

The body that I had considered normal was now revealed to be anything but. My jeans showed no mercy; every untoned millimeter of my belly hung over my waistband like an overbite in search of an orthodontist. Pants widened my hips, shrank my legs, and made my waist disappear. In India, I'd been above average in height. In the States, I was short (so said the Gap). From a tall, thin Women's, I had morphed into a petite, plump Misses'—without gaining or losing a smidgen of flesh.

There ought to be a dictionary entry for those who enter the Western world to find that their bodies are thin no more. My vote goes to "slimmigrant"—for an immigrant who discovers that he or she needs to shed a dozen pounds to be considered unfat.

My quest for asslimilation began with a whimper. I forswore mayonnaise, peanut butter, cheesecake, and tortilla chips—delicacies I'd never sampled before coming to America. I stopped going to those $9.99 Indian buffets with their unlimited helpings of butter chicken. For the first time in my life, I visited a gym, where my whimpers became shrieks of pain.

My extra poundage, however, was like a cockroach; it might disappear for a while, but it could never be eradicated. Potluck lunches, Thanksgiving dinners, and snow days made sure of that.

Two years ago, on my thirtieth birthday, I resolved to remain plump forever rather than go on another diet. And to escape my new homeland, which considered me overweight, I resolved to take a holiday in

Chennai, where salesgirls would hint that garments would drape better if only I were wider, my aunt would insist that I was scrawny, and my mother would feed me restorative spoonfuls of clarified butter. I booked my plane tickets.

Slimmigrants, beware!

Satellite television and globalization had changed the city I grew up in: in the five years I'd been away, skim milk had replaced the heavy cream of middle-class India, and those cushiony Bollywood heroines had been supplanted by supermodels whose hipbones could shred lettuce.

It seemed that every girl in Chennai was wearing trousers (and the girls' waists seemed no bigger round than a CD). The neighborhood video-rental store had become a fitness center. Even my aunt had bought a stationary bike (which she rode very competently in her sari).

My mother said she was glad to see me looking so nice and healthy. Time to go on a diet, I realized. I opted for the Mediterranean one—I love pizza.

QUESTIONS: For Thinking and Writing

1. Is beauty a cultural construction? Why are some physical characteristics admired in some cultures but not in others? Can you think of any physical traits that Americans esteem that other cultures do not?
2. How much do the opinions of others influence your personal view of your body and your concept of beauty? Was the author of this piece influenced by her family members or by American constructs of beauty? Whose opinions mattered more, and why?
3. Is body size a part of who you are? Do we try to pretend body size doesn't matter, while feeling that it really does? Explain.
4. Write about a time in your life when you received criticism or praise for your appearance. What did people notice about your body? How did it make you feel? How did you react?
5. As the author explains, in India, plumpness is a sign of health and beauty. Explore the social and psychological aspects of this idea. What would your life be like if the Indian view of beauty and health were embraced by Western culture? Would you be more comfortable in your own skin or, like the author, encouraged to eat more spoonfuls of clarified butter? Explain.

Get Real

Most people who suffer from eating disorders, such as anorexia nervosa or bulimia, also experience distorted self-perception. The person they see in the mirror differs drastically from their physical reality. The National Eating Disorders Association (NEDA) launched the "Get Real" awareness campaign to portray how distorted the self-image of someone suffering from an eating disorder can be. This print ad was created for NEDA in 2005 by Porter Novelli, a public relations firm known for health promotion campaigns.

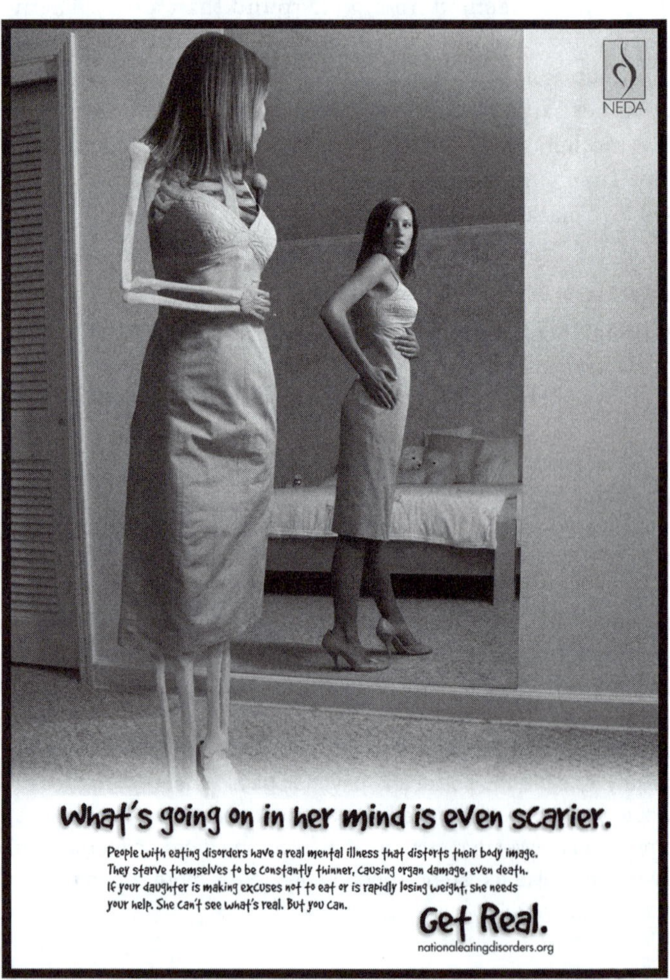

QUESTIONS: For Thinking and Writing

1. If you were leafing through a magazine and saw this ad, would you stop to read it? Why or why not? What catches your eye? How long would you spend looking at the ad? Explain.
2. Visit the NEDA Web site at www.nationaleatingdisorders.org and read about eating disorders in men and women (look at the "Eating Disorder Info" pages). Who is at risk for an eating disorder? What roles do social and cultural pressure play in exacerbating eating disorders? Explain.
3. What is happening in the photo? What is the woman thinking? What does she see? What do we see? What message does the photo convey?
4. Who is the target audience for this ad? Do you think someone with an eating disorder will be persuaded to follow the advice in the ad? If not, who is likely to respond to it? Explain.

ALISA VALDES

My Hips, My Caderas

The saying "beauty is in the eye of the beholder" may be better expressed as "beauty is in the eye of the culture." A feature or characteristic that one culture finds unappealing may be considered beautiful in another. Physical beauty seems to be largely a subjective thing—some cultures artificially elongate the neck, others put plates in their lips, and others prefer tiny feet or high foreheads. As a Latina woman with a white mother and a Cuban father, Alisa Valdes explores the challenges she faces straddling the beauty preferences of two cultures. This piece was published as an online essay on UnderWire MSN *in April 2000.*

My father is Cuban, with dark hair, a cleft in his chin, and feet that can dance the Guaguanco.

My mother is white and American, as blue-eyed as they come.

My voluptuous/big hips are both Cuban and American. And neither. Just like me. As I shift different halves of my soul daily to match whichever cultural backdrop I happen to face, I also carefully prepare myself for how differently my womanly/fat hips will be treated in my two realities.

It all started 15 years ago, when my hips bloomed in Albuquerque, New Mexico, where I was born. I went from being a track club twig—mistaken more than once for a boy—to being a splendidly curving thing that Chicano men with their bandanas down low whistled at as they drove by in their low-riders. White boys in my middle school thought I suddenly had a fat ass, and had no problem saying so.

But the cholos loved me. San Mateo Boulevard . . . I remember it well. Jack in the Box on one corner, me on a splintered wooden bench with a Three Musketeers bar, tight shorts, a hot summer sun, and those catcalls and woof-woofs like slaps. I was 12.

My best friend Stacy and I set out dieting right away that summer, to lose our new hips so boys from the heights, like the nearly albino Tim Fairfield with the orange soccer socks, would like us. In those days, I was too naive to know that dismissing the Chicano guys from the valley and taking French instead of Spanish in middle school were leftovers of colonialism. Taking Spanish still had the stigma of shame, like it would make you a dirty wetback. So Stacy and I pushed through hundreds of leg lifts on her bedroom floor, an open Seventeen magazine as a tiny table for our lemon water, and the sound of cicadas grinding away in the tree outside.

In Spanish, the word for hips is *caderas*—a broad term used to denote everything a real woman carries from her waist to her thighs, all the way around. Belly, butt, it's all part of your caderas. And caderas are a magical sphere of womanhood. In the lyrics of Merengue and Salsa, caderas are to be shaken, caressed, admired, and exalted. The bigger, the better. In Spanish, you eat your rice and beans and sometimes your chicharrones, because you fear your caderas will disappear.

In my work as a Latin music critic for a Boston newspaper, I frequent nightclubs with wood-paneled walls and Christmas lights flashing all year long. I wear short rubber skirts and tall shoes. There, I swing my round hips like a metronome. I become fierce. I strut. In the red disco lights, my hips absolutely torture men. I can see it on their faces.

"Mujeron!" they exclaim as I shimmy past. Much woman. They click their tongues, buy me drinks. They ask me to dance, and I often say "no," because I can. And these men suffer. Ironically, this makes the feminist in me very happy. In these places, my mujeron's hips get more nods than they might at a pony farm.

In English, your hips are those pesky things on the sides of your hipbones. They don't *"menear"* as they do in Spanish: they "jiggle." In

English, hips are something women try to be rid of. Hips are why women bruise themselves in the name of liposuction.

My mother's people hate my hips. They diet. My aunt smokes so she won't eat. And in the gym where I teach step aerobics—a habit I took up in the days when I identified more with my mother's than my father's people—I sometimes hear the suburban anorexics whisper in the front row: "My God, would you look at those hips." Sometimes they walk out of the room even before I have begun teaching, as if hips were contagious. In these situations, I am sad. I drive home and examine my hips in the mirror, hit them for being so imprudent, like great big ears on the side of my body. Sometimes I fast for days. Sometimes I make myself puke up rice and beans. Usually I get over it, but it always comes back.

Sociologists will tell you that in cultures where women are valued for traditional roles of mother and caregiver, hips are in, and that in cultures where those roles have broken down and women try to be like men were in traditional societies—i.e., have jobs—hips are out.

So when I want to be loved for my body, I am a Latina. But most Latino men will not love my mind as they do my body, because I am an Americanized professional. Indeed, they will feel threatened and will soon lose interest in hips that want to *"andar por la calle come un hombre"* (carry themselves like a man).

When I want to be loved for my mind, I flock to liberal intellectuals, usually whites. They listen to my writings and nod . . . and then suggest I use skim milk instead of cream. These men love my fire and passion—words they always use to describe a Latina—but they are embarrassed by my hips. They want me to wear looser pants.

In some ways I am lucky to be able to move between two worlds. At least my hips get acknowledged as beautiful. I can't say the same for a lot of my bulimic friends, who don't have a second set of standards to turn to. But still, I dream of the day when bicultural Latinas will set the standards for beauty and success, when our voluptuous caderas won't bar us from getting through those narrow American doors.

QUESTIONS: For Thinking and Writing

1. Valdes notes that sociologists conjecture that in cultures in which women adhere to the more "traditional" roles of housewife and mother, hips and voluptuous forms are considered beautiful. Evaluate this

theory and its implied inversion—that in societies in which women hold jobs outside the home, small waists and hips are culturally preferred by both sexes.

2. Does the author view the transformation of her hips from her "track club twig" physique to her more womanly shape as a positive or negative change? How does her writing reveal her feelings?
3. Valdes writes, "My mother's people hate my hips." Who are her "mother's people"? Does it seem strange that she would refer to her relatives this way? Compare her description of her mother's side of the family to that of her father's side of the family.
4. How does Valdes's mixed background create conflict in her life? How does she deal with this conflict?
5. Valdes writes, "In cultures where women are valued for traditional roles of mother and caregiver, hips are in." If beauty is a cultural creation, how is it constructed? Explore the idea that social politics influence our cultural sense of beauty in a short essay.

VIEWPOINTS

A Man's Guide to Slimming Couture

Scott McKeen

Why Do We Get to Laugh at Fat Guys?

Catherine Lawson

The next two readings explore different views of the same issue. Although obesity is a sensitive issue for many people, it is also a common theme in humor. Fat guys play funny sidekicks in movies, goofy fathers and husbands in sitcoms, and everybody's pal at the bar. Although the popular media seems to welcome the comedic outlet provided by fat men, the same does not seem to hold true for women. In the first piece, Scott McKeen treats the issue of a potbelly with humor and cunning, as he details eight ways to hide one's middle region. Catherine Lawson, responding to McKeen's article, wonders why it is socially permissible to laugh at fat men but not fat women. After laughing at McKeen's list, Lawson suddenly realizes that she would not be laughing if the article gave advice to fat women. Is this lack of sensitivity to male obesity fair? And why is it more acceptable for men to be fat than for women? McKeen's article appeared in the Edmonton Journal *in December 1999. Lawson's response was first published on December 9 in the* Ottawa Citizen, *and it was updated in February of 2007.*

A Man's Guide to Slimming Couture

Scott McKeen

Trick No. 1: Never, ever wear horizontal stripes. Vertical stripes, in shirts and in suits, are good because they lengthen one's silhouette, which is slimming, don't you know?

Trick No. 2: Always wear a jacket or suit, unless you work near dangerous industrial machinery. Jackets are good because they hide that stuff spilling over your belt.

Trick No. 2A: A double-breasted jacket, with its large lapels, can create a slimming V-shape and is always buttoned, putting a curtain between your gut and the world.

Trick No. 2B: Warning: if a double-breasted jacket is too long, it will shorten your legs visually, and you'll be a fat troll in a blazer. On some men, blazers look tent-like. Ask your wife or girlfriend: "Do I look fat in this?"

Trick No. 2C: A three-button single-breasted jacket is often better than a two-button because the lapels are shorter, making the body of the suit—and you—appear longer and slimmer.

Trick No. 3: Never, ever, tie your necktie too short. It will sit over your belly like a neon motel sign, pointing directly to your straining waistline, screaming "NO VACANCY."

Trick No. 4: The fat man's paradox—a big man squeezed into small clothes will look bigger, what with all the tell-tale strains, wrinkles, rolls, button gaps and—yeesh—underwear lines.

Trick No. 4A: Buy one size too big and you'll look relaxed; your collar won't create an unsightly skin turtleneck, and your clothes will drape properly, hiding those rolls or bulges.

Trick No. 4B: When shopping, don't even look at the suit or waist size. If it fits, it fits. Just because you're now wearing a 42 waist doesn't mean you're not still a great big loveable guy. Honest.

Trick No. 4C: If you scrutinize waist size, pride will take over. You'll walk out with a size 34 waist and in those pants, you'll look stressed, fat, and your vitals will go numb. Hence the stress.

Trick No. 5: Stick with dark, classic, and solid colors—black, blue, and grey. Anything else, especially on a shirt, will draw the eye to your stomach. You don't want eyes on your stomach.

Trick No. 5A: Be mostly monochromatic in your entire ensemble. A dark shirt and trousers create one, long, slimming silhouette. A light shirt with dark trousers draws the eye to the border between the two—your belt line—which, to the observer, looks like the equator.

Trick No. 5B: The same rules apply to a jacket and shirt. Wear an unbuttoned dark jacket with a white shirt and it will be like opening the curtain on an off-Broadway production of Porky's.

Trick No. 5C: Same goes for dark suspenders over a white shirt. The suspenders will frame the bulk like a photo of fat. A dark vest with dark trousers is good, though.

Trick No. 6: Damn the fashions, pleats on pants are good for potbellies. Straight, slim-profile pants contrast with a larger upper half, creating "chicken legs," as one well-known local sartor put it.

Trick No. 7: To tuck or not to tuck? Unless you're in the cast of *Friends*, skinny, or under 25, tuck your shirt into your pants. Anything else screams: FAT GUY HIDING HIS FAT.

Trick No. 8: Don't fret over The Big Question About Potbellies, which is: Where should my belt ride—below the gut, on the gut, or above the gut? Let comfort decide . . . .

Trick No. 8A: But be warned—a belt riding below the gut can cause an unsightly case of cascading corpulence. On the other hand, chest-high pants make it appear as if your shoulders are riding directly atop your butt.

Trick No. 8B: Suspenders can work, especially on bigger pots. They allow for large pants to cross just below the navel—and stay there. No problems then with butt crack, shirttail escape, or that cinched look you get with a too-tight belt across the stomach.

Trick No. 8C: Owners of difficult-to-fit potbellies might want to try a pair of tailored slacks, especially if the proper waist size creates other problems, like an unwieldy crotch. (Don't even go there.) Handmade slacks will cost you so much money, though, that you might actually prefer numb vitals. Ask your wife.

Why Do We Get to Laugh at Fat Guys?

Catherine Lawson

The first time I read Scott McKeen's article on eight tricks to hide a potbelly [above], I laughed all the way through it. I loved its hectoring tone, and the way he didn't mince words on the best way to disguise fat wrinkles, rolls, button gaps, and underwear lines.

Then it hit me: Would I be laughing if these were fashion tips for women? I thought of all the fashion advice for overweight women that I had ever read. The tone is usually deadly serious, and there are terms like "empowerment," "self-acceptance," and "body image" sprinkled liberally throughout. Mr. McKeen, on the other hand, although he dispenses some excellent advice, is playing it for laughs.

So why is it okay to make jokes about fat men, but completely taboo to laugh at fat women? (Heck, I'm not even comfortable putting the words "fat" and "women" together.) Would I have accepted a story for publication that described portly women in double-breasted blazers as looking like fat trolls? Definitely not. Would I have chosen to illustrate a story on fashion for plus-size women with a close-up photo of a stomach encased in a too-tight top? Unthinkable.

It's conventional wisdom that men and women have vastly different body images. If you want to give a chunky man some fashion advice, you cannot be subtle. In a recent episode of *Family Guy,* the corpulent Peter reacts in shock when his doctor tells him he's fat. "Did you just say I was fat? Okay. This is news to me." Then he turns to his trim cartoon wife, Lois. "Did you know this?" Her response is a silent roll of the eyes. We laugh at this because it contains an oversized grain of truth. Men don't spend much time gazing in the mirror. However, even a slightly overweight woman doesn't need to be told she could lose a few pounds, and it's a safe assumption she's hungry for advice on how to look slimmer.

It's likely very few of us remember why Rosie O'Donnell and Donald Trump had that unseemly spat a while back. As the insults flew, none attracted more negative attention than when Trump called O'Donnell fat. He was soon backtracking. "I used the word 'slob,' I used the word 'degenerate,' and I used the words 'not very smart.' The word 'fat' played a very small role, if any, in my description of her."

Taking a look at their respective chins, O'Donnell could just have easily used the f-word to describe Trump; instead, she called him "a comb-over bunny." (Ouch!) Her very female response to Trump's insult was: "I love when people say you're fat, like you don't know."

Of course, plenty of men do know they're fat, and some are very sensitive about it. Yet even they aren't looking for fashion tips to hide those extra pounds. Why should they? Since the dawn of TV history, that poundage hasn't kept men from getting and keeping the (slim) girl. It began with Jackie Gleason on *The Honeymooners* (Gleason, interestingly enough, makes a cameo appearance on that episode of *Family Guy*). The present-day examples are Jim Belushi of *According to Jim* and Kevin James of *King of Queens,* both with svelte wives.

The same Kevin James does even better in the 2005 movie *Hitch,* when he hires "date doctor" Will Smith to help him win the heart of Amber Valletta. Not once does Hitch say the obvious: "You're short and dumpy and you want a supermodel. Are you nuts?" Instead we get his soothing philosophy, "Any man has the chance to sweep any woman off her feet."

So there's back waxing and dance lessons, but no weight-loss program for James's character. *Family Guy*'s Peter doesn't bother dieting either. Instead, he founds the National Association for the Advancement of Fat People. The sign outside the first meeting says, very tellingly, "No fat chicks."

The few fat, or even slightly overweight, women on TV are single. Kirstie Alley may have had her own show, the provocatively named *Fat Actress,* but it ran for a measly seven episodes. Now she's parading her new body in a series of ads for a weight-loss system. The message is clear: The only story arc for a fat woman is to lose the weight, and then she can think about having a life.

Women pick up on that kind of inequity. And it leads us to the stark truth that, in our society, a woman's appearance is still far more important than a man's. We can laugh at fat guys because they are also inherently loveable, well-dressed or not. A woman who fails to dress in a way that disguises those extra pounds is out of the game. If you make a joke about a man's gut, all you've done is made fun of his stomach. Insult a woman's body, and you wound her soul.

I called Scott McKeen to ask if there had been any complaints about his article when it ran in the *Edmonton Journal*. "Not a one," he said.

Many people did ask if the potbelly in the photo is his. He stresses that it definitely is not. You see, fat guys may be funny, but no one aspires to be one.

QUESTIONS: For Thinking and Writing

1. Think of the number of popular movies and television programs featuring fat men as the focal point for humor. Now think of the number of programs that feature fat women. How do the two compare?
2. Answer Lawson's question in your own words: "Why do we get to laugh at fat guys?"
3. Why is Lawson uncomfortable even "putting the words 'fat' and 'women' together"? What is the source of her discomfort?
4. According to Lawson, what are some of the disparities between fat men and fat women? Do you agree or disagree with her assessment? Explain.
5. Lawson comments that if you joke about a man's gut, all you have done is made fun of his stomach. But if you "insult a woman's body, you wound her soul." Write an essay in which you explore this idea.

QUESTIONS: For Further Research and Group Work

1. Make a list of the prime-time comedy shows on television. After compiling the list, identify the overweight characters on each program. What is the male-to-female ratio of these characters? Compare your findings with some of the points made in Lawson's essay, and formulate a response in which you support or question her conclusions.
2. Select two or three non-Western countries and research the cultural perspectives of beauty and health for each. (You may wish to ask international students for their perspectives on this topic.) How do the standards of beauty in the countries you researched compare with Western definitions? In your opinion (and supported by your research) what role, if any, does American popular culture have on body image in these countries?
3. In her article, Alisa Valdes implies that white women feel more pressure to be thin than Latina women do, because Latin culture holds women to a different standard of beauty. In small groups, explore the idea that beauty

is culturally determined—that is, what one group may find beautiful, another may not. Can you find any evidence that the all-American image of beauty is changing?

4. Select two characters from a recent film or popular television program. Write a description of each character's body type and attire. Discuss the connection (if any) between the physical appearance of the characters you selected and the temperament, personality, or nature of the character. What influence, if any, do the characters, or the actors who play them, exert on the fashion world and on our cultural constructions of beauty?
5. Ask at least ten people to respond to this question: If you could be either very beautiful or very wealthy, which would you choose, and why? Based on the multiple responses you receive, can you reach any conclusions about the influence of beauty on men and women in today's society? Explain.
6. Take a look at several popular fashion magazines aimed at men *(Details, GQ, Esquire)*. Different group members may want to focus on different aspects of the magazines—such as advertising, articles, fashion, or advice columns. Do the models in the magazine fit the description in Cloud's article? What do the articles suggest men should aspire to look like? How many articles on improving appearance are featured? After reviewing the magazines, discuss your findings and collaborate on an essay about how men's fashion magazines help define the "ideal" male.

2 CHAPTER

Wanting It, Selling It

ADVERTISING IS EVERYWHERE—TELEVISION, NEWSPAPERS, magazines, the Internet, the sides of buses and trains, highway billboards, T-shirts, sports arenas, and even license plates. It is the driving force of our consumer economy, accounting for 150 billion dollars worth of commercials and print ads each year—more than the gross national product of many countries in the world—and filling a quarter of each television hour and the bulk of most newspapers and magazines. It is everywhere people are, and its appeal goes to the quick of our fantasies: happiness, material wealth, eternal youth, social acceptance, sexual fulfillment, and power. Through carefully selected images and words, it is the most pervasive form of persuasion in America and, perhaps, the single most significant manufacturer of meaning in our consumer society. And many of us are not aware of its astounding influence on our lives.

Most of us are so accustomed to advertising that we hear it without listening and see it without looking. However, if we stop to examine how it works on our subconscious, we would be amazed at how powerful and complex a psychological force it is. This chapter examines how words compel us to buy, how images feed our fantasies, and how the advertising industry tempts us to part with our money.

ROBERT SAMUELSON

Shop 'til We Drop?

The Puritan ethics of humility, industry, and thrift on which America was founded have given way to a "buy now" mentality in which consumption is king. In this essay, Newsweek *columnist Robert Samuelson explores some of the social forces driving American consumer culture. Are Americans in a hedonistic consumer freefall? Why do Americans seem compelled to buy, and what will happen if the money runs out? This essay was published in the Winter 2004 issue of the* Wilson Quarterly.

We shop, therefore we are. This is not exactly the American credo, but it comes close to being the American pastime. Even infants and toddlers quickly absorb the consumer spirit through television and trips to the supermarket ("I want that" is a common refrain). As we age, consumption becomes an engine of envy, because in America, the idea is that everyone should have everything—which means that hardly anyone ever has enough. The notion that wants and needs have reached a limit of material and environmental absurdity, though preached fervently by some social activists and intellectuals, barely influences ordinary Americans. They continue to flock to shopping malls, automobile dealers, cruise ships, and health clubs. There are always, it seems, new wants and needs to be satisfied.

Although consumerism now defines all wealthy societies, it's still practiced most religiously in its country of origin. Indeed, Americans have rarely so indulged the urge to splurge as in the past decade. Look at the numbers. In 2002, consumer spending accounted for 70 percent of U.S. national income (gross domestic product), which is a modern American record—and a much higher figure than in any other advanced nation. In Japan and France, consumer spending in 2002 was only 55 percent of GDP; in Italy and Spain, it was 60 percent. These rates are typical elsewhere. Even in the United States, consumer spending was only 67 percent of GDP as recently as 1994. Three added percentage points of GDP may seem trivial, but in today's dollars, they amount to an extra $325 billion annually.

This spending spree has, in some ways, been a godsend. Without it, the U.S. and world economies would recently have fared much worse. During the 1997–1998 Asian financial crisis, the irrepressible buying of American consumers cushioned the shock to countries that, suddenly unable to borrow abroad, had to curb their domestic spending. Roughly half of U.S. imports consist of consumer goods, automobiles, and food (oil, other raw materials, and industrial goods make up the balance). By selling Americans more shoes, toys, clothes, and electronic gadgets, Asian countries partially contained higher unemployment. U.S. trade deficits exploded. From 1996 to 2000, the deficit of the current account (a broad measure of trade) grew from $177 billion to $411 billion.

Later, the buying binge sustained the U.S. economy despite an onslaught of bad news that, by all logic, should have been devastating: the popping of the stock market "bubble" of the 1990s; rising unemployment (as dot-com firms went bankrupt and business investment—led by telecommunications spending—declined); 9/11; and a string of corporate scandals (Enron, WorldCom, Tyco). But American consumers barely paused, and responded to falling interest rates by prolonging their binge. Car and light-truck sales of 17.1 million units in 2001 gave the automobile industry its second-best year ever, after 2000. The fourth- and fifth-best years were 2002 (16.8 million units) and 2003 (an estimated 16.6 million units). Strong home sales buoyed appliance, furniture, and carpet production.

To some extent, the consumption boom is old hat. Acquisitiveness is deeply embedded in American culture. Describing the United States in the 1830s, Alexis de Tocqueville marveled over the widespread "taste for physical gratification." Still, the ferocity of the latest consumption outburst poses some interesting questions: Why do Americans spend so much more of their incomes than other peoples? How can we afford to do that? After all, economic theory holds that societies become wealthier only by sacrificing some present consumption to invest in the future. And if we aren't saving enough, can the consumer boom continue?

Let's start with why Americans spend so much. One reason is that our political and cultural traditions differ from those of other nations. We do some things in the private market that other societies do through government. Health care, education, and social welfare are good examples. Most middle-class Americans under 65 pay for their own health care, either directly or through employer-provided health insurance (which reduces their take-home pay). That counts as private consumption. In countries with government-run health care systems, similar medical costs are classified as government spending. The same thing is true of education. Although U.S. public schools involve government spending, college tuition (or tuition for private school or preschool) counts as personal consumption. Abroad, governments often pay more of total educational costs.

It's also true that the United States saves and invests less than other nations—investment here meaning money that, though initially channeled into stocks, bonds, or bank deposits, ultimately goes into new factories, machinery, computers, and office buildings. Low U.S. saving and investment rates have often inspired alarm about America's future. In 1990, for instance, Japan's national savings rate was 34 percent of GDP, more than double the U.S. rate of 16 percent. By outinvesting us, Japan (it was said) would become the world's wealthiest nation. That hasn't happened, in part because what matters is not only how much countries invest but how well they invest it. And Americans generally are better investors than others.

Of course, there's waste. The hundreds of billions of dollars invested in unneeded dot-com and telecom networks in the late 1990s are simply the latest reminder of that. But the American business system corrects its blunders fairly quickly. If projects don't show signs of becoming profitable, they usually don't get more capital. Wall Street's obsession with profits—though sometimes deplored as discouraging long-term investment—compels companies to cut costs and improve productivity. If bankrupt firms (Kmart and United Airlines are recent examples) can't improve efficiency, their assets (stores, planes) are sold to others who hope to do better. American banks, unlike Japanese banks, don't rescue floundering companies; neither (usually) does the government, unlike governments in Europe. Getting more bang from our investment buck, we can afford to invest less and consume more.

Our privileged position in the world economy reinforces the effect. Since the 1970s, we've run trade deficits that have allowed us to have our cake and eat it too: All those imports permit adequate investment rates without crimping consumption. We send others dollars; they send us cars, clothes, and computer chips. It's a good deal as long as we're near full employment (when we're not, high imports add to unemployment). The trade gap—now about 5 percent of GDP—persists in part because the dollar serves as the major global currency. Foreigners—companies and individuals—want dollars, so they can conduct trade and make international investments. Some governments hoard dollars, because they'd rather export than import. The strong demand for dollars props up the exchange rate, making our imports less expensive and our exports more expensive. Continuous trade deficits result.

All this suggests that the consumer boom could go on forever, because Americans always feel the need to outdo the Joneses—or at least to stay even with them. No level of consumption ever suffices, because the social competition is constant. The surge in prosperity after World War II briefly fostered the illusion that the competition was ebbing, because so many things that had once been restricted (homes, cars, televisions) became so widely available. "If everyone could enjoy the good things of life—as defined by mass merchandisers—the meanness of class distinctions would disappear," Vance Packard wrote in his 1959 classic *The Status Seekers*. Instead, he found, Americans had developed new distinctions, including bigger homes and flashier clothes.

Four decades later, little has changed. Americans constantly pursue new markers of success and status. In 2002, the median size of a new home was 20 percent larger than in 1987, even though families had gotten smaller. Luxury car sales have soared. According to the marketing research firm of J. D. Power and Associates, in 1980, luxury brands—mainly Cadillacs and Lincolns, along with some Mercedes—accounted for only 4.5 percent of new-vehicle sales. By 2003, luxury brands—a category that now includes Lexus, Infiniti, and Acura, along with Hummers and more BMWs and Mercedes—exceeded 10 percent of sales. Second homes are another way that people separate themselves from the crowd. Perhaps 100,000 to 125,000 such homes are built annually, says economist Gopal Ahluwalia of the National Association of Homebuilders. In the 1990s, comparable figures were between 75,000 and 100,000.

To critics, this "consumption treadmill" is self-defeating, as Cornell University economist Robert H. Frank put it in his 1999 book *Luxury Fever: Money and Happiness in an Era of Excess*. People compete to demonstrate their superiority, but most are frustrated because others continually catch up. Meanwhile, overconsumption—homes that are too big, cars that are too glitzy—actually detracts from people's happiness and society's well-being, Frank argued. Striving to maximize their incomes, workers sacrifice time with family and friends—time that, according to surveys, they would prize highly. And society's reluctance to take money out of consumers' pockets through taxation means too little is spent to solve collective problems, such as poverty and pollution.

As a cure, Frank proposed a progressive consumption tax. People would be taxed only on what they spent, at rates rising to 70 percent above $500,000. Savings (put, for example, into stocks, bonds, and bank deposits) would be exempt. The tax would deter extravagant spending and encourage saving, Frank contended. Total consumption spending would be lower, government spending could be higher, and the competition for status would simply occur at lower levels of foolishness. The "erstwhile Ferrari driver . . . might turn instead to [a] Porsche," he wrote. Whatever their merits, proposals such as this lack political support. Indeed, they do not differ dramatically—except for high tax rates—from the present income tax, which allows generous deductions for savings through vehicles such as 401(k) plans and individual retirement accounts.

Still, America's consumption boom could falter, because it faces three powerful threats: debt, demographics, and the dollar.

Over six decades, we've gone from being a society uneasy with credit to a society that rejoices in it. In 1946, household debt was 22 percent of personal disposable income. Now, it's roughly 110 percent. Both business and government have promoted more debt. In 1950, Diners Club introduced the modern credit card, which could be used at multiple restaurants and stores. (Some department stores and oil companies were already offering cards restricted to their outlets.) New laws—the Fair Housing Act of 1968, the Equal Credit Opportunity Act of 1974—prohibited discriminatory lending. One result was the invention of credit-scoring formulas that evaluate potential borrowers on their past payment of bills, thereby reducing bias against women, the poor, and minorities. Similarly, the federal government encourages home mortgages through Fannie Mae and Freddie Mac, government-created companies that buy mortgages.

This "democratization of credit" has enabled consumer spending to grow slightly faster than consumer income. People simply borrow more. Economist Thomas Durkin of the Federal Reserve notes the following: In 1951, 20 percent of U.S. households had a mortgage, compared with 44 percent in 2001; in 1970, only 16 percent of households had a bank credit card, compared with 73 percent in 2001. The trouble is that this accumulation of debt can't continue forever. Sooner or later, Americans will decide that they've got as much as they can handle. Or lenders will discover that they've exhausted good and even mediocre credit risks. No one knows when that will happen, but once it occurs, consumer spending may rise only as fast as consumer income—and slower still if borrowers collectively repay debts.

What could hasten the turning point is the baby boom. We're now on the edge of a momentous generational shift. The oldest baby boomers (born in 1946) will be 58 in 2004; the youngest (born in 1964) will be 40. For most Americans, peak spending occurs between the ages of 35 and 54, when household consumption is about 20 percent above average, according to Susan Sterne, an economist with Economic Analysis Associates. Then it gradually declines. People don't buy new sofas or refrigerators. They pay off debts. For 15 years or so, the economy has benefited from baby boomers' feverish buying. It may soon begin to suffer from their decreased spending.

Finally, there's the dollar. Should foreign demand for U.S. investments wane—or should American politicians, worried about jobs, press other countries to stop accumulating U.S. Treasury securities—the dollar would decline on foreign exchange markets. There would simply be less demand, as foreigners sold dollars for other currencies. Then our imports could become more expensive, while our exports could become cheaper. Domestic supplies might tighten. Price pressures on consumer goods—cars, electronics, clothes—could intensify. This might cause Americans to buy a little less. But if they continued buying as before, the long-heralded collision between consumption and investment might materialize. (As this article goes to press, the dollar has dropped from its recent highs. The ultimate effects remain to be seen.)

Little is preordained. Sterne thinks retired baby boomers may defy history and become spendthrifts. "They don't care about leaving anything to their kids," she says. "There's no reluctance to go into debt." Their chosen instrument would be the "reverse mortgage," which unlocks home equity. (Under a reverse mortgage, a homeowner receives a payment from the lender up to some percentage of the home's value; upon the owner's death, the loan is repaid, usually through sale of the house.) Maybe. But maybe the post-World War II consumption boom has reached its peak. If the retreat occurs gently, the consequences, at least on paper, should be painless and imperceptible. We'll spend a little less of our incomes and save a little more. We'll import a little less and export a little more. These modest changes shouldn't hurt, but they might. The U.S. and world economies have grown so accustomed to being stimulated by the ravenous appetite of ordinary Americans that you can't help but wonder what will happen if that appetite disappears.

QUESTIONS: For Thinking and Writing

1. Samuelson begins his essay with a declaration, "We shop, therefore we are." What is the original statement from which he adopts this expression? What is the connection between our sense of existence and the things we buy?
2. What is the author's position on American consumer habits? Identify specific statements and words, as well as the author's tone, that reveal his opinion.
3. Samuelson asks, "Why do Americans spend so much more of their incomes than other peoples?" Answer this question drawing from the essay and from your own observations of American consumer culture.
4. What things do you want that money can buy? Do you want a luxury automobile? A designer wardrobe? A flat-screen television? What drives your desire for these things?
5. Samuelson observes that Americans are on a "consumption treadmill," because they buy things to demonstrate their superiority but are frustrated because others continually catch up. Write about your own consumer motivations. What do you want to buy, and why? How could what you buy demonstrate "superiority"? Explain.

PEGGY ORENSTEIN

What's Wrong With Cinderella?

To call princesses a passing fad among little girls is "like calling Harry Potter a book," explains author and noted feminist Peggy Orenstein in this next essay that appeared in the New York Times *in December of 2006. The Disney media engine has been pushing the princess theme intensely in recent years, after practically stumbling upon its popularity in 2001. Disney sales in princess gear exceeds $3 billion. Is the pitch too intense? Is it sending the wrong message to little girls? In the next article, Orenstein describes her reaction to the princess onslaught and her helplessness to stop it from drawing in her own little girl.*

I finally came unhinged in the dentist's office—one of those ritzy pediatric practices tricked out with comic books, DVDs, and arcade games—where I'd taken my 3-year-old daughter for her first exam. Until then, I'd held my tongue. I'd smiled politely every time the supermarket-checkout clerk greeted her with "Hi, Princess;" ignored the waitress at our local breakfast joint who called the funny-face pancakes she ordered her "princess meal;" made no comment when the lady at Long's Drugs said, "I bet I know your favorite color" and handed her a pink balloon, rather than letting her choose for herself. Maybe it was the dentist's Betty Boop inflection that got to me, but when she pointed to the exam chair and said, "Would you like to sit in my special princess throne so I can sparkle your teeth?" I lost it.

"Oh, for God's sake," I snapped. "Do you have a princess drill, too?"

She stared at me as if I were an evil stepmother.

"Come on!" I continued, my voice rising. "It's 2006, not 1950. This is Berkeley, California. Does every little girl really have to be a princess?"

My daughter, who was reaching for a Cinderella sticker, looked back and forth between us. "Why are you so mad, Mama?" she asked. "What's wrong with princesses?"

Diana may be dead and Masako disgraced, but here in America, we are in the midst of a royal moment. To call princesses a "trend" among girls is like calling Harry Potter a book. Sales at Disney Consumer Products, which started the craze six years ago by packaging nine of its female characters under one royal rubric, have shot up to $3 billion globally this year, from $300 million in 2001. There are now more than 25,000 Disney Princess items. "Princess," as some Disney execs call it, is not only the fastest-growing brand the company has ever created; they say it is on its way to becoming the largest girls' franchise on the planet.

Meanwhile, in 2001 Mattel brought out its own "world of girl" line of princess Barbie dolls, DVDs, toys, clothing, home décor, and myriad other products. At a time when Barbie sales were declining domestically, they became instant best sellers. Shortly before that, Mary Drolet, a Chicago-area mother and former Claire's and Montgomery Ward executive, opened Club Libby Lu, now a chain of mall stores based largely in the suburbs in which girls ages 4 to 12 can shop for "Princess Phones" covered in faux fur and attend "Princess-Makeover Birthday Parties." Saks bought Club Libby Lu in 2003 for $12 million and has since expanded it to 87 outlets; by 2005, with only scant local advertising, revenues hovered around the $46 million mark, a 53 percent jump from the previous year. Pink, it seems, is the new gold.

Even Dora the Explorer, the intrepid, dirty-kneed adventurer, has ascended to the throne: in 2004, after a two-part episode in which she turns into a "true princess," the Nickelodeon and Viacom consumer-products division released a satin-gowned "Magic Hair Fairytale Dora," with hair that grows or shortens when her crown is touched. Among other phrases the bilingual doll utters: "Vámonos! Let's go to fairy-tale land!" and "Will you brush my hair?"

As a feminist mother—not to mention a nostalgic product of the Grranimals era—I have been taken by surprise by the princess craze and the girlie-girl culture that has risen around it. What happened to William wanting a doll and not dressing your cat in an apron? Whither Marlo Thomas? I watch my fellow mothers, women who once swore they'd never be dependent on a man, smile indulgently at daughters who warble *So This Is Love* or insist on being called Snow White. I wonder if they'd concede so readily to sons who begged for combat fatigues and mock AK-47s.

More to the point, when my own girl makes her daily beeline for the dress-up corner of her preschool classroom—something I'm convinced she does largely to torture me—I worry about what playing Little Mermaid is teaching her. I've spent much of my career writing about experiences that undermine girls' well-being, warning parents that a preoccupation with body and beauty (encouraged by films, TV, magazines and, yes, toys) is perilous to their daughters' mental and physical health. Am I now supposed to shrug and forget all that? If trafficking in stereotypes doesn't matter at 3, when does it matter? At 6? Eight? Thirteen?

On the other hand, maybe I'm still surfing a washed-out second wave of feminism in a third-wave world. Maybe princesses are in fact a sign of progress, an indication that girls can embrace their predilection for pink without compromising strength or ambition; that, at long last, they can "have it all." Or maybe it is even less complex than that: to mangle Freud, maybe a princess is sometimes just a princess. And, as my daughter wants to know, what's wrong with that?

The rise of the Disney princesses reads like a fairy tale itself, with Andy Mooney, a former Nike executive, playing the part of prince, riding into the company on a metaphoric white horse in January 2000 to save a consumer-products division whose sales were dropping by as much as 30 percent a year. Both overstretched and underfocused, the division had triggered price wars by granting multiple licenses for core products (say, Winnie-the-Pooh undies) while ignoring the potential of new media. What's more, Disney films like *A Bug's Life* in 1998 had yielded few merchandising opportunities—what child wants to snuggle up with an ant?

It was about a month after Mooney's arrival that the magic struck. That's when he flew to Phoenix to check out his first "Disney on Ice" show. "Standing in line in the arena, I was surrounded by little girls dressed head to toe as princesses," he told me last summer in his palatial office, then located in Burbank, and speaking in a rolling Scottish burr. "They weren't even Disney products. They were generic princess products they'd appended to a Halloween costume. And the light bulb went off. Clearly there was latent demand here. So the next morning I said to my team, 'Okay, let's establish standards and a color palette and talk to licensees and get as much product out there as we possibly can that allows these girls to do what they're doing anyway: projecting themselves into the characters from the classic movies.'"

Mooney picked a mix of old and new heroines to wear the Pantone pink No. 241 corona: Cinderella, Sleeping Beauty, Snow White, Ariel, Belle, Jasmine, Mulan, and Pocahontas. It was the first time Disney marketed characters separately from a film's release, let alone lumped together those from different stories. To ensure the sanctity of what Mooney called their individual "mythologies," the princesses never make eye contact when they're grouped: each stares off in a slightly different direction as if unaware of the others' presence.

It is also worth noting that not all of the ladies are of royal extraction. Part of the genius of "Princess" is that its meaning is so broadly constructed that it actually has no meaning. Even Tinker Bell was originally a Princess, though her reign didn't last. "We'd always debate over whether she was really a part of the Princess mythology," Mooney recalled. "She really wasn't." Likewise, Mulan and Pocahontas, arguably the most resourceful of the bunch, are rarely depicted on Princess merchandise, though for a different reason. Their rustic garb has less bling potential than that of old-school heroines like Sleeping Beauty. (When Mulan does appear, she is typically in the kimonolike hanfu, which makes her miserable in the movie, rather than her liberated warrior's gear.)

The first Princess items, released with no marketing plan, no focus groups, no advertising, sold as if blessed by a fairy godmother. To this day, Disney conducts little market research on the Princess line, relying instead on the power of its legacy among mothers, as well as the instant-read sales barometer of the theme parks and Disney Stores. "We simply gave girls what they wanted," Mooney said of the line's success, "although I don't think any of us grasped how much they wanted this. I wish I could sit here and take credit for having some grand scheme to develop this, but all we did was envision a little girl's room and think about how she could live out the princess fantasy. The counsel we gave to licensees was: What type of bedding would a princess want to sleep in? What kind of alarm clock would a princess want to wake up to? What type of television would a princess like to see? It's a rare case where you find a girl who has every aspect of her room bedecked in Princess, but if she ends up with three or four of these items, well, then you have a very healthy business."

Every reporter Mooney talks to asks some version of my next question: Aren't the Princesses, who are interested only in clothes, jewelry, and cadging the handsome prince, somewhat retrograde role models?

"Look," he said, "I have friends whose son went through the Power Rangers phase who castigated themselves over what they must've done wrong. Then they talked to other parents whose kids had gone through it. The boy passes through. The girl passes through. I see girls expanding their imagination through visualizing themselves as princesses, and then they pass through that phase and end up becoming lawyers, doctors, mothers or princesses, whatever the case may be."

Mooney has a point: There are no studies proving that playing princess directly damages girls' self-esteem or dampens other aspirations. On the other hand, there is evidence that young women who hold the most conventionally feminine beliefs—who avoid conflict and think they should be perpetually nice and pretty—are more likely to be depressed than others and less likely to use contraception. What's more, the 23 percent decline in girls' participation in sports and other vigorous activity between middle and high school has been linked to their sense that athletics is unfeminine. And in a survey released last October by Girls Inc., school-age girls overwhelmingly reported a paralyzing pressure to be "perfect": not only to get straight As and be the student body president, editor of the newspaper, and captain of the swim team, but also to be "kind and caring," "please everyone, be very thin, and dress right." Give those girls a pumpkin and a glass slipper and they'd be in business.

At the grocery store one day, my daughter noticed a little girl sporting a Cinderella backpack. "There's that princess you don't like, Mama!" she shouted.

"Um, yeah," I said, trying not to meet the other mother's hostile gaze.

"Don't you like her blue dress, Mama?"

I had to admit, I did.

She thought about this. "Then don't you like her face?"

"Her face is all right," I said, noncommittally, though I'm not thrilled to have my Japanese-Jewish child in thrall to those Aryan features. (And what the heck are those blue things covering her ears?) "It's just, Honey, Cinderella doesn't really do anything."

Over the next 45 minutes, we ran through that conversation, verbatim, approximately 37 million times, as my daughter pointed out Disney Princess Band-Aids, Disney Princess paper cups, Disney Princess lip balm, Disney Princess pens, Disney Princess crayons, and Disney Princess notebooks—all cleverly displayed at the eye level of a 3-year-old trapped in a shopping cart—as well as a bouquet of Disney Princess balloons bobbing over the checkout line. The repetition was excessive, even for a preschooler. What was it about my answers that confounded her? What if, instead of realizing: Aha! Cinderella is a symbol of the patriarchal oppression of all women, another example of corporate mind control and power-to-the-people! my 3-year-old was thinking, Mommy doesn't want me to be a girl?

According to theories of gender constancy, until they're about 6 or 7, children don't realize that the sex they were born with is immutable. They believe that they have a choice: they can grow up to be either a mommy or a daddy. Some psychologists say that until permanency sets in, kids embrace whatever stereotypes our culture presents, whether it's piling on the most spangles or attacking one another with light sabers. What better way to assure that they'll always remain themselves? If that's the case, score one for Mooney. By not buying the Princess Pull-Ups, I may be inadvertently communicating that being female (to the extent that my daughter is able to understand it) is a bad thing.

Anyway, you have to give girls some credit. It's true that, according to Mattel, one of the most popular games young girls play is Bride, but Disney found that a groom or prince is incidental to that fantasy, a regrettable necessity at best. Although they keep him around for the climactic kiss, he is otherwise relegated to the bottom of the toy box, which is why you don't see him prominently displayed in stores.

What's more, just because they wear the tulle doesn't mean they've drunk the Kool-Aid. Plenty of girls stray from the script, say, by playing basketball in their finery, or casting themselves as the powerful evil stepsister bossing around the sniveling Cinderella. I recall a headline-grabbing 2005 British study that revealed that girls enjoy torturing, decapitating, and microwaving their Barbies nearly as much as they like to dress them up for dates. There is spice along with that sugar after all, though why this was news is beyond me: anyone who ever played with the doll knows there's nothing more satisfying than hacking off all her hair and holding her underwater in the bathtub. Princesses can even be a boon to exasperated parents: in our house, for instance, royalty never whines and uses the potty every single time.

"Playing princess is not the issue," argues Lyn Mikel Brown, an author, with Sharon Lamb, of *Packaging Girlhood: Rescuing Our Daughters From Marketers' Schemes.* "The issue is 25,000 Princess products," says Brown, a professor of education and human development at Colby College. "When one thing is so dominant, then it's no longer a choice: it's a mandate, cannibalizing all other forms of play. There's the illusion of more choices out there for girls, but if you look around, you'll see their choices are steadily narrowing."

It's hard to imagine that girls' options could truly be shrinking, when they dominate the honor roll and outnumber boys in college. Then again, have you taken a stroll through a children's store lately? A year ago, when we shopped for "big girl" bedding at Pottery Barn Kids, we found the "girls" side awash in flowers, hearts, and hula dancers; not a soccer player or sailboat in sight. Across the no-fly zone, the "boys" territory was all about sports, trains, planes, and automobiles. Meanwhile, Baby GAP's boys' onesies were emblazoned with "Big Man on Campus" and the girls' with "Social Butterfly"; guess whose matching shoes were decorated on the soles with hearts and whose sported a "No. 1" logo? And at Toys "R" Us, aisles of pink baby dolls, kitchens, shopping carts, and princesses unfurl a safe distance from the *Star Wars* figures, GeoTrax, and tool chests. The relentless resegregation of childhood appears to have sneaked up without any further discussion about sex roles, about what it now means to be a boy or to be a girl. Or maybe it has happened in lieu of such discussion, because it's easier this way.

Easier, that is, unless you want to buy your daughter something that isn't pink. Girls' obsession with that color may seem like something they're born with, like the ability to breathe or talk on the phone for hours on end. But according to Jo Paoletti, an associate professor of American studies at the University of Maryland, it ain't so. When colors were first introduced to the nursery in the early part of the twentieth century, pink was considered the more masculine hue, a pastel version of red. Blue, with its intimations of the Virgin Mary, constancy, and faithfulness, was thought to be dainty. Why or when that switched is not clear, but as late as the 1930s, a significant percentage of adults in one national survey held to that split. Perhaps that's why so many early Disney heroines—Cinderella, Sleeping Beauty, Wendy, Alice-in-Wonderland—are swathed in varying shades of azure. (Purple, incidentally, may be the next color to swap teams: once the realm of kings and NFL players, it is fast becoming the bolder girl's version of pink.)

It wasn't until the mid 1980s, when amplifying age and sex differences became a key strategy of children's marketing (recall the emergence of " 'tween"), that pink became seemingly innate to girls, part of what defined them as female, at least for the first few years. That was also the time that the first of the generation raised during the unisex phase of feminism—ah, hither Marlo!—became parents. "The kids who grew up in the 1970s wanted sharp definitions for their own kids," Paoletti told me. "I can understand that, because the unisex thing denied everything—you couldn't be this, you couldn't be that, you had to be a neutral nothing."

The infatuation with the girlie girl certainly could, at least in part, be a reaction against the so-called second wave of the women's movement of the 1960s and 1970s (the first wave was the fight for suffrage), which fought for reproductive rights and economic, social, and legal equality. If nothing else, pink and Princess have resuscitated the fantasy of romance that that era of feminism threatened, the privileges that traditional femininity conferred on women despite its costs—doors magically opened, dinner checks picked up. Manolo Blahniks. Frippery. Fun. Why should we give up the perks of our sex until we're sure of what we'll get in exchange? Why should we give them up at all? Or maybe it's deeper than that: the freedoms feminism bestowed came with an undercurrent of fear among women themselves—flowing through *Ally McBeal*, *Bridget Jones's Diary*, *Sex and the City*—of losing male love, of never marrying, of not having children, of being deprived of something that felt essentially and exclusively female.

I mulled that over while flipping through *The Paper Bag Princess,* a 1980 picture book hailed as an antidote to Disney. The heroine outwits a dragon who has kidnapped her prince, but not before the beast's fiery breath frizzles her hair and destroys her dress, forcing her to don a paper bag. The ungrateful prince rejects her, telling her to come back when she is "dressed like a real princess." She dumps him and skips off into the sunset, happily ever after, alone.

There you have it, *Thelma and Louise* all over again. Step out of line, and you end up solo or, worse, sailing crazily over a cliff to your doom. Alternatives like those might send you skittering right back to the castle. And I get that: the fact is, though I want my daughter to do and be whatever she wants as an adult, I still hope she'll find her Prince Charming and have babies, just as I have. I don't want her to be a fish without a bicycle; I want her to be a fish with another fish. Preferably, one who loves and respects her and also does the dishes and half the child care.

There had to be a middle ground between compliant and defiant, between petticoats and paper bags. I remembered a video on YouTube, an ad for a Nintendo game called *Super Princess Peach*. It showed a pack of girls in tiaras, gowns, and elbow-length white gloves sliding down a zip line on parasols, navigating an obstacle course of tires in their stilettos, slithering on their bellies under barbed wire, then using their telekinetic powers to make a climbing wall burst into flames. "If you can stand up to really mean people," an announcer intoned, "maybe you have what it takes to be a princess."

Now here were some girls who had grit as well as grace. I loved Princess Peach even as I recognized that there was no way she could run in those heels, that her peachiness did nothing to upset the apple cart of expectation: she may have been athletic, smart, and strong, but she was also adorable. Maybe she's what those once-unisex, postfeminist parents are shooting for: the melding of old and new standards. And perhaps that's a good thing, the ideal solution. But what to make, then, of the young women in the Girls Inc. survey? It doesn't seem to be "having it all" that's getting to them; it's the pressure to be it all. In telling our girls they can be anything, we have inadvertently demanded that they be everything. To everyone. All the time. No wonder the report was titled *The Supergirl Dilemma.*

The princess as superhero is not irrelevant. Some scholars I spoke with say that given its post-9/11 timing, princess mania is a response to a newly dangerous world. "Historically, princess worship has emerged during periods of uncertainty and profound social change," observes Miriam Forman-Brunell, a historian at the University of Missouri–Kansas City. Francis Hodgson Burnett's original *Little Princess* was published at a time of rapid urbanization, immigration, and poverty; Shirley Temple's film version was a hit during the Great Depression. "The original folk tales themselves," Forman-Brunell says, "spring from medieval and early modern European culture that faced all kinds of economic and demographic and social upheaval—famine, war, disease, terror of wolves. Girls play savior during times of economic crisis and instability." That's a heavy burden for little shoulders. Perhaps that's why the magic wand has become an essential part of the princess get-up. In the original stories—even the Disney versions of them—it's not the girl herself who's magic; it's the fairy godmother. Now if Forman-Brunell is right, we adults have become the cursed creatures whom girls have the thaumaturgic power to transform.

In the 1990s, third-wave feminists rebelled against their dour big sisters, "reclaiming" sexual objectification as a woman's right—provided, of course, that it was on her own terms, that she was the one choosing to strip or wear a shirt that said "Porn Star" or make out with her best friend at a frat-house bash. They embraced words like "bitch" and "slut" as terms of affection and empowerment. That is, when used by the right people, with the right dash of playful irony. But how can you assure that? As Madonna gave way to Britney, whatever self-determination that message contained was watered down and commodified until all that was left was a gaggle of 6-year-old girls in belly-baring T-shirts (which I'm guessing they don't wear as cultural critique). It is no wonder that parents, faced with thongs for 8-year-olds and Bratz dolls' "passion for fashion," fill their daughters' closets with pink sateen; the innocence of Princess feels like a reprieve.

"But what does that mean?" asks Sharon Lamb, a psychology professor at Saint Michael's College. "There are other ways to express 'innocence'—girls could play ladybug or caterpillar. What you're really talking about is sexual purity. And there's a trap at the end of that rainbow, because the natural progression from pale, innocent pink is not to other colors. It's to hot, sexy pink—exactly the kind of sexualization parents are trying to avoid."

Lamb suggested that to see for myself how *Someday My Prince Will Come* morphs into *Oops! I Did It Again,* I visit Club Libby Lu, the mall shop dedicated to the "Very Important Princess." Walking into one of the newest links in the store's chain, in Natick, Massachusetts, last summer, I had to tip my tiara to the founder, Mary Drolet: Libby Lu's design was flawless. Unlike Disney, Drolet depended on focus groups to choose the logo (a crown-topped heart) and the colors (pink, pink, purple, and more pink). The displays were scaled to the size of a 10-year-old, though most of the shoppers I saw were several years younger than that. The decals on the walls and dressing rooms—"I Love Your Hair," "Hip Chick," "Spoiled"—were written in "girlfriend language." The young sales clerks at this "special secret club for superfabulous girls" are called "club counselors" and come off like your coolest babysitter, the one who used to let you brush her hair. The malls themselves are chosen based on a company formula called the GPI, or "Girl Power Index," which predicts potential sales revenues. Talk about newspeak: "Girl Power" has gone from a riot grrrrl anthem to "I Am Woman, Watch Me Shop."

Inside, the store was divided into several glittery "shopping zones" called "experiences": Libby's Laboratory, now called Sparkle Spa, where girls concoct their own cosmetics and bath products; Libby's Room; Ear Piercing; Pooch Parlor (where divas in training can pamper stuffed poodles, pugs, and Chihuahuas); and the Style Studio, offering "Libby Du" makeover choices, including 'Tween Idol, Rock Star, Pop Star, and, of course, Priceless Princess. Each look includes hairstyle, makeup, nail polish, and sparkly tattoos.

As I browsed, I noticed a mother standing in the center of the store holding a price list for makeover birthday parties—$22.50 to $35 per child. Her name was Anne McAuliffe; her daughters—Stephanie, 4, and 7-year-old twins Rory and Sarah—were dashing giddily up and down the aisles.

"They've been begging to come to this store for three weeks," McAuliffe said. "I'd never heard of it. So I said they could, but they'd have to spend their own money if they bought anything." She looked around. "Some of this stuff is innocuous," she observed, then leaned toward me, eyes wide and stage-whispered: "But . . . a lot of it is horrible. It makes them look like little prostitutes. It's crazy. They're babies!"

As we debated the line between frivolous fun and JonBenét, McAuliffe's daughter Rory came dashing up, pigtails haphazard, glasses askew. "They have the best pocketbooks here," she said breathlessly, brandishing a clutch with the words "Girlie Girl" stamped on it. "Please, can I have one? It has sequins!"

"You see that?" McAuliffe asked, gesturing at the bag. "What am I supposed to say?"

On my way out of the mall, I popped into the 'tween" mecca Hot Topic, where a display of Tinker Bell items caught my eye. Tinker

Bell, whose image racks up an annual $400 million in retail sales with no particular effort on Disney's part, is poised to wreak vengeance on the Princess line that once expelled her. Last winter, the first chapter book designed to introduce girls to Tink and her Pixie Hollow pals spent 18 weeks on the *New York Times* children's best-seller list. In a direct-to-DVD now under production, she will speak for the first time, voiced by the actress Brittany Murphy. Next year, Disney Fairies will be rolled out in earnest. Aimed at 6- to 9-year-old girls, the line will catch them just as they outgrow Princess. Their colors will be lavender, green, turquoise—anything but the Princess's soon-to-be-babyish pink.

To appeal to that older child, Disney executives said, the Fairies will have more "attitude" and "sass" than the Princesses. What, I wondered, did that entail? I'd seen some of the Tinker Bell merchandise that Disney sells at its theme parks: T-shirts reading "Spoiled to Perfection," "Mood Subject to Change Without Notice," and "Tinker Bell: Prettier Than a Princess." At Hot Topic, that edge was even sharper: magnets, clocks, light-switch plates, and panties featured "Dark Tink," described as "the bad girl side of Miss Bell that Walt never saw."

Girl power, indeed.

A few days later, I picked my daughter up from preschool. She came tearing over in a full-skirted frock with a gold bodice, a beaded crown perched sideways on her head. "Look, Mommy, I'm Ariel!" she crowed, referring to Disney's *Little Mermaid*. Then she stopped and furrowed her brow. "Mommy, do you like Ariel?"

I considered her for a moment. Maybe Princess is the first salvo in what will become a lifelong struggle over her body image, a Hundred Years' War of dieting, plucking, painting, and perpetual dissatisfaction with the results. Or maybe it isn't. I'll never really know. In the end, it's not the Princesses that really bother me anyway. They're just a trigger for the bigger question of how, over the years, I can help my daughter with the contradictions she will inevitably face as a girl, the dissonance that is as endemic as ever to growing up female. Maybe the best I can hope for is that her generation will get a little further with the solutions than we did.

For now, I kneeled down on the floor and gave my daughter a hug.

She smiled happily. "But, Mommy?" she added. "When I grow up, I'm still going to be a fireman."

QUESTIONS: For Thinking and Writing

1. Why does the author object so strongly to the idea of princesses and princess toys? Explain.
2. Think about your consumer habits as a child. What did you want to buy and how did you learn about the product? What made you want the product?
3. Lyn Mikel Brown coauthor of *Packaging Girlhood: Rescuing Our Daughters From Marketers' Schemes,* notes "When one thing is so dominant, then it's no longer a choice: it's a mandate, cannibalizing all other forms of play." In what ways has the princess craze "cannablized" other forms of play?
4. This article focuses on how little girls are the targets of marketing gimmicks that channel them to desire certain toys and embrace certain types of play. Can the same argument be made for little boys? Explain.
5. Can popular toys—such as princess gear, Bratz dolls, Lego sets, Matchbox cars—lead children to unconsciously embrace prescribed gender roles? Visit the toy section of a department store such as Target, Wal-Mart, Kmart, and so on, and take a look at the merchandise options. Prepare a short analysis on how the toys you saw could influence gender roles for children.

DOUGLAS RUSHKOFF

Which One of These Sneakers Is Me?

Brand-name products target groups of consumers—sometimes large, diverse populations, such as Pepsi or Coke drinkers, or elite ones, such as consumers of Coach or Gucci. Brands depend on image—the image they promote and the image the consumer believes they will project by using the product. For teens, brands can announce membership in a particular group, value systems, and personality type. Media analyst Douglas Rushkoff explains in this article that the youth generation is more consumer-savvy, forcing retailers to rethink how they brand and market goods. Brands are still very important to young people, but they like to think they are hip to the advertising game. But as Rushkoff explains in this essay published on April 30, 2000 in the London Times, *it is a game they cannot win.*

I was in one of those sports "superstores" the other day, hoping to find a pair of trainers for myself. As I faced the giant wall of shoes, each model categorized by either sports affiliation, basketball star, economic class, racial heritage, or consumer niche, I noticed a young boy standing next to me, maybe 13 years old, in even greater awe of the towering selection of footwear.

His jaw was dropped and his eyes were glazed over—a psychophysical response to the overwhelming sensory data in a self-contained consumer environment. It's a phenomenon known to retail architects as "Gruen Transfer," named for the gentleman who invented the shopping mall, where this mental paralysis is most commonly observed.

Having finished several years of research on this exact mind state, I knew to proceed with caution. I slowly made my way to the boy's side and gently asked him, "What is going through your mind right now?"

He responded without hesitation, "I don't know which of these trainers is 'me.'" The boy proceeded to explain his dilemma. He thought of Nike as the most utilitarian and scientifically advanced shoe, but had heard something about third world laborers and was afraid that wearing this brand might label him as too anti-Green. He then considered a skateboard shoe, Airwalk, by an "indie" manufacturer (the trainer equivalent of a micro-brewery), but had recently learned that this company was almost as big as Nike. The truly hip brands of skate shoe were too esoteric for his current profile at school—he'd look like he was "trying." This left the "retro" brands, like Puma, Converse, and Adidas, none of which he felt any real affinity for, since he wasn't even alive in the seventies, when they were truly and nonironically popular.

With no clear choice and, more importantly, no other way to conceive of his own identity, the boy stood there, paralyzed in the modern youth equivalent of an existential crisis. Which brand am I, anyway?

Believe it or not, there are dozens, perhaps hundreds of youth culture marketers who have already begun clipping out this article. They work for hip, new advertising agencies and cultural research firms who trade in the psychology of our children and the anthropology of their culture. The object of their labors is to create precisely the state of confusion and vulnerability experienced by the young shopper at the shoe wall—and then turn this state to their advantage. It is a science, though not a pretty one.

Yes, our children are the prey and their consumer loyalty is the prize in an escalating arms race. Marketers spend millions developing strategies to identify children's predilections and then capitalize on their vulnerabilities. Young people are fooled for a while, but then develop defense mechanisms, such as media-savvy attitudes or ironic dispositions. Then marketers research these defenses, develop new countermeasures, and on it goes. The revolutionary impact of a new musical genre is coopted and packaged by a major label before it reaches the airwaves. The ability of young people to deconstruct and neutralize the effects of one advertising technique are thwarted when they are confounded by yet another. The liberation children experience when they discover the Internet is quickly counteracted by the lure of e-commerce Web sites, which are customized to each individual user's psychological profile in order to maximize their effectiveness.

The battle in which our children are engaged seems to pass beneath our radar screens, in a language we don't understand. But we see the confusion and despair that results—not to mention the ever-increasing desperation with which even 3-year-olds yearn for the next Pokémon trading card. How did we get in this predicament, and is there a way out? Is it your imagination, you wonder, or have things really gotten worse?

Alas, things seem to have gotten worse. Ironically, this is because things had gotten so much better.

In olden times—back when those of us who read the newspaper grew up—media was a one-way affair. Advertisers enjoyed a captive audience and could quite authoritatively provoke our angst and stoke our aspirations. Interactivity changed all this. The remote control gave viewers the ability to break the captive spell of television programming whenever they wished without having to get up and go all the way up to the set. Young people proved particularly adept at "channel surfing," both because they grew up using the new tool, and because they felt little compunction to endure the tension-provoking narratives of storytellers who did not have their best interests at heart. It was as if young people knew that the stuff on television was called "programming" for a reason and developed shortened attention spans for the purpose of keeping themselves from falling into the spell of advertisers. The remote control allowed young people to deconstruct TV.

The next weapon in the child's arsenal was the video game joystick. For the first time, viewers had control over the very pixels on their monitors. The television image was demystified.

Lastly, the computer mouse and keyboard transformed the TV receiver into a portal. Today's young people grew up in a world where a screen could as easily be used for expressing oneself as for consuming the media of others. Now the media was up for grabs, and the ethic, from hackers to camcorder owners, was "do it yourself."

Of course, this revolution had to be undone. Television and Internet programmers, responding to the unpredictable viewing habits of the newly liberated, began to call our mediaspace an "attention economy." No matter how many channels they had for their programming, the number of "eyeball hours" that human beings were willing to dedicate to that programming was fixed. Not coincidentally, the channel-surfing habits of our children became known as "attention deficit disorder"—a real disease now used as an umbrella term for anyone who clicks away from programming before the marketer wants him to. We quite literally drug our children into compliance. Likewise, as computer interfaces were made more complex and opaque—think Windows—the do-it-yourself ethic of the Internet was undone. The original Internet was a place to share ideas and converse with others. Children actually had to use the keyboard! Now, the Internet encourages them to click numbly through packaged content. Web sites are designed to keep young people from using the keyboard, except to enter in their parents' credit card information.

But young people had been changed by their exposure to new media. They constituted a new "psychographic," as advertisers like to call it, so new kinds of messaging had to be developed that appealed to their new sensibility.

Anthropologists—the same breed of scientists that used to scope out enemy populations before military conquests—engaged in focus groups, conducted "trend watching" on the streets, in order to study the emotional needs and subtle behaviors of young people. They came to understand, for example, how children had abandoned narrative structures for fear of the way stories were used to coerce them. Children tended to construct narratives for themselves by collecting things instead, like cards, bottlecaps called "pogs," or keychains and plush toys. They also came to understand how young people despised advertising—especially when it did not acknowledge their media-savvy intelligence.

Thus, Pokémon was born—a TV show, video game, and product line, where the object is to collect as many trading cards as possible.

The innovation here, among many, is the marketer's conflation of TV show and advertisement into one piece of media. The show and movies are essentially long advertisements. The storyline, such as it is, concerns a boy who must collect little monsters in order to develop his own character. Likewise, the Pokémon video game engages the player in a quest for those monsters. Finally, the card game itself (for the few children who actually play it) involves collecting better monsters—not by playing, but by buying more cards. The more cards you buy, the better you can play.

Kids feel the tug, but in a way they can't quite identify as advertising. Their compulsion to create a story for themselves—in a world where stories are dangerous—makes them vulnerable to this sort of attack. In marketers' terms, Pokémon is "leveraged" media, with "cross promotion" on "complementary platforms." This is ad-speak for an assault on multiple fronts.

Moreover, the time a child spends in the Pokémon craze amounts to a remedial lesson in how to consume. Pokémon teaches them how to want things that they can't or won't actually play with. In fact, it teaches them how to buy things they don't even want. While a child might want one particular card, he needs to purchase them in packages whose contents are not revealed. He must buy blind and repeatedly until he gets the object of his desire.

Worse yet, the card itself has no value—certainly not as a plaything. It is a functionless purchase, slipped into a display case, whose value lies purely in its possession. It is analogous to those children who buy action figures from their favorite TV shows and movies with no intention of ever removing them from their packaging! They are purchased for their collectible value alone. Thus, the imagination game is reduced to some fictional moment in the future where they will, presumably, be resold to another collector. Children are no longer playing. They are investing.

Meanwhile, older kids have attempted to opt out of aspiration altogether. The "15–24" demographic, considered by marketers the most difficult to wrangle into submission, has adopted a series of postures they hoped would make them impervious to marketing techniques. They take pride in their ability to recognize when they are being pandered to, and watch TV for the sole purpose of calling out when they are being manipulated. They are armchair media theorists, who take pleasure in deconstructing and defusing the messages of their enemies.

But now advertisers are making commercials just for them. Soft drink advertisements satirize one another before rewarding the cynical viewer: "image is nothing," they say. The technique might best be called "wink" advertising for its ability to engender a young person's loyalty by pretending to disarm itself. "Get it?" the ad means to ask. If you're cool, you do.

New magazine advertisements for jeans, such as those created by Diesel, take this even one step further. The ads juxtapose imagery that actually makes no sense—ice cream billboards in North Korea, for example. The strategy is brilliant. For a media-savvy young person to feel good about himself, he needs to feel he "gets" the joke. But what does he do with an ad where there's obviously something to get that he can't figure out? He has no choice but to admit that the brand is even cooler than he is. An ad's ability to confound its audience is the new credential for a brand's authenticity.

Like the boy at the wall of shoes, kids today analyze each purchase they make, painstakingly aware of how much effort has gone into seducing them. As a result, they see their choices of what to watch and what to buy as exerting some influence over the world around them. After all, their buying patterns have become the center of so much attention!

But however media-savvy kids get, they will always lose this particular game. For they have accepted the language of brands as their cultural currency and the stakes in their purchasing decisions as something real. For no matter how much control kids get over the media they watch, they are still utterly powerless when it comes to the manufacturing of brands. Even a consumer revolt merely reinforces one's role as a consumer, not an autonomous or creative being.

The more they interact with brands, the more they brand themselves.

QUESTIONS: For Thinking and Writing

1. When you were a teenager, did you have particular brands to which you were most loyal? Did this loyalty change as you got older? Why did you prefer certain brands over others? What cultural and social influences contributed to your desire for that brand?
2. Look up the phrase *"Gruen transfer"* on the Internet. Were you aware of this angle of marketing practice? Does it change the way you think about how products are sold to you?
3. While the boy's dilemma in Rushkoff's introduction is humorous on the surface, it is a serious situation for the teen. Why is his choice of

sneaker so important to him? What expectations does he seem to connect with his choice? What could happen if he picks the wrong shoe?

4. Rushkoff notes that the youth generation "constitutes a new psychographic." What makes this generation different from previous generations of consumers? If you are a part of this generation (ages 12–21), explain why you think you do or do not represent a "new psychographic."
5. Teens and young adults covet certain brand name clothing because they believe it promotes a particular image. What defines brand image? Is it something created by the company or by the people who use the product? How does advertising influence the social view we have of ourselves and the brands we use? Write about the connections between advertising and our cultural values of what is popular and what is not.

JAMES B. TWITCHELL

Lux Populi

While media and academic critics question the methods of advertising agencies and lament the sacrifice of values in the name of consumerism, professor James B. Twitchell openly embraces the media-driven world of advertising. In the next piece, he explores the joys of luxury and challenges the academic criticism that condemns our material instincts as shallow and self-centered. He realizes that his viewpoint may not be popular, but it is honest; because the truth is we love nice stuff. Is that so wrong? This essay, published in the winter 2007 issue of the Wilson Quarterly, *is adapted from Twitchell's book* Living It Up: America's Love Affair With Luxury.

> *At length I recollected the thoughtless saying of a great prince who, on being informed that the country had no bread, replied, "Let them eat cake."*
>
> —*Jean-Jacques Rousseau, Confessions*

Well, okay, so Marie Antoinette never said, "Let them eat cake." When Rousseau wrote those words, Marie was just 11 years old and living in Austria. But Americans used to like the story that, when the French queen was told by an official that the people were angry because they had no bread, she responded, "*Qu'ils mangent de la brioche.*" We liked to imagine her saying it with a snarl and a curled lip. She was a luxury bimbo whose out-of-control spending grated on the poor and unfortunate French people. We fought a revolution to separate ourselves from exactly that kind of uppercrustiness. She got her just "desserts."

But that was 200 years ago. Now cake is one of *our* favorite foods, part of the fifth food group, a totally unnecessary luxury consumption. We're not talking about a few crumbs, but the real stuff. Brioche by the loaf. Not for nothing has Marie become a favorite subject for current infotainment. Novelists, historians, biographers, and even hip young filmmaker Sofia Coppola are telling her story, not because we want her reviled, but because we want to be like her.

And we're doing a pretty good job. Luxury spending in the United States has been growing more than four times as fast as overall spending, and the rest of the West is not far behind. You might think that modern wannabe Maries are grayhairs with poodles. Not so. This spending is being done by younger and younger consumers. Take a walk up Fifth Avenue, and then, at 58th, cross over and continue up Madison. You'll see who is swarming through the stores with names we all recognize: Louis Vuitton, Gucci, Prada, Dior, Coach. . . . Or cruise Worth Avenue or Rodeo Drive, and you'll see the same furious down-marketing and up-crusting. This is the Twinkiefication of deluxe.

You don't have to go to these streets of dreams to see who's on a sugar high. Take a tour of your local Costco or Sam's Club discount warehouse and you'll see the same stuff, only a day old and about to become stale, being consumed by a slightly older crowd. Observe the parking lot, where shiny new imported sedans and SUVs are parked beside aging subcompacts. Or spend an hour watching the Home Shopping Network, a televised flea market for impulse buyers. Its call centers now have some 23,000 incoming phone lines capable of handling up to 20,000 calls a minute. The network no longer sells cubic zirconia rings. It sells Gucci handbags.

We've developed a powerful desire to associate with recognized objects of little intrinsic but high positional value, which is why Martha Stewart, our faux Marie, is down at Kmart introducing her Silver Label goods; why a courtier the likes of Michael Graves is designing toasters for Target (pronounced by wits, with an ironic French flair, TarZHAY);

why the Duke of Polo, Ralph Lauren, is marketing house paint; and why suave Cole Porter-brand furniture is appearing on the floor at Ethan Allen stores.

Look around, and you will see that almost every category of consumables has cake at the top. This is true not just for expensive products such as town cars and McMansions, but for everyday objects. In bottled water, for instance, there is Evian, advertised as if it were a liqueur. In coffee, there's Starbucks; in ice cream, Häagen-Dazs; in sneakers, Nike; in wine, Chateau Margaux; in cigars, Arturo Fuente Hemingway, and well, you know the rest. Having a few TVs around the house is fine, but what you really need is a home entertainment center worthy of Versailles, with a JBL Ultra Synthesis One audio system, a Vidikron Vision One front projector, a Stewart Ultramatte 150 screen, a Pioneer DV-09 DVD player, and an AMX ViewPoint remote control. Hungry for chow with your entertainment? Celebrity chef Wolfgang Puck has his own line of TV dinner entrées.

Ironically, what this poaching of deluxe by the middle class has done is make things impossible for the truly rich. Ponder this: A generation ago, the Duke and Duchess of Windsor surrounded themselves with the world's finest goods—from jewelry to bed linens to flatware. The duchess, the twice-divorced American Wallis Simpson, would never be queen, but that didn't prevent her from carrying off a passable imitation of Marie. In the Windsor household, the coasters were Cartier and the placemats were Porthault, and the pooches ate from silver-plated Tiffany bowls.

When Sotheby's auctioned more than 40,000 items from the Windsors' Paris home in 1997, the remnants of their royal life went out for bid. Most of the items listed in the Sotheby's catalog are still being made, either in the same form or in an updated version. In other words, the duchess's precious things are within your grimy reach. From her point of view, she might just as well take 'em to the dump.

- Chanel faux-pearl earrings given to the duchess by the duke can be picked up for about $360 at Chanel stores.
- The duchess's Cartier love bracelet in 18-karat gold with screw closure, which was presented by the president of Cartier to the Windsors and other "great lovers" in 1970 (among the other

recipients: Elizabeth Taylor and Richard Burton, Sophia Loren and Carlo Ponti), is yours for $3,625 at Cartier boutiques.

- T. Anthony luggage, the Windsors' favorite (they owned 118 such trunks), is still being manufactured and can be bought in Manhattan.
- Hand-embroidered Porthault linens are stocked at your local mall.
- The Windsors' stationery from the Mrs. John L. Strong company, complete with handengraved monogrammed pieces on pure cotton paper, can be yours for $80 to $750, depending on the ornamentation.
- The duke's velvet slippers can be purchased for $188 at Brooks Brothers, which owns the London company that made them. Instead of an *E* for "Edward" below the embroidered crown, the slippers have a *BB*.
- Okay, okay, you'll never own as many scarves and gloves as the duchess did, but Hermes and Balenciaga sell exactly the same ones she wore for upward of $300 a pop.

Here's the takeaway: There is very little cake a rich person once gorged on that a middle-class person can't get on his plate. You name it; I can taste it. So I can't afford a casita on Bermuda, but I can get in on a time-share for a weekend. No, I can't own a stretch limo, but I can rent one by the hour. Maybe Venice is out this year, but I'll go to the Venetian in Vegas instead. I can't afford an Armani suit, but what about these eyeglasses with Giorgio's name plastered on them? Commodore Vanderbilt said that if you have to ask how much a yacht costs, you can't afford one, but check out my stateroom on my chartered Majestic Princess. True, I don't have my own Gulfstream V jet, but I can upgrade to first class on Delta with the miles I "earn" by using my American Express card. Is that my own Lexus out front? Or is it on lease from a used car dealer? You'll never know.

Lux populi may be the end of deluxe. "Real" luxury used to be for the "happy few," but in the world of the supra-12,000 Dow Jones industrial average, there are only the minted many. "Sudden Wealth Syndrome," as the *Los Angeles Times* has called it, is not just for dot-com innovators or contestants on *Who Wants to Be a Millionaire* but for a generation that is inheriting its wealth through the steady attrition of the Generation Who Fought the War. The "wealth effect," as former Federal Reserve chairman Alan Greenspan termed it, drives more and more money to chase after goods whose production can hardly be called beneficial and cannot now even be called positional.

There's a story, perhaps apocryphal, that when Tom Ford, chief designer for Gucci in the 1990s, was passing through the Newark airport (what the hell was he doing there?!), he saw one of his swanky T-shirts on the tummy of a portly prole. He immediately canceled the clothing line. Too late. Perhaps the social construction of luxury as a material category has already been deconstructed into banality.

The very unreachableness of old luxe made it safe, like an old name, old blood, old land, an old coat of arms, or old service to the crown. Primogeniture, the cautious passage and consolidation of wealth to the firstborn male, made the anxiety of exclusion from luxe somehow bearable. After all, you knew your place from the moment of birth and had plenty of time to make your peace. If you drew the short straw, not to worry. A comfortable life as a vicar would await you. Or the officer corps.

The application of steam, then electricity, to the engines of production brought a new market to status objects, an industrial market made up of people who essentially bought their way into having a bloodline. These were the people who so disturbed economist Thorstein Veblen, and from them, this new generation of consumer has descended. First the industrial rich, then the inherited rich, and now the incidentally rich, the accidentally rich, the golden-parachute rich, the buyout rich, the lottery rich.

Call them yuppies, yippies, bobos, nobrows, or whatever, the consumers of the new luxury have a sense of entitlement that transcends social class, a conviction that the finest things are their birthright. Never mind that they may have been born into a family whose ancestral estate is a tract house in the suburbs, near the mall, not paid for, and whose family crest was downloaded from the Internet. Ditto the signet ring design. Language reflects this hijacking. Words such as *gourmet, premium, boutique, chic, accessory,* and *classic* have loosened from their elite moorings and now describe such top-of-category items as popcorn, hamburgers, discount brokers, shampoo, scarves, ice cream, and trailer parks. "Luxury for all" is an oxymoron, all right, the aspirational goal of modern culture, and the death knell of the real thing.

These new *customers* for luxury are younger than *clients* of the old luxe used to be, there are far more of them, they make their money much sooner, and they are far more flexible in financing and fickle in choice. They do not stay put. When Richie Rich starts buying tulips by the ton, Nouveau Riche is right there behind him picking them up by the pound.

In a sense, the filthy rich have only two genuine luxury items left: time and philanthropy. As the old paradox goes, the rich share the luxury of too much time on their hands with the very people on whom they often bestow their philanthropy. Who knows, maybe poverty will become the new luxury, as the philosophes predicted. Wonder Bread becomes the new cake. Once you've ripped out all the old patinaed hardware, once you've traded in the Bentley for a rusted-out Chevy, once you've carted all the polo pony shirts to Goodwill, once you've given the Pollock to the Met, once you've taken your last trip up Everest and into the Amazon, there's not much left to do to separate yourself but give the rest of the damned stuff away. Competitive philanthropy has its allure. Why do you think there are more than 20 universities with multibillion-dollar pledge campaigns? Those bobos sure as hell can't do it. Little wonder that Warren Buffett dumped his load rather casually on top of a pile amassed by another modern baron, almost as if to say, "Top that." Now that's a show stopper. Even The Donald can't trump that.

QUESTIONS: For Thinking and Writing

1. Why is materialism so criticized, yet obviously so wholeheartedly embraced by American society? If we are basically lovers of luxury, why are we so quick to condemn advertising and consumerism?
2. Twitchell refers to Marie Antoinette in his opening paragraphs. Why does he choose her to demonstrate the American thirst for luxury? Explain.
3. Evaluate Twitchell's tone and style in this piece. What can you surmise from his tone and use of language? Does it make him more or less credible? Explain.
4. According to Twitchell, why is luxury so important to Americans? What is the connection between desire and social status? In what ways is luxury "socially constructed"? Explain.
5. Write a brief narrative about a time you experienced a decadent spending situation—either for yourself or with someone else. What motivated your spending? How did you feel afterward?

VIEWPOINTS

With These Words, I Can Sell You Anything

William Lutz

The Language of Advertising

Charles A. O'Neill

Words such as "help" and "virtually" and phrases such as "new and improved" and "acts fast" seem like innocuous weaponry in the arsenal of advertising. But not to William Lutz, who analyzes how such words are used in ads—how they misrepresent, mislead, and deceive consumers. In this essay, he alerts us to the special power of "weasel words," those familiar and sneaky little critters that "appear to say one thing when in fact they say the opposite, or nothing at all." The real danger, Lutz argues, is how such language debases reality and the values of the consumer. Lutz's essay is an excerpt from his book, Doublespeak. *Marketing executive Charles A. O'Neill, in his original essay, challenges Lutz's criticism of advertising doublespeak. Although admitting to some of the craftiness of his profession, O'Neill defends the huckster's language—both verbal and visual—against claims that it distorts reality. Examining some familiar television commercials and magazine ads, he explains why the language may be charming and seductive but far from brainwashing.*

With These Words, I Can Sell You Anything

William Lutz

One problem advertisers have when they try to convince you that the product they are pushing is really different from other, similar products is that their claims are subject to some laws. Not a lot of laws, but there are some designed to prevent fraudulent or untruthful claims in advertising. Even during the happy years of nonregulation under President Ronald Reagan, the FTC did crack down on the more blatant abuses in advertising claims. Generally speaking, advertisers have to be careful in what they say in their ads and in the claims they make for the products they advertise. Parity claims are safe because they are legal and supported by a number of court decisions. But beyond parity claims, there are weasel words.

Advertisers use weasel words to appear to be making a claim for a product when in fact they are making no claim at all. Weasel words get their name from the way weasels eat the eggs they find in the nests of other animals. A weasel will make a small hole in the egg, suck out the insides, then place the egg back in the nest. Only when the egg is examined closely is it found to be hollow. That's the way it is with weasel words in advertising: Examine weasel words closely, and you'll find that they're as hollow as any egg sucked by a weasel. Weasel words appear to say one thing, when in fact they say the opposite or nothing at all.

"Help"—The Number One Weasel Word

The biggest weasel word used in advertising doublespeak is "help." Now "help" only means to aid or assist, nothing more. It does not mean to conquer, stop, eliminate, end, solve, heal, cure, or anything else. But once the ad says "help," it can say just about anything after that, because "help" qualifies everything coming after it. The trick is that the claim that comes after the weasel word is usually so strong and so dramatic that you forget the word "help" and concentrate only on the dramatic claim. You read into the ad a message that the ad does not contain. More importantly, the advertiser is not responsible for the claim that you read into the ad, even though the advertiser wrote the ad so you would read that claim into it.

The next time you see an ad for a cold medicine that promises that it "helps relieve cold symptoms fast," don't rush out to buy it. Ask yourself what this claim is really saying. Remember, "helps" means only that the medicine will aid or assist. What will it aid or assist in doing? Why, "relieve" your cold "symptoms." "Relieve" only means to ease, alleviate, or mitigate, not to stop, end, or cure. Nor does the claim say how much relieving this medicine will do. Nowhere does this ad claim it will cure anything. In fact, the ad doesn't even claim it will do anything at all. The ad only claims that it will aid in relieving (not curing) your cold symptoms, which are probably a runny nose, watery eyes, and a headache. In other words, this medicine probably contains a standard decongestant and some aspirin. By the way, what does "fast" mean? Ten minutes, one hour, one day? What is fast to one person can be very slow to another. *Fast* is another weasel word.

Ad claims using "help" are among the most popular ads. One says, "Helps keep you young looking," but then a lot of things will help keep you young looking, including exercise, rest, good nutrition, and a facelift. More importantly, this ad doesn't say the product will keep you young, only "young looking." Someone may look young to one person and old to another.

A toothpaste ad says, "Helps prevent cavities," but it doesn't say it will actually prevent cavities. Brushing your teeth regularly, avoiding sugars in foods, and flossing daily will also help prevent cavities. A liquid cleaner ad says, "Helps keep your home germ free," but it doesn't say it actually kills germs, nor does it even specify which germs it might kill.

"Help" is such a useful weasel word that it is often combined with other action-verb weasel words such as "fight" and "control." Consider the claim, "Helps control dandruff symptoms with regular use." What does it really say? It will assist in controlling (not eliminating, stopping, ending, or curing) the symptoms of dandruff, not the cause of dandruff nor the dandruff itself. What are the symptoms of dandruff? The ad deliberately leaves that undefined, but assume that the symptoms referred to in the ad are the flaking and itching commonly associated with dandruff. But just shampooing with any shampoo will temporarily eliminate these symptoms, so this shampoo isn't any different from any other. Finally, in order to benefit from this product, you must use it regularly. What is "regular use"—daily, weekly, hourly? Using another shampoo "regularly" will have the same effect. Nowhere does this advertising claim say this particular shampoo stops, eliminates, or cures dandruff. In fact, this claim says nothing at all, thanks to all the weasel words.

Look at ads in magazines and newspapers, listen to ads on radio and television, and you'll find the word "help" in ads for all kinds of products. How often do you read or hear such phrases as "helps stop . . .," "helps overcome . . .," "helps eliminate . . .," "helps you feel . . .," or "helps you look . . ."? If you start looking for this weasel word in advertising, you'll be amazed at how often it occurs. Analyze the claims in the ads using "help," and you will discover that these ads are really saying nothing.

There are plenty of other weasel words used in advertising. In fact, there are so many that to list them all would fill the rest of this book. But, in order to identify the doublespeak of advertising and understand the real meaning of an ad, you have to be aware of the most popular weasel words in advertising today.

Virtually Spotless

One of the most powerful weasel words is "virtually," a word so innocent that most people don't pay any attention to it when it is used in an advertising claim. But watch out. "Virtually" is used in advertising claims that appear to make specific, definite promises when there is no promise. After all, what does "virtually" mean? It means "in essence of effect, although not in fact." Look at that definition again. "Virtually" means not in fact. It does not mean "almost," or "just about the same as," or anything else. And before you dismiss all this concern over such a small word, remember that small words can have big consequences.

In 1971 a federal court rendered its decision on a case brought by a woman who became pregnant while taking birth control pills. She sued the manufacturer, Eli Lilly and Company, for breach of warranty. The woman lost her case. Basing its ruling on a statement in the pamphlet accompanying the pills, which stated that, "When taken as directed, the tablets offer virtually 100 percent protection," the court ruled that there was no warranty, expressed or implied, that the pills were absolutely effective. In its ruling, the court pointed out that, according to Webster's *Third New International Dictionary*, "virtually" means "almost entirely" and clearly does not mean "absolute" (*Whittington v. Eli Lilly and Company*, 333 F. Supp. 98). In other words, the Eli Lilly company was really saying that its birth control pill, even when taken as directed, did not in fact provide 100 percent protection against pregnancy. But Eli Lilly didn't want to put it that way, because then many women might not have bought Lilly's birth control pills.

The next time you see the ad that says that this dishwasher detergent "leaves dishes virtually spotless," just remember how advertisers twist the meaning of the weasel word "virtually." You can have lots of spots on your dishes after using this detergent, and the ad claim will still be true, because what this claim really means is that this detergent does not in fact leave your dishes spotless. Whenever you see or hear an ad claim that uses the word "virtually," just translate that claim into its real meaning. So the television set that is "virtually trouble free" becomes the television set that is not in fact trouble free, the "virtually foolproof operation" of any appliance becomes an operation that is in fact not foolproof, and the product that "virtually never needs service" becomes the product that is not in fact service free.

New and Improved

If "new" is the most frequently used word on a product package, "improved" is the second most frequent. In fact, the two words are almost always used together. It seems just about everything sold these days is "new and improved." The next time you're in the supermarket, try counting the number of times you see these words on products. But you'd better do it while you're walking down just one aisle, otherwise you'll need a calculator to keep track of your counting.

Just what do these words mean? The use of the word "new" is restricted by regulations, so an advertiser can't just use the word on a product or in an ad without meeting certain requirements. For example, a product is considered new for about six months during a national advertising campaign. If the product is being advertised only in a limited test market area, the word can be used longer, and in some instances has been used for as long as two years.

What makes a product "new"? Some products have been around for a long time, yet every once in a while you discover that they are being advertised as "new." Well, an advertiser can call a product new if there has been "a material functional change" in the product. What is "a material functional change," you ask? Good question. In fact it's such a good question, it's being asked all the time. It's up to the manufacturer to prove that the product has undergone such a change. And if the manufacturer isn't challenged on the claim, then there's no one to stop it. Moreover, the change does not have to be an improvement in the product. One manufacturer added an artificial lemon scent to a cleaning product and called it "new and improved," even though the product did not clean any better than without the lemon scent.

The manufacturer defended the use of the word "new" on the grounds that the artificial scent changed the chemical formula of the product and therefore constituted "a material functional change."

Which brings up the word "improved." When used in advertising, "improved" does not mean "made better." It only means "changed" or "different from before." So, if the detergent maker puts a plastic pour spout on the box of detergent, the product has been "improved," and away we go with a whole new advertising campaign. Or, if the cereal maker adds more fruit or a different kind of fruit to the cereal, there's an improved product. Now you know why manufacturers are constantly making little changes in their products. Whole new advertising campaigns, designed to convince you that the product has been changed for the better, are based on small changes in superficial aspects of a product. The next time you see an ad for an "improved" product, ask yourself what was wrong with the old one. Ask yourself just how "improved" the product is. Finally, you might check to see whether the "improved" version costs more than the unimproved one. After all, someone has to pay for the millions of dollars spent advertising the improved product.

Of course, advertisers really like to run ads that claim a product is "new and improved." While what constitutes a "new" product may be subject to some regulation, "improved" is a subjective judgment. A manufacturer changes the shape of its stick deodorant, but the shape doesn't improve the function of the deodorant. That is, changing the shape doesn't affect the deodorizing ability of the deodorant, so the manufacturer calls it "improved." Another manufacturer adds ammonia to its liquid cleaner and calls it "new and improved." Since adding ammonia does affect the cleaning ability of the product, there has been a "material functional change" in the product, and the manufacturer can now call its cleaner "new," and "improved" as well. Now the weasel words "new and improved" are plastered all over the package and are the basis for a multimillion-dollar ad campaign. But after six months the word "new" will have to go, until someone can dream up another change in the product. Perhaps it will be adding color to the liquid, or changing the shape of the package, or maybe adding a new, dripless pour spout, or perhaps a   . The "improvements" are endless, and so are the new advertising claims and campaigns.

"New" is just too useful and powerful a word in advertising for advertisers to pass it up easily. So they use weasel words that say "new" without really saying it. One of their favorites is "introducing," as in "Introducing improved Tide," or "Introducing the stain remover." The first is simply saying, here's our improved soap; the second, here's our new advertising campaign for our detergent. Another favorite is "now," as in, "Now there's Sinex," which simply means that Sinex is available. Then there are phrases like "Today's Chevrolet," "Presenting Dristan," and "A fresh way to start the day." The list is really endless, because advertisers are always finding new ways to say "new" without really saying it. If there is a second edition of this book, I'll just call it the "new and improved" edition. Wouldn't you really rather have a "new and improved" edition of this book rather than a "second" edition?

Acts Fast

"Acts" and "works" are two popular weasel words in advertising, because they bring action to the product and to the advertising claim. When you see the ad for the cough syrup that "Acts on the cough control center," ask yourself what this cough syrup is claiming to do. Well, it's just claiming to "act," to do something, to perform an action. What is it that the cough syrup does? The ad doesn't say. It only claims to perform an action or do something on your "cough control center." By the way, what and where is your "cough control center"? I don't remember learning about that part of the body in human biology class.

Ads that use such phrases as "acts fast," "acts against," "acts to prevent," and the like, are saying essentially nothing, because "act" is a word empty of any specific meaning. The ads are always careful not to specify exactly what "act" the product performs. Just because a brand of aspirin claims to "act fast" for headache relief doesn't mean this aspirin is any better than any other aspirin. What is the "act" that this aspirin performs? You're never told. Maybe it just dissolves quickly. Since aspirin is a parity product, all aspirin is the same and therefore functions the same.

Works Like Anything Else

If you don't find the word "acts" in an ad, you will probably find the weasel word "works." In fact, the two words are almost interchangeable in advertising. Watch out for ads that say a product "works against," "works like," "works for," or "works longer." As with "acts," "works" is the same meaningless verb used to make you think that this product really does something, and maybe even something special or unique. But "works," like "acts," is basically a word empty of any specific meaning.

Like Magic

Whenever advertisers want you to stop thinking about the product and to start thinking about something bigger, better, or more attractive than the product, they use that very popular weasel word, "like." The word "like" is the advertiser's equivalent of a magician's use of misdirection. "Like" gets you to ignore the product and concentrate on the claim the advertiser is making about it. "For skin like peaches and cream" claims the ad for a skin cream. What is this ad really claiming? It doesn't say this cream will give you peaches-and-cream skin. There is no verb in this claim, so it doesn't even mention using the product. How is skin ever like "peaches and cream"? Remember, ads must be read literally and exactly, according to the dictionary definition of words. (Remember "virtually" in the Eli Lilly case.) The ad is making absolutely no promise or claim whatsoever for this skin cream. If you think this cream will give you soft, smooth, youthful-looking skin, you are the one who has read that meaning into the ad.

The wine that claims "It's like taking a trip to France" wants you to think about a romantic evening in Paris as you walk along the boulevard after a wonderful meal in an intimate little bistro. Of course, you don't really believe that a wine can take you to France, but the goal of the ad is to get you to think pleasant, romantic thoughts about France and not about how the wine tastes or how expensive it may be. That little word "like" has taken you away from crushed grapes into a world of your own imaginative making. Who knows, maybe the next time you buy wine, you'll think those pleasant thoughts when you see this brand of wine, and you'll buy it. Or, maybe you weren't even thinking about buying wine at all, but now you just might pick up a bottle the next time you're shopping. Ah, the power of "like" in advertising.

How about the most famous "like" claim of all, "Winston tastes good like a cigarette should"? Ignoring the grammatical error here, you might want to know what this claim is saying. Whether a cigarette tastes good or bad is a subjective judgment, because what tastes good to one person may well taste horrible to another. Not everyone likes fried snails, even if they are called escargot. (*De gustibus non est disputandum*, which was probably the Roman rule for advertising, as well as for defending the games in the Colosseum.) There are many people who say all cigarettes taste terrible, other people who say only some cigarettes taste all right, and still others who say all cigarettes taste good. Who's right? Everyone, because taste is a matter of personal judgment.

Moreover, note the use of the conditional, "should." The complete claim is, "Winston tastes good like a cigarette should taste." But should cigarettes taste good? Again, this is a matter of personal judgment and probably depends most on one's experiences with smoking. So, the Winston ad is simply saying that Winston cigarettes are just like any other cigarette: Some people like them and some people don't. On that statement, R. J. Reynolds conducted a very successful multimillion-dollar advertising campaign that helped keep Winston the number-two-selling cigarette in the United States, close behind number one, Marlboro.

Can't It Be up to the Claim?

Analyzing ads for doublespeak requires that you pay attention to every word in the ad and determine what each word really means. Advertisers try to wrap their claims in language that sounds concrete, specific, and objective, when in fact the language of advertising is anything but. Your job is to read carefully and listen critically so that when the announcer says that "Crest can be of significant value . . ." you know immediately that this claim says absolutely nothing. Where is the doublespeak in this ad? Start with the second word.

Once again, you have to look at what words really mean, not what you think they mean or what the advertiser wants you to think they mean. The ad for Crest only says that using Crest "can be" of "significant value." What really throws you off in this ad is the brilliant use of "significant." It draws your attention to the word "value" and makes you forget that the ad only claims that Crest "can be." The ad doesn't say that Crest is of value, only that it is "able" or "possible" to be of value, because that's all that "can" means.

It's so easy to miss the importance of those little words, "can be." Almost as easy as missing the importance of the words "up to" in an ad. These words are very popular in sale ads. You know, the ones that say, "Up to 50 percent off!" Now, what does that claim mean? Not much, because the store or manufacturer has to reduce the price of only a few items by 50 percent. Everything else can be reduced a lot less, or not even reduced. Moreover, don't you want to know 50 percent off of what? Is it 50 percent off the "manufacturer's suggested list price," which is the highest possible price? Was the price artificially inflated and then reduced? In other ads, "up to" expresses an ideal situation. The medicine that works "up to ten times faster," the battery that lasts "up to twice as long," and the soap that gets you "up to twice as clean"—all are based on ideal situations for using those products, situations in which you can be sure you will never find yourself.

Unfinished Words

Unfinished words are a kind of "up to" claim in advertising. The claim that a battery lasts "up to twice as long" usually doesn't finish the comparison—twice as long as what? A birthday candle? A tank of gas? A cheap battery made in a country not noted for its technological achievements? The implication is that the battery lasts twice as long as batteries made by other battery makers, or twice as long as earlier model batteries made by the advertiser, but the ad doesn't really make these claims. You read these claims into the ad, aided by the visual images the advertiser so carefully provides.

Unfinished words depend on you to finish them, to provide the words the advertisers so thoughtfully left out of the ad. Pall Mall cigarettes were once advertised as "A longer, finer, and milder smoke." The question is, longer, finer, and milder than what? The aspirin that claims it contains "Twice as much of the pain reliever doctors recommend most" doesn't tell you what pain reliever it contains twice as much of. (By the way, it's aspirin. That's right; it just contains twice the amount of aspirin. And how much is twice the amount? Twice of what amount?) Panadol boasts that "nobody reduces fever faster," but, since Panadol is a parity product, this claim simply means that Panadol isn't any better than any other product in its parity class. "You can be sure if it's Westinghouse," you're told, but just exactly what it is you can be sure of is never mentioned. "Magnavox gives you more" doesn't tell you what you get more of. More value? More television? More than they gave you before? It sounds nice, but it means nothing, until you fill in the claim with your own words, the words the advertisers didn't use. Since each of us fills in the claim differently, the ad and the product can become all things to all people, and not promise a single thing.

Unfinished words abound in advertising, because they appear to promise so much. More importantly, they can be joined with powerful visual images on television to appear to be making significant promises about a product's effectiveness without really making any promises. In a television ad, the aspirin product that claims fast relief can show a person with a headache taking the product and then, in what appears to be a matter of minutes, claiming complete relief. This visual image is far more powerful than any claim made in unfinished words. Indeed, the visual image completes the unfinished words for you, filling in with pictures what the words leave out. And you thought that ads didn't affect you. What brand of aspirin do you use?

Some years ago, Ford's advertisements proclaimed "Ford LTD—700 percent quieter." Now, what do you think Ford was claiming with these unfinished words? What was the Ford LTD quieter than? A Cadillac? A Mercedes Benz? A BMW? Well, when the FTC asked Ford to substantiate this unfinished claim, Ford replied that it meant that the inside of the LTD was 700 percent quieter than the outside. How did you finish those unfinished words when you first read them? Did you even come close to Ford's meaning?

Combining Weasel Words

A lot of ads don't fall neatly into one category or another, because they use a variety of different devices and words. Different weasel words are often combined to make an ad claim. The claim, "Coffee-Mate gives coffee more body, more flavor," uses Unfinished Words ("more" than what?) and also uses words that have no specific meaning ("body" and "flavor"). Along with "taste" (remember the Winston ad and its claim to taste good), "body" and "flavor" mean nothing, because their meaning is entirely subjective. To you, "body" in coffee might mean thick, black, almost bitter coffee, while I might take it to mean a light brown, delicate coffee. Now, if you think you understood that last sentence, read it again, because it said nothing of objective value; it was filled with weasel words of no specific meaning: "thick," "black," "bitter," "light brown," and "delicate." Each of those words has no specific, objective meaning, because each of us can interpret them differently.

Try this slogan: "Looks, smells, tastes like ground-roast coffee." So, are you now going to buy Taster's Choice instant coffee because of this ad? "Looks," "smells," and "tastes" are all words with no specific meaning and depend on your interpretation of them for any meaning. Then there's that great weasel word "like," which simply suggests a comparison but does not make the actual connection between the product and the quality. Besides, do you know what "ground-roast" coffee is? I don't, but it sure sounds good. So, out of seven words in this ad, four are definite weasel words, two are quite meaningless, and only one has any clear meaning.

Remember the Anacin ad—"Twice as much of the pain reliever doctors recommend most"? There's a whole lot of weaseling going on in this ad. First, what's the pain reliever they're talking about in this ad? Aspirin, of course. In fact, any time you see or hear an ad using those words "pain reliever," you can automatically substitute the word "aspirin" for them. (Makers of acetaminophen and ibuprofen pain relievers are careful in their advertising to identify their products as nonaspirin products.) So, now we know that Anacin has aspirin in it. Moreover, we know that Anacin has twice as much aspirin in it, but we don't know twice as much as what. Does it have twice as much aspirin as an ordinary aspirin tablet? If so, what is an ordinary aspirin tablet, and how much aspirin does it contain? Twice as much as Excedrin or Bufferin? Twice as much as a chocolate chip cookie? Remember those unfinished words and how they lead you on without saying anything.

Finally, what about those doctors who are doing all that recommending? Who are they? How many of them are there? What kind of doctors are they? What are their qualifications? Who asked them about recommending pain relievers? What other pain relievers did they recommend? And there are a whole lot more questions about this "poll" of doctors to which I'd like to know the answers, but you get the point. Sometimes, when I call my doctor, she tells me to take two aspirin and call her office in the morning. Is that where Anacin got this ad?

Read the Label, or the Brochure

Weasel words aren't just found on television, on the radio, or in newspaper and magazine ads. Just about any language associated with a product will contain the doublespeak of advertising. Remember the Eli Lilly case and the doublespeak on the information sheet that came with the birth control pills. Here's another example.

Estée Lauder cosmetics company announced a new product called "Night Repair." A small brochure distributed with the product stated that

"Night Repair was scientifically formulated in Estée Lauder's U.S. laboratories as part of the Swiss Age-Controlling Skincare Program. Although only nature controls the aging process, this program helps control the signs of aging and encourages skin to look and feel younger." You might want to read these two sentences again, because they sound great but say nothing.

First, note that the product was "scientifically formulated" in the company's laboratories. What does that mean? What constitutes a scientific formulation? You wouldn't expect the company to say that the product was casually, mechanically, or carelessly formulated, or just thrown together one day when the people in the white coats didn't have anything better to do. But the word "scientifically" lends an air of precision and promise that just isn't there.

It is the second sentence, however, that's really weasely, both syntactically and semantically. The only factual part of this sentence is the introductory dependent clause—"only nature controls the aging process." Thus, the only fact in the ad is relegated to a dependent clause, a clause dependent on the main clause, which contains no factual or definite information at all and indeed purports to contradict the independent clause. The new "skincare program" (notice it's not a skin cream but a "program") does not claim to stop or even retard the aging process. What, then, does Advanced Night Repair, at a price of over $85 dollars for a one-ounce bottle, do? According to this brochure, nothing. It only "helps," and the brochure does not say how much it helps. Moreover, it only "helps control," and then it only helps control the "signs of aging," not the aging itself. Also, it "encourages" skin not to be younger but only to "look and feel" younger. The brochure does not say younger than what. Of the sixteen words in the main clause of this second sentence, nine are weasel words. So, before you spend all that money for Night Repair, or any other cosmetic product, read the words carefully, and then decide if you're getting what you think you're paying for.

Other Tricks of the Trade

Advertisers' use of doublespeak is endless. The best way advertisers can make something out of nothing is through words. Although there are a lot of visual images used on television and in magazines and newspapers, every advertiser wants to create that memorable line that will stick in the public consciousness. I am sure pure joy reigned in one advertising agency when a study found that children who were asked to spell the word "relief" promptly and proudly responded "r-o-l-a-i-d-s."

The variations, combinations, and permutations of doublespeak used in advertising go on and on, running from the use of rhetorical questions ("Wouldn't you really rather have a Buick?" "If you can't trust Prestone, who can you trust?") to flattering you with compliments ("The lady has taste."

“We think a cigar smoker is someone special.” “You’ve come a long way, Baby.”). You know, of course, how you’re supposed to answer those questions, and you know that those compliments are just leading up to the sales pitches for the products. Before you dismiss such tricks of the trade as obvious, however, just remember that all of these statements and questions were part of very successful advertising campaigns.

A more subtle approach is the ad that proclaims a supposedly unique quality for a product, a quality that really isn’t unique. “If it doesn’t say Goodyear, it can’t be Polyglas.” Sounds good, doesn’t it? Polyglas is available only from Goodyear because Goodyear copyrighted that trade name. Any other tire manufacturer could make exactly the same tire but could not call it “Polyglas,” because that would be copyright infringement. “Polyglas” is simply Goodyear’s name for its fiberglass-reinforced tire.

Since we like to think of ourselves as living in a technologically advanced country, science and technology have a great appeal in selling products. Advertisers are quick to use scientific doublespeak to push their products. There are all kinds of elixirs, additives, scientific potions, and mysterious mixtures added to all kinds of products. Gasoline contains “HTA,” “F-130,” “Platformate,” and other chemical-sounding additives, but nowhere does an advertisement give any real information about the additive. Shampoo, deodorant, mouthwash, cold medicine, sleeping pills, and any number of other products all seem to contain some special chemical ingredient that allows them to work wonders. “Certs contains a sparkling drop of Retsyn.” So what? What’s “Retsyn”? What’s it do? What’s so special about it? When they don’t have a secret ingredient in their product, advertisers still find a way to claim scientific validity. There’s “Sinarest. Created by a research scientist who actually gets sinus headaches.” Sounds nice, but what kind of research does this scientist do? How do you know if she is any kind of expert on sinus medicine? Besides, this ad doesn’t tell you a thing about the medicine itself and what it does.

The World of Advertising

In the world of advertising, people wear “dentures,” not false teeth; they suffer from “occasional irregularity,” not constipation; they need deodorants for their “nervous wetness,” not for sweat; they use “bathroom tissue,” not toilet paper; and they don’t dye their hair, they “tint” or “rinse” it. Advertisements offer “real counterfeit diamonds” without the slightest hint of embarrassment, or boast of goods made out of “genuine imitation leather” or “virgin vinyl.”

In the world of advertising, the girdle becomes a “body shaper,” “form persuader,” “control garment,” “controller,” “outerwear enhancer,” “body garment,” or “antigravity panties” and is sold with such trade names as “The Instead,” “The Free Spirit,” and “The Body Briefer.”

A study some years ago found the following words to be among the most popular used in U.S. television advertisements: *new, improved, better, extra, fresh, clean, beautiful, free, good, great,* and *light.* At the same time, the following words were found to be among the most frequent on British television: *new, good-better-best, free, fresh, delicious, full, sure, clean, wonderful,* and *special.* While these words may occur most frequently in ads, and while ads may be filled with weasel words, you have to watch out for all the words used in advertising, not just the words mentioned here.

Every word in an ad is there for a reason; no word is wasted. Your job is to figure out exactly what each word is doing in an ad—what each word really means, not what the advertiser wants you to think it means. Remember, the ad is trying to get you to buy a product, so it will put the product in the best possible light, using any device, trick, or means legally allowed. Your only defense against advertising (besides taking up permanent residence on the moon) is to develop and use a strong critical reading, listening, and looking ability. Always ask yourself what the ad is really saying. When you see ads on television, don't be misled by the pictures, the visual images. What does the ad say about the product? What does the ad not say? What information is missing from the ad? Only by becoming an active, critical consumer of the doublespeak of advertising will you ever be able to cut through the doublespeak and discover what the ad is really saying.

The Language of Advertising

Charles A. O'Neill

His name was Joe Camel. On the billboards and in the magazine ads, he looked like a cartoonist's composite sketch of the Rolling Stones, lounging around in a celebrity waiting area at MTV headquarters in New York. He was poised, confident, leaning against a railing or playing pool with his friends. His personal geometry was always just right. He often wore a white suit, dark shirt, sunglasses. Cigarette in hand, wry smile on his lips, his attitude was distinctly confident, urbane.

He was very cool and powerful. So much so that more than 90 percent of 6-year-olds matched Joe Camel with a picture of a cigarette, making him as well-known as Mickey Mouse.[1]

Good advertising, but bad public relations.

Finally, after extended sparring with the tobacco company about whether Joe really promoted smoking, the Federal Trade Commission brought the ads to an end. President Clinton spoke for the regulators when he said, "Let's stop pretending that a cartoon camel in a funny costume is trying to sell to adults, not children."

Joe's 23-year-old advertising campaign was stopped, because it was obvious that he could turn kids into lung cancer patients. That's bad enough. But beneath the surface, the debate about Joe typifies something more interesting and broad-based: the rather uncomfortable, tentative acceptance of advertising in our society. We recognize the legitimacy—even the value—of advertising, but on some level we can't quite fully embrace it as a "normal" part of our experience.

At best, we view advertising as distracting. At worst, we view it as dangerous to our health and a pernicious threat to our social values. One notable report acknowledged the positive contribution of advertising (e.g., provides information, supports worthy causes, and encourages competition and innovation), then added, "In the competition to attract even larger audiences . . . communicators can find themselves pressured . . . to set aside high artistic and moral standards and lapse into superficiality, tawdriness, and moral squalor."[2]

How does advertising work? Why is it so powerful? Why does it raise such concern? What case can be made for and against the advertising business?

In order to understand advertising, you must accept that it is not about truth, virtue, love, or positive societal values. It is about money. It is about moving customers through the sales process. Sometimes the words and images are concrete; sometimes they are merely suggestive. Sometimes ads provide useful information; sometimes they convince us that we need to spend money to solve a problem we never knew we had. Ads are designed to be intrusive. We're not always pleased about the way they clutter our environment and violate our sense of private space. We're not always happy with the tactics they use to impose themselves upon us.

Whatever the product or creative strategy, advertisements derive their power from a purposeful, directed combination of images. These can take the form of text in a magazine or newspaper, images on television, interactive games on Web pages or mini-documentaries on YouTube. Whatever the means of expression, the combination of images is the language of advertising, a language unlike any other.

Everyone who grows up in the civilized world knows that advertising language is different from other languages. Read this aloud: "With Nice 'n Easy, it's color so natural, the closer he gets, the better you look." Many children would be unable to explain how this classic ad for Clairol's Nice 'n Easy hair coloring differs from "ordinary language," but they would say it sounds like an ad.

The language of advertising changes with the times. Styles and creative concepts come and go. But there are at least four distinct, general characteristics of the language of advertising that make it different from other languages. They lend advertising its persuasive power:

1. The language of advertising is edited and purposeful.
2. The language of advertising is rich and arresting; it is specifically intended to attract and hold our attention.

3. The language of advertising involves us; in effect, *we* complete the message.
4. The language of advertising is simple and direct. It holds no secrets from us.

Edited and Purposeful

In his famous book, *Future Shock,* Alvin Toffler describes various types of messages we receive from the world around us each day. He observed that there is a difference between normal "coded" messages and "engineered" messages. Much of normal, human experience is "uncoded." When a man walks down a street, for example, he sees where he is going and hears random sounds. These are mental images, but they are not messages "designed by anyone to communicate anything, and the man's understanding of it does not depend directly on a social code—a set of agreed-upon signs and definitions."[3]

In contrast, the language of advertising is "coded." It exists in the context of our society. It is also carefully engineered and ruthlessly purposeful. When he wrote in the 1960s, Toffler estimated that the average adult was exposed to 560 advertising messages each day. Now, our homes are equipped with 400-channel, direct-broadcast satellite television, the Internet, video streaming mobile devices, and other new forms of mass media. We're literally swimming in a sea of information. We're totally wired and wireless. We're overwhelmed by countless billboards in subway stations, stickers on light poles, 15-second spots on television, and an endless stream of spam and pop up messages online.

Demanding Attention

Among the hundreds of advertising messages in store for us each day, very few will actually command our conscious attention. The rest are screened out. The people who design and write ads know about this screening process; they anticipate and accept it as a premise of their business.

The classic, all-time favorite device used to breach the barrier is sex. There was a time, many years ago, when advertisers used some measure of subtlety and discretion in their application of sexual themes to their mass media work. No more. Sensuality has been replaced by in-your-face, unrestrained sexuality. One is about romance and connection; the other, physical connection and emotional distance.

A poster promotes clothing sold by the apparel company, French Connection group, United Kingdom: (FCUK). Large type tells us, "Apparently there are more important things in life than fashion. Yeah, right." This text is accompanied by a photo of two young people in what has become a standard set up: A boy. A girl. She is pretty, in a detached, vapid sort of way.

He has not shaved for 48 hours. They are sharing physical space, but there is no sense of human contact or emotion. The company name appears on the lower right hand side of the poster. The headline is intended to be ironic: "Of course there are things that are more important than fashion, but right now, who cares?" The company maintains that they are "not trying to shock people." As absurd as it may seem, this is actually the truth. This company is not in the business of selling shock. They are selling clothes. They are making a lot of money selling clothes, because they know what motivates their teenaged customers—a desire to separate from their parents and declare their membership in the tribe of their peers.

Fortunately, advertisers use many other techniques to attract and hold the attention of the targeted consumer audience. The strategy may include strong creative execution, humor, or a plain, straightforward presentation of product features and customer benefits. Consider this random cross section of advertisements from popular media:

- An ad for SalesForce.com used a photo of the Dalai Lama beneath the headline, "There is no software on the path to enlightenment." (What does this mean? "Salesforce.com provides computer services, so I won't have to buy software myself.")
- An ad for Chevrolet HHR automobiles sports a headline, "We're innocent in every way like apple pie and Chevrolet—Mötley Crüe" (Another use of irony. Most readers of Rolling Stone are unlikely to consider the band to be a paragon of innocence, and by extension, neither is the car.)
- Some ads entertain us and are effective, even though they don't focus much on the product. They work because we remember them. Geico is an automobile insurance company, but they use angst-ridden cavemen and a cute little lizard—appropriately enough, a Gecko—as characters in their ads.
- Some ads tell us we have problems—real or imagined—that we'd better solve right away. Do you have dry skin or "unsightly eyebrow hairs?" (Causing the hapless reader to think, "I never really noticed, but now that they mention it. . . .")

Soft drink companies are in an advertising category of their own. In the archetypical version of a soft drink TV spot, babies frolic with puppies in the sunlit foreground, while their youthful parents play touch football. On the porch, Grandma and Pops quietly smile as they wait for all of this affection to transform the world into a place of warmth, harmony, and joy.

Dr. Pepper ads say, "Be you!" and feature dancers prancing around singing songs about "individuality." In Coke's ads, the singer Maya tells us this can of syrupy fizz is "real." And Pepsi has Britney Spears singing, "Pepsi: for those who think young!" The message: If you are among the millions of people who see the commercial and buy the product, you will become "different." You will find yourself transformed into a unique ("Be you," "individuality," "real"), hip ("young") person.[4]

These "slice of life" ads seduce us into feeling that if we drink the right combination of sugar, preservatives, caramel coloring, and a few secret ingredients, we'll fulfill our yearning for a world where folks from all nations, creeds, and sexual orientations live together in a state of perfect bliss. At least for the five minutes it takes to pour the stuff down our parched, fast-food-filled throats. If you don't buy this version of the American Dream, look around. You are sure to find a product that promises to help you gain prestige in whatever posse you do happen to run with.

When the connection is made, the results can be very powerful. Starbucks has proven that a commodity product like coffee can be artfully changed from a mere beverage into an emotional experience.

Ad campaigns and branding strategies do not often emerge like Botticelli's Venus from the sea, flawless and fully grown. Most often, the creative strategy is developed only after extensive research. "Who will be interested in our product? How old are they? Where do they live? How much money do they earn? What problem will our product solve?" The people at Starbucks did not decide to go to China on a whim. The people at French Connection did not create their brand name simply to offend everyone who is old-fashioned enough to think that some words don't belong on billboards, T-shirts, and storefronts.

Involving

We have seen that the language of advertising is carefully engineered; we have discovered a few of the devices it uses to get our attention. Coke and Pepsi have entranced us with visions of peace and love. An actress offers a winsome smile. Now that they have our attention, advertisers present information intended to show us that their product fills a need and differs from the competition. Advertisers exploit and intensify product differences when they find them and invent them when they do not.

As soon as we see or hear an advertisement, our imagination is set in motion, and our individual fears and aspirations, quirks, and insecurities come out to play.

It was common not long ago for advertisers in the fashion industry to make use of gaunt, languid models. To some observers, these ads promoted "heroin chic." Perhaps only a few were substance abusers, but something was most certainly unusual about the models appearing in ads for Prada and Calvin Klein products. A young woman in a Prada ad projects no emotion whatsoever. Her posture suggests that she is in a trance or drug-induced stupor. In a Calvin Klein ad, a young man, like the woman from Prada, is gaunt beyond reason. He is shirtless. As if to draw more attention to his peculiar posture and "zero body fat" status, he is shown pinching the skin next to his navel. To some, this also suggests that he is preparing to insert a needle.

The fashion industry backed away from the heroin theme. Now the models look generally better fed. But they are, nonetheless, still lost in a world of ennui and isolation. In an ad by Andrew Mark NY, we see a young woman wearing little leather shorts. Her boyfriend's arm is wrapped around her, his thumb pushing ever-so-slightly below the waistband of her pants. What does he look like? He appears to be dazed. He is wearing jeans, an unzipped leather jacket. He hasn't shaved for a couple of days. We are left with the impression that either something has just happened here or is about to. It probably has something to do with sex.

Do these depictions of a decadent lifestyle exploit certain elements of our society—the young, insecure, or clueless? Or did these ads, and others of their ilk, simply reflect profound bad taste? Most advertising is about exploitation—the systematic, deliberate identification of our needs and wants, followed by the delivery of a carefully constructed promise that the product will satisfy them.

Advertisers make use of a variety of techniques and devices to engage us in the delivery of their messages. Some are subtle, making use of warm, entertaining, or comforting images or symbols. Others, as we've seen, are about as subtle as an action sequence from Quentin Tarantino's latest movie. Although it may seem hard to believe, advertising writers did not invent sex. They did not invent our tendency to admire and seek to identify ourselves with famous people. Once we have seen a famous person in an ad, we associate the product with the person. When we buy Coke, we're becoming a member of the Friends of Maya Club. The logic is faulty, but we fall for it just the same. Advertising works, not because Maya and Britney have discriminating taste, or the nameless waif in the clothing ad is a fashion diva, but because we participate in it.

Keeping It Simple

Advertising language differs from other types of language in another important respect: it is simple by design. To measure the simplicity of an ad, calculate its Fog Index. Robert Gunning[5] developed this formula to determine the comparative ease with which any given piece of communication can be read. The resulting number is intended to correspond with grade level.

- Calculate the number of words in an average sentence.
- Count the number of words of three or more syllables in a typical 100-word passage, omitting words that are capitalized, combinations of two simple words, or verb forms made into three-syllable words by the addition of -ed or -es.
- Add the two figures (the average number of words per sentence and the number of three-syllable words per 100 words), then multiply the result by 0.4.

Consider the text of this ad for Geico automobile insurance:

```
"The Gecko speaks out." (Headline)

     "I love to entertain, but I'm here to save
you money on car insurance. Get a FREE rate quote.
Fifteen minutes could save you 15 percent or
more." (Body copy)

1. Words per sentence:            10
2. Three syllable words/100:      2
3. Subtotal:                      12
4. Multiply by 0.4:               4.8
```

According to Gunning's scale, you should be able to comprehend this ad if you are just about to finish the fourth grade. Compare this to comic books, which typically weigh in at the sixth grade level, or *Atlantic Monthly*, at the twelfth.

Why do advertisers favor simple language? The answer lies with the consumer. As a practical matter, we would not notice many of these messages if length or eloquence were counted among their virtues. Today's consumer cannot take the time to focus on anything for long, much less blatant advertising messages. Every aspect of modern life runs at an accelerated pace. Voice mail, text messaging, cellular phones, e-mail, the Internet—the world is always awake, always switched on, and hungry for more information. Time is dissected into increasingly smaller segments.

Who Is Responsible?

Some critics view the advertising industry as a cranky, unwelcomed child of commerce—a noisy, whining, brash truant who must somehow be kept in line but can't just yet be thrown out of the house. In reality, advertising mirrors the fears, quirks, and aspirations of the society that creates it (and is, in turn, sold by it). This alone exposes advertising to parody and ridicule. The overall level of acceptance and respect for advertising is also influenced by the varied quality of the ads themselves. Critics have declared advertising guilty of other failings as well:

1. Advertising encourages unhealthy habits.
2. Advertising feeds on human weaknesses and exaggerates the importance of material things, encouraging "impure" emotions and vanities.
3. Advertising sells daydreams—distracting, purposeless visions of lifestyles beyond the reach of the majority of the people who are most exposed to advertising.

4. Advertising warps our vision of reality, implanting in us groundless fears and insecurities.
5. Advertising downgrades the intelligence of the public.
6. Advertising debases English.
7. Advertising perpetuates racial and sexual stereotypes.

What can be said in advertising's defense? Does it encourage free-market competition and product innovation? Sure. But the real answer is simply this: Advertising is, at heart, only a reflection of society.

What can we say about the charge that advertising debases the intelligence of the public? Exactly how intelligent is "the public?" Sadly, evidence abounds that the public at large is not particularly intelligent after all. Americans now get 31 percent of their calories from junk food and alcoholic beverages.[6] Michael can't read. Jessica can't write. And the entire family spends the night in front of the television, watching people eat living insects in the latest installment of a "reality" show.

Ads are effective because they sell products. They would not succeed if they did not reflect the values and motivations of the real world. Advertising both reflects and shapes our perception of reality. Ivory Snow is pure. Federal Express won't let you down. Absolut is cool. Sasson is sexy. Mercedes represents quality. Our sense of what these brand names stand for may have as much to do with advertising as with the objective "truth."

Good, responsible advertising can serve as a positive influence for change, while fueling commerce. But the obverse is also true: Advertising, like any form of mass communication, can be a force for both "good" and "bad." It can just as readily reinforce or encourage irresponsible behavior, ageism, sexism, ethnocentrism, racism, homophobia, heterophobia—you name it—as it can encourage support for diversity and social progress.

As Pogo once famously said, "We have met the enemy, and he is us."[7]

Notes

1. Internet: http://www.joechemo.org.
2. Pontifical Council for Social Communications, "Ethics in Advertising," published 2/22/97.
3. Alvin Toffler, *Future Shock* (New York Random House, 1970), p. 146.
4. Shannon O'Neill, a graduate student at the University of New Hampshire, contributed this example and others cited here.
5. Curtis D. MacDougall, *Interpretive Reporting* (New York: Macmillan, 1968), p. 94.
6. 2000 study by the American Society for Clinical Nutrition (*Boston Globe*, 7/29/93).
7. Walt Kelly, *Pogo* cartoon (1960s); referring to the Vietnam War.

QUESTIONS: For Thinking and Writing

1. Consider the phrases used in advertising, such as "new and improved" and "cleans like a dream." Do we think about such advertising phrases? How much do such phrases influence you as a consumer? Explain.
2. Describe an experience in which you purchased a product because you were influenced by its advertising language. For example, did you buy a hair, beauty, or electronic product because of the promises made by its ad? Explain.
3. Consider Lutz's argument that advertisers are trying to "trick" consumers with their false promises and claims. How much are our expectations of product performance influenced by the claims and slogans of advertising? How do you think O'Neill would respond to Lutz's accusation?
4. A "weasel word" is a word so hollow it has no meaning. Consider your own reaction to weasel words when you hear them. Try to identify as many weasel words as you can. What are the words, and what do consumers think they mean?
5. O'Neill believes that advertising language mirrors the fears, quirks, and aspirations of the society that creates it. Do you agree or disagree with this statement? Explain your perspective in a brief essay supporting your response with examples.

A Portfolio of Advertisements

The next section features five recently published magazine advertisements. Diverse in content and style, some ads use words to promote the product, while others depend on emotion, name recognition, visual appeal, or association. They present a variety of sales pitches and marketing techniques. The ads are followed by questions to help you analyze how they work their appeal to promote their products. When studying them, consider how they target our social perception and basic desires for happiness, beauty, and success. Approach each as a consumer, an artist, a social scientist, and a critic with an eye for detail.

Gap

QUESTIONS: For Thinking and Writing

1. What is the expression of the woman in this ad? How does her expression contribute to the tone the ad wishes to set?

2. Do you know who the woman in the ad is? What sort of person do you imagine her to be? What is she wearing? Is what she is wearing important in promoting the product, a line of clothing? How does her role in pop culture promote the product?
3. What is this woman known for? Why do you think she is pictured without the equipment she uses as part of her profession?
4. Who would you say is the target audience for this ad? Why? Consider age, gender, lifestyle, and so on in your response.
5. Consider the different angles at which the photograph included in this ad might have been taken. How would its impact be different if it were shot from above? What if the woman in the photo was looking directly at the camera? Explain.

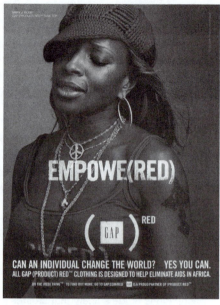

Weallhaveaids.Com

QUESTIONS: For Thinking and Writing

1. Do you find this ad particularly compelling? Why or why not? What kind of an impact does the universal statement made by the group have on the reader? Explain.
2. Who are the people in this advertisement? What is their connection to the "product"? How are they dressed and posed? Do these photographic elements make the ad more effective? If so, why?
3. If you were leafing through a magazine and saw this ad, would you stop to look at it? Why or why not?
4. What message is this ad trying to convey? To whom is it addressed? What action does it want consumers to take?

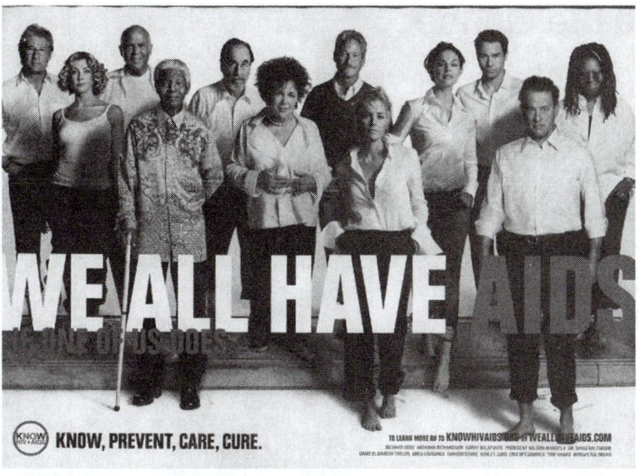

M&Ms

QUESTIONS: For Thinking and Writing

1. What is this ad mimicking? Explain.
2. None of the text in this advertisement is serious; that is, the advertisers do not speak to the audience about the product. Evaluate the use of text in this ad. How does it complement the picture? Is anything lost by not telling the audience about the product? Why or why not?
3. Would you stop and look at this ad? Why or why not?
4. Evaluate the personification of the candy in this ad. Does this seem like an effective vehicle to promote the product? Explain.
5. Who is the target audience for this ad? Is it likely to appeal to a broad group of people, or a specific group?

Absolute On Ice

QUESTIONS: For Thinking and Writing

1. What is the purpose of this ad? What is it "selling?"
2. How does this ad rely on our previously established expectations regarding the product it satirizes and how that product has been marketed?
3. Visit the Absolut Vodka Web site at www .absolutvodka. com to see real ads produced by this company. How does the spoof ad incorporate elements of the real ads? Explain.
4. What are your gut reactions to this ad? Do you find it disturbing? Offensive? Effective? Enlightening? Explain.
5. Evaluate the effectiveness of photographic decisions in this ad. Would it be as effective if the ad featured an entire body? A face? Explain.

Ad council: Girl Scouts

QUESTIONS: For Thinking and Writing

1. Who is the person in the picture? What is she doing? How does the text above the photo help us understand what the ad is trying to do?
2. What is the purpose of this advertisement, and who is it trying to reach? What can you determine about the intended audience based on the picture, language, and message?

3. If there were no text in this ad, what other things could it promote? Explain.
4. Visit the Web site (www. girlsgotech. org). Would the ad lead you to look up the Web site? How useful is this site to the intended audience? Explain.

QUESTIONS: For Further Research And Group Work

1. Identify some recent advertising campaigns that created controversy (Abercrombie and Fitch, Dove's "Real Beauty," PETA, Dolce and Gabbana, or Snickers). What made them controversial? How did the controversial campaigns impact sales?
2. Charles O'Neill notes that sometimes advertisers use symbols to engage their audience. Compile a list of brand symbols or logos, their corresponding products, and the lifestyle we associate with the logo or symbol. Are some logos more popular or prestigious? Explain.
3. Working in a group, develop a slogan and advertising campaign for one of the following products: sneakers, soda, a candy bar, or jeans. How would you apply the principles of advertising language to market your product? After completing your marketing plan, "sell" your product to the class. If time permits, explain the reasoning behind your selling technique.
4. As a class or group project, make a list of standard appliances, equipment, and possessions that people have in their homes—refrigerators, microwave ovens, pocketbooks, personal planners, fans, coffeemakers, DVD players, computers, VCRs, televisions, stereos (include components), iPods, blow-dryers, scooters, and so on. Compile a list of at least 30 items, then rank each item as a necessary, desirable, or luxury item. For example, you may decide a refrigerator is a necessary item but list an air conditioner as a luxury item. Do not look at how other members of your group rank the items until you are all finished. Compare your list with others in your group. Do the lists match, or are there some surprising discrepancies? Discuss the similarities and differences between your lists.
5. Develop a marketing plan to the youth market for a long-established product, such as Levi's jeans, Adidas sneakers, or Dr. Pepper cola. Refer to points made by Rushkoff in his essay as you develop your plan. After creating your marketing plan, explain why you chose this strategy and why it is likely to appeal to the youth market.
6. Research how popular culture media and marketing, including the Internet and television, sell products to children. Locate Web sites and identify television programs that target children. How do theme parks, such as Disneyland and Disneyworld, and merchandise, such as DVDs and books, also influence children? Report your findings to the class as part of a broader group discussion on this issue.

3 CHAPTER

The American Family in Flux

THE AMERICAN FAMILY IS ALWAYS IN A STATE OF CHANGE. How we perceive the very concept of family is based largely on where we come from and what values we share. We have a tendency to base our views on traditional constructs—models that are generations old and perpetuated by media archetypes. As a result, sociologists tell us, our vision of family is usually not based on realistic examples but on political ideals and media images. Yet the traditional family is obviously changing. Stepfamilies, same-sex relationships, single-parent households, and extended families with several generations living in one home all force us to redefine, or at least reexamine, our traditional definitions of family.

From traditional "nuclear family" models of husband, wife, and children to same-sex unions, this chapter takes a look at how our concept of marriage and family has changed over the last several decades. Divorce, for example, is a widely accepted reality of life and is no longer viewed as a deviation from the norm. Single motherhood is no longer ascribed the social stigma it had 30 or 40 years ago. Some states have legalized same-sex marriage. A census report issued in 2007 revealed that only 24 percent of households are comprised of what many politicians refer to as the "model family" of husband, wife, and children. Clearly, the American family unit has changed, and with it, our expectations and social collective consciousness have changed. Readings in this chapter examine the changing face of the American family and the state of marriage in the United States today.

BETTY G. FARRELL

Family: Idea, Institution, and Controversy

Although the family has always been in a state of transition, many politicians expound that the family is not just in a state of change; it is in a state of decline—to the detriment of society. And whether this is true or not, it seems that many people agree that most of society's ills are directly connected to the "decline" of the family. The truth is, the American family is more than an icon in our culture. It is an American institution, subject to intense scrutiny and criticism. Professor Betty G. Farrell, in this excerpt from her book, The Making of an Idea, an Institution, and a Controversy in American Culture, *explores the importance of the institution of family in American culture and how this importance is inextricably linked to our social and political consciousness.*

Q: What did Eve say to Adam on being expelled from the Garden of Eden?

A: "I think we're in a time of transition."

The irony of this joke is not lost as we begin a new century and anxieties about social change seem rife. The implication of this message, covering the first of many subsequent periods of transition, is that change is normal; there is, in fact, no era or society in which change is not a permanent feature of the social landscape. Yet, on the eve of the twenty-first century, the pace of change in the United States feels particularly intense, and a state of "permanent transition" hardly seems a contradiction in terms at all. To many, it is an apt description of the economic fluctuations, political uncertainties, social and cultural upheaval, and fluidity of personal relationships that characterize the times. For a large segment of the population, however, these transitions are tinged with an acute sense of loss and nostalgia. Moral values, communities, even the American way of life seem in decline. And at the core of that decline is the family.

In a nationwide poll conducted by the *Los Angeles Times*, May 26, 1996, 78 percent of respondents said they were dissatisfied with today's moral values, and nearly half of that group identified divorce, working parents, and undisciplined children as the key problems. Only 11 percent of the respondents believed that their own behavior had contributed to the moral problems in the United States, and a resounding 96 percent believed that they were personally doing an excellent or good job of teaching moral values to their children. Conversely, 93 percent thought that other parents were to blame for the inadequate moral upbringing of their children. The sense of loss and decline many Americans feel today is filled with such contradictions. Americans want their families to offer unconditional love yet also to enforce and uphold strict moral values. They want flexibility, mobility, and autonomy in their personal lives but yearn for traditional communities and permanently stable families. When the substance of the debate over families is this ambiguous and contradictory, it is important to look more closely at the underlying issues in this time of transition.

For most people in most eras, change seems anything but normal. Periods of social change can evoke much social anxiety, because the unknown is inherently unsettling, and because many people are stakeholders in the status quo. Those who seek change generally want to affect a shift in the relations of power, either for themselves or for others. But such shifts are always unpredictable, and they can seem treacherous to those who hold the reins of power, as well as to those who feel their social, economic, or political power eroding. The groups with eroding power are the ones most likely to resist, through active strategies and passive resistance, the ideas, values, symbols, and behavior associated with change. This describes such groups in the contemporary United States as militias who see minorities, foreigners, and new cultural values as a threat to the American way of life; whites who see blacks, Latinos, and Asians as challenging their privileges and claims on limited resources in a zero-sum game; pro-life advocates who see pro-choice supporters as threatening traditionally defined family roles; and antigay proponents who see gays and lesbians as subverting the gendered social order. Although social structural forces are ultimately responsible for the realignment of prestige and power among social groups in any society, these forces are always complex, abstract, intangible, and invisible. So those who symbolize or represent the forces of the new—women, minorities, immigrants, the poor, and other marginalized groups—tend to be singled out and blamed for the disruptions and upheaval associated with change. Social psychologists identify this process as *scapegoating,* the act of displacing generalized anxiety onto a conveniently visible and available target. Scapegoats have been identified in every era; but in periods in which the pace of change is particularly fast and a sense of unsettling disruption is acute, those social newcomers who challenge established values and behavior can all too readily become the targets of the rage, fear, and ambivalence of people feeling the earthquake tremors of social change.

Popular Perspectives on the Family

The family values debate has been generated against just such a backdrop in the late-twentieth-century United States. Fundamental changes in the expectations, meanings, and practices defining American family life have characterized much of the twentieth century, but especially the final 30 years. Consequently, concern about the family has moved to the center of the political arena. Threats to the family, on the one hand, and salvation through the family, on the other, are the two most prominent themes in the recent family politics discourse. That the American family is broken and in need of repair is a common assumption of many social observers. Its complement is that families are worth fixing, because making them strong (again) is the key to solving most of society's ills. Neither of these assumptions has been subject to much critical scrutiny, nor has the historical image of the strong, vital, central family institution of the past on which they rest. Longing for order is one of the impulses behind the current turn to family politics in the United States; and feminists, gays and lesbians, single-parent mothers, absent fathers, pregnant teenagers, and gang-oriented youth, among others, have all at one time or another been made the scapegoats for family decline in the United States.

Longing for a more orderly, mythic past is most commonly associated with the conservative position on the family politics spectrum, and it would be easy to caricature the nostalgia for a family modeled on the classic 1950s television sitcom as the sum total of this side of the family values debate. But if we assume that concerns about The Family, writ large, are only those of conservative politicians attempting to manipulate public sentiment, we would overlook the vast reservoir of social anxiety about contemporary family life that is also being tapped by many others from a variety of political and social perspectives:

working mothers who are consumed with worry about child care; white Christian men who, by the tens of thousands in the late 1990s, attended Promise Keepers revivals that focused on renewing their traditional roles as husbands and fathers; adolescents seeking the emotional attachment of family ties among peers and in gangs, when it is found lacking in their own homes; committed gay and lesbian couples fighting for inclusion in the legal definition of family, even as they retain a skeptical stance toward this fundamentally heterosexual institution. Why such concern about the family? One reason is that the metaphor evoked by family is a powerful one. A family is defined not so much by a particular set of people as by the quality of relationships that bind them together. What seems to many to be the constant feature of family life is not a specific form or structure but the meanings and the set of personal, intimate relationships families provide against the backdrop of the impersonal, bureaucratized world of modern society.

The core sentiments of family life that define the nature and meaning of this social institution for most Americans are unconditional love, attachment, nurturance, and dependability. The hope that these qualities are common to family relationships accounts for the shock with which we react to reports of violence, abuse, and neglect occurring inside the sanctuary of the private home. In popular culture as in real life, stories of families beset by jealousy, envy, lust, and hatred, rather than by the ideals of love, loyalty, and commitment, provide an endless source of titillation and fascination. Family stories are not only the stuff of life we construct through our daily experience but the narrative form used to entice us as consumers into a marketplace adept at presenting all sorts of products as invested with emotional qualities and social relationships.

The widely promoted "Reach Out and Touch Someone" advertising campaign developed by AT&T in 1978 was a prototype of this genre. In this set of ads, a powerful multinational company hoped to pull at the heartstrings and the pocketbooks of the consuming public by promoting itself as the crucial communication link between family members separated by great global distances. The copy in the print advertisements told heartwarming personal tales of mothers and sons, uncles and nephews, and grandmothers and grandchildren reunited by AT&T's implied commitment to family values, albeit at long distance phone rates. The family metaphor works as an advertising ploy, because there is widespread sentimentality in American society about family life. What makes families so compelling for those of us who actively choose to live in them, as well as for those of us who just as actively reject them as oppressively confining, is that families reside at the intersection of our most personal experience and of our social lives. They are institutions we make, yet they are in no small part also constructed by cultural myths and social forces beyond any individual's control.

A desire for the kind of care and connection provided by the ideal family cuts across class, race, and ethnic lines in the United States. A commitment to family seems to be so widely shared across groups of all kinds in the hybrid mix that makes up American culture as to be nearly universal. It therefore comes as some surprise that the qualities many accept as natural components of family ties today—unconditional love, warmth, enduring attachment—were not the same expectations most American families had until 150 years ago. The historical variations in family life challenge the claim that the family, even within the same culture, has had the same meaning or has offered the same timeless experiences to its members.

Assumptions about American family life in the past are widely shared. These include the beliefs that families were large and extended, with most people living in multigenerational households; that marriages occurred at an early age and were based on permanent, unwavering commitment between spouses; that the ties between kin were stronger and closer than those experienced today; and that family life in the past was more stable and predictable than it is currently. These assumptions about the family of the past have collectively produced an image that one sociologist has called "the Classical Family of Western Nostalgia." It is the image upon which politicians and advertisers, among others, routinely draw as they explain contemporary social problems by reference to family breakdown, or as they tap consumer desires by associating a product with positive family values and warm family feeling. The family is a potent symbol in contemporary American society, because it touches our emotional needs for both intimate, personal attachments and a sense of embeddedness in a larger community.

Is there truth to the fears that family values are weaker today than in the past—that children are more vulnerable, adolescents more intractable, adults less dependable, and the elderly more needy? In both popular culture and political discourse, sentimentality and nostalgia about the family have often prevailed, and a social and historical context for framing the issues has largely been missing. It is important to challenge the popular understanding of the family as an institution that is biologically based, immutable, and predictable with a more culturally variable and historically grounded view. Because families are central to the way we talk about ourselves and about our social and political lives, they deserve to be studied in their fullest scope, attached to a real past as well as a present and future.

Academic Perspectives on the Family

Assumptions about the nature of the family abound not only in popular culture but in social science as well. The disciplines of anthropology, sociology, history, and psychology all have particular orientations to the institution of the family that define their theoretical positions and research agendas. Among sociologists and anthropologists, for example, a starting premise about the family has been that it is one of the central organizing institutions of society. Its centrality comes from having the capacity to organize social life quite effectively by regulating sexuality, controlling reproduction, and ensuring the socialization of children who are born within the family unit. Many social science disciplines start with the question, how is society possible? And they recognize that the organization of individuals into family units is a very effective means of providing social regulation and continuity. Through the institution of the family, individuals are joined together and given the social and legal sanction to perpetuate their name and traditions through their offspring. Whole societies are replenished with future generations of leaders and workers.

In the early twentieth century, the anthropologist Bronislaw Malinowski made the argument that the most universal characteristic of family life in all cultures and all time periods was the "principle of legitimacy." He noted that the rules for sexual behavior varied widely across cultures but that control over reproduction was a common feature of every social order. Every society made the distinction between those children (legitimate) born to parents who had been culturally and legally sanctioned to reproduce and those children (illegitimate) whose parents were not accorded this sanction. The function of the principle of legitimacy, according to Malinowski, was to ensure that a child born into a society had both an identifiable mother and father. The father might, in fact, not be biologically related to the child, but his recognized sociological status as father was the affiliation that gave the child a set of kin and a social placement in that social order.

In addition to being the only sanctioned setting for reproduction, families are important sources of social continuity, because they are most often the setting in which children are cared for and raised. The power of social forces is such that parents normally can be counted on to provide long-term care for their dependent children, because the emotional closeness of family bonds makes them want to do so. Families are therefore particularly effective institutions, because they press people into service for their kin by the dual imperatives of love and obligation. Although it is possible that food, shelter, physical care, and emotional nurturance could be provided through alternative means by the state or other centrally administered bureaucratic agencies, it would require considerable societal resources and effort to ensure that these needs were effectively met for a majority of individuals in a society. What families seem to provide naturally, societies would otherwise have to coordinate and regulate at great cost.

To argue that families are effective or efficient as social institutions is not, however, to claim that they are necessary or inevitable. One common fallacy that some sociologists have promoted in studying the family at the societal level is the equation of its prevalence with the idea that it is functionally necessary. The assumption that societies "need" families in order to continue, based on the observation that some form of family exists in all known societies, ignores the range of variation in or the exceptions to this institution. Individuals and subgroups within all societies have constructed alternative arrangements to the traditional family of parents and their children. But the very fact that they are considered alternatives or experimental social organizations suggests how powerful the dominant family norm continues to be.

Another assumption that is shared across several social science disciplines is that family harmony and stability constitute the basis for order and control in the larger society. From this perspective, the family is a microcosm of the larger society, and social regulation in the domestic sphere helps promote order and control at all social levels. Individual social analysts might alternatively celebrate or lament the kind of control, regulation, and social order that was understood to begin in the family and radiate outward to the larger society; but the assumption that society was built on the foundation of the family was rarely challenged.

As a microcosm, or a miniature society, of the rulers and the ruled who are bound together by reciprocal rights and obligations, the family helps maintain social order first by its capacity to place people in the social system. It does so by providing them with identifiable kin and establishing the lines of legitimate succession and inheritance that mark their economic, political, and social position in society. Because individuals are located in an established social hierarchy by their birth or adoption into a particular family group, the nature of power and access to resources in a society remain largely intact from one generation to the next. Thus, one meaning of the family as a central institution of the social order is that it reinforces the political and economic status quo. Families ensure that the distribution of resources both to the advantaged and disadvantaged will remain relatively stable, since the transmission of wealth, property, status, and opportunity is channeled along the lines of kinship.

In another important way, families help to regulate the social order. Family life, according to both law and custom, prescribes roles for men, women, and children. Although these roles are really the products of social and cultural forces rather than biological imperatives and are therefore highly fluid in times of change, they appear to most people to be prescribed by stable and immutable rules governing everyday life. The meaning of "traditional" family life is that people are conscripted into established roles. Everyone knows his or her place and tends to keep to it by the pressures of community norms and social sanctions. But such traditional family roles exact a toll as well. What promotes social harmony and order to the advantage of some produces severe constraints on others. Women and children, whose roles in the family have traditionally been subordinate to those of men, have sometimes resisted such prescriptive expectations and have led the charge for social change in both overt and covert ways. It is not surprising that in times of rapid social change the family has been identified as an inherently conservative institution, one that not only helps to perpetuate the status quo but is perceived as being oppressively restrictive to many of its own members.

Although many changes have characterized American family life over time, we should be mindful of important continuities as well. The most striking continuity is the importance that the family holds for so many people. The reasons that the family is important have varied historically, but there is no doubt that it has been a central institution, one on which people have pinned all manner of beliefs, values, and prejudices, as well as fears about and hopes for the future. Families reside at the intersection of private and public experience. We are all experts, since most of us have lived within one or more families at some point in our lives. Families can house both our highest hopes and our greatest disappointments, and their fragility or resilience therefore carries great personal meaning, in addition to social significance. The novelist Amos Oz has called the family "the most mysterious, most secret institution in the world." Its mysteries and secrets are not fully revealed in the social and historical record, but in reconstructing some of the patterns of family life, we can begin to understand why it has continued to play such a central role in American culture as an organizing social institution, a lived experience, and a powerful metaphor.

QUESTIONS: For Thinking and Writing

1. Social scientists and family historians often comment that the American family is in a "state of transition." What do they mean? What is transition? Is it a positive or negative thing?
2. Farrell notes that in a 1996 poll on moral values, 78 percent of respondents said that they were dissatisfied with today's moral values, but that only 11 percent believed that their own behavior had contributed to this moral decline. What is your own opinion about today's moral values, and how does your own behavior fit in with these values?
3. Farrell comments that our social concern for "The Family" is rooted in the "metaphor evoked by family". What does she mean? How does she define family, and how does this definition connect to our social concerns about the decay of the family in general? Explain.
4. At the end of her essay, Farrell quotes novelist Amos Oz, who calls the family "the most mysterious, most secret institution in the world." Explore this idea. How is the family "secret"? If almost everyone has a family and understands what the term implies, how can it be "mysterious"? Support your position with information from Farrell's article as well as your own personal perspective.
5. In a letter to a politician or public figure of your choice, discuss the current state of the family as it applies to the concept of family as an

institution in American culture. In your letter, you should make specific references to the politiciatance on the state of the family.

JAMES Q. WILSON

The Decline of Marriage

Recent decades have witnessed a shift in how society views single parenthood. High divorce rates and changing attitudes toward unwed motherhood are partially responsible for this shift. But is this greater acceptance of single parenthood good for children and their parents? In this essay, professor and author James Q. Wilson of Pepperdine University discusses the decline of marriage in the United States—and its cultural implications as a contributor to poverty and unemployment. This essay was published in the City Journal *on February 17, 2002.*

Everyone knows that the rising proportion of women who bear and raise children out of wedlock has greatly weakened the American family system. This phenomenon, once thought limited predominantly to African Americans, now affects whites as well, so much so that the rate at which white children are born to an unmarried mother is now as high as the rate for black children in the mid 1960s, when Daniel Patrick Moynihan issued his famous report on the black family.

"For whites, the rate is one-fifth; for blacks, it is over one-half."

Almost everyone agrees that children in mother-only homes suffer harmful consequences: these youngsters are more likely than those in two-parent families to be suspended from school, have emotional problems, become delinquent, suffer from abuse, and take drugs. Some of these problems may arise from the economic circumstances of these one-parent families, but the best studies show that low income can explain, at most, about half of the differences between single-parent and two-parent families. The rest are explained by a mother living without a husband. And single moms, by virtue of being single, are more likely to be poor than are married moms.

Now, not all children born out of wedlock are raised by a single mother. Some are raised by a man and woman who, though living together, are not married; others are raised by a mother who gets married shortly after the birth. Nevertheless, there has been a sharp increase in children who are not only born out of wedlock but are raised without a father. In the United States, the percentage of children living with an unmarried mother has tripled since 1960.

Why has this happened? I think there are two possible explanations to consider: money and culture.

Money readily comes to mind. If a welfare system pays unmarried mothers enough to have their own apartment, some women will prefer babies to husbands. When government subsidizes something, we get more of it. But for many years, American scholars discounted this possibility. Since the amount of welfare paid per mother had declined in inflation-adjusted terms, and since the amount paid in each state showed no correlation with each state's illegitimacy rate, surely money could not have caused the increase in out-of-wedlock births.

There are three arguments against this view. First, what counted was the inflation-adjusted value of all of the benefits an unmarried mother might receive—not only welfare, but also food stamps and Medicaid. By adding these in, welfare kept up with inflation. Second, what counted was not how much money each state paid out, but how much it paid compared to the cost of living in that state. Third, comparing single-parent families and average spending levels neglects the real issue: how attractive is welfare to a low-income unmarried woman in a given locality?

When economist Mark Rosenzweig asked this question of women who are part of the national longitudinal survey of youth, he found that a 10 percent increase in welfare benefits made the chances that a poor young woman would have a baby out of wedlock before the age of 22 go up by 12 percent. And this was true for whites as well as blacks. Welfare made a difference.

But how big a difference?

AFDC began in 1935, but by 1960 only 4 percent of the children getting welfare had a mother who had never been married; the rest had mothers who were widows or had been separated from their husbands. By 1996 that had changed dramatically: now approximately two thirds of the welfare children had an unmarried mom and hardly any were the offspring of widows.

To explain this staggering increase, we must turn to culture. In this context, what I mean by culture is simply that being an unmarried mother and living on welfare has lost its stigma. At one time, living on the dole was shameful; now it is much less so.

Consider these facts: Women in rural communities who go on welfare leave it much sooner than the same kind of women who take welfare in big cities, and this is true for both whites and blacks and regardless of family size. In a small town, everyone knows who is on welfare, and welfare recipients do not have many friends in the same situation with whom they can associate. But in a big city, welfare recipients are not known to everyone, and each one can easily associate with other women living the same way.

American courts have made clear that welfare laws cannot be used to enforce stigma. When Alabama tried in 1960 to deny welfare to an unmarried woman who was living with a man who was not her husband, the U.S. Supreme Court objected. Immorality, it implied, was an outdated notion. If the state is concerned about immorality, it will have to rehabilitate the women by other means.

How did the stigma get weakened by practice and undercut by law, when Americans favor marriage and are skeptical of welfare?

Let me suggest that beneath the popular support for marriage there has slowly developed, almost unnoticed, a subversion of it: whereas marriage was once thought to be about a social union, it is now about personal preferences. At one time, law and opinion enforced the desirability of marriage without inquiring into what went on in that union; today law and opinion enforce the desirability of individual happiness without worrying too much about maintaining a formal relationship. Marriage was once a sacrament, then it became a contract, and now it is an arrangement. Once religion provided the sacrament, then the law enforced the contract, and now personal preferences define the arrangement.

The cultural change that made this happen was the same one that gave us science, technology, freedom, and capitalism: the Enlightenment. The Enlightenment made human reason the measure of all things, throwing off ancient rules if they fell short. What the king once ordered, what bishops once enforced, what tradition once required was to be set aside in the name of scientific knowledge and personal self-discovery.

I am a great admirer of the Enlightenment. But it entailed costs. I take great pride in the vast expansion in human freedom that the Enlightenment conferred on so many people, but I also know that the Enlightenment spent little time worrying about those cultural habits that make freedom meaningful. The family was one of these.

It was in the world most affected by the Enlightenment that we find both its good and bad legacies. There we encounter both remarkable science and personal self-indulgence. There we find human freedom and high rates of crime. There we find democratic governments and frequent divorces. There we find regimes concerned about the poor and a proliferation of single-parent families.

Single-parent families are most common in those nations—England, America, Canada, Australia, France, the Netherlands—where the Enlightenment had its greatest effect. It was in the Enlightened nations that nuclear rather than extended families became common, that individual consent and not clan control was the basis of a marriage contract, and that divorce first became legal.

The Enlightenment did not change the family immediately, because everyone took family life for granted. The most important Enlightenment thinkers assumed marriage and denounced divorce. That assumption—and in time that denunciation—slowly lost force, as people slowly experienced the widening of human freedom. The laws, until well into the twentieth century, made it crystal clear that, though a child might be conceived by an unmarried couple, once born, it had to have two parents. There was no provision for the state to pay for a single-parent child, and public opinion strongly endorsed that policy.

But by the end of the nineteenth century and the early years of the twentieth, policies changed, and then, slowly, opinion changed. Two things precipitated the change: first, a compassionate desire to help needy children and, second, a determination to end the legal burdens under which women suffered.

The first was a powerful force, especially since the aid to needy children was designed to help those who had lost their fathers owing to wars or accidents. Slowly, however, a needy child was redefined to include those of any mother without a husband, and not just any who had become a widow.

The emancipation of women was also a desirable process. In America and England, nineteenth-century women already had more rights than those in most of Europe, but when married, they still could not easily own property, file for a divorce, or conduct their own affairs. By the 1920s most of these restrictions had ended, and once women got the vote, there was no chance of these limitations ever being reinstated.

We should therefore not be surprised that the twenties were an enthusiastic display of unchaperoned dating, provocative dress, and exhibitionist behavior. Had it not been for a timeout imposed by the Great Depression and the Second World War, we would no longer be referring to the sixties as an era of self-indulgence; we would be talking about the legacy of the twenties.

The sixties reinstated trends begun half a century earlier, but now without effective opposition. No-fault divorce laws were passed throughout most of the West, the pill and liberalized abortion laws dramatically reduced the chances of unwanted pregnancies, and popular entertainment focused on pleasing the young. As a result, family law lost its moral basis. It was easier to get out of a marriage than a mortgage. This change in culture was made crystal clear by court decisions. At the end of the nineteenth century, the Supreme Court referred to marriage as a "sacred obligation." By 1965, the same court described marriage as "an association of two individuals."

People still value marriage; but it is only that value—and very little social pressure or legal obligation—that sustains it.

But there is another part of the cultural argument, and it goes to the question of why African-Americans have such high rates of mother-only families. When black scholars addressed this question, as did W. E. B. Dubois in 1908, they argued that slavery weakened the black family. When Daniel Patrick Moynihan repeated this argument in 1965, he was denounced for "blaming the victim."

An intense scholarly effort to show that slavery did little harm to African-American families followed that denunciation; instead, what really hurt them was migrating to big cities where they encountered racism and oppression.

It was an astonishing argument. Slavery, a vast system of organized repression that, for over two centuries, denied to blacks the right to marry, vote, sue, own property, or take an oath; that withheld from them the proceeds of their own labor; that sold them and their children on the auction block; that exposed them to brutal and unjust punishment: all of this misery had little or no effect on family life, but moving as free people to a big city did. To state the argument is to refute it.

But since some people take academic nonsense seriously, let me add that we now know that this argument was empirically wrong. The scholars who made it committed some errors. In calculating what percentage of black mothers had husbands in the nineteenth century, they accepted many women's claims that they were widows, when we now know that such claims were often lies, designed to conceal that the respondents had never married. In figuring out what proportion of slaves were married, these scholars focused on large plantations, where the chance of having a spouse was high, instead of on small ones, where most slaves lived but where the chance of having a spouse was low. On these small farms, only about one fifth of the slaves lived in a nuclear household.

The legacy of this sad history is twofold. First, generations of slaves grew up without having a family, or without having one that had any social and cultural meaning. Second, black boys grew up aware that their fathers were often absent or were sexually active with other women, giving the boys poor role models for marriage.

There remains at least one more puzzle to solve. Culture has shaped how we produce and raise children, but that culture surely had its greatest impact on how educated people think. Yet the problem of weak, single-parent families is greatest among the least educated people. Why should a culture that is so powerfully shaped by upper-middle-class beliefs have so profound an effect on poor people? If white culture has weakened marriage, why should black culture follow suit? I suspect that the answer may be found in Myron Magnet's book, "The Dream and the Nightmare." When the haves remake a culture, the people who pay the price are the have-nots. Let me restate his argument with my own metaphor. Imagine a game of crack-the-whip, in which a line of children, holding hands, starts running in a circle. The first few children have no problem keeping up, but near the end of the line, the last few must run so fast that many fall down. Those children who did not begin the turning suffer most from the turn.

There are countless examples of our cultural crack-the-whip. Heroin and cocaine use started among elites and then spread down the social scale. When the elites wanted to stop, they could hire doctors and therapists; when the poor wanted to stop, they could not hire anybody. People who practiced contraception endorsed loose sexuality in writing and movies; the poor practice loose sexuality without contraception. Divorce is more common among the affluent than the poor. The latter, who can't afford divorce, deal with unhappy marriages by not getting married in the first place. My only trivial quarrel with Magnet is that I believe these changes began a century ago and even then built on more profound changes that date back centuries.

Now you probably expect me to tell you what we can about this, but if you believe, as I do, in the power of culture, you will realize that there is very little one can do. As a University of Chicago professor once put it, if you succeed in explaining why something is so, you have probably succeeded in explaining why it must be so. He implied what is in fact often the case: change is very hard. Moreover, there are many aspects of our culture that no one, least of all I, wants to change.

We do not want fewer freedoms or less democracy. Most of us do not want to change any of the gains women have made in establishing their moral and legal standing as independent actors with all of the rights that men once enjoyed alone.

We can talk about tighter divorce laws, but it is not easy to design one that both protects people from ending a marriage too quickly with an easy divorce and at the same time makes divorce for a good cause readily available. The right and best way for a culture to restore itself is for it to be rebuilt, not from the top down by government policies, but from the bottom up by personal decisions.

On the side of that effort, we can find churches—or at least many of them—and the common experience of adults that the essence of marriage is not sex, or money, or even children: it is commitment.

QUESTIONS: For Thinking and Writing

1. What is your opinion of single parenthood? Has society become too accepting of parents who decide to raise children out of wedlock?
2. Wilson notes that American courts have made it clear that welfare laws cannot be used to enforce a stigma on unwed mothers. Should the government encourage unwed parents to marry? Why or why not? What is your viewpoint on this issue?
3. What cultural and social reasons does Wilson cite for why women in rural communities leave welfare more rapidly than women in urban areas? Do you agree with his analysis?
4. According to Wilson, what factors have contributed to the decline of the American family? Make a list of the social and cultural forces influencing the family.
5. Write a response to Wilson's essay, addressing some of the arguments he makes with which you agree or disagree in whole or in part. You may select a particular aspect of his argument, such as the role of welfare or the role of the stigma of childbearing out of wedlock, to address in depth.

STEPHANIE COONTZ

For Better, For Worse

As Betty G. Farrell explained in the first essay in this chapter, many Americans feel that the family and marriage in general is in a state of decline. Underlying this feeling is that there is a loss of "traditional family values" that have contributed to the decay of marriage. How much of this belief is rooted in fact and how much in hype? Stephanie Coontz maintains that the problem is that we are longing for a social construction that is based on a false memory, rather than fact. Culturally, we can't "go back," and Coontz wonders why we would even want to. This editorial appeared in the May 1, 2005 edition of The Washington Post.

Thirteen years ago, Vice President Dan Quayle attacked the producers of TV sitcom *Murphy Brown* for letting her character bear a child out of wedlock, claiming that the show's failure to defend traditional family values was encouraging America's youth to abandon marriage. His speech kicked off more than a decade of outcries against the "collapse of the family." Today, such attacks have given way to a kinder, gentler campaign to promote marriage, with billboards declaring that "Marriage Works" and books making "the case for marriage." What these campaigns have in common is the idea that people are willfully refusing to recognize the value of traditional families and that their behavior will change if we can just enlighten them.

But recent changes in marriage are part of a worldwide upheaval in family life that has transformed the way people conduct their personal lives as thoroughly and permanently as the Industrial Revolution transformed their working lives 200 years ago. Marriage is no longer the main way in which societies regulate sexuality and parenting or organize the division of labor between men and women. And although some people hope to turn back the tide by promoting traditional values, making divorce harder or outlawing gay marriage, they are having to confront a startling irony: The very factors that have made marriage more satisfying in modern times have also made it more optional.

The origins of modern marital instability lie largely in the triumph of what many people believe to be marriage's traditional role—providing love, intimacy, fidelity, and mutual fulfillment. The truth is that for centuries, marriage was stable precisely because it was not expected to provide such benefits. As soon as love became the driving force behind marriage, people began to demand the right to remain single if they had not found love or to divorce if they fell out of love.

Such demands were raised as early as the 1790s, which prompted conservatives to predict that love would be the death of marriage. For the next 150 years, the inherently destabilizing effects of the love revolution were held in check by women's economic dependence on men, the unreliability of birth control, and the harsh legal treatment of children born out of wedlock, as well as the social ostracism of their mothers. As late as the 1960s, two thirds of college women in the United States said they would marry a man they didn't love if he met all their other, often economic, criteria. Men also felt compelled to marry if they hoped for promotions at work or for political credibility.

All these restraints on individual choice collapsed between 1960 and 1980. Divorce rates had long been rising in Western Europe and the United States, and although they had leveled off following World War II, they climbed at an unprecedented rate in the 1970s, leading some to believe that the introduction of no-fault divorce laws, which meant married couples could divorce if they simply fell out of love, had caused the erosion of marriage.

The so-called divorce revolution, however, is just one aspect of the worldwide transformation of marriage. In places where divorce and unwed motherhood are severely stigmatized, the retreat from marriage simply takes another form. In Japan and Italy, for example, women are far more likely to remain single than in the United States. In Thailand, unmarried women now compete for the title of "Miss Spinster Thailand." Singapore's strait-laced government has resorted to sponsoring singles nights in an attempt to raise marriage rates and reverse the birth strike by women.

In the United States and Britain, divorce rates fell slightly during the 1990s, but the incidence of cohabitation and unmarried child raising continues to rise, as does the percentage of singles in the population.

Both trends reduce the social significance of marriage in the economy and culture. The norms and laws that traditionally penalized unwed mothers and their children have weakened or been overturned, ending centuries of injustice but further reducing marriage's role in determining the course of people's lives. Today, 40 percent of cohabiting couples in the United States have children in the household, almost as high a proportion as the 45 percent of married couples who have kids, according to the 2000 Census. We don't have a TV show about that yet, but it's just a matter of time.

The entry of women into the workforce in the last third of the twentieth century was not only a U.S. phenomenon. By the 1970s, women in America and most of Europe could support themselves if they needed to. The 1980s saw an international increase in unmarried women having babies (paving the way for Murphy Brown), as more people gained the ability to say no to shotgun marriages, and humanitarian reforms lowered the penalties for out-of-wedlock births. That decade also saw a big increase in couples living together before marriage.

Almost everywhere, women's greater participation in education has raised the marriage age and the incidence of nonmarriage. Even in places where women's lives are still largely organized through marriage, fertility rates have been cut in half and more wives and mothers work outside the home.

From Turkey to South Africa to Brazil, countries are having to codify the legal rights and obligations of single individuals and unmarried couples raising children, including same-sex couples. Canada and the Netherlands have joined Scandinavia in legalizing same-sex marriage, and such bastions of tradition as Taiwan and Spain are considering following suit.

None of this means that marriage is dead. Indeed, most people have a higher regard for the marital relationship today than when marriage was practically mandatory. Marriage as a private relationship between two individuals is taken more seriously and comes with higher emotional expectations than ever before in history.

But marriage as a public institution exerts less power over people's lives, now that the majority of Americans spend half their adult lives outside marriage and almost half of all kids spend part of their childhood in a household that does not include their two, married, biological parents. And unlike the past, marriage or lack of marriage does not determine people's political and economic rights.

Under these conditions, it is hard to believe that we could revive the primacy of marriage by promoting traditional values. People may revere the value of universal marriage in the abstract, but most have adjusted to a different reality. The late Pope John Paul II was enormously respected for his teaching about sex and marriage. Yet during his tenure, premarital sex, contraception use, and divorce continued to rise in almost all countries. In the United States, the Bible Belt has the highest divorce rate in the nation. And although many American teens pledged abstinence during the 1990s, 88 percent ended up breaking that pledge, according to the National Longitudinal Study of Adolescent Youth that was released in March.

Although many Americans bemoan the easy accessibility of divorce, few are willing to waive their personal rights. In American states where "covenant" marriage laws allow people to sign away their right to a no-fault divorce, fewer than 3 percent of couples choose that option. Divorce rates climbed by the same percentage in states that did not allow no-fault divorce as in states that did. By 2000, Belgium, which had not yet adopted no-fault divorce, had the highest divorce rates in Europe outside of Finland and Sweden.

Nor does a solution lie in preaching the benefits of marriage to impoverished couples or outlawing unconventional partnerships. A poor single mother often has good reason not to marry her child's father, and poor couples who do wed have more than twice the divorce risk of more affluent partners in the United States. Banning same-sex marriage would not undo the existence of alternatives to traditional marriage. Five million children are being raised by gay and lesbian couples in this country. Judges everywhere are being forced to apply many principles of marriage law to those families, if only to regulate child custody should the couple part ways.

We may personally like or dislike these changes. We may wish to keep some and get rid of others. But there is a certain inevitability to almost all of them.

Marriage is no longer the institution where people are initiated into sex. It no longer determines the work men and women do on the job or at home, regulates who has children and who doesn't, or coordinates care-giving for the ill or the aged. For better or worse, marriage has been displaced from its pivotal position in personal and social life and will not regain it short of a Taliban-like counterrevolution.

Forget the fantasy of solving the challenges of modern personal life by reinstitutionalizing marriage. In today's climate of choice, many people's choices do not involve marriage. We must recognize that there are healthy as well as unhealthy ways to be single or to be divorced, just as there are healthy and unhealthy ways to be married. We cannot afford to construct our social policies, our advice to our own children, and even our own emotional expectations around the illusion that all commitments, sexual activities, and caregiving will take place in a traditional marriage. That series has been canceled.

QUESTIONS: For Thinking and Writing

1. In your opinion, is marriage in danger of becoming an obsolete institution? Why do people marry today? Is marriage a goal for you in your life plan? Why or why not?
2. Coontz states, "For better or worse, marriage has been displaced from its pivotal position in personal and social life and will not regain it short of a Taliban-like counterrevolution." Respond to this statement in your own words. Do you agree with her? Is her statement a generalization or is it based largely on social fact? Explain.
3. Based on her essay, summarize Coontz's view of marriage. Cite specific areas of the text to support your summary.
4. How do you think James Wilson would respond to Coontz's argument? Explain.
5. Write a personal narrative in which you describe the structure of your family during your childhood, focusing specifically on the role of marriage in your family. Were your parents married? Divorced? If you could have changed anything about your parent's marital relationship, what would it have been?

DAVID POPENOE AND BARBARA DAFOE WHITEHEAD

The Cultural Devaluation of Child Rearing

It used to be that the American dream involved a house, a spouse, at least two kids, and a dog. Nowadays, the dream is shifting and kids are increasingly less likely to be part of the picture. National Marriage Project directors David Popenoe and Barbara Dafoe Whitehead believe that a general devaluation of the nobility of child rearing has contributed to the opinion that having children is undesirable. This phenomenon, coupled with a media glamorization of the single life, is creating a cultural shift that the authors fear could have dire ramifications for the American family. The National Marriage Project is a nonprofit initiative at Rutgers University that provides research and analysis on the state of marriage in America, specifically addressing the social, economic, and cultural conditions affecting marriage. The article below is an excerpt from an essay appearing in the Project's 2006 annual report.

In American society, there is a popular tradition of paying tribute to the work and sacrifice of parents—and especially the steadfast heroism of American mothers. This tradition is waning. Indeed, if the popular culture were the only source of knowledge about American parenthood, one would quickly conclude that being a parent is one of the least esteemed and most undesirable roles in the society. From the newsstands to the blogosphere, reports of parents behaving badly abound.

Several stereotypes have emerged. There are the hypercompetitve sports parents, who scream at their own kids, yell obscenities at players on rival teams, assault referees, and attack parents rooting for the opposing team. There are aggressive urban parents, who use Mack-truck-sized Bugaboo strollers to plow their way down narrow sidewalks. There are the self-entitled parents, who let their kids run wild in coffeehouses and restaurants while ignoring, or staring down, annoyed patrons. Most famously, there are the helicopter parents, who not only hover over their children, but also swoop down to rescue them from the consequences of their own bad behavior.

Television has long made fun of fathers. Now, in a dramatic departure from television tradition, it has turned to ridiculing mothers. The Unfit Mom has become a reality show staple. In the shows *Nanny 911* and *Supernanny*, mothers can't get their kids to eat, go to bed, or pick up their toys. They sob that they are "bad" mothers. Meanwhile, the kids wheedle and manipulate and fight. It takes a British nanny, schooled in modern child-rearing techniques, to teach these shell-shocked American moms how to discipline their kids. In two other reality shows, *Wife Swap* and *Meet Your New Mom*, mothers exchange households and families. The mothers represent starkly opposing and equally unattractive types: the negligent vs. overindulgent; the slob vs. the neatnik; the game hunter vs. the gun control advocate; the meat-eater vs. the vegan; the moralizing Christian vs. the New Age wacko.

The unappealing image of life with children is all the more striking when it is contrasted with the appealing image of life before children. Television shows like *Friends* and *Sex and the City* have sexualized and glamorized the life of young urban singles. The characters in these hugely popular shows hang out with friends, hook up for sex, and spend enormous amounts of free time in restaurants, clubs, and coffee bars.

The empty nest years have undergone a similar makeover. The AARP—once self-styled as the political voice of millions of fixed income pensioners—has changed its image. It has retired the word "retired" in order to appeal to aging baby boomers, a demographic group that famously refuses to grow old. It has mothballed the name of its flagship magazine, once known as *Modern Maturity*, in favor of the more age-neutral *AARP Magazine*. Most telling of all, it has revised the content of the magazine to include features on sex, dating, romantic relationships, and "having a baby after 50." Borrowing the language of teen magazines, it has developed its own list of the 50 Hot People over 50—including "babelicious baldies," like Bruce Willis; "fetching newshounds," like Ed Bradley, and "sexy scribes," like Terry McMillan.

AARP is not alone in the effort to remake the image of older adulthood. A raft of recent books on women's "second half of life" has transformed the post-menopausal years from frumpy to fabulous. Television ads for the denture adhesive, Fixodent, used to tout the product's effectiveness in removing blueberry stains from false teeth. Now the Fixodent spots feature a handsome, well-seasoned couple in evening clothes locking lips in the back seat of a taxicab.

Of course, the media images of the non–child-rearing years do not accurately describe the real life experience of most American adults. Life without children is rarely as sexy or liberating as the popular portraits suggest. Nonetheless, fantasy can be more powerful than reality in shaping cultural aspirations. And in this case, the fantasy is revealing: in what is a major cultural shift, the child-free years are portrayed as more attractive, even superior to, the child-rearing years.

The cultural devaluation of child rearing is especially harmful in the American context. In other advanced Western societies, parents' contributions are recognized and compensated with tangible work and family benefits. In American society, the form of compensation has been mainly cultural. Parents have been rewarded (many would argue inadequately) for the unpaid work of caring for children with respect, support, and recognition from the larger society. Now this cultural compensation is disappearing. Indeed, in recent years, the entire child-rearing enterprise has been subject to a ruthless debunking. Most notably, the choice of motherhood is now contested terrain, with some critics arguing that the tasks of mothering are unworthy of educated women's time and talents. Along with the critique of parenthood, a small but aggressively vocal "child-free" movement is organizing to represent the interests of nonparents.

It is hard enough to rear children in a society that is organized to support that essential social task. Consider how much more difficult it becomes when a society is indifferent at best, and hostile at worst, to those who are caring for the next generation.

QUESTIONS: For Thinking and Writing

1. According to the authors, in what ways has the media contributed to the "devaluation" of child rearing? Explain.
2. The authors note that recent television programs not only make fun of fathers but, now, mothers, portraying women with children as inept, ineffectual, and stupid. Do you think programs such as the ones cited by Dafoe Whitehead and Popenoe indeed influence our cultural perceptions of parenthood? Of children? Why or why not?
3. Dafoe Whitehead and Popenoe observe that "fantasy can be more powerful than reality in shaping cultural aspirations." What do they mean? Explain.
4. If you have not started a family yourself, do you expect to later? What circumstances will precede your decision to have children? Do you experience any of the ambivalence towards having children that the authors in this article describe? If so, why? Are you influenced by media messages? Personal experience? Other factors? Explore your perspective in a well-considered essay.
5. You are an analyst working for the National Marriage Project. Write a short report providing recommendations for change to improve the perception of child rearing in the United States.

VIEWPOINTS

Why the "M" Word Matters to Me

Andrew Sullivan

The Case Against Same Sex Marriage

Margaret A. Somerville

This chapter's Viewpoints section addresses the issue of gay marriage, which has been hotly argued, as some states ban and others begin to permit same-sex marriage. The Commonwealth of Massachusetts made headlines at the end of 2003 when its highest court ruled four to three that same-sex marriage was permissible under its state Constitution. Much of the debate hinges on how we define marriage—is it a partnership between two loving, consenting adults or a sanctified or legal union between a man and a woman? Many arguments, such as the one presented here by Andrew Sullivan, focus on the issue of love—if two people love each other, goes the argument, they should be allowed to marry. Opponents to this view, such as Margaret A. Somerville in this section, contend that marriage is about more than love—it has traditionally been a legal and social bond between a man and a woman foremost to support the upbringing of children. To redefine this definition of marriage would be to undermine the institution itself and threaten the family. Should couples of the same gender be legally allowed to marry? What problems and benefits might result? Sullivan's essay first appeared in the February 8, 2004 issue of TIME. *Somerville's report, from which this piece is excerpted, was submitted to the Canadian Standing Committee on Justice and Human Rights on April 29, 2003. Some references to Canadian legal cases have been omitted. The document in its entirety can be found online.*

Why the "M" Word Matters to Me

Andrew Sullivan

What's in a name?

Perhaps the best answer is a memory.

As a child, I had no idea what homosexuality was. I grew up in a traditional home—Catholic, conservative, middle class. Life was relatively simple: education, work, family. I was brought up to aim high in life, even though my parents hadn't gone to college. But one thing was instilled in me. What matters is not how far you go in life, how much money you make, how big a name you make for yourself. What really matters is family, and the love you have for one another. The most important day of your life was not graduation from college or your first day at work or a raise or even your first house. The most important day of your life was when you got married. It was on that day that all your friends and all your family got together to celebrate the most important thing in life: your happiness, your ability to make a new home, to form a new but connected family, to find love that puts everything else into perspective.

But as I grew older, I found that this was somehow not available to me. I didn't feel the things for girls that my peers did. All the emotions and social rituals and bonding of teenage heterosexual life eluded me. I didn't know why. No one explained it. My emotional bonds to other boys were one-sided; each time I felt myself falling in love, they sensed it, pushed it away. I didn't and couldn't blame them. I got along fine with my buds in a nonemotional context; but something was awry, something not right. I came to know almost instinctively that I would never be a part of my family the way my siblings one day might be. The love I had inside me was unmentionable, anathema—even, in the words of the Church I attended every Sunday, evil. I remember writing in my teenage journal one day: "I'm a professional human being. But what do I do in my private life?"

So, like many gay men of my generation, I retreated. I never discussed my real life. I couldn't date girls and so immersed myself in schoolwork, in the debate team, school plays, anything to give me an excuse not to confront reality. When I looked toward the years ahead, I couldn't see a future. There was just a void. Was I going to be alone my whole life? Would I ever have a "most important day" in my life? It seemed impossible, a negation, an undoing. To be a full part of my family, I had to somehow not be me. So like many gay teens, I withdrew, became neurotic, depressed, at times close to suicidal. I shut myself in my room with my books, night after night, while my peers developed the skills needed to form real relationships, and loves. In wounded pride, I even voiced a rejection of family and marriage. It was the only way I could explain my isolation.

It took years for me to realize that I was gay, years later to tell others, and more time yet to form any kind of stable emotional bond with another man. Because my sexuality had emerged in solitude—and without any link to the idea of an actual relationship—it was hard later to reconnect sex to love and self-esteem. It still is. But I persevered, each relationship slowly growing longer than the last, learning in my twenties and thirties what my straight friends found out in their teens. But even then, my parents and friends never asked the question they would have asked automatically if I were straight: so when are you going to get married? When is your relationship going to be public? When will we be able to celebrate it and affirm it and support it? In fact, no one—no one—has yet asked me that question.

When people talk about "gay marriage," they miss the point. This isn't about gay marriage. It's about marriage. It's about family. It's about love. It isn't about religion. It's about civil marriage licenses—available to atheists as well as believers. These family values are not options for a happy and stable life. They are necessities. Putting gay relationships in some other category—civil unions, domestic partnerships, civil partnerships, whatever—may alleviate real human needs, but, by their very euphemism, by their very separateness, they actually build a wall between gay people and their own families. They put back the barrier many of us have spent a lifetime trying to erase.

It's too late for me to undo my own past. But I want above everything else to remember a young kid out there who may even be reading this now. I want to let him know that he doesn't have to choose between himself and his family anymore. I want him to know that his love has dignity, that he does indeed have a future as a full and equal part of the human race. Only marriage will do that. Only marriage can bring him home.

The Case Against Same Sex Marriage

Margaret A. Somerville

Marriage as Culture

Marriage is, and has been for millennia, the institution that forms and upholds for society the cultural and social values and symbols related to procreation. That is, it establishes the values that govern the transmission of human life to the next generation and the nurturing of that life in the basic societal unit, the family. Through marriage our society marks out the relationship of two people, who will together transmit human life to the next generation and nurture and protect that life. By institutionalizing the relationship that has the inherent capacity to transmit life—that between a man and a woman—marriage symbolizes and engenders respect for the transmission of human life.

To change the definition of marriage to include same-sex couples would destroy its capacity to function in the ways outlined above, because it could no longer represent the inherently procreative relationship of opposite-sex pair bonding. It would be to change the essence and nature of marriage as the principal societal institution establishing the norms that govern procreation. Marriage involves public recognition of the spouses' relationship and commitment to each other. But that recognition is for the purpose of institutionalizing the procreative relationship in order to govern the transmission of human life and to protect and promote the well-being of the family that results. It is not a recognition of the relationship just for its own sake or for the sake of the partners to the marriage, as it would necessarily become were marriage to be extended to include same-sex couples.

Reproduction is the fundamental occurrence on which, ultimately, the future of human life depends. That is the primary reason why marriage is important to society. In our highly individualistic societies, we tend to look only at its importance to individuals. That is necessary but not sufficient in deciding on the future of marriage.

People advocating same-sex marriage argue that we should accept that the primary purpose of marriage is to give social and public recognition to an intimate relationship between two people and, therefore, to exclude same-sex couples is discrimination. They are correct if the primary purpose of marriage is to protect an intimate pair-bond. But they are not correct if its primary purpose is to protect the inherently procreative relationship of opposite-sex pair bonding or to protect an intimate relationship for the purposes of its procreative potential. When marriage is limited to opposite-sex couples, there is no need to choose between these purposes, because they are compatible with each other and promote the same goal. The same is not true if marriage is extended to include same-sex couples. That would necessarily eliminate marriage's role in symbolizing and protecting the procreative relationship. We now need the procreative symbolism of marriage more than in the past because of new technoscience possibilities for transmitting life, if we believe that, ethically, there should be limits on the use of these technologies.

Culture is what marks us as human; it is what distinguishes us and allows us to distinguish ourselves from other animals and, in the future, from intelligent machines. In the past, we used religion as an important forum and force in the foundation of culture—we did so by finding shared values through religion. That is not possible in a secular society; one result is that it makes it more difficult to find consensus on values.

To form a society, we must create a societal-cultural paradigm—the collection of values, principles, attitudes, beliefs, and myths, the "shared story" through which we find values and meaning in life as both individuals and society. In establishing a societal-cultural paradigm, all human societies have focused on the two great events of every human life: birth and death. Marriage is a central part of the culture—values, attitudes, beliefs—that surrounds birth. We require a culture related to birth in a secular society, at least as much as in a religious one, and must establish it through secular means. That is one reason why the legal recognition of marriage is important.

One argument in favor of same-sex marriage is that the culture of marriage has changed over the years and that recognizing same-sex marriage is just another change. A common example given is the change in the status of the woman partner, in that marriage is now seen as a union of equals. But that change goes to a collateral feature of marriage, not its essential nature or essence as recognizing same-sex marriage would. In short, these two changes are not analogous; rather, they are fundamentally different in kind.

Advocates of same-sex marriage also argue that restricting marriage to opposite-sex couples based on society's need for an institution that symbolizes the inherently procreative relationship between a man and a woman means that opposite-sex couples who cannot or do not want to have children should be excluded from marriage or, more extremely, that only a man and a woman who produce a child should be allowed to marry.

Marriage between opposite-sex partners symbolizes, however, the reproductive potential that exists, at a general level, between a man and a woman. Even if a particular man and woman cannot or do not want to have a child, their getting married does not damage this general symbolism. The reproductive potential of opposite-sex couples is assumed at a general level and is not investigated in individual cases. To do otherwise would be a serious and unjustifiable breach of privacy. It is also sometimes argued that the absence of a reproductive potential is obvious "on the face of the record" when a woman well past the age of childbearing enters a marriage and yet we recognize such marriages. But again, these marriages do not damage the reproductive symbolism of marriage in the way that same-sex marriages would. Indeed, they continue this symbolism at the grandparent level and, therefore, across the generations.

Marriage's role in upholding respect for the transmission of human life, which is the first event in procreation, is of unusual importance at present. We are facing unprecedented challenges to that respect because of new technoscience that opens up unprecedented modes of transmission of life. That is another reason why marriage should remain limited to opposite-sex couples. Without it, we would have no institution that establishes a social-sexual ecology of human reproduction and symbolizes respect for the transmission of human life through sexual reproduction, as compared, for example, through asexual replication (cloning).

Recognizing that a fundamental purpose of marriage is to engender respect for the transmission of human life provides a corollary insight: Excluding same-sex couples from marriage is not related to those people's homosexual orientation, or to them as individuals, or to the worth of their relationships. Rather, the exclusion of their relationship is related to the fact that it is not inherently procreative, and, therefore, if it is encompassed within marriage, marriage cannot institutionalize and symbolize respect for the transmission of life. To recognize same-sex marriage (which is to be distinguished from same-sex partnerships that do not raise this problem) would unavoidably change and eliminate this function of marriage.

The alternative view is that new reproductive technoscience means that same-sex couples will be able to reproduce as a couple, so they should be included in marriage as the institution that institutionalizes, recognizes, and protects procreative relationships. I discuss this argument in the next section.

The inherently procreative relationship institutionalized in marriage is fundamental to society and requires recognition as such. Marriage carries important norms and values, "memes" (long standing units of deep cultural information passed on from generation to generation) related to reproduction. Marriage makes present in the present the deep, collective human memory concerning the norms and values surrounding reproduction. Extending marriage to include same-sex couples (or delegislating marriage, which I discuss shortly) would seriously harm all of these societal-level functions of the institution of marriage.

. . .

Mutual Respect

The reason for excluding same-sex couples from marriage matters: If the reason for denying same-sex marriage is that we have no respect for homosexuals and their relationships, or want to give the message that homosexuality is wrong, then the exclusion of same-sex couples from marriage is not ethically acceptable from the perspective of respect for homosexuals and their relationships. It is also discrimination.

On the other hand, if the reason is to keep the very nature, essence, and substance of marriage intact, and that essence is to protect the inherently procreative relationship, then excluding same-sex couples from marriage is ethically acceptable from the perspective of respect for them and their relationships. And such a refusal is not discrimination.

Respect for others' religious beliefs in a multicultural society can raise complex issues. Some people object to same-sex marriage on the basis of their religious beliefs. These beliefs are often profound, and the people who hold them see a complex interplay in marriage between its voluntary formation, religious sanction, social legitimation, and natural origin. Even if we do not agree with these beliefs, indeed even more so if we do not, we need to understand what they are in order to understand the impact on the people who hold them of legally recognizing same-sex marriage.

We must also likewise take into account the impact on same-sex couples of refusing to recognize their relationships as marriage. We are in a situation of competing sorrows or harms.

We must ask which approach to marriage best accommodates mutual respect. Both sides in this debate must recognize that they can only demand respect from their opponents if they give it; that is, if respect is to be present at all, it will only be so in a context of mutual respect. To the extent that we can avoid transgressing people's religious beliefs, even though we do not agree with them, we should not transgress them out of respect for the people who hold them, not out of respect for those beliefs. The same is true for people who oppose homosexuality on moral grounds, in relation to their having respect for homosexuals, if not for their beliefs. Ethics requires us to take the least invasive, least restrictive alternative reasonably available and likely to be effective in achieving a justified goal. Maintaining traditional marriage and legally recognizing same-sex partnerships fulfills that ethical requirement.

Note: this same accommodation of respect for beliefs in the formation of public policy would not apply to beliefs, based on religion, about the wrongfulness of homosexuality. While such beliefs may be privately held, they are not acceptable as the basis for public policy decision making in a secular society, if only because the harm of recognizing such beliefs far outweighs the harm of not doing so. That is the reason why opposing same-sex marriage on the basis that it involves recognizing a homosexual relationship is not valid, but opposition based on such recognition necessarily destroying the essence of marriage is a valid reason. There is a major difference between not destroying the essence of marriage for people who will enter into that institution and whose religious beliefs mean that recognizing same-sex marriage would destroy it, and recognizing, at any public policy level, the same people's antihomosexual beliefs. The latter is unacceptable, because it directly denigrates homosexuals, rather than seeking a justified goal (maintaining marriage); and because others' sexual orientation, unlike the recognition of same-sex marriage, in no way directly affects the people who regard homosexuality as morally wrong.

Attributing Homophobia

Being against same-sex marriage is frequently alleged by proponents of same-sex marriage to be proof of homophobia. A useful comparison can be made with people who take the view that being against infant male circumcision (IMC) is proof of anti-Semitism. (I, personally, have been subject to both sets of allegations in the public square.)

The strategy adopted in both cases is to shame those who are against same-sex marriage or IMC into silence. The choice of language and framing of the issues is carefully crafted to achieve this result. This strategy also involves using "*ad hominem*" arguments, that is, derogatorily labeling those who oppose same-sex marriage as homophobic or as religious (which is seen by some as a derogatory label), and claiming, therefore, their arguments against same-sex marriage should not be given any weight. The substance of these arguments, however, is not addressed.

Use of Law

The use of law can never be neutral, whether we are enacting, changing, or repealing it. We use law in postmodern, secular societies to challenge or uphold our most important societal values. Same-sex marriage cases are already in the courts and the issue is before this committee. We cannot avoid the decisions of judges regarding same-sex marriage affecting the values related to marriage—either to uphold or change them. One of the options that has been proposed, of repealing the laws on marriage and abandoning the area of marriage, would not be a neutral act. It would necessarily change the values and symbolism associated with marriage. We legislate about matters associated with our most important societal values, therefore delegislating marriage would be to detract from its importance and the values associated with it.

If marriage were not available as a societal institution but only as a religious (quasi-private) one, to mark out and mark off the intrinsically procreative relationship from other types of relationship, there would be no societally sanctioned way these people could symbolize for themselves, others close to them, and society that their relationship had changed, because they were becoming or had become parents. That would be particularly true for people who were not religious.

But what about homosexuals who bring children into their relationship, shouldn't those adults have access to marriage? This is the most powerful argument, in my view, for recognizing same-sex marriage, but I do not believe it justifies extending marriage to same-sex couples.

First, marriage institutionalizes and symbolizes for society the inherently procreative relationship. It cannot do that if it is changed to include same-sex couples.

Second, the joint reproductive incapacity of a same-sex couple must not be addressed through reproductive technologies. I believe that a child has a right not to be created from the genetic patrimony of two men or two women, or by cloning, or from multiple genetic parents. Therefore, same-sex relationships should not be included within an institution that symbolizes an inherently procreative relationship.

Third, bringing children into a same-sex relationship should not be seen as within the norm, but rather as an exception to it. Although it is considered a radical view by some people, and often seen as politically incorrect, I believe that a child needs a mother and a father and if possible, and unless there are good reasons to the contrary, preferably its own biological mother and father as its raising parents. (Adopted children's search for their birth parents and current moves to give children born through reproductive technologies, using donated gametes, access to the gamete donors' identity shows a deep human need to know our biological family origins.) Recognizing same-sex marriage would make bringing children into a same-sex relationship part of the norm, rather than the exception.

We should recognize same-sex relationships and legally protect them and any children involved, but not by recognizing the same-sex couples' relationship as marriage.

Finally, within the context of the legal issues related to recognizing same-sex marriage, we must ask what the private, international-law impact of changing the law would be on all marriages, not just same-sex ones.

Discrimination

Homosexuals are not excluded from marriage, but their intimate pair-bonding relationships are. It is argued that is discrimination on the basis of sexual orientation. If that is correct, we must consider whether the discrimination is justified. I believe it is.

One way the justification can be articulated is in terms of the doctrine of "double effect": The primary intent in restricting marriage to opposite-sex couples is to maintain marriage as the institution that fulfills society's need to protect the inherently procreative relationship and its functions for society and is not to exclude homosexual relationships because they are homosexual. The discrimination involved in the exclusion is a secondary effect, which is not desired but unavoidable, and it is justified or excused by the primary purpose which otherwise cannot be realized.

A useful comparison can be made with the discrimination involved in affirmative action. That shows that sometimes discrimination and the harm it involves can be justified when it is to achieve a greater good that cannot otherwise be achieved.

It is also argued by those advocating same-sex marriage that excluding same-sex couples from marriage is the same act of discrimination as prohibiting interracial marriage, which has rightly been recognized as a serious breach of human rights. That argument is not correct. Because an interracial marriage between a man and a woman does symbolize the procreative relationship, its prohibition is based on racial discrimination, which is wrong. In contrast, not extending the definition of marriage to include same-sex couples is not based on the sexual orientation of the partners, but the absence of a feature of their relationship, which is an essential feature of marriage.

Conclusion

In conclusion, society needs marriage to establish cultural meaning, symbolism, and moral values around the inherently procreative relationship between a man and a woman and thereby protect that relationship and the children who result from it. That is more necessary than in the past, when alternatives to sexual reproduction were not available. Redefining marriage to include same-sex couples would affect its cultural meaning and function and in doing so damage its ability, and thereby society's capacity, to protect the inherently procreative relationship and the children who result from it, whether those children's' future sexual orientation proves to be homosexual or heterosexual.

QUESTIONS: For Thinking and Writing

1. In your opinion, should same-sex couples be permitted to legally marry? Are you likely to be swayed by hearing different points of view on the subject? Why or why not?
2. Identify the primary points of argument Sullivan uses to support his case. Make a list of his reasons, and respond to each one. How do you think Somerville would respond to Sullivan's points in an editorial?
3. How does Sullivan's description of his childhood and his troubled adolescence reach out to his reader? Is his story likely to make his audience more sympathetic? Is it likely to make them better understand his point of view? Explain.
4. Somerville opens her essay with a statement avowing that for thousands of years, marriage has been an institution that forms and

upholds society. In what ways has the institution of marriage served as the foundation of society—intellectually, religiously, politically, economically, and culturally? Explain.

5. Most of the arguments supporting gay marriage note that gay couples are in committed, loving relationships and wish to legitimize their relationship with a marriage license. Can you think of other, less idealistic reasons why people marry? Based on these other reasons, including the practical and the shady, could these reasons undermine the movement legalizing homosexual marriage? For example, what if two female heterosexual friends, one employed the other not, wished to marry for health insurance? Could such alliances be avoided if same-sex marriage were legal? Explain.

God-Ordained Marriage

One argument against gay marriage is that it goes against the Biblical definition of marriage as a union between a man and a woman. This photo, which originally appeared in the Quad City Times, *features young Hawken Runquist as he joins his family members during a rally against the legalization of gay marriage on February 14, 2004, in front of the Clinton County Courthouse in Clinton, Iowa.*

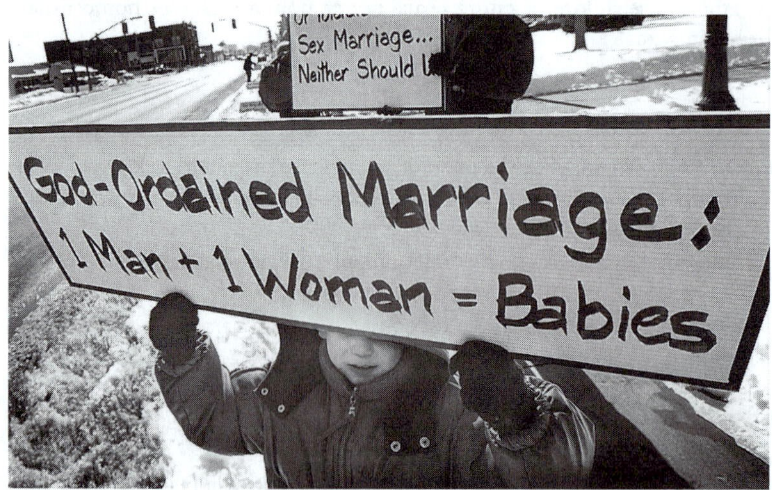

Photo: AP/Quad City Times

QUESTIONS: For Critical Thinking and Writing

1. What argument does the child's sign present against gay marriage? Is this a valid argument on this issue? How might opponents respond to the claim the sign makes?
2. Is it likely that the child in the photo is responsible for the sign's content? Do you think it is an appropriate sign for the child to hold? What can you determine about the child based upon what you see in this photo? Explain.
3. What is the "God-Ordained" definition of marriage? Does your religious background influence your opinion of the gay-marriage issue? Explain.
4. Have you ever taken part in a protest for a cause you believed in? If so, what was the cause, and what was your role in the protest? Is the participation of a young child, such as in this photo, an effective way to protest this particular issue? Why or why not?

QUESTIONS: For Further Research and Group Work

1. Design and administer a poll to people outside your class. Ask for opinions on the health of the American family versus its decline, the ideal role each family member should play in family structure, the desirability of day care, and so on. Also ask for anonymous information about each participant's age, economic status, education, political affiliation, religion, and race. After you have assembled the data you collected as a group, analyze the results. Do any groups seem more or less optimistic about the state of the American family? If so, in what ways? Are some groups more traditional? Explain.
2. Working in small groups, discuss and compare the structures of families within your own experiences. Think about the families you grew up in, the families you know well, and the families you may have started. Evaluate the kinds of families you find. These may include two-earner families, traditional families, families with no children, blended families with stepparents and children, children raised by other relatives, and other groupings. Compare notes with your group.
3. Using free association (writing down anything that comes to mind), brainstorm with your group to develop a list of terms associated with the term "single mother." The list could include anything from "latchkey kids" to "welfare" to "independent" and "community networking." Once you have developed a list, try and locate the source of the association, such as television, opinion editorials, government, political speeches, religion, and news media. What sources are grounded in modern fact, and what sources are not? What role does changing social opinion have on these associations? Explain.

4. Should marriage be a public and political institution? Alternatively, should it be a religious, private, and moral institution? Should it have certain features of each type? List the qualities that a marriage draws from each of these realms. After you have compiled your list, discuss with your group what marriage should be and for whom.
5. Create a survey that you will administer anonymously to other members of your class or to students in the student union, asking for their opinions on gay marriage. Design your survey to allow people to formulate opinions and express their views while incorporating some of the ideas presented in the Viewpoints section. Collect the surveys and discuss them.

CHAPTER 4

Television Troubles

TELEVISION IS THE PRIME MOVER OF MODERN CULTURE. In five decades, it has become the country's foremost source of entertainment and news. More than any other medium, television regulates commerce, lifestyles, and social values. But the medium is also the object of considerable scorn. For years, television has been blamed for nearly all of our social ills—the rise in crime, increased divorce rates, lower voter turnouts, racism, falling SAT scores, increased sexual promiscuity, drug addiction, and the collapse of the family. In short, it has been cited as the cause of the decline of Western civilization.

Certainly, television can be blamed for piping into America's homes hours of brain-numbing, excessively violent, exploitative trash. And given the fact that the average 20-year-old viewer will have spent nearly 3 years of his or her life in front of the television set, it plays a significant and influential role in our daily lives. But to categorically condemn the medium is to be blind to some of the quality programming television is capable of producing—and not just those produced by PBS and educational channels such as TLC, Discovery, and the History Channel. The essays in this chapter explore some of the ways television is a part of our lives—for better or worse—and will examine the areas in which television appears to have failed, and where it shines.

JANE ROSENZWEIG

Can TV Improve Us?

Although television is often cited as the source of many social ills—from teen violence to the decline of the family—many people point out that it also teaches, informs, and entertains us. This article takes the debate one step further by postulating that TV can actually improve us. This essay by Jane Rosenzweig, published in the July/August 1999 issue of the American Prospect, *describes some of the ways in which television has forced us to think about social issues and has promoted moral values. And although television may not be the ideal vehicle to advocate values, it may be the best one we have.*

It's eight o'clock Wednesday evening, and a rumor is circulating at a small-town high school in Massachusetts that a student named Jack is gay. Jack's friends—one of whom is a 15-year-old girl who has been sexually active since she was 13, and another of whom has a mother who has recently committed adultery—assure him it would be okay with them if he were, but admit their relief when he says he isn't. An hour later, in San Francisco, a woman named Julia is being beaten by her boyfriend. Meanwhile, in Los Angeles, a young stripper who has given birth out of wedlock learns that her own mother locked her in a basement when she was three years old, an experience that she thinks may explain her inability to love her own child.

A typical evening in America? If a visitor from another planet had turned on the television today with the aim of learning about our society, he would likely conclude that it is made up pretty exclusively of photogenic young people with disintegrating nuclear families and liberal attitudes about sex. It's obviously not an accurate picture, but what might our visitor have learned from the programs he watched? Would all the sex, violence, and pathology he saw teach him antisocial behavior? Or might he glean from prime-time dramas and sitcoms the behavior and attitudes that he would do well to adopt if he intended to go native in America?

This is not an idle question—not because aliens might be watching American television, but because people are, particularly impressionable children and teenagers. In a time when 98 percent of U.S. households own at least one television set—a set which is turned on for an average of nearly seven hours a day—the degree to which people learn from and emulate the behavior of the characters they see on TV is an academic cottage industry. Some evidence does support the widespread belief that children and teenagers are affected by violence and other antisocial behavior in the media. When Dan Quayle made his infamous comments in 1992 about Murphy Brown having a baby out of wedlock, he was merely doing what numerous concerned parents, ethnic groups, religious organizations, gun-control advocates, and others were already doing—blaming television for encouraging certain types of behavior.

But if television contributes to poor behavior, might it also be a vehicle for encouraging good behavior? In 1988, Jay Winsten, a professor at the Harvard School of Public Health and the director of the school's Center for Health Communication, conceived a plan to use television to introduce a new social concept—the "designated driver"—to North America. Shows were already dealing with the topic of drinking, Winsten reasoned, so why not add a line of dialogue here and there about not driving drunk? With the assistance of then-NBC chairman Grant Tinker, Winsten met with more than 250 writers, producers, and executives over six months, trying to sell them on his designated driver idea.

Winsten's idea worked; the "designated driver" is now common parlance across all segments of American society and in 1991 won entry into a Webster's dictionary for the first time. An evaluation of the campaign in 1994 revealed that the designated driver "message" had aired on 160 prime-time shows in four seasons and had been the main topic of 25 thirty-minute or sixty-minute episodes. More important, these airings appear to have generated tangible results. In 1989, the year after the "designated driver" was invented, a Gallup poll found that 67 percent of adults had noted its appearance on network television. What's more, the campaign seems to have influenced adult behavior: polls conducted by the Roper Organization in 1989 and 1991 found significantly increasing awareness and use of designated drivers. By 1991, 37 percent of all U.S. adults claimed to have refrained from drinking at least once in order to serve as a designated driver, up from 29 percent in 1989. In 1991, 52 percent of adults younger than 30 had served as designated drivers, suggesting that the campaign was having greatest success with its target audience.

In 1988 there were 23,626 drunk driving fatalities. By 1997 the number was 16,189. While the Harvard Alcohol Project acknowledges that some of this decline is due to new laws, stricter anti-drunk driving enforcement, and other factors, it claims that many of the 50,000 lives saved by the end of 1998 were saved because of the designated driver campaign. (The television campaign was only a part of the overall campaign; there were strong community-level and public service components as well.) As evidence, the project cites statistics showing the rapid decline in traffic fatalities per 100 million vehicle miles traveled in the years during and immediately following the most intensive period of the designated driver campaign. Officials at the National Highway Traffic and Safety Administration have stated that the only way to explain the size of the decline in drinking-related traffic fatalities is the designated driver campaign.

Following the success of the Harvard Alcohol Project's campaign, various other advocacy groups—the majority of them with progressive leanings—have begun to work within the existing structures of the television industry in a similar fashion, attempting to influence programming in a positive direction. In truth, there are limits to the effect any public interest group can have on what gets broadcast. Commercial television's ultimate concerns are Nielsen ratings and advertisers. Thus there will always be a hefty quantity of sex and violence on network television. As Alfred Schneider, the former vice president of policy and standards for ABC, asserts in his contribution to the forthcoming anthology Advocacy Groups and the Television Industry, "While [television] can raise the consciousness of the nation, it should not be considered as the major vehicle for social relief or altering behavior." But why not?

Other groups remain optimistic, emulating Winsten's method of treating television as a potential ally rather than an adversary and approaching writers and producers likely to be receptive to particular ideas. When writers and producers for the WB network's critically acclaimed new drama *Felicity* were working on the script for a two-part story about date rape, they wanted to make sure they got the details right. They sought the advice of experts from the Kaiser Family Foundation, a nonprofit that focuses on education about health issues; its Program on Entertainment Media and Public Health offers briefings, research services, and a hotline for script writers with health-related questions. "We were really aware of the message we were sending out," the show's executive producer Ed Redlich told me recently. "Given that our audience is teenage girls, we wanted to be correct. At the same time, we didn't want it to be an extended public service announcement." As the scripts went through revisions, the show's writers sat down to discuss date rape with representatives from Kaiser, who had previously offered their services to the WB. In whom might a young woman confide after being raped?

What kind of advice might a rape counselor provide? What physical tests would the woman undergo? What kind of message would the show be sending if the rapist didn't use a condom?

Meanwhile, WB network executive Susanne Daniels sought input on the *Felicity* scripts from Marisa Nightingale at the National Campaign to Prevent Teen Pregnancy, an advocacy group formed in 1995 with the goal of reducing teen pregnancies by one-third by the year 2005. Nightingale, the manager of media programs, spends her days meeting with writers and producers to offer statistics, information on birth control methods, and suggestions for how to incorporate pregnancy prevention into storylines. "I can't knock on every door in the country and discuss safe sex with teenagers," she says, "but if Bailey and Sarah on [the Fox network's] *Party of Five* discuss it, that's the next best thing."

According to a recent Kaiser Foundation survey, 23 percent of teens say they learn about pregnancy and birth control from television and movies. Clearly, we should be mindful of what exactly teenagers are watching. On a recent episode of *Dawson's Creek* two 16-year-olds contemplating sex ran into each other at a drugstore only to discover they were standing in front of a condom display, which led to a frank discussion about safe sex. An episode of *Felicity* featured the title character researching birth control methods and learning the proper way of putting on a condom. Once prepared, Felicity then decided in the heat of the moment she wasn't quite ready to have sex. A young woman's decision to put off having sex is rarely portrayed in prime time, but Felicity is a strong character and her reasoning is probably convincing to a teenage audience. She may well have more influence on teenage girls than a public service announcement.

Of course, making television an explicit vehicle for manipulating behavior has its dangers. My idea of the good may not be yours; if my ideas have access to the airwaves but yours don't, what I'm doing will seem to you like unwanted social engineering. We can all agree that minimizing drunk driving is a good thing—but not everyone agrees on the messages we want to be sending to, say, teenage girls about abstinence versus condoms, about having an abortion, or about whether interfaith marriages are okay. Television's power to mold viewers' understanding of the world is strong enough that we need to be aware that embedding messages about moral values or social behavior can have potent effects—for good or for ill.

For the moment, Hollywood's liberal tilt (yes, it really has one) makes it likely that the messages and values it chooses to incorporate into its television programs will be agreeable to progressives. But how active a role do we want television to play in the socialization of our youth? If advocacy groups can gain access to Hollywood with messages that seem like positive additions to existing fare, then they may someday be able to do the opposite—to instill, say, values of a particular religion or an intolerant political group through television.

Consider the popularity of CBS's *Touched by an Angel*, which has just completed its fifth season and has secured a regular place among the top ten Nielsen-rated programs. The show, which features angels—not winged creatures, but messengers of God who arrive to help mortals in times of crisis—has sparked a mini trend in prime time. Along with its spin-off, *Promised Land*, and the WB's *7th Heaven*, *Touched by an Angel* has carved out a new niche in family-hour entertainment: fare that's endorsed by many groups on the religious right (as well as, to be fair, by people not of the Christian right who are seeking wholesome television entertainment).

7th Heaven's producer, Brenda Hampton, who created the show for Aaron Spelling's production company (the creative force behind such racier fare as Beverly Hills 90210 and Melrose Place), emphasizes in interviews that she is not influenced by religious groups and that her goal is simply to create entertaining television. But Martha Williamson, the producer of *Touched by an Angel*, is very outspoken about her Christianity. While Williamson, too, emphasizes that she aims primarily to entertain, the program's religious message is unmistakably in the foreground. Williamson says she is regularly contacted by viewers, who say the show helped them make a decision—to get in touch with a long-estranged relative or to stop smoking.

On its face there's nothing objectionable about this; in fact, it's probably good. And there's no evidence that *Touched by an Angel* is actively converting people, or making unwilling Jews or atheists into Christians. Still, the show does proselytize for a set of values that some viewers might find alienating or offensive. A more extreme version could become Big Brotherish propaganda, beamed into the homes and receptive minds of the seven-hour-a-day TV watchers. At this point, the most offensive thing about *Touched by an Angel* is its saccharine writing (even some religious groups have criticized it on these grounds). But it is perhaps telling that a Republican Congress has awarded Williamson a "Freedom Works Award" for "individuals and groups who seek the personal reward of accepting and promoting responsibility without reliance on or funding from the federal government."

Given that writers have to create 22 episodes each season, it's not surprising that they are receptive to outside groups pitching socially redeeming story ideas. *Dawson's Creek* producer Paul Stupin estimates he sits down with three to five advocacy groups at the beginning of each season and always finds the meetings useful. The fact that large numbers of writers and producers attend briefings sponsored by Kaiser, the National Campaign to Prevent Teen Pregnancy, or Population Communications International (which recently sponsored a "Soap Summit") suggests that others feel the same way.

The strongest evidence that advocates can effect change through partnerships with the television industry comes from the success of the designated driver campaign. While there are as of yet no large-scale studies exploring the effects of public health advocacy through television, a survey conducted by the Kaiser Foundation is enlightening. On April 10, 1997, NBC aired an episode of *ER* focusing on morning-after contraception, put together with the help of Kaiser Foundation research. Before the show aired, independent researchers interviewed 400 of the show's regular viewers about their knowledge of options for preventing unwanted pregnancy even after unprotected sex. In the week after the show aired, 305 more viewers were interviewed. The number of *ER* viewers who said they knew about morning-after contraception went up by 17 percent after the episode aired. The study concluded that up to six million of the episode's 34 million viewers learned about emergency contraception for the first time from the show (and 53 percent of *ER* viewers say they learn important health care information from the show).

Even the limited evidence provided by the *ER* study suggests the scope of television's power to educate and influence. And additional Kaiser studies suggest that the lobbying of public health groups advocating safe sex and birth control is not yet having nearly enough of a beneficial effect. While 25 percent of teenagers say they have learned "a lot" about pregnancy and birth control from TV shows and movies, and 40 percent say they have gotten ideas about how to talk to their boyfriend or girlfriend about sex from TV and movies, 76 percent say that one reason teens feel comfortable having sex at young ages is that TV shows and movies "make it seem normal" to do so.

Another problem: According to Kaiser, while 67 percent of *ER* viewers knew about morning-after contraception when questioned immediately following the show, only 50 percent knew about it when questioned two-and-a-half months later. This suggests that the 17 percent who gained new information about contraception from the episode may not have retained it. Jay Winsten says that because new information fades without repetition, for a single message to take hold the way the designated driver campaign did will require a barrage of appearances on a wide range of TV shows, over an extended period of time.

The role of advocacy groups as a resource for Hollywood writers and producers is growing, and it's worth taking seriously. Their approach—presenting ideas to a creative community that is constantly in need of ideas—is proving effective. Yes, the messages are diluted to fit sitcom or drama formats. Yes, for every "good value" that makes its way onto the small screen, a flurry of gunshots on another network will partly counteract it. And yes, when *TIME* cites Ally McBeal as a factor in the demise of feminism, it is placing absurdly disproportionate responsibility on a television character and on the creative community that invented her. Yet if the college women on *Felicity* practice safe sex, or if a prime-time parent talks about drugs—or adoption, or eating disorders, or the Holocaust—with a child, the message is likely to resonate with an audience comprised of people who relate to their favorite television characters as if they knew them.

Is television the ideal forum for a culture to define its values? No. As long as television remains a profit-driven industry, the best we can hope to do—especially those of us who have views in common with those who create television content (and fortunately for liberals, we tend to)—is to work within the existing system to make it better. We do need to be realistic about the limits of television in packaging messages to fit this format. To turn *Friends* into a show about capital punishment would be ineffective, as well as dramatically unconvincing; but to encourage the producers of *Dawson's Creek* to portray young people facing the realistic consequences of adult decisions just might work.

QUESTIONS: For Thinking and Writing

1. Think about how television can increase awareness about a particular issue or promote certain values in audiences. What social or moral themes can you recall that were recently featured in popular television programs?
2. Assess Rosenzweig's question, "if television contributes to poor behavior, might it also be a vehicle for encouraging good behavior?" What assumptions does Rosenzweig make about her audience by phrasing the question this way?
3. Rosenzweig states in a side comment that Hollywood "really has" a liberal tilt. On what evidence does she base this statement? Do you agree or disagree with her view?
4. In her introduction, Rosenzweig questions what visitors from another planet would think about our society based on what they learned from watching television on one specific evening. Pretend you are such a visitor, and you know nothing about American culture or social values. Based on an evening's television viewing (you may hop between several programs), what conclusions would you make about our culture? Cite specific examples in your analysis.
5. Has a television program ever made you think about a social or moral issue that you would not otherwise have thought about had you not watched the program? Write a personal narrative about a television program that influenced, or even changed, how you felt about a social or moral issue.

ANDREW O'HEHIR

The Myth of Media Violence

Media critics often cite television and movie violence as a catalyst for violent behavior in children and teens. But the next essay, which includes a book review of Harold Schechter's 2006 book, Savage Pastimes, *explains why we may be misplacing the blame. The truth is, explains Andrew O'Hehir, television is no more violent today than it was 50 years ago. But if television isn't to blame, what is? The answer may be more disturbing than we thought. This essay appeared in the online magazine,* Salon, *in March of 2005.*

Kids these days. They're all wasting their spare hours, or so we're told, with immoral trash like *Grand Theft Auto*, the now-notorious series of slickly decorated and powerfully addictive video games. As Senator Hillary Clinton explained at a forum hosted by the Kaiser Family Foundation, "They're playing a game that encourages them to have sex with prostitutes and then murder them."

Fans of "GTA" claim this is a typical nongamer's misinterpretation—it might be possible to kill hookers in the game, but it won't necessarily help you win—but let's let that go. There's no doubt that GTA allows you, for example, to play the role of an ex-con trying to take over a vice-addled city by gunning down drug lords, cops, low-flying aircraft and pretty much everything and everybody else. These games revel in their pseudo-noir amorality, and they're basically designed to be loathed by parents, school principals and tweedy psychologists.

Clinton's attack on the latest manifestation of the Media Demon—you know, the evil force within video games, action movies, rap songs, comic books, dime novels, Judas Priest records played backward and, I don't know, Javanese puppet theater and cave hieroglyphics—is a depressingly familiar ploy in American politics. When you can't make any progress against genuine social problems, or, like Senator Clinton, you seem religiously committed to triangulating every issue and halving the distance between yourself and Jerry Falwell, you go after the people who sell fantasy to teenagers.

What might be most interesting about this latest vapidity, in fact, is what Clinton didn't say. Five years ago, in the wake of the Columbine massacre, we were told that there was no serious debate about whether media violence contributed to teenage crime in the real world. A clear link had been established, the case was closed, and the only question was what we were going to do about it. By contrast, Clinton's comments were surprisingly mild and almost entirely subjective. She called violent and debauched entertainment a "silent epidemic," essentially arguing that it has effects, but we don't quite know what they are.

Over the long haul, Clinton said, violent media might teach kids "that it's okay to dis people because they're women or they're a different color or they're from a different place." Perhaps more to the point, she added: "Parents worry their children will not grow up with the same values they did because of the overwhelming presence of the media." That was it—no claims that we were breeding a nation of perverts and murderers, and no mention of all the supposed science indicating a link between simulated mayhem and the real thing. Playing GTA and watching Internet porn might lead your kids to "dis" somebody, or to grow up with different values from yours (or anyway to make you concerned that they might). Katy, bar the door!

As dopey as Clinton's remarks are, I don't mean to ridicule parents and educators for their legitimate concerns. Of course, I'm not certain that violent movies and games (or, for that matter, dumb-ass sitcoms and vapid reality shows) are harmless. My own kids are still too young for this question to matter much, but of course, I hold onto the naive hope that they'll spend their formative years hiking the Appalachians and reading about the Byzantine Empire, rather than vegetating in media sludge. But it's long past time to face the fact that, while it's legitimate not to like violent media, or to believe it's psychologically deadening in various ways, the case that it directly leads to real-life violence has pretty much collapsed.

Hillary Clinton's equivocation may be something of a compulsive family trait, but it also reflects how muddy this issue has become since the summer of 2000, when the American Medical Association, the American Psychiatric Association, the American Academy of Child and Adolescent Psychiatry, and several other professional busybody organizations issued a joint statement proclaiming that "well over 1,000 studies" had shown a direct connection between media violence and "juvenile aggression." In 2002, Harvard psychologist Steven Pinker wrote that it had become an article of faith "among conservative politicians and liberal health professionals alike . . . that violence in the media is a major cause of American violent crime."

Actually, there never was any such consensus in the academic fields of psychology, criminology, or media studies. And there weren't well over a thousand studies of media violence either—that was one of the many myths and legends that sprung up around this question. In the years since then, the mavericks have been increasingly heard from. Even in the theatrical United States Senate hearings convened a few days after the Columbine shootings in 1999, MIT professor Henry Jenkins observed that the idea that violent entertainment had consistent and predictable effects on viewers was "inadequate and simplistic," adding almost poetically that most young people don't absorb entertainment passively, but rather move "nomadically across the media landscape, cobbling together a personal mythology of symbols and stories taken from many different places."

Jenkins was a lonely voice at the time, but more recently the edifice of mainstream certainty has begun to crumble. Psychologists like

Pinker, Jonathan Freedman, Jonathan Kellerman, and Melanie Moore have counterattacked against their own establishment, arguing that media-violence research to date has been flawed and inconclusive at best, and a grant-funding scam at worst. Some have gone further, suggesting that violent entertainment provides a valuable fantasy outlet for the inevitable rage of childhood and adolescence, and probably helps more children than it hurts. . . .

We've also heard from criminologists, lawyers, and literary scholars as the tide of counterarguments has swelled. The latest of these last is Harold Schechter, a professor at Queens College in New York whose book, *Savage Pastimes*, provides an eye-opening survey of gruesome entertainment throughout the history of Western civilization. Schechter's main point concerns what scholars call the "periodicity" of campaigns like Senator Clinton's latest screed. Every time a technological shift occurs (such as from books to movies, radio to TV, movies to video games), he argues, it produces a new medium for gruesome entertainment aimed at adolescent audiences, and produces a renewed outrage among the self-appointed guardians of civilization.

One remarkable example not cited by Schecter: In 1948, there was an enormous uproar in Canada over a meaningless killing committed by two boys, ages 13 and 11. Pretending to be highwaymen, they hid near a road with a stolen rifle and shot at a passing car, killing a passenger. When it was revealed that they were avid readers of crime comic books, the anticomics movement swelled. This story bears an uncanny similarity to a recent case, examined in *Salon*, in which two boys, ages 15 and 13, stole their father's rifle, hid near a highway, and shot at a passing car, killing a passenger. The youths defended themselves on the grounds that playing *Grand Theft Auto* made them do it.

The Jeremiahs who condemn violent entertainment, whether crime comics or *Grand Theft Auto*, also invariably lament the passage of a golden age, generally contemporaneous with their own childhoods, when entertainment was healthful and wholesome, suitable for infants and grannies alike. I don't mean to impugn Granny, who may have a healthy appetite for phony bloodshed, but these moral guardians' sunny views of the past either reflect fuzzy memories or whopping hypocrisy.

Schechter offers an amusing catalog of the outrageous bloodshed and mayhem found in popular entertainment since time immemorial, from the classics (as he observes, the onstage blinding of Gloucester in

"King Lear"—"out, vile jelly"—is one of the most traumatic acts of violence in any medium) to the pornographic sadism of Grand-Guignol theater, the lurid sensationalism of turn-of-the-century "penny papers," and the ugly misogyny of Mickey Spillane's best-selling pulp novels. Undoubtedly Hillary Clinton would prefer that today's kids read books instead of playing GTA, and Schechter might suggest "*Seth Jones:* or, *The Captives of the Frontier*," a wilderness adventure that was one of the best-selling kids' books of the nineteenth century. In one scene, the hero comes upon the corpse of a man who has been tied to a tree by Indians and burned to death: "Every vestige of the flesh was burned off to the knees, and the bones, white and glistening, dangled to the crisp and blackened members above! The hands, tied behind, had passed through the fire unscathed, but every other part of the body was literally roasted!" Seth is greatly relieved, however, to discover that the victim was not a white man. As Schechter says, it's impossible to imagine anyone publishing this as kiddie lit today, both for its gore quotient and its casual racism.

In another dime novel of the period, a rattling Western adventure called *Deadwood Dick on Deck*, Schechter reports that more than 100 people are killed in the first two chapters, a figure that fans of *Resident Evil* and *Doom* can only view with awe and veneration. Then there's the gruesome "comic" yarn Schechter digs up from 1839, in which that authentic American hero, Davy Crockett, engages in a "scentiforous fight" with an individual referred to as "a pesky great bull nigger" (and also as "Blackey," "Mr. Nig" and "snow-ball"). Crockett ends the battle by gouging out one of his adversary's eyes, feeling "the bottom of the socket with end of my thum."

Schechter knows what you're thinking: At least those kids were reading, and as reprehensible by our standards as those books may have been, there's really no comparison between the printed page and the "hyperkinetic visuals of movies and computer games." The only answer to this is maybe and maybe not; critics of pop culture always assume that new technologies have rendered kids incapable of telling the difference between reality and fantasy, and so far they've always been wrong. Schechter writes that for children who had never seen a movie or a video game, "the printed page *was* a PlayStation, and penny dreadfuls were state-of-the-art escapism, capable of eliciting a shudder or thrill every bit as intense as the kind induced by today's high-tech entertainment." The relativist position that each generation is equally affected by the media available to it is supported by ample historical evidence, from the way that the audiences at early film screenings rose in panic when on-screen trains bore down upon them to the wildly Dionysian effect of that hypersexual, morals-corroding music, swing.

If Senator Clinton might prefer an outdoor family activity in the sunny American heartland, there's always the example of Owensboro, Kentucky, where on August 14, 1936, some 20,000 citizens of all ages crowded into the courthouse square. It was a "jolly holiday," according to newspaper reports. Hot dogs, popcorn, and soft drinks were sold, and there was a mixture of cheers and catcalls—but no general disorder, as the local paper angrily insisted—when sheriff's deputies brought a man named Rainey Bethea out to the scaffold, where he was hanged.

Schechter cites the infamous opening pages of Michel Foucault's *Discipline and Punish*, which recount the horrible tortures inflicted in 1757 on Robert François Damiens, the attempted assassin of Louis XV. In 1305 in London, Scottish rebel William Wallace was hanged and revived, castrated and disemboweled while still alive, and finally decapitated and dismembered, with the pieces coated in boiling tar and strung up in various public places. (When Mel Gibson played Wallace in *Braveheart*, we saw none of that.) Sometimes it's the little things that tell the story: During the Reign of Terror in revolutionary France, children were given 2-foot-tall toy guillotines they could use to behead birds and mice.

Schechter doesn't bring up the Bethea execution to paint white Kentuckians of the Depression as depraved rubes; his point is that we actually have come a long way in seven decades. We're free to regard violent movies and video games as loathsome, but we also have to admit they reflect at least a partially successful sublimation of what William James called "our aboriginal capacity for murderous excitement." Few of us are eager for the return of public executions (except perhaps the programming executives at Fox) and no real cops or prostitutes were harmed during the creation of *Grand Theft Auto*. Although a few juveniles charged with murder, or their victims' families, have argued that video games were responsible for murder, kids who play video-game shooters aren't outside gunning down the neighbors, possibly because that would mean getting off their butts and leaving behind the overlit universe of their TV or computer screen.

As Schechter says, there are two linked assumptions that underpin all the hysteria about purported media-influenced violence in the last 20 years, if not longer. Assumption No. 1 is that we live in an especially violent time in human history, surrounded by serial killers, hardened teenage "superpredators," genocidal atrocities, and all sorts of amoral mayhem. Assumption No. 2 is that our popular entertainment is far more violent than the entertainment of the past, and presents that violence in more graphic and bloodthirsty detail. For critics of media violence, from the Clintons to Dave Grossman to the leadership of the child-psychiatry establishment, these assumptions go essentially unchallenged, and the conclusion they draw is that there is a causal or perhaps circular relationship between these "facts": Media violence breeds real violence, which leads to ever more imaginative media violence, and so on.

A longtime crime buff who has written several books about notorious murderers, Schechter mounts an impressive case in *Savage Pastimes* that, if anything, our pop culture is less bloody-minded than that of the past. Anyone who looks back at the 1950s, when Schechter himself was a child, and remembers only *Leave It to Beaver* and Pat Boone needs to read his discourse on the hugely popular *Davy Crockett* miniseries of 1954, "whose level of carnage," he writes, "remains unsurpassed in the history of televised children's entertainment." This series, with its barrage of "shootings, stabbings, scalpings, stranglings," was broadcast on Wednesday nights at 7:30 PM, and presented as the acme of wholesome family fare.

In fact, as Schechter demonstrates, fifties TV was profoundly rooted in guns and gunfire, to a degree that would provoke widespread outrage today. But there are factors he doesn't consider, or considers only in passing, that fuel people's perceptions that the past was less violent, both in real and symbolic terms. Those fifties TV shows were mostly westerns, of course, which meant that they presented themselves as instructive fables of American history in [their] most masculine, individualistic form. They were racially and politically uncomplicated; *Gunsmoke* and *Bonanza* developed a social conscience in the sixties, but the white screen cowboys of the fifties were heroes, and the whites, Indians, and Mexicans around them were clearly divided into good guys and bad.

In other words, while *Davy Crockett* and *Have Gun Will Travel* and *The Rifleman* were loaded with violence, it was mostly reassuring violence, presented without splatter and without moral consequences. The graphic media violence of our age, whether in *Taxi Driver* or *Reservoir Dogs* or *CSI* or *Grand Theft Auto*, is deliberately unsettling, meant to fill viewers with dread and remind them that life is an uncertain, morally murky affair. This might put us closer to the murder-obsessed Victorian age than to the scrubbed fifties, and in examining both eras, it's important to remember that this message can be delivered badly or well, used for a cheap roller-coaster effect or a tremendous *King Lear* catharsis. (It's also worth pointing out that Jib Fowles disagrees with Schecter, arguing, "It does appear that television violence has been slowly growing in volume and intensity since 1950.")

But if Assumption No. 2 looks questionable, Assumption No. 1 is just flat-out false. As Fowles painstakingly details in *The Case for Television Violence*, violence has clearly been decreasing in the Western world for the last 500 years; as far as we can tell from uneven record keeping, the murder rate in medieval Europe was several times higher than it is today, even in relatively violent societies like the United States. While the twentieth century has seen some spikes in violent crime—correlating less to the arrival of television than to the proportion of young men in the population—the downward trend since about 1980 has reinforced the general tendency. As Rhodes puts it, "We live in one of the least violent eras in peacetime human history."

Again, there are some complicating ambiguities here, although they don't make the absolute numbers look any different. If you're convinced that we live amid a psychotic crime wave, well, blame the media. Murder has become an increasingly rare crime, and most of it is pretty unglamorous—poor people, many of them black and brown, killing each other in petty disputes over love affairs or insultingly small amounts of money. But whenever something truly ghoulish happens—a serial killer hacks up some white girls or a mom drowns her kids in the tub—we're exposed to so many pseudo-news stories and movies of the week that it seems as if society is totally out of its gourd and such things are happening every day.

I don't think there's any question that the sense of dislocation this produces, while unmeasurable by social science, can be profound. We know this as the "mean world" syndrome, and it's the reason why, for instance, my wife's 90-something grandparents not only don't go outside after dark but also refuse to answer the phone. (Apparently the depraved criminals roaming the suburban streets can teleport themselves through the phone lines.) Our obsession with violent crime may indeed be at an all-time high, even as crime itself keeps becoming rarer. Perhaps TV has made us so frightened that we've mostly stopped killing each other.

There's far more that one could and perhaps should say about the essentially adolescent character of our civilization, fatally torn between the impulses of Eros and Thanatos. But the point I'm struggling toward is that while you can't prove that media violence *doesn't* lead to real violence—and only an idiot would assert that no one has ever been inspired to commit a crime by a book or movie or video game—our definitions of "media" and "violence" may need some rethinking. And as a general proposition, the simplistic consensus of a few years ago stands on exceedingly shaky ground. "This whole episode of studying television violence," as Fowles told Rhodes in 2000, "is going to be seen by history as a travesty. It's going to be used in classes as an example of how social science can just go totally awry."

Most likely it will be seen in the same way that we now see psychologist Frederic Wertham's infamous fifties campaign against horror comics—as an understandable, if in retrospect laughable, response to the unknown. Wertham interviewed juvenile offenders and found that most of them read comic books; ergo, comics led to juvenile crime. There was widespread panic about juvenile delinquency in that decade (which actually saw record lows in crime of all kinds), and he had found an appropriately disreputable scapegoat. While Wertham focused his ire on the gore-drenched horror comics, with their rotting zombies and sadistic scientists, he also wrote that Wonder Woman was a lesbian, Batman and Robin were a man-boy couple and Superman was a fascist. (So he got those right, at least.)

Attorney and author Marjorie Heins has pointed out that the conflict between pop culture and its critics is literally as old as Western civilization: Plato thought that unsavory art should be censored, while Aristotle argued that violent and upsetting drama had a cathartic effect and helped purge the undesirable emotions of spectators. Jib Fowles suggests that these periodic culture wars are mostly a way of displacing anxieties about class, race, and gender, as well as, most obviously, a proxy war between middle-aged adults and the succeeding generations whose culture they can't quite understand.

Perhaps the most sensible words on this subject that I've discovered come from comics author Gerard Jones, in a 2000 *Mother Jones* article that became, in part, the basis for his book *Killing Monsters.* "I'm not going to argue that violent entertainment is harmless," he wrote. "I am going to argue that it's helped hundreds of people for every one it's hurt, and that it can help far more if we learn to use it well. I am going to argue that our fear of 'youth violence' isn't well-founded on reality, and that the fear can do more harm than the reality. We act as though our highest priority is to prevent our children from growing up into murderous thugs—but modern kids are far more likely to grow up too passive, too distrustful of themselves, too easily manipulated."

That expresses, I suspect, exactly what many parents of more or less my generation feel about their kids and the media. To be fair, I also think it's a more honest, less red-state-coded version of what Hillary Clinton was trying to say. We know that the media stew most of us marinate in is tremendously powerful, but we don't understand its power, so we fear it. Furthermore, even if violent entertainment has always been with us, as Harold Schechter argues, it's *supposed* to scare us, because it calls up emotions and impulses we don't usually want to think about, because it summons demons from below our conscious minds and before our approved history. That's its job.

Ultimately, we can't protect our kids from being frightened or unsettled by things they will inevitably encounter, whether while reading Dostoevsky or playing the latest zombie-splattering incarnation of *Resident Evil.* We can't stop them from forging their own culture out of fragments and shards they collect along the way, a culture specifically intended to confuse and alienate us. But I think Jones is right: Most of us don't have to worry about breeding little homicidal maniacs. What's far more plausible, and more dangerous, is that we'll raise a pack of sedentary, cynical little button-pushing consumption monsters who never go outside. Now that's scary.

QUESTIONS: For Thinking and Writing

1. Think about the level of violence in the programs you watch on television. Is violence a common theme? Does it make an impression on you? Why or why not?
2. Why does the author call media critics who condemn violent entertainment "Jeremiahs"?
3. O'Hehir includes references to video-game violence in addition to television violence as an often cited source of aggressive behavior in teens. Do you think that video game violence contributes to violent behavior? Why or why not?

4. O'Hehir observes that television and movies have historically presented violent material. How valid is this circumstance to his overall argument? How might critics respond?
5. O'Hehir concludes his essay with an observation by Harold Schechter that violent entertainment is "supposed to scare us, because it calls up emotions and impulses we don't usually want to think about." Write a short essay exploring the possible beneficial aspects of violent entertainment.

JASON KELLY

The Great TV Debate

Many parents struggle with the question of how much television is too much. Is it fair to restrict our children's television time, while we fail to curtail our own? Is television promoting illiteracy, as some critics warn, or are we overreacting to hype? In the next essay, writer Jason Kelly worries about his son's viewing habits. This essay was first published by the online magazine PopPolitics *in December 2001.*

I worry about a lot of things related to my son. September 11 brought almost more than I could bear. Today, for instance, I'm worried that he's pushing other kids at his day care center. Alas, there are a few constant worries, including this one: Am I already letting him turn his brain to mush?

When I got this assignment, I set out to try and understand the latest salvos in the great TV debate. I'd planned to do a sensibly journalistic, fully objective treatment of both sides. Then I realized that, especially as a dad, that's nearly, if not totally, impossible.

My wife and I have operated under the notion that I'd ascribe to most people—we allow our son, Owen, age 2, to watch some television, though we worry about him watching too much. We'll give into the pressure a little too often, pushing in a Teletubbies or Elmo video when we need a mental break, or need to actually get something done.

It's worth confessing here that I like TV, and maybe slightly more than the average bear. I watch enough shows regularly to have strong opinions about, and feelings for, fake people: Carrie on *Sex and the City*, Jack on *Will and Grace*, Donna on *West Wing*. I do feel like I know them. I, of course, hide behind my occupation as a "writer," tricking myself (but not others, I'm afraid) into thinking that watching these shows is really work, as if talking about them in important terms—"Sorkin's gift for writing that crisp, banter-y dialogue makes these shows feel more like plays than movies"—will make them important, will turn them into high art.

And so, actually, I feel slightly ashamed of my own viewing habits. Why not include my son in my neuroses ("Paging Dr. Frasier Crane")? These overlapping guilts lead to a creeping sense of hypocrisy, whereby I deprive my son of watching *Clifford: The Big Red Dog* but, when he leaves the room, quickly switch over to *Today*, so I can see Katie banter with Matt about listening to the *Shrek* soundtrack in her minivan. At least Clifford's got a "big idea of the day"—usually something like "respect" or "sharing"—on at the end of every show. Katie and Matt just have Willard and his jelly jars every few days.

In the great American spirit of rationalization, I've convinced myself that my son—who goes to day care during the week—actually watches less TV than a kid who stays at home full-time with a parent or a nanny. I know that occasionally his teachers roll in the television and slip in a video, but it's certainly not every day. Owen has always been somewhat fickle about watching TV, and in this I see the tendencies that stay with you through adulthood. Sometimes, the dude just wants to chill out and watch the Teletubbies (or, in his lingo, simply "Tubbies"). Other times, he's far too busy, and actually walks over and turns it off in favor of reading a book, coloring or building Lego towers.

I spent hours on the Web sifting through searches on "Kids and TV," looking for guidance. While on the Cartoon Network site, I came across a link for "TV Parental Guidelines." That's the site for the classification system that puts the little box on the screen that says "TV-MA (mature audiences only)," for example. The guidelines, at least for me, have become more or less invisible; they're pretty broad and based on the quite-flawed Motion Picture Association of America guidelines, which say it's okay for 13-year-olds to both see and hear the F-bomb.

The Fox Kids TV site was suitably frightening to me, with its animation and teasers—"It's the stinkiest Ripping Friends ever!!" The site for the PBS shows (for better or worse, the only shows we let Owen watch) was similarly predictable in its "We're really about education here" language. Drilling through the Teletubbies, I noted the repeated use of carefully chosen words like "safe," "friendly," and "stimulating."

After wading through the positive messages from the purveyors themselves, I found the Washington, D.C.-based TV-Turnoff Network, which appears to have a reputable staff and advisory board. I gave them a call, and they mailed me a packet of materials supporting a TV-free lifestyle, including the requisite bumper stickers. The one that made me chuckle was designed to mimic the warnings on cigarette boxes: "Surgoen Generel's Warnig: Telivison Promots Iliteracy." They also feature some startling statistics, like the fact that the average 2- to 17-year-old viewer watches nearly 20 hours of TV per week. And that 73 percent of American parents would like to limit their kids' TV-watching.

Writing this story forced the topic to the front of my mind, and as I chatted with friends and colleagues, even interview subjects for other stories, about various other topics, I often tried to sneak this one in. One friend told me that his kids watch about an hour of TV a month. It took me a full minute to stop saying "Wow." He and his wife both work and have had a full-time nanny since their now-7- and 9-year-old children were born. The nanny knows that no TV is the rule. "And the nanny's a TV junkie" in her off-hours, my friend tells me.

In an odd turn of events, two days later we go with another family on a Sunday outing, loading three adults and three kids comfortably into their family minivan, one of the new, decked-out Honda Odysseys. The high-end versions of these veritable cruise ships on wheels have a VCR and video screen installed; the player sits in the middle console up front, and the screen flips down from the ceiling just behind the front seats. Our hour-plus trip was nearly silent. We could've ridden for days it seemed, despite the fact that we had three sub-6-year-olds in the car.

Somewhere in the middle of these two extremes is where I fall, and, by the looks of it, so does a lot of America. Schools across the country embrace the idea of using TV as a learning tool and are aided by groups like Cable in the Classroom and Channel One, which provide special programming. The latter is the much-ballyhooed 11-year-old network that broadcasts to roughly 12,000 American middle, junior, and high schools; the network claims those schools represent more than 8 million students and 400,000 educators. There is, however, a catch: Channel One also broadcasts commercials. So while the kids are learning more about, say, life in space, they're also being told to eat Mars bars.

More pointedly, many of the kids TV shows—led by the granddaddy of educational TV, *Sesame Street*—encourage kids to read. *Clifford the Big Red Dog*, we're told at the end of his PBS show, wants us to "be the best-read dog on the block." And in fact, Clifford was born as a book character himself, then migrated to PBS. *Teletubbies* and others took the reverse path. But they all stress the value of reading. My own son seems to have no problem reading and watching TV, often at the same time. It's a brand of multitasking I'm sure my wife and I have encouraged by example, as we talk on the phone, listen to the radio, cook dinner, and read a magazine, all in one fluid, continuous motion.

I'm starting to come to grips with the idea that this is just how it is, that we live in an information and media-drenched society. We can't stop it, as the wise man said, we can only hope to contain it. Then, as I'm putting all my thoughts together, I come across one more thing that makes me throw my hands up.

Neil Postman's *Amusing Ourselves to Death* is a book I read in college that paints a stark picture of what TV is doing to us and our children. He spends 163 pages undermining just about every idea set forth by the Cable in the Classrooms and PBS's of the world, namely that "educational television" is a contradiction in terms. While his data is old—the book was published in 1985—his arguments likely have more, not less, relevance.

And his voice, while somewhat histrionic, does echo in my ears: "Like the alphabet or the printing press, television has by its power to control the time, attention, and cognitive habits of our youth gained the power to control their education."

And so I end much like I began—pretty damn confused, with my finger poised uncertainly in front of the "play" button.

QUESTIONS: For Thinking and Writing

1. Do you think parents have a responsibility to teach their children how to watch television? If so, what skills do they need to teach, and how should they go about teaching their children?
2. Kelly admits that he likes to watch television, "maybe slightly more than the average bear." What role does TV play in your daily life? Could you easily go without it, or would your quality of life be compromised, and why?
3. Why is Kelly "ashamed" of his own television viewing habits? What is the social stigma of enjoying television? Have you ever lied about how much television you watch? If so, explain.
4. Kelly comments on his astonishment that his friends' children, ages 7 and 9, only watch about an hour of television a month. Do you think this is admirable, as Kelly seems to imply? Is it unrealistic? Harmful? What would your response be to this parent? Explain.

5. PBS children's programming has a reputation for being more acceptable than programs aired by other networks. What accounts for this reputation? Why do you think Kelly makes the side comment that "for better or worse," these are the only programs he lets his child watch? Explain.

HEATHER HAVRILESKY

Three Cheers for Reality TV

While reality television programs are fodder for critics, there is no denying their popularity. Far from a passing fad, there are more reality television programs than ever before. Several programs have emerged as constant hits, including Survivor, The Bachelor, *and* American Idol. *In this essay, published in* Salon *magazine on September 13, 2004, Heather Havrilesky explains why reality television is so popular today. The pundits, she explains, can tut-tut all they want, but reality shows rule television for a simple reason: The best of them are far more compelling than the worn-out sitcoms and crime dramas the networks keep churning out.*

> *"[S]ifting through so-called reality TV has become like rummaging through a landfill: There seems to be no end to the quantity and types of trash you'll find. . . . [I]f we're going to start setting taste standards for reality TV, there's going to be a lot of dead air time."*
>
> [Myrtle Beach Sun News, 9/2/04]

> *"This is not just bad television in the sense that it's mediocre, pointless, puerile even. It's bad because it's damaging."*
>
> [*BBC journalist John Humphrys, in a speech to U.K. TV executives,* Reuters U.K., 8/27/04]

> *"Reality TV is so cheap because you don't need writers, actors, directors . . . it is killing off new talent and we are all worse off for that."*
>
> [*Rebecca of Cambridge, U.K., posting on* BBC News, 8/28/04]

> *"Reality TV, in particular, mocks committed relationships and makes trust seem foolish, some teens said. So teens tend to 'hook up' with friends to get a sexual fix without the responsibility of a relationship."*
>
> [Richmond Times-Dispatch, 9/7/04]

Welcome to the modern world, where we're all sucking on the same pop-cultural crack pipe, but only the unrefined among us will admit that they inhale. Reality TV earns its reputation as the dangerous street drug du jour mostly by aiming its lens at human behavior—we're far less photogenic than we imagine ourselves to be. While shows run the gamut from high-quality, dramatically compelling work to silly, exploitative trash, pundits consistently point to programs at the bottom of the barrel and cast aspersions on those foolish enough to watch them. Thanks to this stigma, it's not always easy to get a clear picture of how many people genuinely enjoy reality shows and aren't about to give them up.

Instead, every few months, a new survey announces that reality is on its way out. Last March, an *Insider Advantage* survey found that "67 percent of Americans" were "becoming tired of so-called reality programs." This year, a survey by Circuit City concluded that 58 percent of viewers are "getting tired" of reality TV. (What are they excited about? Why, HDTV, of course—they just can't wait to purchase their new HDTV-capable sets!) Can you expect accurate results when you ask people if they're "getting tired" of anything? But even while many people take their cue from the media and bemoan the evils of reality, they're still watching. Just as there are those who claim to read *Penthouse* for the fine articles, no matter how "sad, rather than engaging" reality TV might be, audiences have yet to drop off as predicted.

"Reality TV is not going away," says Marc Berman, television analyst for *Mediaweek*. "This summer, reality dominated. In terms of total viewers during the regular season, three of the top five shows [*The Apprentice, American Idol* and *Survivor*] were reality shows." Berman predicts that we'll see these same reality shows pull in big numbers in the fall, along with frequent time-slot winners like *The Bachelor* and whichever new reality programs draw in big audiences. "The bottom line is that the genre is absolutely exploding," Berman says.

Instead of writing off millions of viewers as the unenlightened consumers of lowbrow entertainment, shouldn't we ask why they're attracted to reality TV in the first place?

First of all, viewers have been exposed to the same half-hour and hour episodic plot structures, implemented in roughly the same ways, for decades now, setting the stage for a less conventional format. Even once-groundbreaking, high-quality dramas like *ER* and *The West Wing* have evolved into parodies of themselves, with all the usual suspects striding through halls and corridors, spitting out the same clever quips until the next big tragedy hits. Meanwhile, traditional sitcoms are faring even worse, as the networks spend millions each fall to develop shows that don't stick. While those in the industry bemoan the fact that the networks have whittled their sitcom offerings down to two or three shows, that makes perfect sense when you recognize how bad TV executives have been at locating genuinely good shows, and how expensive it is just to develop a handful of episodes. *Two and a Half Men*, one of the only sitcoms to make it to another season, is considered a hit, yet it's not remotely funny. And the best sitcoms—*Everybody Loves Raymond, Will and Grace* and *That '70s Show*—all wrapped up.

That's not to say that the world of scripted entertainment is dead—far from it. Instead, new formats are taking hold: one-camera sitcoms like *Arrested Development* and *Entourage*, sketch comedies like *Chappelle's Show* and *Da Ali G Show*, and unconventional twists on old formulas, like *Deadwood* and *The Wire*. But unconventional means risky, which is why none of those shows are on the Big Three networks, which seem as faithful to old-formula fiction as Joanie was to Chachi.

Ultimately, though, it's not the basic format of the traditional sitcom or drama that's to blame, it's the lack of original, high-quality writing. By now everyone knows that HBO, a channel not poisoned by the copycat mentality of the networks, is behind most of the best shows on television. Many producers and writers report that quality scripts and ideas are out there, but the networks aren't necessarily looking for quality. What seems familiar about those wisecracking characters on their couches isn't the setting or the format, it's the mediocre jokes and story lines that simply mimic the story lines of other better—but not necessarily great—shows. Sadly, as the networks continue the impossible search for guaranteed hits and sure things, they limit their scope to the sorts of shows that have succeeded before instead of seeking original voices with something to say. This is why we'll end up watching soggy star vehicles like John Goodman's *Center of the Universe* and Jason Alexander's *Listen Up* (It worked with Charlie Sheen, right?) this fall instead of encountering truly original comedies with fresh, surprising characters.

Will we be watching? The truth is, the best reality shows feature exactly the kinds of fresh, surprising characters that most sitcoms and dramas lack. For those who care about the quality of reality shows they produce, the bar has been set very high by Mark Burnett. At a time when reality TV appeared to be shackled to the somewhat shallow teenage-bitch-slap tradition of *The Real World*, Burnett insisted on bringing the same intelligent editing and beautiful cinematography to *Survivor* that he brought to *Eco Challenge.* He recognized that, beyond painstakingly careful casting and crafting of dramatically compelling story lines, viewers would want to get a real feel for the show's exotic setting. As fleeting as those aerial and wildlife shots can seem, they add an inestimable dimension to the viewer's experience. Anyone who watched the first few episodes of *Survivor* knew that the show was bound to be a hit, and the reason for that had more to do with sparkling shots of cornflower-blue water than it had to do with Richard Hatch (although having a naked, backstabbing provocateur around certainly helped).

If reality offerings were limited to claustrophobic, repetitive, aesthetically irritating shows like *Elimidate* or *The Bachelor*, it would be easy to write off the entire genre as the work of sensationalistic producers churning out trash for a quick buck. Instead, a few sharp producers like Burnett saw the enormous potential of the form and approached it with a passion, creating a vicarious experience for the viewer. They recognized that reality TV could truly engage audiences, pulling them into a time and place, populated by real human beings. As long as the cast and the settings were a little larger than life, as long as the stories were edited to make the viewer feel like a personal confidante to each of the competitors, audiences would find themselves swept into the action, investing far more of their emotions in the competition than they imagined was possible.

The Amazing Race followed in the footsteps of *Survivor* in terms of quality, but conquered the most difficult production challenges imaginable. Ten teams of two scamper across the globe, racing to complete various tasks, but you never, ever spot a single camera, not when several teams are running across a beach to the finish line, not when they're hang gliding or walking teams of dogs or eating two pounds of Russian caviar. Produced by Jerry Bruckheimer and edited with so many suspense-inducing tricks it's impossible not to get caught up in the action, *The Amazing Race* took Burnett's high standards of human drama and visual appeal and built on them. Lumping together an intensely difficult, expensive, painstakingly produced show like *The Amazing Race* with meandering, silly shows like *The Ultimate Love Test* is an insult to the sharp, talented people who seem to set the bar higher each season.

Of course, meandering, silly shows have a certain charm of their own. Fox's *Paradise Hotel* stumbled on accidental genius with its hyperaggressive cast of frat boys and neurotics. Originally intended as a sleazy dating show where those guests who didn't "hook up" would get thrown out of Paradise "forever!" as the voice-over put it, *Paradise Hotel* evolved into a nasty battle between two cliques, with the producers scrambling to mold their "twists" and promos to fit the bizarre clashes arising on the set. There's something to be said for a show that evolves based on the strange behavior of its cast, thanks mostly to the fact that its cast is made up of belligerent drunks. Sadly, *Paradise Hotel*'s success was purely accidental. The producers foolishly moved the show away from its original location, a gorgeous Mexican resort with brilliant white walls that lit every scene beautifully, making all of the inhabitants appear larger than life. They renamed the show, cast it with bland, empty-headed Neanderthals, added an even-more-awful host and some pointless twists, and the magic was over. The ironically titled *Forever Eden* was canceled before the season ended.

But part of the joy of watching, for true reality aficionados, is witnessing such false starts and mesmerizingly entertaining mistakes. While those who've never seen much of the genre bemoan the foolishness of most shows, it's the newness of the form that makes it so exciting. When not even the producers can predict how the characters on a show will react, audiences feel like they're a part of something that's evolving before their eyes. The second season of *The Joe Schmo Show*, titled *Joe Schmo 2*, epitomized this state. The show lures two individuals into thinking that they're contestants on a dating show called *Last Chance for Love*, when in fact, their fellow contestants are really actors, paid to create absurd, funny scenarios.

To the dismay of the show's producers and crew, a few episodes in, one of the two Schmos named Ingrid figured out that something was very wrong, and kept asking the actors around her if they had memorized the things they were saying, or if there was "some kind of *Truman Show* thing going on." Instead of declaring the show a failure, the producers chose to reveal the truth to Ingrid and then enlisted her as an actor for the rest of the show. This kind of behind-the-scenes, seat-of-the-pants improvisation is such completely new territory, it's not hard to understand why audiences are intrigued.

Furthermore, if our obsession with celebrities tends to rise and fall and rise again in cycles, then it makes sense that reality TV would become popular in the wake of the late nineties, when celebrity obsession reached new levels of absurdity. Audiences bored with Brad and Jennifer or Jennifer and Ben or Paris and Nicole suddenly found themselves with more knowable, less remote personalities to root for. Instead of focusing all their attention on those far too privileged to comprehend or relate to, audiences could embrace no-nonsense, surprisingly open-minded Rudy of *Survivor* or despise the outspoken-but-bellicose Susan Hawk. Reality "stars" like lovable couple Chip and Kim from *The Amazing Race* or country-boy Troy from *The Apprentice* offer us a chance to admire real people for qualities that go beyond choosing the perfect dress for the Oscars or smiling sweetly for the cameras.

Plus, now that magazines like *InStyle* make it clear that a major celebrity's image and personality are essentially created by a team of stylists, interior designers, assistants, managers and publicists, it's no wonder we crave an exploration of the little quirks and flaws of ordinary people. And when it comes to making enemies, anyone can throw a temper tantrum and then stalk offstage, but how many ordinary humans can manage the messy explosion of insults and accusations set off by Omarosa of *The Apprentice*? Who knew that "Now there's the pot calling the kettle black!" was a racial slur?

Many have argued that self-consciousness will be the death of the genre. As more and more contestants who appear on the shows have been exposed to other reality shows, the argument goes, their actions and statements will become less and less "real." What's to blame here is the popular use of the word "reality" to describe a genre that's never been overtly concerned with realism or even with offering an accurate snapshot of the events featured. In fact, the term "reality TV" may have sprung from *The Real World*, in which the "real" was used both in the sense of "the world awaiting young people after they graduate from school," and in the sense of "getting real," or, more specifically, getting all up in someone's grill for eating the last of your peanut butter.

The truth is, part of the entertainment offered by reality TV lies in separating the aspects of subjects' behavior that are motivated by an awareness of the cameras from the aspects that are genuine. You can't expect someone who's surrounded by cameras to act naturally all of the time, and as the genre has evolved, editors and producers have become aware that highlighting this gap between the real self and the camera-ready self not only constitutes quality entertainment but may be the easiest shortcut to creating the villain character that any provocative narrative requires. When *Big Brother 5*'s Jason pouts his lips, flexes his muscles, and adjusts his metrosexual headband in the mirror, then confides to the camera that every idiotic thing he's done in the house so far has been part of a master plan to confuse his roommates, he not only makes a great enemy for the more seemingly grounded members of the house, but he also hints at narcissistic and sociopathic streaks that reality TV has demonstrated may be a defining characteristic of the modern personality. Either an alarming number of reality show contestants are self-obsessed and combative, or the common character traits found in young people have shifted dramatically.

In our self-conscious, media-savvy culture, such posturing and preening are a worthy subject for the camera's gaze, documenting as they do the flavor of the times. When young kids talk about marketing themselves properly and "breaking wide," it makes perfect sense to shine a light on the rampant self-consciousness and unrelenting self-involvement of these characters. When we see Puck of *The Real World* screeching at the top of his lungs or Richard Hatch of *Survivor* confiding to the cameras that he considers the other players beneath him, we may be glimpsing behavior that's more true of the average American than any of us would like to believe.

But then, no matter how premeditated many of the words and actions of reality show stars can be, the proper events and tasks eventually conspire to create cracks in the shiny veneer, revealing flaws and personality tics they'd clearly wish to hide. If even the smooth operators of *The Apprentice* stumble on their words, bare their claws, and show their less polished selves regularly, you have to figure that keeping your true self hidden from the camera is more difficult than it looks. Katrina, for example, started the first season appearing smooth and polished, then slowly unraveled as the personalities and tactics of the players around her seemed to erode her sense of self. And who can forget Rupert on *Survivor*, who went from lovable teddy bear to snarling grizzly whenever someone crossed him? Real people are surprising. The process of getting to know the characters, of discovering the qualities and flaws that define them, and then discussing these discoveries with other viewers creates a simulation of community that most people don't finding in their everyday lives. That may be a sad commentary on the way we're living, but it's not the fault of these shows, which unearth a heartfelt desire to make connections with other human beings. Better that we rediscover our interest in other, real people than sink ourselves into the mirage of untouchable celebrity culture or into some überhuman, ultraclever, fictional *Friends* universe.

Naturally, there will always be those shows that heedlessly propagate crass televised stunts without any socially redeeming qualities. *The Swan*, which turns normal, attractive women into hideous plasticized demons with lots of pricey plastic surgery, then pits the demons against each other in a beauty contest, is more freakishly dehumanizing than anything George Orwell could've dreamed up. *Gana La Verde*, a *Fear Factor*-style competition in which immigrants compete for a green card, or at least for the use of lawyers who might win them a green card, makes you wonder if we're not one step away from feeding the underprivileged to the lions on live TV. But the lowest rung on the reality ladder has nothing to do with the sharp, fascinating shows at the top. The best reality shows transform ordinary places and people into dramatic settings populated by lovable heroes and loathsome enemies, and in the process of watching and taking sides and comparing the characters' choices to the ones we might make, we're reacquainted with ourselves and each other. Great fictional TV has the power to engage us, too, but the networks aren't creating much of that these days. When was the last time *CSI* sparked a little self-examination? Does *Still Standing* make you giggle in recognition at life's merry foibles?

Lowbrow or not, all most of us want from TV is the chance to glimpse something true, just a peek at those strange little tics and endearing flaws that make us human. While the networks' safe little formulas mostly seem devoid of such charms, reality shows have the power to amuse, anger, appall, surprise, but most of all, engage us. Isn't that the definition of entertainment?

QUESTIONS: For Thinking and Writing

1. Do you watch reality TV programs? If so, which ones? What inspires you to watch these programs? What is their appeal?
2. In her introductory comments, Havrilesky compares reality television to using drugs. Why does she make this connection? How does it set the tone for her essay? Does she approve of reality television, or not? Explain.
3. In what ways does reality television programming hold up the camera lens on human behavior?

4. Why does Havrilesky presume that the surveys done on the popularity of reality television are likely to be skewed? What questions would you ask to accurately determine the popularity of this type of programming?
5. Havrilesky observes that reality programs span from quality to trash. Make a list of as many reality programs as you can think of, and rate them on a scale of 1 to 5, with 5 indicating the highest quality. Then comment on the programs you enjoy the most. Do you find yourself drawn to the "quality," or the "trashy," or neither?

TV-Turnoff Week

Founded in 1994, TV-Turnoff Week is a grassroots nonprofit project run by the TV-Turnoff Network. Supported or endorsed by the American Medical Association, the National Education Association, and the American Academy of Pediatrics (AAP), Turn Off Your TV Week encourages families to turn off the set and reconnect with each other and "return to real life." The poster below promotes the network's 2007 campaign.

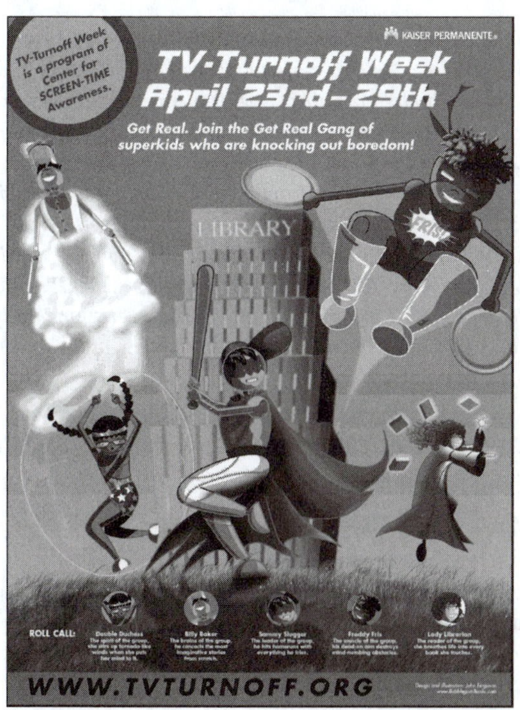

QUESTIONS: For Thinking and Writing

1. Who is the target audience for this poster? Where would you expect to see it? What does it urge the viewer to do?
2. What does this poster promote? What are the characters in the poster doing? How do the actions of the characters compare to the poster's charge to "TV-Turnoff Week"?
3. In what ways might this poster be considered ironic? Explain.
4. Do you think this poster is an effective way to reach kids? Do you think it will inspire them to not watch television the week of April 23rd? Why or why not?

VIEWPOINTS

AAP Discourages Television for Very Young Children

American Academy of Pediatrics

TV Can Be a Good Parent

Ariel Gore

The American Academy of Pediatrics (AAP) advises parents to avoid exposing their children under the age of 2 years to television of any kind and to carefully monitor viewing in children over that age. It further recommends that pediatricians ask parents questions about their children's television exposure in routine health visits. Although the policy seems to make some sense, some parents question the sweeping judgments it makes about the use of television in American homes. One such parent, Ariel Gore, argues that television can be a good co-parent, giving parents, especially working or single ones, needed relief from the demands of parenting. Although she agrees with the AAP's claim that young children need direct interaction with adults to grow mentally and socially, she questions how this assessment translates into a policy advocating no television exposure at all.

AAP Discourages Television for Very Young Children

American Academy of Pediatrics

A new policy from the American Academy of Pediatrics (AAP) urges parents to avoid television for children under 2 years old.

"While certain television programs may be promoted to this age group, research on early brain development shows that babies and toddlers have a critical need for direct interactions with parents and other significant caregivers for healthy brain growth and the development of appropriate social, emotional, and cognitive skills," the policy says. The new AAP statement on media education also suggests parents create an "electronic media-free" environment in children's rooms and avoid using media as an electronic babysitter. In addition, it recommends pediatricians incorporate questions about media into routine child health visits, as education can reduce harmful media effects.

"With an educated understanding of media images and messages, users can recognize media's potential effects and make good choices about their and their children's media exposure," states the new policy.

According to the AAP, a media educated person understands that:

- all media messages are constructed;
- media messages shape our understanding of the world;
- individuals interpret media messages uniquely; and
- mass media has powerful economic implications.

Research strongly suggests that media education may result in young people becoming less vulnerable to negative aspects of media exposure, the AAP says. In some studies, heavy viewers of violent programming were less accepting of violence or showed decreased aggressive behavior after a media education intervention. Another study found a change in attitudes about wanting to drink alcohol after a media education program. Canada, Great Britain, Australia, and some Latin American countries have successfully incorporated media education into school curricula, the statement says. "Common sense would suggest that increased media education in the United States could represent a simple, potentially effective approach to combating the myriad of harmful media messages seen or heard by children and adolescents."

In addition, the AAP emphasized that media education should not be used as a substitute for careful scrutiny of the media industry's responsibility for its programming.

TV Can Be a Good Parent

Ariel Gore

Let me get this straight.

The corporations have shipped all the living-wage jobs off to the developing world, the federal government has "ended welfare" and sent poor women into subminimum wage "training programs," while offering virtually no child-care assistance, the rent on my one-bedroom apartment just went up to $850 a month, the newspapers have convinced us that our kids can't play outside by themselves until they're 21, and now the American Academy of Pediatrics wants my television?

I don't think so.

Earlier this month, the AAP released new guidelines for parents recommending that kids under the age of 2 not watch TV. They say the box is bad for babies' brains and not much better for older kids. Well, no duh.

When I was a young mom on welfare, sometimes I needed a break. I needed time to myself. I needed to mellow out to avoid killing my daughter for pouring bleach on the Salvation Army couch. And when I was at my wits' end, Barney the Dinosaur and Big Bird were better parents than I was. My daughter knows that I went to college when she was a baby and preschooler. She knows that I work. And, truth be told, our television set has been a helpful co-parent on rainy days when I've been on deadline. Because I'm the mother of a fourth-grader, Nickelodeon is my trusted friend.

There was no TV in our house when I was a kid. My mother called them "boob tubes." But that was in the 1970s. My mother and all of her friends were poor—they were artists—but the rent she paid for our house on the Monterey (California) Peninsula was $175 a month, and my mother and her friends helped each other with the kids. The child care was communal. So they could afford to be poor, to stay home, to kill their televisions. I, on the other hand, cannot.

Now the AAP is saying I'm doing my daughter an injustice every time I let her watch TV. The official policy states that "Although certain television programs may be promoted to [young children], research on early brain development shows that babies and toddlers have a critical need for direct interactions with parents and other significant caregivers for healthy brain growth and the development of appropriate social, emotional, and cognitive skills. Therefore, exposing such young children to television programs should be discouraged."

Maybe my brain has been warped by all my postchildhood TV watching, but I'm having a little trouble getting from point A to point B here. Babies and toddlers have a critical need for direct interactions with actual people. I'm with them on this. "Therefore, exposing such young children to television programs should be discouraged." This is where they lose me. I can see "Therefore, sticking them in front of the TV all day and all night should be discouraged." But the assumption that TV-watching kids don't interact with their parents or caregivers is silly. Watching TV and having one-on-one interactions with our kids aren't mutually exclusive.

I've been careful to teach my daughter critical thinking in my one-woman "mind over media" campaign. It started with fairytales: "What's make-believe?" and "How would you like to stay home and cook for all those dwarves?" Later we moved on to the news: "Why was it presented in this way?" and "What's a stereotype?" But if you think I was reading *Winnie the Pooh* to my toddler when I thought up these questions, think again. I was relaxing with a cup of coffee and a book on feminist theory, while Maia was riveted to PBS.

I read to my daughter when she was little. We still read together. But even a thoughtful mama needs an electronic babysitter every now and again. Maybe especially a thoughtful mama.

Not surprisingly, the television executives feel there's plenty of innocuous programming on television to entertain young kids without frying their brains. "It's a bunch of malarkey," said Kenn Viselman, president of the Itsy Bitsy Entertainment Company, about the new policy. Itsy Bitsy distributes the British show *Teletubbies,* which is broadcast on PBS. While I prefer Big Bird to Tinky Winky, I have to agree with him when he says, "Instead of attacking shows that try to help children, the pediatricians should warn parents that they shouldn't watch *The Jerry Springer Show* when kids are in the room."

The AAP's policy refers to all television, of course, but it's hard not to feel like they're picking on PBS. *Teletubbies* is the only program currently shown on noncable television marketed toward babies and toddlers. Just two weeks ago, the station announced a $40 million investment to develop six animated programs for preschoolers. The timing of the AAP's report is unfortunate.

Cable stations offer a wider variety of kid programming. Take for example Nick Jr., an offshoot of the popular Nickelodeon channel. On weekdays from 9 AM to 2 PM, the programming is geared specifically toward the preschool set. "Our slogan for Nick Jr. is 'Play to Learn'," Nickelodeon's New York publicity manager, Karen Reynolds, told me. "A child is using cognitive skills in a fun setting. It's interactive. With something like *Blues Clues,* kids are talking back to the TV. They are not just sitting there."

Still, the station has no beef with the new AAP policy on toddlers. "Nick Jr. programs to preschool children ages 2 to 5, but we are aware that children younger than 2 may be watching television," said Brown Johnson, senior vice president of Nick Jr. "We welcome a study of this kind because it encourages parents to spend more time bonding and playing with their children."

In addition to telling parents that young children shouldn't watch television at all and that older kids shouldn't have sets in their bedrooms, the AAP is recommending that pediatricians ask questions about media consumption at annual checkups. The difference between recommending less TV watching and actually mandating that it be monitored by the medical community is where this could become a game of hardball with parents. What would this "media file" compiled by our doctors be used for? Maybe television placement in the home will become grounds for deciding child custody. ("I'm sorry, your honor, I'll move the set into the bathroom immediately.") Or maybe two decades from now Harvard will add TV abstention to their ideal candidate profile. ("*Teletubbies* viewers need not apply.") Better yet, Kaiser could just imprint "Poor White Trash" directly onto my family's medical ID cards. Not that those cards work at the moment. I'm a little behind on my bill.

I called around, but I was hard-pressed to find a pediatrician who disagreed with the academy's new policy. Instead, doctors seemed to want their kids to watch less TV, and they're glad to have the AAP's perhaps over-the-top guidelines behind them. "If all your kids did was an hour of Barney and *Sesame Street* a day, I don't think that the academy would have come out with that statement," said a pediatrician at La Clinica de la Raza in Oakland, California, who asked not to be named. "It's not the best learning tool." And he scoffs at the notion of "interactive" TV. "It's not a real human interaction. When you're dealing with babies and toddlers, this screen is an integral part of their reality. You want kids to be able to understand interaction as an interaction. It's like the Internet. We're getting to a place where all of your relationships are virtual relationships."

Fair enough.

I'm not going to say that TV is the greatest thing in the world for little kids—or for anyone. I'm not especially proud of the hours I spend watching television. Mostly I think American television is a string of insipid shows aired for the sole purpose of rounding up an audience to buy tennis shoes made in Indonesian sweatshops.

But it seems that there is a heavy middle-class assumption at work in the AAP's new policy—that all of us can be stay-at-home moms, or at least that we all have partners or other supportive people who will come in and nurture our kids when we can't.

I say that before we need a policy like this one, we need more—and better—educational programming on TV. We need to end the culture of war and the media's glorification of violence. We need living-wage jobs. We need government salaries for stay-at-home moms so that all women have a real career choice. We do not need "media files" in our pediatricians' offices or more guilt about being bad parents. Give me a $175 a month house on the Monterey Peninsula and a commune of artists to share parenting responsibilities, and I'll kill my TV without any provocation from the AAP at all. Until then, long live Big Bird, *The Brady Bunch*, and all their very special friends!

QUESTIONS: For Thinking and Writing

1. Think about some of the children's television programs popular today. Who is responsible for developing and distributing these programs?
2. On what criteria does the AAP base its new policy? Does the policy seem logical and sound? What is the basic point of the AAP's new policy?
3. Gore explains that when she called to ask pediatricians for their viewpoint on the new AAP policy, she was "hard-pressed" to find a pediatrician who disagreed with it. How does she respond to this reaction?
4. Gore questions the AAP's recommendation that pediatricians ask parents questions about media in the home in their routine child health examinations. Do her fears of "media files" seem reasonable? Does the AAP policy allow for any flexibility in this type of questioning?

5. In this essay, Gore analyzes and responds to the AAP's policy statement that young children should not watch television. In your own words, respond to the AAP's statement by explaining your viewpoint on this issue. Like Gore, support your stance by analyzing the wording of the AAP's policy and your personal experience.

QUESTIONS: For Further Research and Group Work

1. Rosenzweig notes that although the issue of drunk driving was easy for Hollywood to incorporate into its programming, other issues have met with less success. Make a list of the issues that television programming has addressed in your viewing experience. After reviewing the list, expand it to include other important, but less "exciting" issues, such as the hole in the ozone layer or recycling. Develop a story line together for a popular program dealing with one of these less stimulating issues and present it to the class.
2. Using a television weekly programming guide for reference, try to identify the political "tilt" of prime-time programs with the members of your group. In your analysis, include television dramas, news programs, and sitcoms. Based on your results, personal experience, and the information provided by articles in this unit, participate in a class discussion on the social and political influences of television programming.
3. As a group, discuss your personal viewing habits and the role television plays in your daily life. Each group member should describe how much television they watch, when the television is on during the day or evening, what programs they tend to watch, and viewing habits of roommates that may influence their own viewing. After each group member has presented their history, discuss your impressions of this essay. Is television indeed "addictive"? Is this a bad thing?
4. Conduct a class experiment. All students in your class should give up television entirely for one full week. (While television viewing by roommates may be impossible to avoid, class members should try to minimize exposure and not look at the set while it is on.) Keep a daily journal of what the experience was like, including any symptoms of withdrawal, frustration, or disappointment at missing a cherished program. At the end of the week, share your journal entries with the rest of the class. Was the experiment more difficult for some members than others? What did you learn about television and its influence on your own life?
5. With your group, compare the children's television programs aired on PBS to those aired on other channels, such as Nickelodeon, Fox Kids,

and the major networks. With your group, develop a checklist of program elements that make a children's program superior, such as "teaches a lesson," "encourages reading," "fosters critical thinking," "teaches (math) (alphabet)," and so on. Different group members should watch and critique several children's programs for discussion. Determine whether your group's observations support or refute Kelly's claim, or inference, that PBS programs are better than those of other channels.

6. Develop your own reality television program plot. Include the show's premise, its object and goal, why people would want to watch it, and who would be a typical contestant. Outline the program and present it to the class. The class should vote on which program it finds the most engaging.

CHAPTER 5

The Global Warming Debate

THE ISSUE OF GLOBAL WARMING IS AT THE FOREFRONT of political and public policy debates. Natural disasters, human health, biodiversity, endangered species, water resources, international trade, financial services, transportation networks, agriculture—virtually any area of human experience is in some way affected by climate. Environmental models predict that the Earth's temperature is likely to rise from anywhere between 2 and 11 degrees Fahrenheit (1–6 degrees Celsius) by 2100. And while most scientists and politicians agree that the earth is indeed getting warmer, they disagree on why and what it means.

The debate focuses on the cause of global warming, what—if anything—should be done about it, and what it means for the environment in years to come. An increase in global temperatures may lead to other changes in our ecosystem, such as a rising sea level, altered weather patterns, and the extinction of species of animals. Agricultural yields and coastal communities are also at risk.

A majority of scientists postulate that global warming is caused by the human use of fossil fuels, including coal, oil, and natural gas, which release carbon into the atmosphere and increase the greenhouse effect. They warn that if humans do not make changes and reduce greenhouse emissions, we could face catastrophic environmental consequences. On the other hand, some scientists and politicians question whether humans are even the cause of increased greenhouse gases and postulate that rising temperatures are simply a normal aspect of a dynamic earth.

Scientists Roger Pielke, Jr. and Daniel Sarewtiz describe the debate as the "Cassandras versus the Dorothies." The Cassandras—named for the Greek heroine cursed to predict the future but never to be believed—foretell of a doomed planet, if we do not make radical policy changes immediately. The Dorothies—so named for the character in *The Wizard of Oz*—see themselves as the revealers of truth, who pull away the curtain to expose the wizards, who manipulate scientific models for political gain. The reality, however, may lie somewhere in between. This chapter explores the complexities of this pressing issue.

AL GORE

Global Warming Is an Immediate Crisis

Former U.S. Vice President Al Gore explains that he has studied the environment and climatic change for over 30 years. His concern about the issue of global warming led to his participation in the 2006 Academy Award winning-film An Inconvenient Truth. *Gore explains in the introduction to this film, "Whether you are a Democrat or a Republican, whether you voted for me or not, I very much hope that you will sense that my goal is to share with you both my passion for the Earth and my deep sense of concern for its fate. It is impossible to feel one without the other when you know all the facts . . . The climate crisis is, indeed, extremely dangerous. In fact it is a true planetary emergency." This next piece, outlining much of Gore's position and recommendations concerning global warming, is a speech he made in September 2006 to a group of students at the New York University School of Law.*

A few days ago, scientists announced alarming new evidence of the rapid melting of the perennial ice of the north polar cap, continuing a trend of the past several years that now confronts us with the prospect that human activities, if unchecked in the next decade, could destroy one of the earth's principle mechanisms for cooling itself. Another group of scientists presented evidence that human activities are responsible for the dramatic warming of sea surface temperatures in the areas of the ocean where hurricanes form. A few weeks earlier, new information from yet another team showed dramatic increases in the burning of forests throughout the American West, a trend that has increased decade by decade, as warmer temperatures have dried out soils and vegetation. All these findings come at the end of a summer with record-breaking temperatures and the hottest twelve-month period ever measured in the United States, with persistent drought in vast areas of our country. *Scientific American* introduces the lead article in its special issue this month with the following sentence: "The debate on global warming is over."

Many scientists are now warning that we are moving closer to several "tipping points" that could—within as little as ten years—make it impossible for us to avoid irretrievable damage to the planet's habitability for human civilization. In this regard, just a few weeks ago, another group of scientists reported on the unexpectedly rapid increases in the release of carbon and methane emissions from frozen tundra in Siberia, now beginning to thaw because of human-caused increases in global temperature. The scientists tell us that the tundra in danger of thawing contains an amount of additional global warming pollution that is equal to the total amount that is already in the earth's atmosphere. Similarly, earlier this year, yet another team of scientists reported that the previous 12 months saw 32 glacial earthquakes on Greenland between 4.6 and 5.1 on the Richter scale—a disturbing sign that a massive destabilization may now be underway deep within the second largest accumulation of ice on the planet, enough ice to raise sea level 20 feet worldwide if it broke up and slipped into the sea. Each passing day brings yet more evidence that we are now facing a planetary emergency—a climate crisis that demands immediate action to sharply reduce carbon dioxide emissions worldwide in order to turn down the earth's thermostat and avert catastrophe.

The serious debate over the climate crisis has now moved on to the question of how we can craft emergency solutions in order to avoid this catastrophic damage.

This debate over solutions has been slow to start in earnest, not only because some of our leaders still find it more convenient to deny the reality of the crisis, but also because the hard truth for the rest of us is that the maximum that seems politically feasible still falls far short of the minimum that would be effective in solving the crisis. This no-man's land—or no-politician zone—falling between the farthest reaches of political feasibility and the first beginnings of truly effective change is the area that I would like to explore in my speech today.

T. S. Eliot once wrote: "Between the idea and the reality, Between the motion and the act, Falls the Shadow. Between the conception and the creation, Between the emotion and the response, Falls the Shadow."

My purpose is not to present a comprehensive and detailed blueprint—for that is a task for our democracy as a whole—but rather to try to shine some light on a pathway through this terra incognita that lies between where we are and where we need to go. Because, if we acknowledge candidly that what we need to do is beyond the limits of our current political capacities, that really is just another way of saying that we have to urgently expand the limits of what is politically possible.

I have no doubt that we can do precisely that, because having served almost three decades in elected office, I believe I know one thing about America's political system that some of the pessimists do not: it shares something in common with the climate system; it can appear to move only at a slow pace, but it can also cross a tipping point beyond which it can move with lightning speed. Just as a single tumbling rock can trigger a massive landslide, America has sometimes experienced sudden avalanches of political change that had their beginnings with what first seemed like small changes. Two weeks ago, Democrats and Republicans joined together in our largest state, California, to pass legally binding, sharp reductions in CO_2 emissions. Two hundred ninety-five American cities have now independently "ratified" and embraced CO_2 reductions called for in the Kyoto Treaty. Eighty-five conservative evangelical ministers publicly broke with the Bush-Cheney administration to call for bold action to solve the climate crisis. Business leaders in both political parties have taken significant steps to position their companies as leaders in this struggle and have adopted a policy that not only reduces CO_2 but makes their companies zero-carbon companies. Many of them have discovered a way to increase profits and productivity by eliminating their contributions to global warming pollution.

Many Americans are now seeing a bright light shining from the far side of this no-man's land that illuminates not sacrifice and danger, but instead a vision of a bright future that is better for our country in every way—a future with better jobs, a cleaner environment, a more secure nation, and a safer world.

After all, many Americans are tired of borrowing huge amounts of money from China to buy huge amounts of oil from the Persian Gulf to make huge amounts of pollution that destroys the planet's climate. Increasingly, Americans believe that we have to change every part of that pattern.

When I visit port cities like Seattle, New Orleans, or Baltimore, I find massive ships, running low in the water, heavily burdened with foreign cargo or foreign oil, arriving by the thousands. These same cargo ships and tankers depart riding high with only ballast water to keep them from rolling over.

One-way trade is destructive to our economic future. We send money, electronically, in the opposite direction. But, we can change this by inventing and manufacturing new solutions to stop global warming right here in America. I still believe in good old-fashioned American ingenuity. We need to fill those ships with new products and technologies that we create to turn down the global thermostat. Working together, we can create jobs and stop global warming. But we must begin by winning the first key battle—against inertia and the fear of change.

In order to conquer our fear and walk boldly forward on the path that lies before us, we have to insist on a higher level of honesty in America's political dialogue. When we make big mistakes in America, it is usually because the people have not been given an honest accounting of the choices before us. It also is often because too many members of both parties who knew better did not have the courage to do better.

Our children have a right to hold us to a higher standard when their future—indeed the future of all human civilization—is hanging in the balance. They deserve better than the spectacle of censorship of the best scientific evidence about the truth of our situation and harassment of honest scientists who are trying to warn us about the looming catastrophe. They deserve better than politicians who sit on their hands and do nothing to confront the greatest challenge that humankind has ever faced—even as the danger bears down on us.

We in the United States of America have a particularly important responsibility, after all, because the world still regards us—in spite of our recent moral lapses—as the natural leader of the community of nations. Simply put, in order for the world to respond urgently to the climate crisis, the United States must lead the way. No other nation can.

Developing countries like China and India have gained their own understanding of how threatening the climate crisis is to them, but they will never find the political will to make the necessary changes in their growing economies unless and until the United States leads the way. Our natural role is to be the pace car in the race to stop global warming.

So, what would a responsible approach to the climate crisis look like if we had one in America?

Well, first of all, we should start by immediately freezing CO_2 emissions and then beginning sharp reductions. Merely engaging in high-minded debates about theoretical future reductions while continuing to steadily increase emissions represents a self-delusional and reckless approach. In some ways, that approach is worse than doing nothing at all, because it lulls the gullible into thinking that something is actually being done, when in fact it is not.

An immediate freeze has the virtue of being clear, simple, and easy to understand. It can attract support across partisan lines as a logical starting point for the more difficult work that lies ahead. I remember a quarter century ago, when I was the author of a complex nuclear arms control plan to deal with the then rampant arms race between our country and the former Soviet Union. At the time, I was strongly opposed to the nuclear freeze movement, which I saw as simplistic and naive. But, three-quarters of the American people supported it—and as I look back on those years, I see more clearly now that the outpouring of public support for that very simple and clear mandate changed the political landscape and made it possible for more detailed and sophisticated proposals to eventually be adopted.

When the politicians are paralyzed in the face of a great threat, our nation needs a popular movement, a rallying cry, a standard, a mandate that is broadly supported on a bipartisan basis.

A responsible approach to solving this crisis would also involve joining the rest of the global economy in playing by the rules of the world treaty that reduces global warming pollution by authorizing the trading of emissions within a global cap.

At present, the global system for carbon emissions trading is embodied in the Kyoto Treaty. It drives reductions in CO_2 and helps many countries that are a part of the treaty to find the most efficient ways to meet their targets for reductions. It is true that not all countries are yet on track to meet their targets, but the first targets don't have to be met until 2008, and the largest and most important reductions typically take longer than the near term in any case.

The absence of the United States from the treaty means that 25 percent of the world economy is now missing. It is like filling a bucket with a large hole in the bottom. When the United States eventually joins the rest of the world community in making this system operate well, the global market for carbon emissions will become a highly efficient closed system, and every corporate board of directors on earth will have a fiduciary duty to manage and reduce CO_2 emissions in order to protect shareholder value.

Many American businesses that operate in other countries already have to abide by the Kyoto Treaty anyway, and unsurprisingly, they are the companies that have been most eager to adopt these new principles here at home as well. The United States and Australia are the only two countries in the developed world that have not yet ratified the Kyoto Treaty. Since the Treaty has been so demonized in America's internal debate, it is difficult to imagine the current Senate finding a way to ratify it. But the United States should immediately join the discussion that is now underway on the new, tougher treaty that will soon be completed. We should plan to accelerate its adoption and phase it in more quickly than is presently planned.

Third, a responsible approach to solutions would avoid the mistake of trying to find a single, magic "silver bullet" and recognize that the answer will involve what Bill McKibben has called "silver-buckshot"—numerous important solutions, all of which are hard, but no one of which is, by itself, the full answer for our problem.

One of the most productive approaches to the "multiple solutions" needed is a road map designed by two Princeton professors, Rob Socolow and Steven Pacala, which breaks down the overall problem into more manageable parts. Socolow and Pacala have identified 15 or 20 building blocks (or "wedges") that can be used to solve our problem effectively—even if we only use seven or eight of them. I am among the many who have found this approach useful as a way to structure a discussion of the choices before us.

Over the next year, I intend to convene an ongoing broad-based discussion of solutions that will involve leaders from government, science, business, labor, agriculture, grass-roots activists, faith communities, and others.

I am convinced that it is possible to build an effective consensus in the United States, and in the world at large, on the most effective approaches to solve the climate crisis. Many of those solutions will be found in the building blocks that currently structure so many discussions. But I am also certain that some of the most powerful solutions will lie beyond our current categories of building blocks and "wedges." Our secret strength in America has always been our capacity for vision. "Make no little plans," one of our most famous architects said over a century ago, "they have no magic to stir men's blood."

I look forward to the deep discussion and debate that lies ahead. But there are already some solutions that seem to stand out as particularly promising:

First, dramatic improvements in the efficiency with which we generate, transport, and use energy will almost certainly prove to be the single biggest source of sharp reductions in global warming pollution. Because pollution has been systematically ignored in the old rules of America's marketplace, there are lots of relatively easy ways to use new and more efficient options to cheaply eliminate it. Since pollution is, after all, waste, business and industry usually become more productive and efficient when they systematically go about reducing pollution. After all, many of the technologies on which we depend are actually so old that they are inherently far less efficient than newer technologies that we haven't started using. One of the best examples is the internal combustion engine. When scientists calculate the energy content in BTUs of each gallon of gasoline used in a typical car, and then measure the amounts wasted in the car's routine operation, they find that an incredible 90 percent of that energy is completely wasted. One engineer, Amory Lovins, has gone further and calculated the amount of energy that is actually used to move the passenger (excluding the amount of energy used to move the several tons of metal surrounding the passenger) and has found that only 1 percent of the energy is actually used to move the person. This is more than an arcane calculation or a parlor trick with arithmetic. These numbers actually illuminate the single biggest opportunity to make our economy more efficient and competitive, while sharply reducing global warming pollution.

To take another example, many older factories use obsolete processes that generate prodigious amounts of waste heat that actually has tremendous economic value. By redesigning their processes and capturing all of that waste, they can eliminate huge amounts of global warming pollution, while saving billions of dollars at the same time.

When we introduce the right incentives for eliminating pollution and becoming more efficient, many businesses will begin to make greater use of computers and advanced monitoring systems to identify even more opportunities for savings. This is what happened in the computer chip industry, when more powerful chips led to better computers, which in turn made it possible to design even more powerful chips, in a virtuous cycle of steady improvement that became known as "Moore's Law." We may well see the emergence of a new version of "Moore's Law" producing steadily higher levels of energy efficiency at steadily lower cost.

There is yet another lesson we can learn from America's success in the information revolution. When the Internet was invented—and I assure you I intend to choose my words carefully here—it was because defense planners in the Pentagon 40 years ago were searching for a way to protect America's command and communication infrastructure from being disrupted in a nuclear attack. The network they created—known as ARPANET—was based on "distributed communication" that allowed it to continue functioning even if part of it was destroyed.

Today, our nation faces threats very different from those we countered during the Cold War. We worry today that terrorists might try to inflict great damage on America's energy infrastructure by attacking a single vulnerable part of the oil distribution or electricity distribution network. So, taking a page from the early pioneers of ARPANET, we should develop a distributed electricity and liquid fuels distribution network that is less dependent on large, coal-fired generating plants and vulnerable oil ports and refineries.

Small windmills and photovoltaic solar cells distributed widely throughout the electricity grid would sharply reduce CO_2 emissions and at the same time increase our energy security. Likewise, widely dispersed ethanol and biodiesel production facilities would shift our transportation fuel stocks to renewable forms of energy, while making us less dependent on and vulnerable to disruptions in the supply of expensive crude oil from the Persian Gulf, Venezuela, and Nigeria, all of which are extremely unreliable sources upon which to base our future economic vitality. It would also make us less vulnerable to the impact of a category five hurricane hitting coastal refineries, or to a terrorist attack on ports or key parts of our current energy infrastructure.

Just as a robust information economy was triggered by the introduction of the Internet, a dynamic new renewable-energy economy can be stimulated by the development of an "electranet," or smart grid, that allows individual homeowners and business owners anywhere in America to use their own renewable sources of energy to sell electricity into the grid when they have a surplus and purchase it from the grid when they don't. The same electranet could give homeowners and business owners accurate and powerful tools with which to precisely measure how much energy they are using where and when, and identify opportunities for eliminating unnecessary costs and wasteful usage patterns.

A second group of building blocks to solve the climate crisis involves America's transportation infrastructure. We could further increase the value and efficiency of a distributed energy network by retooling our failing auto giants—GM and Ford—to require and assist them in switching to the manufacture of flex-fuel, plug-in, hybrid vehicles. The owners of such vehicles would have the ability to use electricity as a principle source of power and to supplement it by switching from gasoline to ethanol or biodiesel. This flexibility would give them incredible power in the marketplace for energy to push the entire system to much higher levels of efficiency and, in the process, sharply reduce global warming pollution.

This shift would also offer the hope of saving tens of thousands of good jobs in American companies that are presently fighting a losing battle, selling cars and trucks that are less efficient than the ones made by their competitors in countries where they were forced to reduce their pollution and thus become more efficient.

It is, in other words, time for a national oil change. That is apparent to anyone who has looked at our national dipstick.

Our current ridiculous dependence on oil endangers not only our national security but also our economic security. Anyone who believes that the international market for oil is a "free market" is seriously deluded. It has many characteristics of a free market, but it is also subject to periodic manipulation by the small group of nations controlling the largest recoverable reserves, sometimes in concert with companies that have great influence over the global production, refining, and distribution network.

It is extremely important for us to be clear among ourselves that these periodic efforts to manipulate price and supply have not one but two objectives. They naturally seek to maximize profits. But even more significantly, they seek to manipulate our political will. Every time we come close to recognizing the wisdom of developing our own independent sources of renewable fuels, they seek to dissipate our sense of urgency and derail our effort to become less dependent. That is what is happening at this very moment.

Shifting to a greater reliance on ethanol, cellulosic ethanol, butanol, and green diesel fuels will not only reduce global warming pollution and enhance our national and economic security, it will also reverse the steady loss of jobs and income in rural America. Several important building blocks for America's role in solving the climate crisis can be found in new approaches to agriculture. As pointed out by the "25 by 25" movement (aimed at securing 25 percent of America's power and transportation fuels from agricultural sources by the year 2025), we can revitalize the farm economy by shifting its mission from a focus on food, feed, and fiber to a focus on food, feed, fiber, fuel, and ecosystem services. We can restore the health of depleted soils by encouraging and rewarding the growing of fuel-source crops, like switchgrass and saw-grass, using no-till cultivation and scientific crop rotation. We should also reward farmers for planting more trees and sequestering more carbon, and recognize the economic value of their stewardship of resources that are important to the health of our ecosystems.

Similarly, we should take bold steps to stop deforestation and extend the harvest cycle on timber to optimize the carbon sequestration that is most powerful and most efficient with older trees. On a worldwide basis, two-and-a-half trillion tons of the ten trillion tons of CO_2 emitted each year come from burning forests. So, better management of forests is one of the single most important strategies for solving the climate crisis.

Biomass—whether in the form of trees, switchgrass, or other sources—is one of the most important forms of renewable energy. And renewable sources make up one of the most promising building blocks for reducing carbon pollution.

Wind energy is already fully competitive as a mainstream source of electricity and will continue to grow in prominence and profitability.

Solar photovoltaic energy is—according to researchers—much closer than it has ever been to a cost-competitive breakthrough, as new nanotechnologies are being applied to dramatically enhance the efficiency with which solar cells produce electricity from sunlight, and as clever new designs for concentrating solar energy are used with new approaches, such as Stirling engines, that can bring costs sharply down.

Buildings, both commercial and residential, represent a larger source of global warming pollution than cars and trucks. But new architecture and design techniques are creating dramatic new opportunities for huge savings in energy use and global warming pollution. As an example of their potential, the American Institute of Architecture and the National Conference of Mayors have endorsed the "2030 Challenge," asking the global architecture and building community to immediately transform building design to require that all new buildings and developments be designed to use one half the fossil fuel energy they would typically consume for each building type, and that all new buildings be carbon neutral by 2030, using zero fossil fuels to operate. A newly constructed building at Oberlin College is producing 30 percent more energy than it consumes. Some other countries have actually required a standard calling for zero carbon-based energy inputs for new buildings.

The rapid urbanization of the world's population is leading to the prospective development of more new urban buildings in the next 35 years than have been constructed in all previous human history. This startling trend represents a tremendous opportunity for sharp reductions in global-warming pollution through the use of intelligent architecture and design and stringent standards.

Here in the United States, the extra cost of efficiency improvements, such as thicker insulation and more efficient window coatings, have traditionally been shunned by builders and homebuyers alike, because they add to the initial purchase price—even though these investments typically pay for themselves, by reducing heating and cooling costs, and then produce additional savings each month for the lifetime of the building. It should be possible to remove the purchase-price barrier for such improvements through the use of innovative mortgage finance instruments that eliminate any additional increase in the purchase price by capturing the future income from the expected savings. We should create a Carbon Neutral Mortgage Association to market these new financial instruments and stimulate their use in the private sector by utilities, banks, and homebuilders. This new "Connie Mae" (CNMA) could be a valuable instrument for reducing the pollution from new buildings.

Many believe that a responsible approach to sharply reducing global warming pollution would involve a significant increase in the use of nuclear power plants as a substitute for coal-fired generators. While I am not opposed to nuclear power and expect to see some modest increased use of nuclear reactors, I doubt that they will play a significant role in most countries as a new source of electricity. The main reason for my skepticism about nuclear power playing a much larger role in the world's energy future is not the problem of waste disposal or the danger of reactor operator error or the vulnerability to terrorist attack. Let's assume for the moment that all three of these problems can be solved. That still leaves two serious issues that are more difficult constraints. The first is economics; the current generation of reactors is expensive, takes a long time to build, and only comes in one size—extra large. In a time of great uncertainty over energy prices, utilities must count on great uncertainty in electricity demand—and that uncertainty causes them to strongly prefer smaller incremental additions to their generating capacity that are each less expensive and quicker to build than are large, 1000-megawatt light-water reactors. Newer, more scalable and affordable reactor designs may eventually become available, but not soon. Secondly, if the world as a whole chose nuclear power as the option of choice to replace coal-fired generating plants, we would face a dramatic increase in the likelihood of nuclear weapons proliferation. During my eight years in the White House, every nuclear weapons proliferation issue we dealt with was connected to a nuclear reactor program. Today, the dangerous weapons programs in both Iran and North Korea are linked to their civilian reactor programs. Moreover, proposals to separate the ownership of reactors from the ownership of the fuel-supply process have met with stiff resistance from developing countries who want reactors. As a result of all these problems, I believe that nuclear reactors will only play a limited role.

The most important set of problems that must be solved in charting solutions for the climate crisis have to do with coal, one of the dirtiest sources of energy that produces far more CO_2 for each unit of energy output than oil or gas. Yet, coal is found in abundance in the United States, China, and many other places. Because the pollution from the burning of coal is currently excluded from the market calculations of what it costs, coal is presently the cheapest source of abundant energy. And its relative role is growing rapidly day by day.

Fortunately, there may be a way to capture the CO_2 produced as coal is burned and sequester it safely to prevent it from adding to the climate crisis. It is not easy. This technique, known as carbon capture and sequestration (CCS), is expensive, and most users of coal have resisted the investments necessary to use it. However, when the cost of not using it is calculated, it becomes obvious that CCS will play a significant and growing role as one of the major building blocks of a solution to the climate crisis.

Interestingly, the most advanced and environmentally responsible project for capturing and sequestering CO_2 is in one of the most forbidding locations for energy production anywhere in the world—in the Norwegian portions of the North Sea. Norway, as it turns out, has hefty CO_2 taxes; and, even though there are many exceptions and exemptions, oil production is not one of them. As a result, the oil producers have found it quite economical and profitable to develop and use advanced CCS technologies in order to avoid the tax they would otherwise pay for the CO_2 they would otherwise emit. The use of similar techniques could be required for coal-fired generating plants and can be used in combination with advanced approaches, like integrated gasification combined cycle (IGCC). Even with the most advanced techniques, however, the economics of carbon capture and sequestration will depend upon the availability of and proximity to safe, deep-storage reservoirs. Nevertheless, it is time to recognize that the phrase "clean coal technology" is devoid of meaning, unless it means "zero carbon emissions" technology.

CCS is only one of many new technological approaches that require a significant increase by governments and business in advanced research and development to speed the availability of more effective technologies that can help us solve the climate crisis more quickly. But it is important to emphasize that even without brand new technologies, we already have everything we need to get started on a solution to this crisis.

In a market economy like ours, however, every one of the solutions that I have discussed will be more effective and much easier to implement if we place a price on the CO_2 pollution that is recognized in the marketplace. We need to summon the courage to use the right tools for this job.

For the last 14 years, I have advocated the elimination of all payroll taxes—including those for social security and unemployment compensation—and the replacement of that revenue in the form of pollution taxes, principally on CO_2. The overall level of taxation would remain exactly the same. It would be, in other words, a revenue-neutral tax swap. But, instead of discouraging businesses from hiring more employees, it would discourage businesses from producing more pollution.

Global-warming pollution, indeed all pollution, is now described by economists as an "externality." This absurd label means, in essence: we don't to keep track of this stuff, so let's pretend it doesn't exist.

And sure enough, when it's not recognized in the marketplace, it does make it much easier for government, business, and all the rest of us to pretend that it doesn't exist. But what we're pretending doesn't exist is the stuff that is destroying the habitability of the planet. We put 70 million tons of it into the atmosphere every 24 hours, and the amount is increasing day by day. Penalizing pollution instead of penalizing employment will work to reduce that pollution. When we place a more accurate value on the consequences of the choices we make, our choices get better. At present, when business has to pay more taxes in order to hire more people, it is discouraged from hiring more people. If we change that, and discourage them from creating more pollution, they will reduce their pollution. Our market economy can help us solve this problem, if we send it the right signals, and tell ourselves the truth about the economic impact of pollution.

Many of our leading businesses are already making dramatic changes to reduce their global-warming pollution. General Electric, Dupont, Cinergy, Caterpillar, and Wal-Mart are among the many who are providing leadership for the business community in helping us devise a solution for this crisis.

Leaders among unions, particularly the steel workers, have also added momentum to this growing movement.

Hunters and fishermen are also now adding their voices to the call for a solution to the crisis. In a recent poll, 86 percent of licensed hunters and anglers said that we have a moral obligation to stop global warming to protect our children's future.

And young people, as they did during the Civil Rights Revolution, are confronting their elders with insistent questions about the morality of not moving swiftly to make these needed changes.

Moreover, the American religious community—including a group of 85 conservative evangelicals, and especially the U.S. Conference of

Catholic Bishops—has made an extraordinary contribution to this entire enterprise. To the insights of science and technology, it has added the perspectives of faith and values, of prophetic imagination, spiritual motivation, and moral passion without which all our plans, no matter how reasonable, simply will not prevail. Individual faith groups have offered their own distinctive views. And yet, uniquely in religious life at this moment and even historically, they have established common ground and resolve across tenacious differences. In addition to reaching millions of people in the pews, they have demonstrated the real possibility of what we all now need to accomplish: how to be ourselves, together, and how to discover, in this process, a sense of vivid, living spirit and purpose that elevates the entire human enterprise.

Individual Americans of all ages are becoming a part of a movement, asking what they can do as individuals and what they can do as consumers and as citizens and voters. Many individuals and businesses have decided to take an approach known as "zero carbon." They are reducing their CO_2 as much as possible and then offsetting the rest with reductions elsewhere, including by the planting of trees. At least one entire community—Ballard, a city of 18,000 people in Washington State—is embarking on a goal of making the entire community zero carbon.

This is not a political issue: This is a moral issue. It affects the survival of human civilization. It is not a question of left versus right; it is a question of right versus wrong. Put simply, it is wrong to destroy the habitability of our planet and ruin the prospects of every generation that follows ours.

What is motivating millions of Americans to think differently about solutions to the climate crisis is the growing realization that this challenge is bringing us unprecedented opportunity. I have spoken before about the way the Chinese express the concept of crisis. They use two symbols, the first of which, by itself, means danger. The second, in isolation, means opportunity. Put them together, and you get "crisis." Our single word conveys the danger but doesn't always communicate the presence of opportunity in every crisis. In this case, the opportunity presented by the climate crisis is not only the opportunity for new and better jobs, new technologies, new opportunities for profit, and a higher quality of life. It gives us an opportunity to experience something that few generations ever have the privilege of knowing: a common moral purpose compelling enough to lift us above our limitations and motivate us to set aside some of the bickering to which we as human beings are naturally vulnerable. America's so-called "greatest generation" found such a purpose, when they confronted the crisis of global fascism and won a war in Europe and in the Pacific simultaneously. In the process of achieving their historic victory, they found that they had gained new moral authority and a new capacity for vision. They created the Marshall Plan and lifted their recently defeated adversaries from their knees and assisted them to a future of dignity and self-determination. They created the United Nations and the other global institutions that made possible many decades of prosperity, progress, and relative peace. In recent years, we have squandered that moral authority, and it is high time to renew it by taking on the highest challenge of our generation. In rising to meet this challenge, we too will find self-renewal and transcendence and a new capacity for vision to see other crises in our time that cry out for solutions: 20 million HIV/AIDS orphans in Africa alone, civil wars fought by children, genocides and famines, the rape and pillage of our oceans and forests, an extinction crisis that threatens the web of life, and tens of millions of our fellow humans dying every year from easily preventable diseases. And, by rising to meet the climate crisis, we will find the vision and moral authority to see them not as political problems but as moral imperatives.

This is an opportunity for bipartisanship and transcendence, an opportunity to find our better selves and, in rising to meet this challenge, create a better brighter future—a future worthy of the generations who come after us and who have a right to be able to depend on us.

QUESTIONS: For Thinking and Writing

1. What words does Gore use to describe global warming? How does his description of the potential impact of global warming compare to Richard Lindzen's in the next essay? Explain.
2. In what ways does this speech appeal to the emotions? In what ways does it appeal to the intellect? In what ways does Gore leverage his political background in this speech? Explain.
3. How compelling is Gore's argument? Does the fact that he is a former vice president of the United States influence your reception of his speech? Does his reputation and background make him more or less credible? Explain.

4. Were there any points raised by Gore that came as a surprise to you, or did he repeat information that is generally known? Explain.
5. Write a letter to your congressional representative in which you make an appeal for action on the issue of global warming. You may take any position on this issue you wish, but support your viewpoint with some data gathered from Gore's speech or data from another essay in this chapter.

RICHARD S. LINDZEN

Don't Believe the Hype

Despite claims made by global-warming activists, such as Al Gore, that the "debate is over" on the issue of global warming, some researchers argue that we are still only guessing about the future impact of global warming on our ecosystem. Richard S. Lindzen, a professor of meteorology at the Massachusetts Institute of Technology, asserts in this next essay that Al Gore is wrong. There's no "consensus" on global warming, and he's proof. This piece first appeared on the editorial pages of the July 2, 2006 edition of The Wall Street Journal.

According to Al Gore's new film, "An Inconvenient Truth," we're in for "a planetary emergency": melting ice sheets, huge increases in sea levels, more and stronger hurricanes, and invasions of tropical disease, among other cataclysms—unless we change the way we live now.

Bill Clinton has become the latest evangelist for Mr. Gore's gospel, proclaiming that current weather events show that he and Mr. Gore were right about global warming, and we are all suffering the consequences of President Bush's obtuseness on the matter. And why not? Mr. Gore assures us that "the debate in the scientific community is over."

That statement, which Mr. Gore made in an interview with George Stephanopoulos on ABC, ought to have been followed by an asterisk. What exactly is this debate that Mr. Gore is referring to? Is there really a scientific community that is debating all these issues and then somehow agreeing in unison? Far from such a thing being over, it has never been clear to me what this "debate" actually is in the first place.

The media rarely help, of course. When *Newsweek* featured global warming in a 1988 issue, it was claimed that all scientists agreed.

Periodically thereafter it was revealed that although there had been lingering doubts beforehand, now all scientists did indeed agree. Even Mr. Gore qualified his statement on ABC only a few minutes after he made it, clarifying things in an important way. When Mr. Stephanopoulos confronted Mr. Gore with the fact that the best estimates of rising sea levels are far less dire than he suggests in his movie, Mr. Gore defended his claims by noting that scientists "don't have any models that give them a high level of confidence" one way or the other and went on to claim—in his defense—that scientists "don't know. . . . They just don't know."

So, presumably, those scientists do not belong to the "consensus." Yet their research is forced, whether the evidence supports it or not, into Mr. Gore's preferred global-warming template—namely, shrill alarmism. To believe it requires that one ignore the truly inconvenient facts. To take the issue of rising sea levels, these include: that the Arctic was as warm or warmer in 1940; that icebergs have been known since time immemorial; that the evidence so far suggests that the Greenland ice sheet is actually growing on average. A likely result of all this is increased pressure, pushing ice off the coastal perimeter of that country, which is depicted so ominously in Mr. Gore's movie. In the absence of factual context, these images are perhaps dire or alarming. They are less so otherwise. Alpine glaciers have been retreating since the early nineteenth century and were advancing for several centuries before that. Since about 1970, many of the glaciers have stopped retreating, and some are now advancing again. And, frankly, we don't know why.

The other elements of the global-warming scare scenario are predicated on similar oversights. Malaria, claimed as a byproduct of warming, was once common in Michigan and Siberia and remains common in Siberia—mosquitoes don't require tropical warmth. Hurricanes, too, vary on multidecadal time scales; sea-surface temperature is likely to be an important factor. This temperature itself varies on multidecadal time scales. However, questions concerning the origin of the relevant sea-surface temperatures and the nature of trends in hurricane intensity are being hotly argued within the profession.

Even among those arguing, there is general agreement that we can't attribute any particular hurricane to global warming. To be sure, there is one exception: Greg Holland of the National Center for Atmospheric Research in Boulder, Colorado, who argues that it must be global warming, because he can't think of anything else. While arguments like these, based on lassitude, are becoming rather common in climate assessments, such claims, given the primitive state of weather and climate science, are hardly compelling.

A general characteristic of Mr. Gore's approach is to assiduously ignore the fact that the earth and its climate are dynamic; they are always changing even without any external forcing. To treat all change as something to fear is bad enough; to do so in order to exploit that fear is much worse. Regardless, these items are clearly not issues over which debate is ended—at least not in terms of the actual science.

A clearer claim as to what debate has ended is provided by the environmental journalist Gregg Easterbrook. He concludes that the scientific community now agrees that significant warming is occurring, and that there is clear evidence of human influences on the climate system. This is still a most peculiar claim. At some level, it has never been widely contested. Most of the climate community has agreed, since 1988, that global mean temperatures have increased on the order of 1 degree Fahrenheit over the past century, having risen significantly from about 1919 to 1940, decreased between 1940 and the early 1970s, increased again until the 1990s, and remaining essentially flat since 1998.

There is also little disagreement that levels of carbon dioxide in the atmosphere have risen from about 280 parts per million by volume in the nineteenth century to about 387 ppmv today. Finally, there has been no question whatever that carbon dioxide is an infrared absorber (i.e., a greenhouse gas—albeit a minor one), and its increase should theoretically contribute to warming. Indeed, if all else were kept equal, the increase in carbon dioxide should have led to somewhat more warming than has been observed, assuming that the small observed increase was in fact due to increasing carbon dioxide, rather than a natural fluctuation in the climate system. Although no cause for alarm rests on this issue, there has been an intense effort to claim that the theoretically expected contribution from additional carbon dioxide has actually been detected.

Given that we do not understand the natural internal variability of climate change, this task is currently impossible. Nevertheless there has been a persistent effort to suggest otherwise, and with surprising impact. Thus, although the conflicted state of the affair was accurately presented in the 1996 text of the Intergovernmental Panel on Climate

Change, the infamous "summary for policy makers" reported ambiguously that "The balance of evidence suggests a discernible human influence on global climate." This sufficed as the smoking gun for Kyoto.

The next IPCC report again described the problems surrounding what has become known as the attribution issue: that is, to explain what mechanisms are responsible for observed changes in climate. Some deployed the lassitude argument—we can't think of an alternative—to support human attribution. But the "summary for policy makers" claimed in a manner largely unrelated to the actual text of the report that "In the light of new evidence, and taking into account the remaining uncertainties, most of the observed warming over the last 50 years is likely to have been due to the increase in greenhouse gas concentrations."

In a similar vein, the National Academy of Sciences issued a brief (15-page) report responding to questions from the White House. It again enumerated the difficulties with attribution, but again the report was preceded by a front end that ambiguously claimed that "The changes observed over the last several decades are likely mostly due to human activities, but we cannot rule out that some significant part of these changes is also a reflection of natural variability." This was sufficient for CNN's Michelle Mitchell to presciently declare that the report represented a "unanimous decision that global warming is real, is getting worse, and is due to man. There is no wiggle room." Well, no.

More recently, a study in the journal *Science*, by the social scientist Nancy Oreskes, claimed that a search of the ISI Web of Knowledge Database for the years 1993 to 2003, under the key words "global climate change," produced 928 articles, all of whose abstracts supported what she referred to as the consensus view. A British social scientist, Benny Peiser, checked her procedure and found that only 913 of the 928 articles had abstracts at all, and that only 13 of the remaining 913 explicitly endorsed the so-called consensus view. Several actually opposed it.

Even more recently, the Climate Change Science Program, the Bush administration's coordinating agency for global-warming research, declared it had found "clear evidence of human influences on the climate system." This, for Mr. Easterbrook, meant: "Case closed." What exactly was this evidence? The models imply that greenhouse warming should impact atmospheric temperatures more than surface temperatures, and yet satellite data showed no warming in the atmosphere since 1979. The report showed that selective corrections to the atmospheric data could lead to some warming, thus reducing the conflict between observations and the model's descriptions of what greenhouse warming should look like. That, to me, means the case is still very much open.

So what, then, is one to make of this alleged debate? I would suggest at least three points.

First, nonscientists generally do not want to bother with understanding the science. Claims of consensus relieve policy types, environmental advocates, and politicians of any need to do so. Such claims also serve to intimidate the public and even scientists—especially those outside the area of climate dynamics. Secondly, given that the question of human attribution largely cannot be resolved, its use in promoting visions of disaster constitutes nothing so much as a bait-and-switch scam. That is an inauspicious beginning to what Mr. Gore claims is not a political issue but a "moral" crusade.

Lastly, there is a clear attempt to establish truth, not by scientific methods, but by perpetual repetition. An earlier attempt at this was accompanied by tragedy. Perhaps Marx was right. This time around, we may have farce—if we're lucky.

QUESTIONS: For Thinking and Writing

1. How does Lindzen summarize Al Gore's position on global warming? Is it an accurate synopsis of Gore's viewpoint?
2. On what grounds does Lindzen object to Gore's statement that the scientific community has reached a consensus on the issue of global warming? Does he have a point?
3. As an academic and a meteorologist, does Lindzen's pedigree make him a more credible authority on the issue of global warming? Why or why not?
4. According to the author, what are the "inconvenient facts" that counter Gore's argument on global warming? Do you agree that the facts Lindzen cites do indeed undermine Gore's position? Why or why not?
5. Lindzen states, "It has never been clear to me what this 'debate' actually is in the first place." Drawing from his essay and others in this chapter, summarize the debate on global warming in your own words.

ANNE CASSELMAN

Earth's Before and After Pictures

Biologists Richard Primack and Abraham Miller-Rushing looked in an odd place to study the biological effects of global warming: old photographs. By comparing contemporary photos with shots from a century ago, "you can literally see that trees are leafing out and the plants are flowering earlier now," says Primack, of Boston University. He hopes their study, published in the *American Journal of Botany*, will spur citizens to dig up more climate-change data from their old photo albums and journals.

The duo examined 286 dated photographs of the Arnold Arboretum in Boston and Concord, Massachusetts. They found that plants are flowering and trees are leafing ten days earlier today than they were 100 years ago. Primack credits the 3 degree Fahrenheit temperature rise in eastern Massachusetts over the past century with jump-starting plant development in the spring.

"These kinds of changes are already being seen in Boston, and they will be seen in the rest of the United States in the next 100 years," he says. "We're going to see enormous changes in the distribution of plants and animals, agricultural patterns, and patterns of rainfall." Some plants may even begin flowering before pollinators are around

A Memorial Day observance for Civil War soldiers in Lowell, Massachusetts. May 30, 1868

The same location in 2005 looks summer lush. May 30, 2005
Courtesy of *American Journal of Botany*

to fertilize them. Hay fever could blossom, too, cautions Primack: "Plants may have a longer season of pollen production, which may extend the allergy season."

PEW RESEARCH CENTER FOR THE PEOPLE AND THE PRESS

Global Warming: A Divide on Causes and Solutions

Many of the articles in this chapter present the views of politicians and scientists on the issue of global warming and what we should do about it. But what does the American public think? A recent survey by the Pew Research Center reveals that, despite unusual weather patterns over the last decade, the public is quite divided on the issue. While scientists may have reached a "consensus," the American people have not. The Pew Research Center is an independent opinion research group that studies attitudes toward the press, politics, and public policy issues. They conduct regular national surveys and polls that measure public trends in values and fundamental political and social attitudes. Results for this survey are based on telephone interviews conducted among a nationwide sample of 1,708 adults, 18 years of age or older, from January 10 through January 15, 2007.

Summary of Findings

President Bush's mention in his State of the Union Message of the "serious challenge of global climate change" was directed at an American public, many of whom remain lukewarm about the importance of the issue. The unusual weather affecting the nation this winter may have reinforced the widely held view that the phenomenon of rising temperatures is real (77 percent of Americans believe that), but the public continues to be deeply divided over both its cause and what to do about it. But there is considerably less agreement over its cause, with about half (47 percent) saying that human activity, such as the burning of fossil fuels, is mostly to blame for the earth getting warmer.

Moreover, there are indications that most Americans do not regard global warming as a top-tier issue. In Pew's annual list of policy priorities for the president and Congress, global warming ranked fourth lowest of

Global Warming a Polarizing Issue

	Total %	Cons Rep %	Mod/Lib Rep %	Ind %	Cons/Mod Dem %	Lib Dem %
Believe that...						
Earth is getting warmer	77	54	78	78	83	92
Due to human activity	47	20	46	47	54	71
How serious a problem is global warming?						
Very serious	45	18	35	46	52	73
Somewhat serious	32	33	39	35	31	20
Not too serious	12	29	15	9	20	5
Not a problem	8	17	10	8	4	2
DK/refused	3	3	1	2	3	*
	100	100	100	100	100	100
*Global warming requires immediate govt. action?**						
Yes	55	22	51	58	61	81
No	31	54	37	29	29	14
Not a problem**	11	20	12	10	7	1
DK/refused	3	4	*	3	3	4
	100	100	100	100	100	100

*Asked of those who said global warming is a problem.
**Includes those who answered don't know on whether global warming is a problem.

23 items tested, with only about four in ten (38 percent) rating it a top priority. A survey last year by the Pew Global Attitudes Project showed that the public's relatively low level of concern about global warming sets the United States apart from other countries. That survey found that only 19 percent of Americans who had heard of global warming expressed a great deal of personal concern about the issue. Among the 15 countries surveyed, only the Chinese expressed a comparably low level of concern (20 percent).

Stable Views of Global Warming

	June 2006 %	July 2006 %	Aug 2006 %	Jan 2007 %
Solid evidence that the earth is warming?				
Yes, solid evidence	70	79	77	77
Due to human activity	41	50	47	47
Due to natural patterns	21	23	20	20
No, no solid evidence	20	17	17	16
Mixed/Don't know	10	4	6	7
	100	100	100	100

The latest national survey by the Pew Research Center for the People and the Press, conducted January 10 to January 15 among 1,708 Americans, finds a majority (55 percent) saying that global warming is a problem that requires immediate government action. But the percentage of Americans expressing this view has declined a bit since August, when 61 percent felt global warming was a problem that required an immediate government response.

The survey finds deep differences between Republicans and Democrats—and within both political parties—over virtually every issue related to global warming. These disagreements extend even to the question of whether the earth is getting warmer. Just 54 percent of conservative Republicans say there is solid evidence that average temperatures have been getting warmer over the past few decades; by contrast, more than three-quarters of both moderate and liberal Republicans and independents (78 percent each), and even higher percentages of Democrats, believe the earth has been getting warmer.

The political divisions are still greater over the issue of whether global warming is a problem that requires immediate government action. About half of moderate and liberal Republicans (51 percent) express this view, compared with just 22 percent of conservative Republicans. The differences among Democrats are somewhat smaller; 81 percent of liberal Democrats, and 61 percent of moderate and conservative Democrats, say global warming is a problem that requires immediate government action.

Education and Party

There also are striking educational differences in partisans' views of global warming. Among Republicans, higher education is linked to greater skepticism about global warming—fully 43 percent of Republicans with a college degree say that there is no evidence of global warming, compared with 24 percent of Republicans with less education.

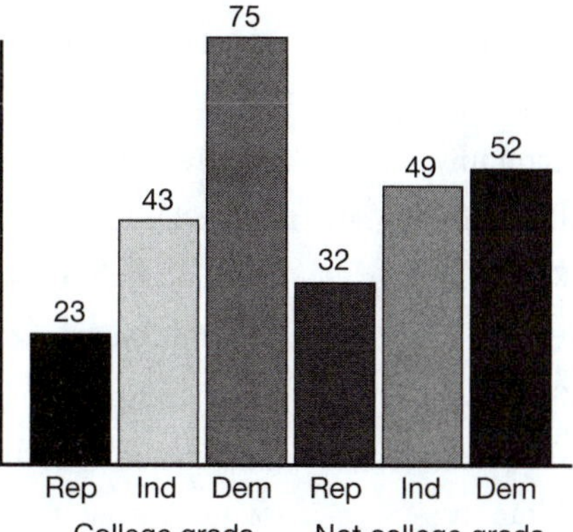

But among Democrats, the pattern is the reverse. Fully 75 percent of Democrats with college degrees say that there is solid evidence of global warming and that it is caused by human activities. This is far higher than among Democrats with less education, among whom 52 percent say the same. Independents, regardless of education levels, fall in between these partisan extremes.

Global Warming Not a High Priority

Roughly twice as many Democrats as Republicans say that dealing with global warming should be a top priority for the president and Congress this year (48 percent versus 23 percent). However, the issue is a relatively low priority for members of both parties, as well as for independents.

The issue of dealing with global warming rates near the bottom of the priorities list for both Democrats and independents and is the lowest priority for Republicans. Notably, there is much greater support, across the political spectrum, for the broader goal of protecting the environment. Two-thirds of Democrats (67 percent) view protecting the environment as a top priority, and it ranks near the middle of their policy priorities list. Many more independents and Republicans also rate protecting the environment an important priority than say the same about dealing with global warming.

Global Warming Lags as a Policy Priority

Percent rating each as a 'top priority'

Republicans		Democrats		Independents	
Terrorism	93	Health care costs	77	Terrorism	77
Education	65	Economy	77	Education	66
Economy	65	Terrorism	74	Health care costs	66
Illegal immigration	63	Education	74	Medicare	61
Social Security	62	Social Security	72	Economy	60
Health care costs	58	Minimum wage	71	Social Security	60
Stronger military	56	Medicare	70	Job situation	60
Crime	56	Health insurance	70	**Environment**	**59**
Morality	54	Crime	69	Energy	58
Medicare	53	**Environment**	**67**	Crime	57
Tax cuts	49	Poverty	67	Budget deficit	53
Poverty	48	Job situation	67	Health insurance	52
Energy	45	Energy	64	Minimum wage	50
Health insurance	44	Budget deficit	57	Illegal immigration	49
Budget deficit	42	Tax cuts	54	Poverty	46
Environment	**41**	Illegal immigration	48	Stronger military	45
Job situation	39	**Global warming**	**48**	Morality	42
Int'l Trade	33	Morality	45	Tax cuts	41
Minimum wage	28	Govt. ethics*	44	**Global warming**	**40**
Govt. ethics*	28	Stronger military	42	Govt. ethics*	35
Global warming	**23**	Int'l Trade	35	Int'l Trade	31

*Reducing the influence of lobbyists and special interests in Washington

QUESTIONS: For Thinking and Writing

1. The Pew Research Center reports that the American public is "lukewarm" on the issue of global warming. In your opinion, what accounts for the lack of interest in this issue?
2. How might politicians and scientists use the information in this report? Explain.

3. How do political party affiliations and platforms influence public opinion of global warming? Explain.
4. What issues, according to the Pew survey, are considered more pressing for Americans than global warming? Provide your own ranking of the priorities listed below in order of most important to least important to you.

Budget deficit	Global warming	Minimum wage
Crime	Government ethics	Morality
Economy	Health care	Poverty
Education	Health insurance	Social security
Employment	Illegal immigration	Stronger military
Energy	International trade	Taxes
Environment	Medicare	Terrorism

   How does your ranking compare to the political affiliations cited?
5. Using the information provided in the graphs and charts accompanying this article, prepare a short report on the public perception on global warming, interpreting what the data mean in terms of policy change and action in the coming decade.

VIEWPOINTS

No Change in Political Climate

Ellen Goodman

On Comparing Global Warming Denial to Holocaust Denial

Dennis Prager

Several authors in this section, including Al Gore, allude to the issue of global warming, and the need to take action to stop it, as a moral charge. Is this issue one of moral "right and wrong"? The next two editorials address the ethics of global warming and the language used to couch the argument. First, liberal columnist Ellen Goodman charges that the evidence for global warming is so overwhelming that those who doubt it are in the same category as Holocaust deniers. Conservative radio talk-show host Dennis Prager challenges her viewpoint and her language choice. To make this parallel, he fears, is to make the issue one of good and evil, with anyone who dares to question whether we need to do anything about global warming on par with Nazis. He also fears a time when voicing an unpopular opinion could be a criminal offense. Ellen Goodman's editorial appeared in the Boston Globe, on February 9, 2007. Dennis Prager's rebuttal was published online at Townhall.com four days later, on February 13, 2007.

No Change in Political Climate

Ellen Goodman

On the day that the latest report on global warming was released, I went out and bought a light bulb. Okay, an environmentally friendly, compact fluorescent light bulb.

No, I do not think that if everyone lit just one little compact fluorescent light bulb, what a bright world this would be. Even the Prius in our driveway doesn't do a whole lot to reduce my carbon footprint, which is roughly the size of the Yeti lurking in the (melting) Himalayas.

But it was either buying a light bulb or pulling the covers over my head. And it was too early in the day to reach for that kind of comforter.

By every measure, the UN's Intergovernmental Panel on Climate Change raises the level of alarm. The fact of global warming is "unequivocal." The certainty of the human role is now somewhere over 90 percent. Which is about as certain as scientists ever get.

I would like to say we're at a point where global warming is impossible to deny. Let's just say that global-warming deniers are now on a par with Holocaust deniers, though one denies the past and the other denies the present and future.

But light bulbs aside—I now have three and counting—I don't expect that this report will set off some vast political uprising. The sorry fact is that the rising world thermometer hasn't translated into political climate change in America.

The folks at the Pew Research Center clocking public attitudes show that global warming remains twentieth on the annual list of 23 policy priorities. Below terrorism, of course, but also below tax cuts, crime, morality, and illegal immigration.

One reason is that while poles are melting and polar bears are swimming between ice floes, American politics has remained polarized. There are astonishing gaps between Republican science and Democratic science. Try these numbers: Only 23 percent of college-educated Republicans believe the warming is due to humans, while 75 percent of college-educated Democrats believe it.

This great divide comes from the science-be-damned-and-debunked attitude of the Bush administration and its favorite media outlets. The day of the report, Big Oil Senator James Inhofe of Oklahoma actually described it as "a shining example of the corruption of science for political gain." Speaking of corruption of science, the American Enterprise Institute, which has gotten $1.6 million over the years from Exxon Mobil, offered $10,000 last summer to scientists who would counter the IPCC report.

But there are psychological as well as political reasons why global warming remains in the cool basement of priorities. It may be, paradoxically, that framing this issue in catastrophic terms ends up paralyzing instead of motivating us. Remember the *TIME* magazine cover story: "Be Worried. Be Very Worried." The essential environmental narrative is a hair-raising consciousness-raising: This is your Earth. This is your Earth on carbon emissions.

This works for some. But a lot of social science research tells us something else. As Ross Gelbspan, author of *The Heat is On*, says, "when people are confronted with an overwhelming threat and don't see a solution, it makes them feel impotent. So they shrug it off or go into deliberate denial."

Michael Shellenberger, coauthor of *The Death of Environmentalism*, adds, "The dominant narrative of global warming has been that we're responsible and have to make changes or we're all going to die. It's tailor-made to ensure inaction."

So how many scientists does it take to change a light bulb?

American University's Matthew Nisbet is among those who see the importance of expanding the story beyond scientists. He is charting the reframing of climate change into a moral and religious issue—*see the greening of the evangelicals*—and into a corruption-of-science issue—*see big oil*—and an economic issue—*see the newer, greener technologies.*

In addition, maybe we can turn denial into planning. "If the weatherman says there's a 75 percent chance of rain, you take your umbrella," Shellenberger tells groups. Even people who clutched denial as their last, best hope can prepare, he says, for the next Katrina. Global-warming preparation is both his antidote for helplessness and a goad to collective action.

The report is grim stuff. Whatever we do today, we face long-range global problems with a short-term local attention span. We're no happier looking at this global thermostat than we are looking at the nuclear doomsday clock.

Can we change from debating global warming to preparing? Can we define the issue in ways that turn denial into action? In America what matters now isn't environmental science, but political science.

We are still waiting for the time when an election hinges on a candidate's plans for a changing climate. That's when the light bulb goes on.

On Comparing Global Warming Denial to Holocaust Denial

Dennis Prager

In her last column, *Boston Globe* columnist Ellen Goodman wrote: "Let's just say that global-warming deniers are now on a par with Holocaust deniers. . . ."

This is worthy of some analysis.

First, it reflects a major difference between the way in which the Left and Right tend to view each other. With a few exceptions, those on the Left tend to view their ideological adversaries as bad people (i.e., people with bad intentions), while those on the Right tend to view their adversaries as wrong, perhaps even dangerous, but not usually as bad.

Those who deny the Holocaust are among the evil of the world. Their concern is not history but hurting Jews, and their attempt to rob nearly six million people of their experience of unspeakable suffering gives new meaning to the word "cruel." To equate those who question or deny global warming with those who question or deny the Holocaust is to ascribe equally nefarious motives to them. It may be inconceivable to Al Gore, Ellen Goodman, and their many millions of supporters that a person can disagree with them on global warming and not have evil motives: Such an individual must be paid by oil companies to lie, or lie—as do Holocaust deniers—for some other vile reason.

The belief that opponents of the Left are morally similar to Nazis was expressed recently by another prominent person of the Left, George Soros, the billionaire who bankrolls many leftist projects. At the World Economic Forum in Davos last month, Soros called on America to "de-Nazify," just as Germany did after the Holocaust and World War II. For Soros, America in Iraq is like the Nazis in Poland.

A second lesson to be drawn from the Goodman statement is that it helps us to understand better one of the defining mottos of contemporary liberalism: "Question authority." In reality, this admonition applies to questioning the moral authority of Judeo-Christian religions or of any secular conservative authority, but not of any other authority. The UN and other experts tell us that there is global warming; such authority is not to be questioned.

Third, the equation of global warming denial to Holocaust denial trivializes Holocaust denial. If questioning global warming is on "a par" with questioning the Holocaust, how bad can questioning the Holocaust really be? The same holds true with regard to Nazism and the George Soros statement. Claiming that America in the Iraq War is morally equivalent to Nazi Germany in World War II trivializes the unparalleled evil of the Nazis.

Fourth, the lack of response (thus far) of any liberal or left individual or organization—except to defend Ellen Goodman—or from the Anti-Defamation League, the organization whose primary purpose has been to defend Jews, is telling. Just imagine if, for example, an equally prominent Christian figure had written that denying America is a Christian country is on a par with denying the Holocaust. It would have been front-page news in the mainstream media, the individual would have been excoriated by just about every major liberal individual and group, and the ADL would have cited this as an example of burgeoning Christian anti-Semitism and Holocaust trivialization. But not a word at the ADL on Soros's comments about de-Nazifying America or Goodman's Holocaust-denial comment.

Fifth, and finally, the Ellen Goodman quote is only the beginning of what is already becoming one of the largest campaigns of vilification of decent people in history—the global condemnation of a) anyone who questions global warming; or b) anyone who agrees that there is global warming but who argues that human behavior is not its primary cause; or c) anyone who agrees that there is global warming, and even agrees that human behavior is its primary cause, but does not believe that the consequences will be nearly as catastrophic as Al Gore does.

If you don't believe all three propositions, you will be lumped with Holocaust deniers, and it would not be surprising that soon, in Europe, global-warming deniers will be treated as Holocaust deniers and prosecuted. Just watch. That is far more likely than the oceans rising by 20 feet. Or even 10. Or even 3.

QUESTIONS: For Thinking and Writing

1. What do Goodman's first two paragraphs reveal about her and her likely position on global warming? Explain.
2. What does Goodman mean when she states "I would like to say we're at a point where global warming is impossible to deny. Let's just say that global-warming deniers are now on a par with Holocaust deniers, though one denies the past and the other denies the present and future." Are they indeed the same? Is there a difference between denying the past and denying the future? Can one deny what hasn't happened yet?
3. Why does Prager object so strongly to Goodman's analogy of global-warming deniers to Holocaust deniers? Explain.
4. Review Prager's synopsis of the Right and Left in his third paragraph. Who is the "Right" and who is the "Left"? Where do Prager and Goodman fall? Do you agree with Prager's view or Goodman's? Explain.
5. Respond to these two editorials with one of your own, expressing your viewpoint. Quote both writers in your article.

QUESTIONS: For Further Research and Group Work

1. Conduct a poll on global warming to see how informed college students are on the issue. Craft a list of five to ten questions designed to develop a profile on how informed the average college student is on the issue of global warming and its implications for the future. Give the survey to at least 40 students. Gather the responses and analyze the data to create a "profile." Share this profile with other students in class. Are college students aware of the issues surrounding global warming? If so, to what extent, and how do they feel about the issue? If not, is this cause for concern? Why or why not?
2. Gore notes that as an insider to the workings of government, he knows that we are capable of enacting radical change. As a group, review his speech and make a list of the solutions/changes Gore proposes. Using your collective knowledge, discuss the feasibility of his solutions.

3. Several essays in this chapter reference the Kyoto Treaty, also known as the Kyoto Protocol. Gore notes that the United States is one of the few nations that did not ratify the treaty. Look up the details on the Kyoto Protocol. Prepare an argument for in-class debate in which you explain why you believe the United States should or should not ratify it. In addition to the treaty itself, you may reference the reasons other nations have cited for ratifying the treaty or not ratifying it, as in the case of Australia.
4. At what point can "consensus" be defined? Discuss the meaning of the word. Is it when everyone agrees, or when a majority does? How much influence should a consensus carry in a democratic society? For example, if a majority of people—especially experts on an issue—assume a particular position, does it follow that laws and policies should be based on their opinion? Why or why not?

CHAPTER 6

Exploring the Gender Gap

WE HAVE WITNESSED ENORMOUS CHANGES IN THE SOCIAL and professional lives of men and women over the past century. Traditional ways of defining others and ourselves along gender lines have been irrevocably altered. Only 100 years ago, the full financial responsibility of a family was squarely on the shoulders of men. Women could not vote and had limited legal resources at their disposal. Sex was something that happened within the confines of marriage. Women were expected to remain at home, relegated to housework and child rearing. Men were expected to be the disciplinarians of family life, with limited involvement in the daily lives of their children. Now, women may pursue many different career options and lifestyles. Men are not expected to be the sole breadwinner, and men and women together often share financial responsibilities. Sexual mores have relaxed, and both men and women enjoy greater freedoms socially, professionally, and intellectually than they ever have before.

Most college-age men and women were born after the "sexual revolution" and the feminist movement of the 1970s. But it was largely the movements of the 1960s and 1970s that have shaped the way men and women interact, view each other, evaluate opportunity, and envision the future. However, while much has changed, and we have moved toward greater gender equality, vestiges of gender bias and sexism remain.

The essays in this chapter examine how society has changed its expectations of gender and how these changes have affected men and women as they continue to define themselves, their relationships with each other, and society as a whole.

MADELEINE BEGUN KANE

My Most Attractive Adversary

Women may seem to have made tremendous progress professionally and academically, but they are held back by indirect sexist comments and attitudes. They are caught in a catch-22. If they react against these seemingly small slights, they appear to be overreacting or too sensitive; but to let them pass may signal that such comments are somehow acceptable. In the next essay, humorist and self-described "recovering lawyer" Madeleine Begun Kane holds that subtle sexism maintains gender differences. This essay appeared in Women's Village *in 2002.*

"Our Portia has come up with an excellent solution." A trial judge said this about me several years ago in open court, when I was still a full-time litigator. I've never forgotten it. Not because it was a compliment to be compared to so formidable a lawyer as Shakespeare's Portia, although I think he meant it as a compliment. But what I really remember is my discomfort at being singled out as a woman in what, even today, remains a predominantly male world.

Despite our progress in the battle against workplace discrimination, the fact of being a female is almost always an issue. It may not be blatant, but it usually lurks just below the surface. We are not lawyers, executives, and managers. We are female lawyers, female executives, and female managers. Just when we are lulled into believing otherwise, something happens to remind us, and those around us, of our gender in subtle yet unsettling ways.

Men often use physical compliments to call attention to the fact that we are different. References to "my lovely opponent" or "my most attractive adversary" remain remarkably common. It's a clever technique, because any response other than a gracious "thank you" seems like a petty overreaction.

Consequently, unless the remark is obviously offensive, as in references to certain unmentionable body parts, a simple nod or "thank you" is usually the prudent response. Of course if you're feeling less cautious, you may want to return the compliment. Done with a slight note of irony, this can be an effective way to get your point across. But saying, "You look very handsome yourself, Your Honor," is probably not a good idea.

Concern for the tender female sensibility rivals compliments in the subtle sexism department. I've experienced this most often during business meetings—high-powered meetings where a lone female is surrounded by her peers and superiors. At some point during the meeting the inevitable will happen. One of the men will use an expletive—a minor one in all likelihood. The expedient course is to ignore it. She is a woman of the world. She has heard and possibly used such language—and even worse.

But is she allowed to ignore it? Of course not! That would be too easy. The curser inevitably turns to the lone female (who until this moment has somehow managed not to blush) and apologizes. This singles her out as a delicate female who doesn't quite belong and needs to be protected. This also reminds everyone that the rest of the group would be ever so much more comfortable, at ease, and free to be themselves, if only a woman hadn't invaded their turf.

This has happened to me more times than I care to recall. And I still don't know the proper response. Should I ignore both the profanity and the apology? Is it best to graciously accept the apology, as if one were appropriate? Or should I say what I'm always tempted to say: "That's all right, I swear like a sailor too."

Most women, myself included, overlook these subtle forms of sexism. I'm troubled by this, and I worry that by being silent, I'm giving up an opportunity to educate. For while some men use these tactics deliberately, others don't even know they're being offensive. Nevertheless, I usually smile discreetly and give a gracious nod. And wonder if I'm doing the right thing, or if I'm mistaking cowardice for discretion.

QUESTIONS: For Thinking and Writing

1. Do we have certain ingrained gender expectations when it comes to job positions? For example, do we expect men to be mechanics or lawyers or firefighters and women to be teachers or nurses or secretaries? Are these expectations changing, or are they still common assumptions?
2. Kane opens her essay with a story about how she was called "Portia" by a judge. Who is Portia? Why is Kane uncomfortable with what she believes to be a compliment by the judge? Explain.

3. Kane objected to physical compliments made by male professionals, such as "my lovely opponent," and "my most attractive adversary." How do such compliments undermine her role as a lawyer and a professional? Do you think the men intended to slight her? Why or why not?
4. Write about a time when you felt awkward because of your gender. Describe the situation, the experience, and why you felt uncomfortable. With a critical eye, analyze the situation and think about how social expectations of gender may have contributed to your feelings of discomfort.
5. In her second paragraph, Kane states that women are not "lawyers, executives, and managers." Instead, they are "female lawyers, female executives, and female managers." Interview a woman who holds a professional position in law, medicine, or business and ask her about this observation. Does she feel that the word "female" floats in front of her professional title, unspoken but still "lurking beneath the surface"? Summarize your interview and analyze the discussion.

SCOTT RUSSELL SANDERS

The Men We Carry in Our Minds

Statistically, men tend to hold more positions of power and wealth than women do. Many women feel that simply being born male automatically confers status and power, or at the very least, makes life easier. This cultural assumption, however, may only apply to a very small segment of the male population. Is it fair to stereotype men this way? Writer Scott Russell Sanders grew up in rural Tennessee and Ohio, where men aged early from lives of punishing physical labor or died young in military service. When he got to college, Sanders was baffled when the daughters of lawyers, bankers, and physicians accused him and his gender of "having cornered the world's pleasures." In this essay, Sanders explores the differences between the men and women in his life and how male power is often dependent on class and social influence.

"This must be a hard time for women," I say to my friend Anneke. "They have so many paths to choose from, and so many voices calling them."

"I think it's a lot harder for men," she replies.

"How do you figure that?"

"The women I know feel excited, innocent, like crusaders in a just cause. The men I know are eaten up with guilt."

"Women feel such pressure to be everything, do everything," I say. "Career, kids, art, politics. Have their babies and get back to the office a week later. It's as if they're trying to overcome a million years' worth of evolution in one lifetime."

"But we help one another. And we have this deep-down sense that we're in the right—we've been held back, passed over, used—while men feel they're in the wrong. Men are the ones who've been discredited, who have to search their souls."

I search my soul. I discover guilty feelings aplenty—toward the poor, Native Americans, the whales, an endless list of debts. But toward women I feel something more confused, a snarl of shame, envy, wary, tenderness, and amazement. This muddle troubles me. To hide my unease I say, "You're right, it's tough being a man these days."

"Don't laugh," Anneke frowns at me. "I wouldn't be a man for anything. It's much easier being the victim. All the victim has to do is break free. The persecutor has to live with his past."

How deep is that past? I find myself wondering. How much of an inheritance do I have to throw off?

When I was a boy growing up on the back roads of Tennessee and Ohio, the men I knew labored with their bodies. They were marginal farmers, just scraping by, or welders, steelworkers, carpenters; they swept floors, dug ditches, mined coal, or drove trucks, their forearms ropy with muscle; they trained horses, stoked furnaces, made tires, stood on assembly lines wrestling parts onto cars and refrigerators. They got up before light, worked all day long whatever the weather, and when they came home at night, they looked as though somebody had been whipping them. In the evenings and on weekends, they worked on their own places, tilling gardens that were lumpy with clay, fixing broken-down cars, hammering on houses that were always too drafty, too leaky, too small.

The bodies of the men I knew were twisted and maimed in ways visible and invisible. The nails of their hands were black and split, the hands tattooed with scars. Some had lost fingers. Heavy lifting had given many of them finicky backs and guts weak from hernias. Racing against conveyor belts had given them ulcers. Their ankles and knees ached from years of standing on concrete. Anyone who had worked for long around machines was hard of hearing. They squinted, and the skin of their faces was creased like the leather of old work gloves. There were times, studying them, when I dreaded growing up. Most of them coughed, from dust or cigarettes, and most of them drank cheap wine or whiskey, so their eyes looked bloodshot and bruised. The fathers of my friends always seemed older than the mothers. Men wore out sooner. Only women lived into old age.

As a boy I also knew another sort of men, who did not sweat and break down like mules. They were soldiers, and so far as I could tell, they scarcely worked at all. But when the shooting started, many of them would die. This was what soldiers were for, just like a hammer was for driving nails. Warriors and toilers: those seemed, in my boyhood vision, to be the chief destinies for men. They weren't the only destinies, as I learned from having a few male teachers, from reading books, and from watching television. But the men on television—the politicians, the astronauts, the generals, the savvy lawyers, the philosophical doctors, the bosses who gave orders to both soldiers and laborers—seemed as remote and unreal to me as the figures in Renaissance tapestries. I could no more imagine growing up to become one of these cool, potent creatures than I could imagine becoming a prince.

A nearer and more hopeful example was that of my father, who had escaped from a red dirt farm to a tire factory, and from the assembly line to the front office. Eventually, he dressed in a white shirt and tie. He carried himself as if he had been born to work with his mind. But his body, remembering the earlier years of slogging work, began to give out on him in his fifties, and it quit on him entirely before he turned 65.

A scholarship enabled me not only to attend college, a rare enough feat in my circle, but even to study in a university meant for the children of the rich. Here I met for the first time young men who had assumed from birth that they would lead lives of comfort and power. And for the first time, I met women who told me that men were guilty of having kept all the joys and privileges of the earth for themselves. I was baffled. What privileges? What joys? I thought about the maimed, dismal lives of most of the men back home. What had they stolen from their wives and daughters? The right to go five days a week, 12 months a year, for 30 or 40 years to a steel mill or a coal mine? The right to drop bombs and die in war? The right to feel every leak in the roof, every gap in the fence, every cough in the engine as a wound they must mend? The right to feel, when the layoff comes or the plant shuts down, not only afraid but ashamed?

I was slow to understand the deep grievances of women. This was because, as a boy, I had envied them. Before college, the only people

I had ever known who were interested in art or music or literature, the only ones who read books, the only ones who ever seemed to enjoy a sense of ease and grace were the mothers and daughters. Like the menfolk, they fretted about money, they scrimped and made do. But when the pay stopped coming in, they were not the ones who had failed. Nor did they have to go to war, and that seemed to me a blessed fact. By comparison with the narrow, ironclad days of fathers, there was an expansiveness, I thought, in the days of mothers. They went to see neighbors, to shop in town, to run errands at school, at the library, at church. No doubt, had I looked harder at their lives, I would have envied them less. It was not my fate to become a woman, so it was easier for me to see the graces. I didn't see, then, what a prison a house could be, since houses seemed to be brighter, handsomer places than any factory. I did not realize—because such things were never spoken of—how often women suffered from men's bullying. Even then I could see how exhausting it was for a mother to cater all day to the needs of young children. But if I had been asked, as a boy, to choose between tending a baby and tending a machine, I think I would have chosen the baby. (Having now tended both, I know I would choose the baby.)

So I was baffled when the women at college accused me and my sex of having cornered the world's pleasures. I think something like my bafflement has been felt by other boys (and by girls as well) who grew up in dirt-poor farm country, in mining country, in black ghettoes, in Hispanic barrios, in the shadows of factories, in Third World nations—any place where the fate of men is just as grim and bleak as the fate of women.

When the women I met at college thought about the joys and privileges of men, they did not carry in their minds the sort of men I had known in my childhood. They thought of their fathers, who were bankers, physicians, architects, stockholders, the big wheels of the big cities. They were never laid off, never short of cash at month's end, never lined up for welfare. These fathers made decisions that mattered. They ran the world.

The daughters of such men wanted to share in this power, this glory. So did I. They yearned for a say over their future, for jobs worthy of their abilities, for the right to live at peace, unmolested, whole. Yes, I thought, yes, yes. The difference between me and these daughters was that they saw me, because of my sex, as destined from birth to become like their fathers, and therefore as an enemy to their desires. But I knew better. I wasn't an enemy, in fact or in feeling. I was an ally. If I had known, then, how to tell them so, would they have believed me? Would they now?

QUESTIONS: For Thinking and Writing

1. Consider the view that being male automatically grants one power, status, and privilege. Then think about three men you know well, such as a father, brother, or friend. Do their everyday life experiences bear out this generalization?
2. Sanders states he has feelings of guilt toward a number of minority groups or social causes, but his feelings toward women are more complicated. What do you think might be the reasons for his feelings? Can you identify with this perspective?
3. How do you think women from the different socioeconomic groups Sanders mentions in his essay would respond to his ideas? For example, how would the educated daughters of the lawyers and bankers respond? How about the women from Sanders's hometown?
4. What are the occupations and obligations of the men mentioned in the article? What socioeconomic segment of society is Sanders describing? What does this suggest about the relationship between gender and class?
5. What does it mean to be a man today? Write an essay explaining what you think it means to be male in today's society. How do men factor into current social, intellectual, political, economic, and religious arenas? What opportunities are available—or not available—to men? Do you think it is easier or better to be male in American culture?

ROZ CHAST

Men's Fault Magazine

QUESTIONS: For Thinking and Writing

1. What is happening in this cartoon? What do you think happened first, and what is likely to happen next?
2. This cartoon appeared in the *New Yorker* magazine. How does it appeal to the reading audience of this magazine? Explain.
3. What social conventions does this cartoon tap into to convey its humor? Explain.

LYZ BARANOWSKI

Girls, We Really Are Our Own Worst Enemies

Feminism has paved the way for many young women to pursue life choices that were largely inaccessible or unacceptable to women only a generation ago. As the feminist movement picked up speed in the 1970s, many activists blamed male-dominated social structures for confining women to prescribed social roles. But should women be pointing the finger back at themselves? In the next editorial, Lyz Baranowski, who wrote this essay while a journalism major at Gustavus Adolphus College, argues that women are their own "worst enemies" when it comes to gender equality. She maintains that it is women's criticism of other women, their tendency to judge a woman on her looks or clothing rather than her intellect, that prevents women from truly being liberated. This essay appeared in Baranowski's student newspaper, the Gustavian Weekly, *on May 2, 2003.*

"A woman needs a man like a fish needs a bicycle," is Gloria Steinem's famous declaration of feminism. It asserts the ideology many associate with feminism: no woman needs a man.

Nearly three years ago, Gloria Steinem married a man twice her age, and many feminist activists declared her a hypocrite. In a time when an overwhelming number of young women refuse to call themselves feminist and headlines declare the death of feminism, we have to ask, was it all just wasted bras?

It is clear through the marriage of Steinem and the similar yoking of many strong and admirable women that feminism is no longer a rejection of men. Women need men like a fish needs water and men need women like a toilet needs to flush. The sexes balance one another, we complement and augment, knowing that without black, there can be no white.

This does not always translate into marriage, nor does it have to, but the companionship of a brother, a father, or a friend adds perspective (who else is going to make sure you see *The Matrix: Reloaded*, over and over and over again?).

The truth is that a new generation of women are becoming strong by realizing the balance and the nature of the world is that Adam needed Eve in the garden, so we fish need our water.

Yet, with this new feminist attitude comes a realization that men are no longer the biggest threat; it is ourselves. Feminism isn't just a reaction against men anymore. A study by the University of Chicago found that in a race, women run slower when other women run with them. (The author concluded that women are less responsive to competition.) Merely walking out of your dorm room with two different colored socks on would prove otherwise. Just think about it: who is going to look at you with that "Girl, don't you know what you are doing" look? It is not the men, it's the women.

As a member of the speech and debate team, I am constantly attending tournaments, wearing nice suits, and speaking pretty. The speech and debate crowd is one of people interested in learning, debating, and discussing, so I was not prepared when a judge commented that I needed to use more lipstick. She later thanked me when I did use more lipstick at the next tournament. A friend received a similar comment, and a girl from California gave a speech on how a female judge told her she ought to stop wearing suit pants because they were not professional. She won nationals with that speech. While she may have won, our experiences and the everyday experiences of girls, commenting and gossiping on everything from clothes to the amount of time a girl raises her hand in class, show that women are still losing. The problem is not others, the problem is us.

We are the ones editing *Vogue* and giving girls weight issues and eating disorders; we are the ones backstabbing and gossiping about that outspoken girl who wears weird clothes. Women act relationally aggressive toward each other, as Rachel Simmons points out in her book, *Odd Girl Out.* She explains that women view one another as competition and attack each other in non-physically aggressive ways. While this form of aggression is neither worse nor better than the usually labeled male physical aggression, it is more difficult to discover.

As Phyllis Chesler, author of *Woman's Inhumanity to Woman,* is clear to point out, even that supposed solid and united front of women in the sixties and seventies was fraught with backstabbing and tension. Many argue that this is a symptom of social convention and gender bias, yet Chesler suggests otherwise. She takes the stance that female aggression may in part be biological, while also perpetuated by cultural ideas of gender.

This concept is almost as liberating as the legal use of contraceptives or suffrage, because it allows us to stop blaming other people (i.e., those stupid white males) for our problems, to take matters into our own hands, and to be more responsible for our actions, rather than pawning them off to history and repression. Blaming and criticizing the world for problems we are just as responsible for perpetuating is not feminism, it is just a cycle of self-oppression.

I will tell you what feminism is: pride. Pride in the fact that we are women who can play sports, make millions, and still look good in spaghetti straps. Pride in the fact that we are not men, and we never will be; we are women, and we are a valid, powerful force. Feminism is the realization that no matter what a woman does, even if she is a homemaker, or didn't even graduate from high school, whether she loves babies and can't wait to embrace motherhood, she is just as important and in need of support as the independent woman with an education, a great job, and a loft apartment in New York. Feminism is me, saying I love being a woman, and I wouldn't have it any other way.

QUESTIONS: For Thinking and Writing

1. In this piece, Baranowski notes that many young women refuse to call themselves feminist, although without feminism, they would not be enjoying the freedoms and lifestyle they currently do. What accounts

for this backlash? What has tarnished feminism for these young women?

2. Baranowski opens her essay with a quote from Gloria Steinem. Who is Gloria Steinem? What is her role in the feminist movement? What did her often quoted statement mean? In what context and climate did she say it? Does the fact that Steinem later married change the impact of her words, or does it simply reflect that culture has changed? Explain.
3. Why, according to Baranowski, are some women "their own worst enemies" in terms of promoting gender equality?
4. Baranowski notes that women are more critical of women than men are. In your opinion, is this true? Explain.
5. Baranowski wrote this piece for her student newspaper, the *Gustavian Weekly*. Write a column about feminism from your own perspective, but begin your column by repeating Baranowski's first line, "A woman needs a man like a fish needs a bicycle."

LINDSAY JOHNS

In Search of Notorious PhDs

Deadly shootings, both on the street and in the schools, are putting kids—especially young males—in front of and behind the trigger. Music glorifying violence and promoting "hypermasculinity" is giving a soundtrack to the violent street dramas that unfold daily in the nation's neighborhoods and suburbs. Could hip-hop music and its preoccupation with violence be fueling the fire? In this next essay, Lindsay Johns takes a look at the connection between hip-hop, violence, and black masculinity. This article appeared in the Spring 2007 issue of the New Black Magazine.

Look around. It only takes a nanosecond of exposure to modern mass media to discern a dazzlingly disturbing trend.

From the glistening pecs and ridiculously chiseled abs of LL Cool J on a billboard, to the cringingly pimpilicious demeanor of Snoop Dogg on *MTV Base*, or the tediously priapic and rabidly homophobic lyrics of Beenieman, we are constantly bombarded by stylized images of hypermasculine black men.

Name your cliché. Über-physical, über-feral or über-sexually potent: they all apply. It doesn't take a genius to see what trite, hackneyed, and ultimately depressing images of blackness these all are. What is more, they are unfortunately symptomatic of a much greater social and racial malaise, one which, like a rotten timber supporting the precariously balanced edifice of our society, threatens to bring it crashing down upon our heads very soon.

Heterosexual black masculinity, as a social construction in the twenty-first century, is at best deeply problematic, and at worst hideously flawed.

From Mike Tyson to Tupac, via 50 Cent, Shaquille O'Neill, and Shabba Ranks, black male icons (invariably from the arenas of sports or music) are right now indubitably doing more harm than good.

But what's wrong with the likes of 50, Beenieman, I hear you cry? What's so wrong with being big 'n' buff or being able to handle your business in the bedroom and, in the memorable words of Sean Paul, able *to do the wuk*?

The answer is devastatingly simple yet is constantly ignored.

Black musicians who indulge in representations of hypermasculinity are simply conceding much-sought-after gains in racial equality. Icons such as 50 Cent, Snoop Dogg, and Elephant Man persist in trading racial dignity for a quick buck and are willingly conforming to the oldest, most pernicious (but perhaps the most lucrative) racial stereotype of all, the most execrable of old chestnuts: that black is wholly physical, and that by implication in the system of binary opposition, white is cerebral.

Why does so much contemporary black music persist in presenting to the world at large such a limiting and psychologically harmful (not to mention erroneous) caricature of black hypermasculinity?

The histrionic (and oh-so-easy to be ridiculed by white people) hip-hop hand gestures, the tedious and repetitious physical and verbal posturing, based on empty self-aggrandizement, the trope of mythical sexual prowess, all are images redolent of ignorance, and all are indicative of a deeply troubled psyche, a psyche visibly manifesting the scars and striations of centuries of slavery and oppression.

Where power, control, and authority—traditional definitions of masculinity—have been historically denied to black men since slavery, it is perhaps historically understandable that the knee-jerk reaction is to present oneself as all that one has lacked.

Thus, the rapper or the reggae singer's conscious embrace of a hypermasculine image as a means of resisting the emasculation of racism is understandable, but ultimately misguided. Unwittingly he plays into the arms of the oppressor yet again. At the risk of gaining the physical, he spectacularly concedes the cerebral.

The ubiquitous and seemingly omnipotent MTV-based culture which peddles *ad nauseam* this hyperbolized and grossly distorted image of black masculinity simply reinforces these negative stereotypes in the most harmful, demeaning, and detrimental of ways. Thus a whole generation of both white and black kids has now been successfully indoctrinated to think that the only way for black masculinity to manifest itself is through physical posturing, sexual braggadocio, feral violence, and general antisocial behavior.

Very soon (if not already) a massive tranche of white people will only be able to relate to black men through the prism of hypermasculinity, not to mention the generation of young black men, some barely into their teens, for whom the *pimp roll*, the *Yo, bitch!* and the *bedroom bully* persona are sadly now the only ways of relating to themselves: the elegiac carapaces behind which they hide from an unforgiving, hostile universe.

New York rapper Nas's hit song *Oochie Wally* (despite its infectious hook and chorus) exemplifies the long list of anthemic songs built upon deeply troubling misogynistic and hypermasculine foundations. Let's be honest: "*I long dicked the bitch all night*" might be a great line to share with your boys at the gym in a moment of locker room bravado or *esprit de corps masculin* when regaling them with tales of your bedroom exploits, but seriously people . . . are we making any progress here?

Similarly, Mad Cobra, another legendary luminary firmly ensconced in the pantheon of dancehall deities (famous for hits such as *Flesh Dagger* and *Plant It*) is one of the most sexually brutal lyricists in the reggae business. Yet he is hailed as an avatar of all that is good about dancehall music. Hypermasculinity, and its concomitants misogyny and homophobia, are all decidedly *de rigueur* in reggae culture, and, what is worse, continue to go unchallenged.

And where does this depiction of black hypermasculinity ultimately lead?

Well, in the first instance, it leads to ostentatiously pimp rollin' down the streets, bouncing along as if he has dislocated his pelvis, belligerently kissing his teeth in some old granny's face because he thinks his *respect* has been compromised by her accidental nudge or stray glance. Result: intimidating or laughable, depending on your point of view.

On another level, the endemic gun violence in the black community can be directly traced back to the wholly irresponsible image of black masculinity, which is fed to us through music.

I will happily wager that Miles Davis's *Birth of Cool* or George Benson's *The Guitar Man* are not the musical accompaniments of choice in the majority of drive-by shootings (auto-tuning into Classic FM by accident notwithstanding).

Ceaseless macho posturing and the absorption of violent imagery results in the playing out of violence in real life. Art mirrors life, but also life mirrors art.

As a direct result of the hypermasculine lyrics in garage, grime, hip-hop or reggae music, we are witnessing a culture of deeply ingrained self-loathing, which is imbuing in black youngsters the notion that to be black means to be physical, violent, homophobic, and über macho (with at least three women). From Ludacris' *I've got hos in different area codes* to Beenieman's *Nuff Gal*, the hypermasculine predominates. Anything else is seen as, quite frankly, effeminate.

These nefarious lies of black masculinity, no doubt expediently propagated over the centuries by white opportunists (first antiabolitionists, and now, in their most contemporary guise, the music executives who control the distribution and marketing of black music, knowing that these raw ingredients will ensure more record sales to the white teenagers who are their target audience) need to be swiftly exposed, dispelled, and eradicated.

Is the hypermasculinity expounded in black music a mask for historical pain? It would be both churlish and naive to say that it isn't. It clearly functions as a mask for the pain engendered by centuries of social ostracism, oppression, and cultural alienation dating back to slavery and also as a mask for chronically low self-esteem. But (momentarily lapsing into the vernacular) *wake up, muthafuckaz*!

The days of slavery are over. And what may have been once a *bona fide* psychological crutch is now being lucratively peddled as an expedient sales gimmick. Is it any wonder that so much of the educated black American middle class has a healthy disdain for hip-hop?

It is time to smell the coffee and to realize that, although the physical shackles of slavery are off, we still need liberating from the debilitating mental shackles, and that by falling into the trap of complying with and buying into these heinous stereotypes, black people are themselves setting back the notion of racial equality decades, if not centuries.

So what next?

We need to redefine notions of black masculinity with alacrity and to directly incorporate more progressive ideas of what it means to be black and male into our music. There is, of course, no one monolithic notion of black masculinity. There are as many manifestations of black masculinity as there are shades of black.

But of paramount importance is the need to present more viable and more visibly cerebral alternatives. We urgently need to create new paradigms of black masculinity which do not give voice to the old lie of black as physical and, by implication, white as cerebral.

The sooner we acknowledge that the black male hip-hop or reggae aesthetic is fundamentally limiting and ironically intellectually emasculating, as opposed to actually empowering, then, and only then, we will begin to progress as a people.

Because, hard though it is to hear, whilst these antediluvian beliefs persist, we are still simply playing ourselves. As the conscious rapper Jeru The Damaja so eloquently said back in 1996:

"With all that big willy talk, ya playin' yaself.
With all that big gun talk, ya playin' yaself."

At the dawn of the twenty-first century, if we are to stand even a chance of leveling the playing field and making tangible progress, we need, (as was said of the teaching methods of Cornell West at Harvard) less of *da boyz* and more of DuBois.

In short, we need much less Notorious B. I. G. and much more Notorious Ph.D.

QUESTIONS: For Thinking and Writing

1. What does the author's title mean? What do you need to know about hip-hop to understand the title?
2. Johns comments, "Heterosexual black masculinity, as a social construction in the twenty-first century, is at best deeply problematic, and at worst hideously flawed." In your own words, describe what the image is of black masculinity in America today. Do you agree or disagree with Johns' assessment? Why or why not?
3. Why does Johns feel that hip-hop artists who cash in on hypermasculinity are setting back racial equality? In what ways is the "hypermasculinity" promoted in hip-hop and reggae music, and embraced by young males, limiting and harmful? In what ways can it be viewed as ironic?
4. Johns notes that MTV "peddles ad nauseam" distorted images that reinforce negative stereotypes. In your opinion, is Johns taking MTV culture too seriously, or can this medium be harmful to society?

5. In this essay, Lindsay Johns expresses his concern about the way some hip-hop artists glorify music that conveys the message that "to be black means to be physical, violent, homophobic, and über macho." Express your own viewpoint on this issue. Can lyrics and images be harmful? Are they just in fun, or maybe to shock, but not to be taken seriously? Explain.

VIEWPOINTS

Homeward Bound

Linda Hirshman

The Year of Domesticity

David Brooks

The next two readings address the "mommy-wars debate" concerning women who "opt-out" of work in favor of staying at home to care for their children. The first essay appeared in the November issue of the American Prospect, written by women's studies professor Linda Hirshman. Hirshman outlines what she believes to be the fallacies of "choice feminism" in which women can choose to stay at home or work outside of it. She further argues that this is no choice at all, because it removes women from positions of power and spheres of political and social influence. Hirshman's article set off a firestorm of controversy. In a follow-up article, Hirshman said, "even though I knew the Greeks made Socrates drink poison, the reaction to my judgment took me by surprise." In January 2006, New York Times *columnist David Brooks published an opinion editorial piece challenging Hirshman's views. Are young women making a mistake when they leave work for at-home motherhood? Or is this choice an example of how far women have come?*

Homeward Bound

Linda Hirshman

The Truth about Elite Women

Half the wealthiest, most privileged, best-educated females in the country stay home with their babies, rather than work in the market economy. When in September the *New York Times* featured an article exploring a piece of this story, "Many Women at Elite Colleges Set Career Path to Motherhood," the blogosphere went ballistic, countering with anecdotes and sarcasm. *Slate*'s Jack Shafer accused the *Times* of "weasel words" and of publishing the same story—essentially, "The Opt-Out Revolution"—every few years, and, recently, every few weeks. A month after the flap, the *Times*' only female columnist, Maureen Dowd, invoked the elite-college article in her contribution to the *Times*' running soap, "What's a Modern Girl to Do?" about how women must forgo feminism even to get laid. The colleges article provoked such fury that the *Times* had to post an explanation of the then-student journalist's methodology on its Web site.

There's only one problem: There is important truth in the dropout story. Even though it appeared in the *New York Times*.

I stumbled across the news three years ago, when researching a book on marriage after feminism. I found that among the educated elite, who are the logical heirs of the agenda of empowering women, feminism has largely failed in its goals. There are few women in the corridors of power, and marriage is essentially unchanged. The number of women at universities exceeds the number of men. But, more than a generation after feminism, the number of women in elite jobs doesn't come close.

Why did this happen? The answer I discovered—an answer neither feminist leaders nor women themselves want to face—is that while the public world has changed, albeit imperfectly, to accommodate women among the elite, private lives have hardly budged. The real glass ceiling is at home.

Looking back, it seems obvious that the unreconstructed family was destined to re-emerge after the passage of feminism's storm of social change. Following the original impulse to address everything in the lives of women, feminism turned its focus to cracking open the doors of the public power structure. This was no small task. At the beginning, there were male juries and male Ivy League schools, sex-segregated want ads, discriminatory employers, harassing colleagues. As a result of feminist efforts—and larger economic trends—the percentage of women, even of mothers in full- or part-time employment, rose robustly through the 1980s and early 1990s.

But then the pace slowed. The census numbers for all working mothers leveled off around 1990 and have fallen modestly since 1998. In interviews, women with enough money to quit work say they are "choosing" to opt out. Their words conceal a crucial reality: the belief that women are responsible for child rearing and homemaking was largely untouched by decades of workplace feminism. Add to this the good evidence that the upper-class workplace has become more demanding and then mix in the successful conservative cultural campaign to reinforce traditional gender roles and you've got a perfect recipe for feminism's stall.

People who don't like the message attack the data. True, the *Times* based its college story on a survey of questionable reliability and a bunch of interviews. It is not necessary to give credence to Dowd's book, from which her *Times Magazine* piece was taken, and which seems to be mostly based on her lifetime of bad dates and some e-mails from fellow *Times* reporters, to wonder if all this noise doesn't mean something important is going on in the politics of the sexes.

What evidence is good enough? Let's start with you. Educated and affluent reader, if you are a 30- or 40-something woman with children, what are you doing? Husbands, what are your wives doing? Older readers, what are your married daughters with children doing? I have asked this question of scores of women and men. Among the affluent-educated-married population, women are letting their careers slide to tend the home fires. If my interviewees are working, they work largely part-time, and their part-time careers are not putting them in the executive suite.

Here's some more evidence: During the nineties, I taught a course in sexual bargaining at a very good college. Each year, after the class reviewed the low rewards for child-care work, I asked how the students anticipated combining work with child rearing. At least half the female students described lives of part-time or home-based work. Guys expected their female partners to care for the children. When I asked the young men how they reconciled that prospect with the manifest low regard the market has for child care, they were mystified. Turning to the women who had spoken before, they said, uniformly, "But she chose it."

Even Ronald Coase, Nobel Prize winner in economics in 1991, quotes the aphorism that "the plural of anecdote is data." So how many anecdotes does it take to make data? I—a 1970s member of the National Organization for Women (NOW), a donor to Emily's List, and a professor of women's studies—did not set out to find this. I stumbled across the story when, while planning a book, I happened to watch *Sex and the City*'s Charlotte agonize about getting her wedding announcement in the "Sunday Styles" section of the *New York Times*. What better sample, I thought, than the brilliantly educated and accomplished brides of the "Sunday Styles," circa 1996? At marriage, they included a vice president of client communication, a gastroenterologist, a lawyer, an editor, and a marketing executive. In 2003 and 2004, I tracked them down and called them. I interviewed about 80 percent of the 41 women who announced their weddings over three Sundays in 1996. Around 40 years old, college graduates with careers: Who was more likely than they to be reaping feminism's promise of opportunity? Imagine my shock when I found almost all the brides from the first Sunday at home with their children. Statistical anomaly? Nope. Same result for the next Sunday. And the one after that.

Ninety percent of the brides I found had had babies. Of the 30 with babies, five were still working full time. Twenty-five, or 85 percent, were not working full time. Of those not working full time, ten were working part time but often a long way from their prior career paths. And half the married women with children were not working at all.

And there is more. In 2000, Harvard Business School professor Myra Hart surveyed the women of the classes of 1981, 1986, and 1991 and found that only 38 percent of female Harvard MBAs were working full time. A 2004 survey by the Center for Work–Life Policy of 2,443 women with a graduate degree or very prestigious bachelor's degree revealed that 43 percent of those women with children had taken a time out, primarily for family reasons. Richard Posner, federal appeals court judge and occasional University of Chicago adjunct professor, reports that "the [*Times*] article confirms what everyone associated with such institutions [elite law schools] has long known: that a vastly higher percentage of female than of male students will drop out of the workforce to take care of their children."

How many anecdotes to become data? The 2000 census showed a decline in the percentage of mothers of infants working full-time, part-time, or seeking employment. Starting at 31 percent in 1976, the percentage had gone up almost every year to 1992, hit a high of 58.7 percent in 1998, and then began to drop—to 55.2 percent in 2000, to 54.6 percent in 2002, to 53.7 percent in 2003. Statistics just released showed further decline to 52.9 percent in 2004. Even the percentage of working mothers with children who were not infants declined between 2000 and 2003, from 62.8 percent to 59.8 percent.

Although college-educated women work more than others, the 2002 census shows that graduate or professional degrees do not increase workforce participation much more than even one year of college. When their children are infants (under a year), 54 percent of females with graduate or professional degrees are not working full-time (18 percent are working part-time and 36 percent are not working at all). Even among those who have children who are not infants, 41 percent are not working full-time (18 percent are working part-time and 23 percent are not working at all).

Economists argue about the meaning of the data, even going so far as to contend that more mothers are working. They explain that the bureau changed the definition of "work" slightly in 2000, the economy went into recession, and the falloff in women without children was similar. However, even if there wasn't a falloff but just a leveling off, this represents not a loss of present value but a loss of hope for the future—a loss of hope that the role of women in society will continue to increase.

The arguments still do not explain the absence of women in elite workplaces. If these women were sticking it out in the business, law, and academic worlds, now, 30 years after feminism started filling the selective schools with women, the elite workplaces should be proportionately female. They are not. Law schools have been graduating classes around 40 percent female for decades—decades during which both schools and firms experienced enormous growth. And, although the legal population will not be 40 percent female until 2010, in 2003, the major law firms had only 16 percent female partners, according to the American Bar Association. It's important to note that elite workplaces like law firms grew in size during the very years that the percentage of female graduates was growing, leading you to expect a higher female employment than the pure graduation rate would indicate. The Harvard Business School has produced classes around 30 percent female. Yet only 10.6 percent of Wall Street's corporate officers are women, and a mere nine are Fortune 500 CEOs. Harvard Business School's dean, who extolled the virtues of interrupted careers on *60 Minutes*, has a 20 percent female academic faculty.

It is possible that the workplace is discriminatory and hostile to family life. If firms had hired every childless woman lawyer available, that alone would have been enough to raise the percentage of female law partners above 16 percent in 30 years. It is also possible that women are voluntarily taking themselves out of the elite job competition for lower status and lower-paying jobs. Women must take responsibility for the consequences of their decisions. It defies reason to claim that the falloff from 40 percent of the class at law school to 16 percent of the partners at all the big law firms is unrelated to half the mothers with graduate and professional degrees leaving full-time work at childbirth and staying away for several years after that, or possibly bidding down.

This isn't only about day care. Half my *Times* brides quit before the first baby came. In interviews, at least half of them expressed a hope never to work again. None had realistic plans to work. More importantly, when they quit, they were already alienated from their work or at least not committed to a life of work. One, a female MBA, said she could never figure out why the men at her workplace, which fired her, were so excited about making deals. "It's only money," she mused. Not surprisingly, even where employers offered them part-time work, they were not interested in taking it.

The Failure of Choice Feminism

What is going on? Most women hope to marry and have babies. If they resist the traditional female responsibilities of child rearing and householding, what Arlie Hochschild called "the second shift," they are fixing for a fight. But elite women aren't resisting tradition. None of the stay-at-home brides I interviewed saw the second shift as unjust; they agree that the household is women's work. As one lawyer-bride put it in explaining her decision to quit practicing law after four years, "I had a wedding to plan." Another, an Ivy Leaguer with a master's degree, described it in management terms: "He's the CEO and I'm the CFO. He sees to it that the money rolls in, and I decide how to spend it." It's their work, and they must do it perfectly. "We're all in here making fresh apple pie," said one, explaining her reluctance to leave her daughters in order to be interviewed. The family CFO described her activities at home: "I take my [3-year-old] daughter to all the major museums. We go to little movement classes."

Conservatives contend that the dropouts prove that feminism "failed" because it was too radical, because women didn't want what feminism had to offer. In fact, if half or more of feminism's heirs (85 percent of the women in my *Times* sample), are not working seriously, it's because feminism wasn't radical enough: It changed the workplace, but it didn't change men, and, more importantly, it didn't fundamentally change how women related to men.

The movement did start out radical. Betty Friedan's original call to arms compared housework to animal life. In *The Feminine Mystique* she wrote, "Vacuuming the living room floor—with or without makeup—is not work that takes enough thought or energy to challenge any woman's full capacity. . . . Down through the ages, man has known that he was set apart from other animals by his mind's power to have an idea, a vision, and shape the future to it . . . when he discovers and creates and shapes a future different from his past, he is a man, a human being."

Thereafter, however, liberal feminists abandoned the judgmental starting point of the movement in favor of offering women "choices." The choice talk spilled over from people trying to avoid saying "abortion," and it provided an irresistible solution to feminists trying to duck the mommy wars. A woman could work, stay home, have ten children or one, marry or stay single. It all counted as "feminist" as long as she chose it. (So dominant has the concept of choice become that when Charlotte, with a push from her insufferable first husband, quits her job, the writers at *Sex and the City* have her screaming, "I choose my choice! I choose my choice!")

Only the most radical fringes of feminism took on the issue of gender relations at home, and they put forth fruitless solutions like socialism and separatism. We know the story about socialism. Separatism ran right into heterosexuality and reproduction, to say nothing of the need to earn a living other than at a feminist bookstore. As feminist historian Alice Echols put it, "Rather than challenging their subordination in domestic life, the feminists of NOW committed themselves to fighting for women's integration into public life."

Great as liberal feminism was, once it retreated to choice, the movement had no language to use on the gendered ideology of the family. Feminists could not say, "Housekeeping and child rearing in the nuclear family is not interesting and not socially validated. Justice requires that it not be assigned to women on the basis of their gender and at the sacrifice of their access to money, power, and honor."

The 50 percent of census answerers and the 62 percent of Harvard MBAs and the 85 percent of my brides of the *Times* all think they are "choosing" their gendered lives. They don't know that feminism, in collusion with traditional society, just passed the gendered family on to them to choose. Even with all the day care in the world, the personal is still political. Much of the rest is the opt-out revolution.

What Is to Be Done?

Here's the feminist moral analysis that choice avoided: The family—with its repetitious, socially invisible, physical tasks—is a necessary part of life, but it allows fewer opportunities for full human flourishing than public spheres like the market or the government. This less-flourishing sphere is not the natural or moral responsibility only of women. Therefore, assigning it to women is unjust. Women assigning it to themselves is equally unjust. To paraphrase, as Mark Twain said, "A man who chooses not to read is just as ignorant as a man who cannot read."

The critics are right about one thing: Dopey *New York Times* stories do nothing to change the situation. Dowd, who is many things but not a political philosopher, concludes by wondering if the situation will change by 2030. Lefties keep hoping the Republicans will enact child-care legislation, which probably puts us well beyond 2030. In either case, we can't wait that long. If women's flourishing does matter, feminists must acknowledge that the family is to 2005 what the workplace was to 1964 and the vote to 1920. Like the right to work and the right to vote, the right to have a flourishing life that includes but is not limited to family cannot be addressed with language of choice.

Women who want to have sex and children with men, as well as good work in interesting jobs, where they may occasionally wield real social power, need guidance, and they need it early. Step one is simply to begin talking about flourishing. In so doing, feminism will be returning to its early, judgmental roots. This may anger some, but it should sound the alarm before the next generation winds up in the same situation. Next, feminists will have to start offering young women not choices and not utopian dreams but solutions they can enact on their own. Prying women out of their traditional roles is not going to be easy. It will require rules—rules like those in the widely derided book *The Rules*, which was never about dating but about behavior modification.

There are three rules: prepare yourself to qualify for good work, treat work seriously, and don't put yourself in a position of unequal resources when you marry.

The preparation stage begins with college. It is shocking to think that girls cut off their options for a public life of work as early as college. But they do. The first pitfall is the liberal arts curriculum, which women are good at, graduating in higher numbers than men. Although many really successful people start out studying liberal arts, the purpose of a liberal education is not, with the exception of a miniscule number of academic positions, job preparation.

So the first rule is to use your college education with an eye to career goals. Feminist organizations should produce each year a survey of the most common job opportunities for people with college degrees, along with the average lifetime earnings from each job category and the characteristics such jobs require. The point here is to help women see that yes, you can study art history, but only with the realistic understanding that one day soon you will need to use your arts education to support yourself and your family. The survey would ask young women to select what they are best suited for and give guidance on the appropriate course of study. Like the rule about accepting no dates for Saturday after Wednesday night, the survey would set realistic courses for women, helping would-be curators who are not artistic geniuses avoid career frustration and avoid solving their job problems with marriage.

After college comes on-the-job training or further education. Many of my *Times* brides—and grooms—did work when they finished their educations. Here's an anecdote about the difference: One couple, both lawyers, met at a firm. After a few years, the man moved from international business law into international business. The woman quit working altogether. "They told me law school could train you for anything," she told me. "But it doesn't prepare you to go into business. I should have gone to business school." Or rolled over and watched her husband the lawyer using his first few years of work to prepare to go into a related business. Every *Times* groom assumed he had to succeed in business and was really trying. By contrast, a common thread among the women I interviewed was a self-important idealism about the kinds of intellectual, prestigious, socially meaningful, politics-free jobs worth their incalculably valuable presence. So the second rule is that women must treat the first few years after college as an opportunity to lose their capitalism virginity and prepare for good work, which they will then treat seriously.

The best way to treat work seriously is to find the money. Money is the marker of success in a market economy; it usually accompanies power, and it enables the bearer to wield power, including within the family. Almost without exception, the brides who opted out graduated with roughly the same degrees as their husbands. Yet somewhere along the way, the women made decisions in the direction of less money. Part of the problem was idealism; idealism on the career trail usually leads to volunteer work, or indentured servitude in social-service jobs, which is nice but doesn't get you to money. Another big mistake involved changing jobs excessively. Without exception, the brides who eventually went home had much more job turnover than the grooms did. There's no such thing as a perfect job. Condoleezza Rice actually wanted to be a pianist, and Gary Graffman didn't want to give concerts.

If you are good at work, you are in a position to address the third undertaking: the reproductive household. The rule here is to avoid taking on more than a fair share of the second shift. If this seems coldhearted, consider the survey by the Center for Work–Life Policy. Fully 40 percent of highly qualified women with spouses felt that their husbands create more work around the house than they perform. According to Phyllis Moen and Patricia Roehling's *Career Mystique*, "When couples marry, the amount of time that a woman spends doing housework increases by approximately 17 percent, while a man's decreases by 33 percent." Not a single *Times* groom was a stay-at-home dad. Several of them could hardly wait for Monday morning to come. None of my *Times* grooms took even brief paternity leave when his children were born.

How to avoid this kind of rut? You can either find a spouse with less social power than you or find one with an ideological commitment to gender equality. Taking the easier path first, marry down. Don't think of this as brutally strategic. If you are devoted to your career goals and would like a man who will support that, you're just doing what men throughout the ages have done: placing a safe bet.

In her 1995 book, *Kidding Ourselves: Babies, Breadwinning, and Bargaining Power*, Rhona Mahoney recommended finding a sharing spouse by marrying younger or poorer, or someone in a dependent status, like a starving artist. Because money is such a marker of status and power, it's hard to persuade women to marry poorer. So here's an easier rule: Marry young or marry much older. Younger men are potential high-status companions. Much older men are sufficiently established so that they don't have to work so hard, and they often have enough money to provide unlimited household help. By contrast, slightly older men with bigger incomes are the most dangerous, but even a pure counterpart is risky. If you both are going through the elite-job hazing rituals simultaneously while having children, someone is going to have to give. Even the most devoted lawyers with the hardest-working nannies are going to have weeks when no one can get home other than to sleep. The odds are that when this happens, the woman is going to give up her ambitions and professional potential.

It is possible that marrying a liberal might be the better course. After all, conservatives justified the unequal family in two modes: "God ordained it" and "biology is destiny." Most men (and most women), including the liberals, think women are responsible for the home. But at least the liberal men should feel squeamish about it.

If you have carefully positioned yourself either by marrying down or finding someone untainted by gender ideology, you will be in a position to resist bearing an unfair share of the family. Even then you must be vigilant. Bad deals come in two forms: economics and home economics. The economic temptation is to assign the cost of child care to the woman's income. If a woman making $50,000 per year whose husband makes $100,000 decides to have a baby, and the cost of a full-time nanny is $30,000, the couple reason that, after paying 40 percent in taxes, she makes $30,000, just enough to pay the nanny. So she might as well stay home. This totally ignores that both adults are in the enterprise together and the demonstrable future loss of income, power, and security for the woman who quits. Instead, calculate that all parents make a total of $150,000 and take home $90,000. After paying a full-time nanny, they have $60,000 left to live on.

The home-economics trap involves superior female knowledge and superior female sanitation. The solutions are ignorance and dust. Never figure out where the butter is. "Where's the butter?" Nora Ephron's legendary riff on marriage begins. In it, a man asks the question when looking directly at the butter container in the refrigerator. "Where's the butter?" actually means butter my toast, buy the butter, remember when we're out of butter. Next thing you know you're quitting your job at the law firm, because you're so busy managing the butter. If women never start playing the household-manager role, the house will be dirty, but the realities of the physical world will trump the pull of gender ideology. Either the other adult in the family will take a hand, or the children will grow up with robust immune systems.

If these prescriptions sound less than family-friendly, here's the last rule: Have a baby. Just don't have two. Mothers' Movement Online's Judith Statdman Tucker reports that women who opt out for child-care reasons act only after the second child arrives. A second kid pressures the mother's organizational skills, doubles the demands for appointments, wildly raises the cost of education and housing, and drives the family to the suburbs. But cities, with their Chinese carryouts and all, are better for working mothers. It is true that if you follow this rule, your society will not reproduce itself. But if things get bad enough, who knows what social consequences will ensue? After all, the vaunted French child-care regime was actually only a response to the superior German birth rate.

Why Do We Care?

The privileged brides of the *Times*—and their husbands—seem happy. Why do we care what they do? After all, most people aren't rich and white and heterosexual, and they couldn't quit working if they wanted to.

We care because what they do is bad for them, is certainly bad for society, and is widely imitated, even by people who never get their weddings in the *Times*. This last is called the "regime effect," and it means that even if women don't quit their jobs for their families, they think they should and feel guilty about not doing it. That regime effect created the mystique around *The Feminine Mystique,* too.

As for society, elites supply the labor for the decision-making classes—the senators, the newspaper editors, the research scientists, the entrepreneurs, the policy-makers, and the policy wonks. If the ruling class is overwhelmingly male, the rulers will make mistakes that benefit males, whether from ignorance or from indifference. Media surveys reveal that if only one member of a television show's creative staff is female, the percentage of women on-screen goes up from 36 percent to 42 percent. A world of 84 percent male lawyers and 84 percent female assistants is a different place than one with women in positions of social authority. Think of a big American city with an 86 percent white police force. If role models don't matter, why care about Sandra Day O'Connor? Even if the falloff from peak numbers is small, the leveling off of women in power is a loss of hope for more change. Will there never again be more than one woman on the Supreme Court?

Worse, the behavior tarnishes every female with the knowledge that she is almost never going to be a ruler. Princeton President Shirley Tilghman described the elite colleges' self-image perfectly, when she told her freshmen last year that they would be the nation's leaders, and she clearly did not have trophy wives in mind. Why should society spend resources educating women with only a 50 percent return rate on their stated goals? The American Conservative Union carried a column in 2004 recommending that employers stay away from such women or risk going out of business. Good psychological data show that the more women are treated with respect, the more ambition they have. And vice versa. The opt-out revolution is really a downward spiral.

Finally, these choices are bad for women individually. A good life for humans includes the classical standard of using one's capacities for speech and reason in a prudent way, the liberal requirement of having enough autonomy to direct one's own life, and the utilitarian test of doing more good than harm in the world. Measured against these time-tested standards, the expensively educated upper-class moms will be leading lesser lives. At feminism's dawning, two theorists compared gender ideology to a caste system. To borrow their insight, these daughters of the upper classes will be bearing most of the burden of the work always associated with the lowest caste: sweeping and cleaning bodily waste. Not two weeks after the Yale flap, the *Times* ran a story of moms who were toilet training in infancy by vigilantly watching their babies for signs of excretion 24–7. They have voluntarily become untouchables.

When she sounded the blast that revived the feminist movement 40 years after women received the vote, Betty Friedan spoke of lives of purpose and meaning, better lives and worse lives, and feminism went a long way toward shattering the glass ceilings that limited their prospects outside the home. Now the glass ceiling begins at home. Although it is harder to shatter a ceiling that is also the roof over your head, there is no other choice.

The Year of Domesticity

David Brooks

After a generation of feminist advance, women have more choices. They are freer to pursue a career, stay home, or figure out some combination of both. And this is progress, right?

Wrong, says Linda Hirshman, a retired Brandeis professor, in the December issue of the *American Prospect*. Women who choose to stay home, she writes, stifle themselves and harm society. As she puts it, "The family—with its repetitious, socially invisible, physical tasks—is a necessary part of life, but it allows fewer opportunities for full human flourishing than public spheres like the market or the government."

Hirshman quotes Mark Twain, "A man who chooses not to read is just as ignorant as a man who cannot read," and argues that a woman who chooses to stay home with her kids is just as weak as a woman who can't get out of the house.

Women need to be coached to make better choices, Hirshman advises. First, they need to aim for careers that pay well: "The best way to treat work seriously is to find the money. Money is the marker of success in a market economy; it usually accompanies power, and it enables the bearer to wield power, including within the family."

Second, women need to find husbands who will share domestic drudgery equally: "You can either find a spouse with less social power than you or find one with an ideological commitment to gender equality."

Finally, she writes, "Have a baby. Just don't have two." Women with two kids find it harder to pursue a demanding career.

Women who stay home worrying about diapers have "voluntarily become untouchables," Hirshman concludes. If these women continue to make bad choices, men will perpetually dominate the highest levels of society. It is time, she says, to re-radicalize feminism.

Hirshman's essay really clears the sinuses. It's a full-bore, unapologetic blast of 1975 time-warp feminism, and it deserves one of the 2005 Sidney Awards, which I've created for the best magazine essays of the year, because it is impossible to read this manifesto without taking a few minutes to figure out why she is so wrong.

But of course, she is wrong.

First, she's wrong with her astonishing assertion that high-paying jobs lead to more human flourishing than parenthood. Look back over your life. Which memories do you cherish more, those with your family or those at the office? If Hirshman thinks high-paying careers lead to more human flourishing, I invite her to spend a day as an associate at a big law firm.

Second, she's wrong to assume that work is the realm of power and home is the realm of powerlessness. The domestic sphere may not offer the sort of brutalizing, dominating power Hirshman admires, but it is the realm of unmatched influence. If there is one thing we have learned over the past generation, it is that a child's I.Q., mental habits, and destiny are largely shaped in the first few years of life, before school or the outside world has much influence.

Children, at least, understand parental power. In "Eminem Is Right," a Sidney Award-winning essay in *Policy Review*, Mary Eberstadt notes a striking change in pop music. "If yesterday's rock was the music of abandon, today's is the music of abandonment." An astonishing number of hits, from artists ranging from Pearl Jam to Everclear to Snoop Dogg, are about kids who feel neglected by their parents. This is a need Hirshman passes over.

Her third mistake is to not even grapple with the fact that men and women are wired differently. The Larry Summers flap produced an outpouring of work on the neurological differences between men and women. I'd especially recommend "The Inequality Taboo" by Charles Murray in

Commentary and a debate between Steven Pinker and Elizabeth Spelke in the online magazine *Edge.*

One of the findings of this research is that men are more interested in things and abstract rules while women are more interested in people. (You can come up with your own Darwinian explanation as to why.)

When you look back over the essays of 2005, you find many that dealt with the big foreign policy issues of the year, but also an amazing number that dealt with domesticity. That's because the deeper you get into economic or social problems—national competitiveness, poverty, school performance, incarceration—the more you realize the answers lie with good parenting and good homes.

Hirshman has it exactly backward. Power is in the kitchen. The big problem is not the women who stay there but the men who leave.

QUESTIONS: For Thinking and Writing

1. In your opinion and experience, are women socially pressured to stay at home? Do men want them to stay home once children enter the picture?
2. Hirshman argues that when women leave the workforce, they not only put their own careers at risk, but jeopardize the economic and political power of all women who seek to achieve in high-status jobs. Do you agree or disagree with her argument? Does the "conundrum" of "opting out" put all women at risk? Why or why not?
3. Summarize Hirshman's study of the *New York Times* brides. What did she discover? What conclusions did she draw from the data? Do her conclusions have merit? Does this group of women accurately represent the female body-politic of the United States? Explain.
4. Evaluate Hirshman's recommendations for young women. Do you agree with her plan? Do you think her plan will be received differently by young women than by young men?
5. David Brooks ends his essay with a note that Hirshman has it backward, "Power is in the kitchen." What conventions does he tap into with this statement? How does his statement connect back to Hirshman's point?

QUESTIONS: For Further Research and Group Work

1. You have been asked to write an article about feminism at the beginning of the twenty-first century for inclusion in a time capsule to be opened at the beginning of the next century. Describe your own perception of feminism and include examples from popular culture and your experience. How do you think things will have changed in 100 years? Explain.

2. Thirty years ago, men were expected to earn more than women. Do we still hold such beliefs? Poll your classmates to find out their opinions regarding income status. Do males feel that they should earn more? Would they feel less masculine if their girlfriends or wives earned more then they did? Do females look for higher incomes when they consider a partner? Analyze your results and write an argument that draws conclusions from your survey and its connection to feminism in the twenty-first century.
3. Conduct a survey of men and women on the issue of women "opting out" of careers in favor of staying at home to raise their children. Interview at least 30 men and women for their views. How does your data compare to the information reported by Linda Hirshman? Is there indeed a trend among young college women to opt out of careers once they become mothers? What do men think, and what do they expect their future partners to do? Discuss your data with the rest of the class.
4. Consider the ways Hollywood influences our cultural perspectives of gender and identity. Write an essay exploring the influence, however slight, that film and television have had on your own perceptions of gender. If you wish, interview other students for their opinion on this issue, and address some of their points in your essay.
5. In your own words, define the terms "masculine" and "feminine." You might include library research on the origins of the words or research their changing implications over the years. Develop your own definition for each word, and then discuss with the rest of the class how you arrived at your definitions.
6. View the clips and read about the independent movie *Hip-Hop: Beyond Beats and Rhymes* by lifelong hip-hop fan and former college football quarterback turned activist Byron Hurt. Hurt decided to make a film about the gender politics of hip-hop, the music and the culture that he grew up with. "The more I grew and the more I learned about sexism and violence and homophobia, the more those lyrics became unacceptable to me," he says. After visiting all parts of the Web site www.pbs.org/independentlens/hiphop, prepare a presentation to the class on this issue.

CHAPTER 7

The University System

BY THE TIME YOU HAVE ENTERED THE HALLS OF YOUR college or university as a first-year student, you will have spent over 20,000 hours in school—not including the time used to complete homework or participate in extracurricular activities. Most people would agree that a good education is the key to success later in life, no matter what field they chose, and that a college education is becoming an increasingly important factor for many career paths.

The most obvious benefits of a college education are economic ones—college graduates tend to earn more than high school graduates. According to a U.S. Census Bureau report, the average adult holding a bachelor's degree will earn over a $1 million dollars more over his or her lifetime as compared to an adult holding only a high school diploma. So while the cost of a college education may seem steep at the time you enroll, the benefits are likely to extend over your lifetime.

There are other benefits, too. College graduates, and their future children, tend to enjoy better health and form stronger, more enduring social networks. They enjoy better professional opportunities and a higher quality of life overall. According to a 2002 report published by the Carnegie Foundation, the benefits of higher education include the tendency for college graduates to be "more open-minded, more cultured, more rational, more consistent, and less authoritarian; these benefits are also passed along to succeeding generations."

However, despite its many benefits, college life and a university education are often the subject of controversy. From the minute you take your PSAT as a junior in high school, the questions abound: Does everyone have the right to a college education? Should everyone go? Are admissions policies fair, and are standardized tests a true indicator of future performance and ability? Is today's college curriculum preparing students for the real world? Do the liberal arts matter? Are college campuses truly a haven for the exchange of ideas and free expression, or are some ideas more acceptable than others? And what happens if you express an unpopular point of view? This chapter examines a few of the issues facing university education today.

JEFFREY HART

How to Get a College Education

Most students arrive at college ready to learn. But what happens if they arrive completely unequipped to handle the coursework assigned, because they lack a foundation in literature and history? As senior professor Jeffrey Hart describes, many of today's freshmen cannot connect on many issues, because they don't understand the basics. In this essay, the Dartmouth professor explains how such students can still get an outstanding college education, if they keep their eye on the goal of education. This essay was published in the National Review Online *on September 29, 2006.*

It was in the fall term of 1988 that the truth burst in upon me like something had gone terribly wrong in higher education. It was like the anecdote in Auden, where the guest at a garden party, sensing something amiss, suddenly realizes that there is a corpse on the tennis court.

As a professor at Dartmouth, my hours had been taken up with my own writing and with teaching a variety of courses—a yearly seminar, a yearly freshman composition course (which—some good news—all senior professors in the Dartmouth English Department are required to teach), and courses in my eighteenth-century specialty. Oh, I knew that the larger curriculum lacked shape and purpose, that something was amiss; but I deferred thinking about it.

Yet there does come that moment.

It came for me in the freshman composition course. The students were required to write essays based upon assigned reading—in this case, some Frost poems, Hemingway's *In Our Time*, *Hamlet*. Then, almost on a whim, I assigned the first half of Allan Bloom's surprise best seller *The Closing of the American Mind.* When the time came to discuss the Bloom book, I asked them what they thought of it.

They hated it.

Oh, yes, they understood perfectly well what Bloom was saying: that they were ignorant, that they believed in clichés, that their education so far had been dangerous piffle, and that what they were about to receive was not likely to be any better.

No wonder they hated it. After all, they were the best and the brightest, Ivy Leaguers with stratospheric SAT scores, the Masters of the Universe. Who is Bloom? What is the University of Chicago, anyway?

So I launched into an impromptu oral quiz.

Could anyone (in that class of 25 students) say anything about the Mayflower Compact?

Complete silence.

John Locke?

Nope.

James Madison?

Silentia.

Magna Carta? The Spanish Armada? The Battle of Yorktown? The Bull Moose party? Don Giovanni? William James? The Tenth Amendment?

Zero. Zilch. Forget it.

The embarrassment was acute, but some good came of it. The better students, ashamed that their first 12 years of schooling had mostly been wasted (even if they had gone to Choate or Exeter), asked me to recommend some books. I offered such solid things as Samuel Eliot Morison's *Oxford History of the United States*, Max Farrand's *The Framing of the Constitution*, Jacob Burckhardt's *The Civilization of the Renaissance in Italy.* Several students asked for an informal discussion group, and so we started reading a couple of Dante's *Cantos* per week, Dante being an especially useful author, because he casts his net so widely—the ancient world, the (his) modern world, theology, history, ethics.

I quickly became aware of the utter bewilderment of entering freshmen. They emerge from the near-nullity of K–12 and stroll into the chaos of the Dartmouth curriculum, which is embodied in a course catalogue about as large as a telephone directory.

Sir, what courses should I take? A college like Dartmouth—or Harvard, Princeton, et cetera—has requirements so broadly defined that almost anything goes for degree credit. Of course, freshmen are assigned faculty "advisors," but most of them would rather return to the library or the Bunsen burner.

Thus it developed that I began giving an annual lecture to incoming freshmen on the subject, "What Is a College Education? And How to Get One, Even at Dartmouth."

One long-term reason why the undergraduate curriculum at Dartmouth and all comparable institutions is in chaos is specialization. Since World War II, success as a professor has depended increasingly on specialized publication. The ambitious and talented professor is not eager to give introductory or general courses. Indeed, his work has little or nothing to do with undergraduate teaching. Neither Socrates nor Jesus, who published nothing, could possibly receive tenure at a first-line university today.

But in addition to specialization, recent intellectual fads have done extraordinary damage, viz.:

- So-called postmodernist thought ("deconstruction," etc.) asserts that one "text" is as much worth analyzing as any other, whether it be a movie, a comic book, or Homer. The lack of a "canon" of important works leads to course offerings in, literally, anything.
- "Affirmative Action" is not just a matter of skewed admissions and hiring, but also a mentality or ethos. That is, if diversity is more important than quality in admissions and hiring, why should it not be so in the curriculum? Hence the courses in things like Nicaraguan Lesbian Poetry.

Concomitantly, ideology has been imposed on the curriculum to a startling degree. In part this represents a sentimental attempt to resuscitate Marxism, with assorted victim groups standing in for the old proletariat; in part it is a new identity politics in which being black, lesbian, Latino, homosexual, radical feminist, and so forth takes precedence over any scholarly pursuit. These victimologies are usually presented as "studies" programs outside the regular departments, so as to avoid the usual academic standards. Yet their course offerings carry degree credit.

On an optimistic note, I think that most or all of postmodernism, the affirmative action/multicultural ethos, and the victimologies will soon pass from the scene. The great institutions have a certain sense of self-preservation. Harvard almost lost its Law School to a

Marxist faculty faction, but then cleaned house. Tenure will keep the dead men walking for another 20 years or so, but then we will have done with them.

But for the time being, what these fads have done to the liberal arts and social sciences curriculum since around 1968 is to clutter it with all sorts of nonsense, nescience, and distraction. The entering student needs to be wary lest he waste his time and his parents' money and come to consider all higher education an outrageous fraud. The good news is that the wise student can still get a college education today, even at Dartmouth, Harvard, Yale, and Princeton.

Of course, the central question is one of *telos*, or goal. What is the liberal arts education supposed to produce? Once you have the answer to this question, course selection becomes easy.

I mean to answer that question here. But first, I find that undergraduates and their third-mortgaged parents appreciate some practical tips, such as:

Select the "ordinary" courses. I use *ordinary* here in a paradoxical and challenging way. An ordinary course is one that has always been taken and obviously should be taken—even if the student is not yet equipped with a sophisticated rationale for so doing. The student should be discouraged from putting his money on the cutting edge of interdisciplinary cross-textuality.

Thus, do take American and European history, an introduction to philosophy, American and European literature, the Old and New Testaments, and at least one modern language. It would be absurd not to take a course in Shakespeare, the best poet in our language. There is art and music history. The list can be expanded, but these areas every educated person should have a decent knowledge of—with specialization coming later on.

I hasten to add that I applaud the student who devotes his life to the history of China or Islam, but that too should come later. America is part of the narrative of European history.

If the student should seek out those "ordinary" courses, then it follows that he should avoid the flashy come-ons. Avoid things like Nicaraguan Lesbian Poets. Yes, and anything listed under "studies," any course whose description uses the words "interdisciplinary," "hegemonic," "phallocratic," or "empowerment," anything that mentions "keeping a diary," any course with a title like "Adventures in Film."

Also, any male professor who comes to class without a jacket and tie should be regarded with extreme prejudice, unless he has won a Nobel Prize.

All these are useful rules of thumb. A theoretical rationale for a liberal arts education, however, derives from that telos mentioned above. What is such an education supposed to produce?

A philosophy professor I studied with as an undergraduate had two phrases he repeated so often that they stay in the mind, a technique made famous by Matthew Arnold.

He would say, "History must be told."

History, he explained, is to a civilization what memory is to an individual, an irreducible part of identity.

He also said, "The goal of education is to produce the citizen." He defined the citizen as the person who, if need be, could re-create his civilization.

Now, it is said that Goethe was the last man who knew all the aspects of his civilization (I doubt that he did), but that after him, things became too complicated. My professor had something different in mind. He meant that the citizen should know the great themes of his civilization, its important areas of thought, its philosophical and religious controversies, the outline of its history, and its major works. The citizen need not know quantum physics, but he should know that it is there and what it means. Once the citizen knows the shape, the narrative, of his civilization, he is able to locate new things—and other civilizations—in relation to it.

The narrative of Western civilization can be told in different ways, but a useful paradigm has often been called "Athens and Jerusalem." Broadly construed, "Athens" means a philosophical and scientific view of actuality and "Jerusalem" a spiritual and scriptural one. The working out of Western civilization represents an interaction—tension, fusion, conflict—between the two.

Both Athens and Jerusalem have a heroic, or epic, phase. For Athens, the Homeric poems are a kind of scripture, the subject of prolonged ethical meditation. In time the old heroic ideals are internalized as heroic philosophy in Socrates, Plato, and Aristotle.

For Jerusalem, the heroic phase consists of the Hebrew narratives. Here again, a process of internalization occurs, Jesus internalizing the Mosaic Law. Socrates is the heroic philosopher, Jesus the ideal of heroic holiness, both new ideals in their striking intensity.

During the first century of the Christian Era, Athens and Jerusalem converge under the auspices of Hellenistic thought, most notably in Paul and in John, whose gospel defined Jesus by using the Greek term for order, *logos.*

Athens and Jerusalem were able to converge, despite great differences, because in some ways they overlap. The ultimate terms of Socrates and Plato, for example, cannot be entirely derived from reason. The god of Plato and Aristotle is monotheistic, though still the god of the philosophers. Yet Socrates considers that his rational universe dictates personal immortality.

In the Hebrew epic, there are hints of a law prior to the law of revelation and derived from reason. Thus, when Abraham argues with God over the fate of Sodom and Gomorrah, Abraham appeals to a known principle of justice, which God also assumes.

Thus, Athens is not pure reason and Jerusalem is not pure revelation. Both address the perennial question of why there is something rather than nothing.

From the prehistoric figures in Homer and in Genesis—Achilles, Abraham—the great conversation commences. Thucydides and Virgil seek order in history. St. Augustine tries to synthesize Paul and Platonism. Montaigne's skepticism would never have been articulated without a prior assertion of cosmic order. Erasmus believed Christianity would prevail if only it could be put in the purest Latin. Shakespeare made a world, and transcended Lear's storm with that final calmed and sacramental Tempest. Rousseau would not have proclaimed the goodness of man if Calvin had not said the opposite. Dante held all the contradictions together in a total structure—for a glorious moment. Kafka could not see beyond the edges of his nightmare, but Dostoyevsky found love just beyond the lowest point of sin. The eighteenth-century men of reason knew the worst, and settled for the luminous stability of a bourgeois republic.

By any intelligible standard, the other great civilization was China, yet it lacked the Athens–Jerusalem tension and dynamism. Much more static, its symbols were the Great Wall and the Forbidden City, not Odysseus/Columbus, Chartres, the Empire State Building, the love that moves the sun and the other stars.

When undergraduates encounter the material of our civilization—that is, the liberal arts—then they know that they are going somewhere. They are becoming citizens.

QUESTIONS: For Thinking and Writing

1. What does Hart's use of language and his style of writing reveal about his own education? What expectations does he have of his audience?
2. Does Hart's background as a professor at Dartmouth make him an expert on this issue? Why or why not? How much does his argument rely on the reader's acceptance of his authority on this issue?
3. Take the impromptu quiz Hart poses to his students. How many of the things he cites did you know at least something about? Do not look up

   The Mayflower Compact — The Bull Moose Party
   John Locke — Don Giovanni
   The Magna Carta — William James
   The Spanish Armada — The Tenth Amendment
   The Battle of Yorktown

   any of the items on the list before answering the question.
4. Based on your responses to question three, and learning their subsequent answers (your instructor will provide answers, but you can look them up in advance), how relevant do you think the issues on the list are to your ability to get a good college education? Explain.
5. Hart mentions the bewilderment of college freshman upon embarking on a college curriculum. What courses should you take? Describe your own experience as a new freshman. What guidance did you receive? How confident were you on your course selection? How happy are you with your current course load? Do you feel comfortable, or confused, as Hart describes in his essay?

ALICIA C. SHEPARD

A's for Everyone!

In an era of rampant grade inflation, some college students find it shocking to discover there are five letters in the grading system. It used to be that earning a B *in a course was cause for celebration. But across college campuses nationwide, many students argue that an* A *is the only acceptable grade. Increasingly, students are arguing with their professors to raise lower grades to higher ones, urging professors to consider "hard work," rather than skill, talent, and performance, as the reason for an* A *grade. Today's parents are also putting pressure on their children to achieve high grades, adding to student anxieties. In this next essay, professor Alicia C. Shepard describes in an editorial, published in the June 5, 2005 edition of the* Washington Post, *this trend from the perspective of a teacher and as a parent.*

It was the end of my first semester teaching journalism at American University. The students had left for winter break. As a rookie professor, I sat with trepidation in my office on a December day to electronically post my final grades.

My concern was more about completing the process correctly than anything else. It took an hour to compute and type in the grades for three classes, and then I hit "enter." That's when the trouble started.

In less than an hour, two students challenged me. Mind you, there had been no preset posting time. They had just been religiously checking the electronic bulletin board that many colleges now use.

"Why was I given a *B* as my final grade?" demanded a reporting student via e-mail. "Please respond ASAP, as I have never received a *B* during my career here at AU, and it will surely lower my GPA."

I must say I was floored. Where did this kid get the audacity to so boldly challenge a professor? And why did he care so much? Did he really think a prospective employer was going to ask for his GPA?

I checked the grades I'd meticulously kept on the electronic blackboard. He'd missed three quizzes and gotten an 85 on two of the three main writing assignments. There was no way he was *A* material. I let the grade mar his GPA, because he hadn't done the required work.

I wasn't so firm with my other challenger. She tracked me down by phone while I was still in my office. She wanted to know why she'd received a *B*-plus. Basically, it was because she'd barely said a word in class, so the *B*-plus was subjective. She harangued me until, I'm ashamed to admit, I agreed to change her grade to an *A*-minus. At the time, I thought, "Geez, if it means that much to you, I'll change it." She thanked me profusely, encouraging me to have a happy holiday.

Little did I know the pressure was just beginning.

The students were relentless. During the spring semester, they showed up at my office to insist I reread their papers and boost their grades. They asked to retake tests they hadn't done well on. They bombarded me with e-mails questioning grades. More harassed me to change their final grade. I began to wonder if I was doing something wrong, sending out some sort of newbie signal that I could be pushed around. Then I talked to other professors in the School of Communication. They all had stories.

My colleague Wendy Swallow told me about one student who had managed to sour her Christmas break one year. Despite gaining entry into AU's honors program, the student missed assignments in Swallow's newswriting class and slept through her midterm. Slept through her midterm! Then she begged for lenience.

"I let her take it again for a reduced grade," Swallow says, "but with the warning that if she skipped more classes or missed more deadlines, the midterm grade would revert to the *F* she earned by missing it. She then skipped the last three classes of the semester and turned in all her remaining assignments late. She even showed up late for her final."

Swallow gave the student a C-minus, which meant she was booted out of the honors program. The student was shocked. She called Swallow at home, hysterical about being dropped from the program. To Swallow, the C-minus was a gift. To the student, an undeserved lump of Christmas coal.

"She pestered me for several days by phone," says Swallow, who did not relent and suggested the student file a formal grievance. She didn't. "The whole exchange, though, made for a very unpleasant break. Now I wait to post my grades until the last minute before leaving for the semester, as by then most of the students are gone, and I'm less likely to get those instantaneous complaints."

Another colleague told me about a student she had failed. "He came back after the summer, trying to convince me to pass him because other professors just gave him a C," says Leena Jayaswal, who teaches photography. Never mind that he didn't do her required work.

John Watson, who teaches journalism ethics and communications law at American, has noticed another phenomenon: Many students, he says, believe that simply working hard—though not necessarily doing excellent work—entitles them to an *A*. "I can't tell you how many times I've heard a student dispute a grade, not on the basis of in-class performance," says Watson, "but on the basis of how hard they tried. I appreciate the effort, and it always produces positive results, but not always the exact results the student wants. We all have different levels of talent."

It's a concept that many students (and their parents) have a hard time grasping. Working hard, especially the night before a test or a paper due date, does not necessarily produce good grades.

"At the age of 50, if I work extremely hard, I can run a mile in eight minutes," says Watson. "I have students who can jog through a mile in seven minutes and barely sweat. They will always finish before me and that's not fair. Or is it?"

Last September, AU's Center for Teaching Excellence hosted a lunchtime forum to provide faculty members tips on how to reduce stressful grade confrontations. I eagerly attended.

The advice we were given was solid: Be clear up front about how you grade and what is expected, and, when possible, use a numerical grading system rather than letter grades. If the grade is an 89, write that on the paper rather than a *B*-plus.

"The key," said AU academic counselor Jack Ramsay, "is to have a system of grading that is as transparent as possible."

Yet even the most transparent grading system won't eliminate our students' desperate pursuit of *A*'s. Of the 20 teachers who came to the session, most could offer some tale of grade harassment.

"Most of the complaints that colleagues tell me about come from *B* students," said James Mooney, special assistant to the dean for academic affairs in the College of Arts and Sciences. "They all want to know why they didn't get an *A*. Is there something wrong with a *B*?"

Apparently there is. "Certainly there are students who are victims of grade inflation in secondary school," said Mooney. "They come to college, and the grading system is much more rigorous. That's one of the most difficult things to convey to the students. If you're getting a *B*, you're doing well in a course."

But his interpretation is rarely accepted by students or their parents. And the pressure on professors to keep the *A*'s coming isn't unique to AU. It's endemic to college life, according to Stuart Rojstaczer, a Duke University professor who runs a Web site called Gradeinflation.com. At Duke and many other colleges, *A*'s outnumber *B*'s, and *C*'s have all but disappeared from student transcripts, his research shows.

Last spring, professors at Princeton University declared war on grade inflation, voting to slash the number of *A*'s they award to 25 percent of all grades. At Harvard, where half of the grades awarded are *A*'s, the university announced that it would cut the number of seniors graduating with honors from 91 percent to about 50 percent.

Despite those moves, Rojstaczer doesn't think it will be easy to reverse the rising tide of *A*'s. He points out that in 1969, a quarter of the grades handed out at Duke were *C*'s. By 2002, the number of *C*'s had dropped to less than 10 percent.

Rojstaczer, who teaches environmental science, acknowledged in an op-ed piece he wrote for the *Post* two years ago that he rarely hands out C's, "and neither do most of my colleagues. And I can easily imagine a time when I'll say the same thing about *B*'s."

Arthur Levine, president of Columbia University Teacher's College and an authority on grading, traces what's going on to the Vietnam War. "Men who got low grades could be drafted," Levine says. "The next piece was the spread of graduate schools where only *A*'s and *B*'s were passing grades. That soon got passed on to undergraduates and set the standard."

And then there's consumerism, he says. Pure and simple, tuition at a private college runs, on average, nearly $28,000 a year. If parents pay that much, they expect nothing less than *A*'s in return. "Therefore, if the teacher gives you a *B*, that's not acceptable," says Levine, "because the teacher works for you. I expect *A*'s, and if I'm getting *B*'s, I'm not getting my money's worth."

Rojstaczer agrees: "We've made a transition where attending college is no longer a privilege and an honor; instead, college is a consumer product. One of the negative aspects of this transition is that the role of a college-level teacher has been transformed into that of a service employee."

Levine argues that we "service employees" are doing students a disservice if we cave in to the demand for top grades. "One of the things an education should do is let you know what you do well in and what you don't," he says. "If everybody gets high grades, you don't learn that."

But, as I'd already seen, many students aren't interested in learning that lesson—and neither are their parents. When AU administrator James Mooney polled professors about grade complaints, he was appalled to learn that some overwrought parents call professors directly to complain. "One colleague told me he got a call from the mother of his student and she introduced herself by saying that she and her husband were both attorneys," said Mooney. "He thought it was meant to intimidate him."

Though I haven't received any menacing phone calls from parents, Mom and Dad are clearly fueling my students' relentless demand for *A*'s. It's a learned behavior. I know, because I'm guilty of inflicting on my son the same grade pressure that now plays out before me as a university professor.

Last fall when my Arlington high school senior finally got the nerve to tell me that he'd gotten a C in the first quarter of his AP English class, I did what any self-respecting, grade-obsessed parent whose son is applying to college would do. I cried. Then I e-mailed his teacher and made an appointment for the three of us to meet. My son's teacher was accommodating. She agreed that if my son did *A* work for the second quarter, colleges would see a *B* average for the two quarters, not that ruinous C.

There's a term for the legions of parents like me. The parents who make sure to get the teacher's e-mail and home phone number on Back to School Night. The kind who e-mail teachers when their child fails a quiz. The kind who apply the same determination to making sure their child excels academically that they apply to the professional world.

We are called "helicopter parents," because we hover over everything our kids do like Secret Service agents guarding the president. (My son refers to me as an Apache attack helicopter, and he's Fallujah under siege.) Only we aren't worried about our kids getting taken out by wild-eyed assassins. We just want them to get into a "good" (whatever that means) college.

"Parents today have this intense investment in seeing their kids do well in school," says Peter Stearns, provost at George Mason University and author of *Anxious Parenting: A History of Modern Child Rearing in America*. "This translates into teachers feeling direct and indirect pressure to keep parents off their backs by handing out reasonably favorable grades and making other modifications, like having up to 18 valedictorians."

High school administrators who haven't made those modifications sometimes find themselves defending their grading policies in court. Two years ago, a senior at New Jersey's Moorestown High School filed a $2.7 million lawsuit after she was told she'd have to share being valedictorian with another high-achieving student. A similar episode occurred in Michigan, where a Memphis High School senior who'd just missed being valedictorian claimed in a lawsuit that one of his *A*'s should have been an *A*-plus.

That hyperconcern about grades and class rankings doesn't disappear when kids finally pack for college. Along with their laptops and cell phones, these students bring along the parental anxiety and pressure they've lived with for 18 years.

One of my students, Rachael Scorca, says that her parents have always used good grades as an incentive. And they've continued to do so during college. "In high school, my social life and curfew revolved around *A*'s," explains Scorca, a broadcast journalism major. "I needed over a 90 average in order to go out during the week and keep my curfew as late as it was. Once college came and my parents couldn't control my hours or effort, they started controlling my bank account. If I wasn't getting good grades, they wouldn't put money in my account, and, therefore, I wouldn't have a social life."

But most of my students tell me the pressure to get top grades doesn't come from their parents any longer. They've internalized it. "I'd say most of the pressure just comes from my personal standards," says Molly Doyle. "It's also something I take pride in. When people ask me how my grades are, I like being able to tell them that I've got all *A*'s and *B*'s."

During my second semester of teaching, I received this e-mail from a student who'd taken my fall class on "How the News Media Shape History" and wasn't satisfied with his grade. He (unsuccessfully) tried bribery.

"Professor. I checked my grade once I got here and it is a *B*," he wrote. "I have to score a grade better than a *B+* to keep my scholarship, and I have no idea how I ended up with a *B*. In addition to that, I have brought you something from The GREAT INDIAN CONTINENT."

I invited him to come to my office, so I could explain why he'd gotten a *B*, but after several broken appointments, he faded away.

Other students were more persistent, particularly a bright young man who'd been in the same class as the briber. He'd gotten an *A*-minus and made it clear in an e-mail he wasn't happy with it: "I have seen a number of the students from the class, and we inevitably got to talking about it. I had assumed that you are a tough grader and that earning an *A*-minus from you was a difficult task, but upon talking to other students, it appears that that grade was handed out more readily than I had thought. Not that other students did not deserve a mark of that caliber, but I do feel as though I added a great deal to the class. I feel that my work, class participation, and consistency should have qualified me for a solid *A*."

When I ignored the e-mail, he pestered me a second time: "I know it's a great pain in the ass to have an *A*-minus student complain, but I'm starting to wonder about the way grades are given. I would be very curious to know who the *A* students were. While other students may have outdone me with quiz grades, I made up for it with participation and enthusiasm. I really feel that I deserved an *A* in your class. If I was an *A*-minus student, I assume that you must have handed out a lot of *C*s and *D*s. I don't mean to be a pain—I have never contested anything before. I feel strongly about this, though."

I shouldn't have done it, but I offered to change the grade. My student was thrilled. He wrote, "With grade inflation being what it is, and the levels of competition being so high, students just can't afford to be hurt by small things. I thought that you did a great job with the course."

But when I completed the required paperwork, the grade change was rejected by a university official. Though no one questioned me the first time I did it, grades can be changed only if they are computed incorrectly. "How fair is it to change his grade?" an assistant dean asked me. "What about other kids who might be unhappy but didn't complain?"

I e-mailed my student to let him know that he would have to live with an *A*-minus. "The gods who make these decisions tell me that they rejected it because it's not considered fair to all the other students in the class," I wrote. "The grade you got was based on a numerical formula, and you can only change a grade if you made a mathematical error. I'm sorry."

"That seems illogical to me," he e-mailed back. "If a student feels that a grade was inappropriate and wishes to contest that grade, that student obviously must contact the person who gave it to them. Who was I supposed to contact? What was the process that I was to follow? The lack of logic in all this never fails to amaze me!"

I told him whom to contact. I'm not sure if he ever followed through, but I saw him recently and he smiled and stopped to talk. Nothing was mentioned about the grade.

The day before this spring semester's grades were due, I bumped into another professor racing out of the building. What's the hurry? I asked.

She told me she had just posted her grades and wanted to get off campus fast. But she wasn't quick enough. Within eight minutes, a *B*-minus student had called to complain.

A few hours after I entered my final grades, I got an e-mail from a student, at 1:44 AM. She was unhappy with her *B*. She worked so hard, she told me. This time, though, I was prepared. I had the numbers to back me up, and I wouldn't budge on her grade. No more Professor Softie.

QUESTIONS: For Thinking and Writing

1. Professor Shepard is shocked that a student would challenge the grade she assigned. Have you ever felt that a grade you received was unfair? If so, did you ask your professor for clarification? Did you challenge the professor to change it? Explain.
2. The author changes one grade after the student challenges the subjective nature of class participation. Should class participation be a factor in grade determination? Why or why not?
3. In your opinion, what is a "good grade" and why?
4. Professor Watson notes that many students believe that "working hard" should carry weight when factoring grades. What do you think? Is this a fair system? What is the line between talent and product and effort and earnestness? For example, if writing comes easily to you, and you excel in it, do you deserve a lower grade than someone who works twice as hard but writes half as well?
5. How important are grades? Write a short persuasive essay in which you argue either for or against grading systems in higher education.

JOHN H. MCWHORTER

Who Should Get into College?

In 2003, the Supreme Court sided with the University of Michigan's admissions officers on the right to use race-based admission policies, which often involve different sets of admission criteria for minority students. Most of the arguments for and against race-based admissions hinge on fairness, with supporters claiming that inequalities in education put black students at a disadvantage and detractors claiming that such policies are unfair to white students as well as blacks. Following the Supreme Court's decision, then-Justice Sandra Day O'Connor noted her hope that "25 years from now the use of racial preferences will no longer be necessary." In the next essay, Manhattan Institute scholar John H. McWhorter challenges the practice of race-based admission policies. He says that not only are they unnecessary today, they're actually hurting the people they're supposed to help. His essay appears in the Spring 2003 issue of City Journal.

For many years now, elite colleges—taking their cue from the Supreme Court's 1978 Bakke decision—have justified racial preferences in admissions by saying that they are necessary to ensure campus "diversity." Get rid of preferences, "diversity" fans say, and top colleges will become minority-free enclaves; the spirit of segregation will be on the march again. The losers won't just be the folks with the brown pigmentation, now exiled from the good schools, but all those white students who now will never get to know the unique perspective of people of color.

Nonsense on all counts. Correctly understood, diversity encompasses the marvelous varieties of human excellence and vision in a modern civilization—from musical genius to civic commitment to big-brained science wizardry. People who recognize the folly of racial preferences are no more opposed to diversity in this sense than critics of "gangsta" rap are opposed to music. What they do reject is the condescending notion that a diverse campus demands lower admissions standards for brown students, and that, in 2003 America, brown students need crutches to make it.

With the Supreme Court about to decide a case that could overturn Bakke and require color-blind admissions, once and for all, it's a good time to describe what a post-affirmative-action admissions policy at a top school should look like—and explain why it would be fully compatible with minority success and real diversity.

The raison d'être of the nation's selective universities, at least from the standpoint of the public interest, is to forge a well-educated, national elite. Thus, our post-preferences approach to admissions must be meritocratic. But few people would want schools simply to choose students with the very best SAT scores and grades and call it a day. The image of elite campuses populated solely by 1,600-SAT-scoring Ken Lays or Sam Waksalls, of whatever color, is unappealing.

Back in the early 1980s, at Simon's Rock Early College in Massachusetts, a smattering of my classmates fell into the 1,600 category. But thankfully, the school's administrators grasped that that kind of achievement represents only one of the forms of excellence that smart young people can bring to campus life. The school worked hard to attract a lively mix of students, who vastly enriched my years on campus. My cello playing, for example, took on new depth, because I had the opportunity to play with a brilliant musician whose talents on piano and violin scaled near-professional heights. A roommate was a splendid stage performer, and marinating (unwillingly at first) in his favorite music and historical anecdotes opened up a universe of vintage American popular music and theater that has been part of my life ever since.

At school, I also met my first Mennonite and my first white Southerner—there is no better way to get past a native sense of an accent as "funny," I discovered, than living with someone who speaks with one. There were other blacks among the school's 300 or so students, too. Most, like me, were middle-class kids, but there was one guy who had grown up in crumbling Camden, New Jersey. This student gave a lesson in one form of cultural "blackness" to his white classmates—he had real "street" cred. But far more important, after a rocky start and some coaching, he also proved he could do the schoolwork on the high level the school demanded.

This was real diversity—the full panoply of human variation, not just the tiny, superficial sliver of it represented by skin pigmentation. And Simon's Rock fostered it without surrendering academic standards.

Since my undergraduate days, however, elite universities have come to mean something much different when they speak of "diversity": having as many brown faces on campus as possible, regardless of standards. The origin of the current notion of "diversity," Peter Wood shows in his masterful *Diversity: The Invention of a Concept*, was Justice Lewis Powell's opinion for the court in Bakke. Though strict racial quotas were unconstitutional, Powell argued, schools could still use race as an "important element" in admissions in order to create a "diverse" campus that would enhance the quality of all students' educational experiences by exposing them to minority "opinions."

Powell's argument was, in Wood's terms, a "self-contradictory mess." How, after all, does one make race an "important" factor in admissions while avoiding quotas? It was also dishonest, in that it wasn't at bottom about broadening white students' horizons but providing a rationale for admitting blacks and Hispanics much less qualified than other applicants. The decision has encouraged the Orwellian mindset by which the University of Michigan Law School can defend its admissions process, 234 times more likely to admit black applicants than similarly credentialed whites, as an expression of "diversity," not the obvious quota system it really is.

Even on its own terms, Powell's "diversity" argument is demeaning and offensive to minorities. What would be a black "opinion" on French irregular verbs? Or systolic pressure? The "black" views that most interest diversity advocates, of course, are those that illumine social injustice. But in my experience, white and Asian students are at least as likely to voice such PC opinions—often picked up in multiculturalism workshops when they first hit campus.

Diversity supporters sometimes reverse themselves 180 degrees and say that race preferences are necessary to show white students that there's no such thing as a "black" viewpoint. "By seeing firsthand that all black or Hispanic students in their classes do not act or think alike," argues Jonathan Alger, counsel for the American Association of University Professors, "white students can overcome learned prejudices." One can only hope that a warm corner of hell awaits anyone who would subject a race to lowered standards for a reason so callow.

Black students understandably can find this whole diversity regime repugnant and even racist. "Professor McWhorter," students have asked me, "what about when I am called on for my opinion as a black person in class? Is it fair that I have to deal with that burden?" A continent away, the undergraduate-written *Black Guide to Life at Harvard* insists: "We are not here to provide diversity training for Kate or Timmy before they go out to take over the world." Indeed, students in general are skeptical of the value of "diversity": a recent survey by Stanley Rothman and Seymour Martin Lipset of 4,000 students at 140 campuses shows that the more that racial "diversity" is emphasized on a campus, the less enthusiastic students are about the quality of education a school offers. What's more, Rothman and Lipset found that such "diversity"-focused schools had more reports of discrimination, not less.

The dismal failure of the "diversity" experiment of the last two decades offers an important lesson for a post-affirmative-action admissions policy. Even as we seek diversity in the worthy, Simon's Rock sense, we must recognize that students need to be able to excel at college-level studies. Nobody wins, after all, when a young man or woman of whatever color, unprepared for the academic rigors of a top university, flunks out, or a school dumbs down its curriculum to improve graduation rates. The problem, then, is to find some way to measure a student's potential that still leaves administrators enough leeway to ensure that campus life benefits from a rich variety of excellences and life experiences.

As it turns out, we have—and use—the measure: the Scholastic Aptitude Test. James Conant invented the SAT as a meritocratic tool to smoke out talented individuals from the wide range of life circumstances in American society, not just the WASP elite who made up the vast majority of Ivy League student bodies in the pre-SAT era. Nowadays, a creeping fashion dismisses the SAT as culturally biased, claiming that it assesses only a narrow range of ability and is irrelevant to predicting students' future performance. But while it is true that the SAT is far from perfect—if it were, students wouldn't be able to boost their scores by taking SAT preparatory classes—the exam really does tend to forecast students' future success, as even William Bowen and Derek Bok admit in their valentine to racial preferences, *The Shape of the River.* In their sample of three classes from 1951 to 1989 at 28 selective universities, Bowen and Bok show that SAT scores correlated neatly with students' eventual class ranks.

For gauging student potential in the humanities, the verbal SAT, or SATV, seems particularly useful. Rutgers University English professor William Dowling compared the grades of kids in one of his classes over the years with how they did on the verbal test. "What I found," Dowling notes, "was that the SATV scores had an extraordinarily high correlation with final grades, and that neither, in the many cases where I had come to know my students' personal backgrounds, seemed to correlate very well with socioeconomic status." The reason, Dowling thinks, is painfully obvious: having a strong command of English vocabulary, usually gained through a lifelong habit of reading, is hardly irrelevant to how one engages advanced reading material. As Dowling argues, a student of any socioeconomic background who can't answer correctly a relatively hard SAT question like this one—"The traditional process of producing an oil painting requires so many steps that it seems______to artists who prefer to work quickly: (A) provocative (B) consummate (C) interminable (D) facile (E) prolific"—will be fated to frustration at a selective university, at least in the humanities.

My own experience reinforces Dowling's. I've taught students who, though intelligent, possessed limited reading vocabularies and struggled with the verbal portion of the SAT. I have never known a single one of these students to reach the top ranks in one of my classes. "I think I understand what Locke is saying," one student told me in frustration while preparing for a big exam. But Locke isn't Heidegger—his prose, while sophisticated, is clear as crystal. This student confessed that he was "no reader" and possessed only a "tiny vocabulary." Without the vocabulary, he was at sea. Conversely, my textaholic students are usually the stars, gifted at internalizing material and interpreting it in fresh ways—and this is especially true of students immersed in high literature.

A post-preferences admissions policy, then, must accept that below a certain cut-off point in SAT scores, a student runs a serious risk of failing to graduate. As Thomas Sowell, among others, has shown, placing minorities in schools that expect a performance level beyond what they have been prepared to meet leads to disproportionate dropout rates—41 percent of the black students in Berkeley's class of 1988, to take one typical example, did not complete their education, compared with 16 percent of whites. Many of these students may have flourished at slightly less competitive schools. Moreover, when minority students attend schools beyond their level, note Stephen Cole and Elinor Barber in *Increasing Faculty Diversity*, poor grades often deter them from pursuing graduate degrees, contributing to the dearth of black PhDs. Black and minority students overwhelmed on a too-demanding campus can succumb, too, to the bluster of seeing themselves as "survivors" in a racist country—becoming part of an embittered minority rather than proud members of a national elite. To prevent this kind of damage, the SAT can supply us with the rough parameters within which our admissions search for different kinds of merit—diversity, rightly understood—will proceed. All this makes the recent efforts by the affirmative-action claque to get rid of the SAT misguided in the extreme.

Within our SAT range, and once in a while even a bit outside it, there will be plenty of room for judgment calls. Grades, extracurricular activities, and character will all be key. An applicant with a high GPA and a 1,480 SAT who plays the trumpet like Clifford Brown or who gives every indication of being a unique and charismatic individual may deserve admission over an applicant with a 1,600 SAT but no real interests and the individuality of a spoon. Our top universities seek to create a national elite, so geographical diversity will be important too: our admissions policy will seek a mix of students from all parts of the nation. As long as there is no coterie of students whose grades and test scores would have excluded them from consideration if they were white (or Asian), basic standards of excellence prevail.

And certainly, our admissions procedure won't immediately disqualify a student who is clearly bright and engaged, but whose test scores happen to fall slightly below the official cut-off, or whose GPA took a hit from one bad year, or who matured into a super student only late in his high school career. Fervent recommendation letters, attesting to leadership or virtue or strength of character, a flabbergastingly good writing sample, a demonstrated commitment to a calling—all will be significant in deciding whether to admit students whose grades and test scores put them on the borderline or slightly below.

Our admissions policy will be color-blind, but it won't ignore the working class and the poor (many of whom, as a practical matter, will be blacks or Hispanics). Of course, it's more likely that affluent children, growing up in print-rich homes, will score within our SAT parameters and have the tippy-top grades. But there have always been kids from hardscrabble backgrounds who show academic promise—by nature, by chance, or thanks to the special efforts of parents or other adults. Abraham Lincoln teaching himself to write on the back of a shovel, civil rights activist Fannie Lou Hamer growing up dust poor in the Mississippi Delta loving books—American history records many examples. Disadvantaged students of this stamp will sometimes get the nod in our admissions procedure over well-off applicants whose scores might be more impressive—provided that the disadvantaged kids' SAT scores are within our range (or close to it). That disadvantaged students have shown academic promise may be just a result of good genes, but it's often a sign of good character—a virtue that selective universities should recognize and cultivate.

The University of California at Berkeley, where I teach, is already on the right track here. Not so long ago, the admissions committee I sat on matter-of-factly chose middle-class brown students, essentially "white" culturally, over equally deserving white students. I felt tremendous discomfort over the practice. Since California voted in a 1997 referendum, led by anti-preferences activist Ward Connerly, to ban the use of race in admissions, things have changed. Berkeley still assesses students on grades and scores, of course, but instead of race, it now considers the "hardships" that young men and women may have overcome while excelling at school. We recently gave fellowships, for example, to two needy white students who had shown sterling promise. I felt fundamentally right about these fellowships. "This is a racially blind process," emphasizes Calvin Moore, chair of Berkeley's faculty committee on admissions.

The idea of a "racially blind process" makes today's "diversity" fans shudder, since they believe that it will lead to a tragic resegregation of the best American universities and thus of American society. I'm sorry, but this is manipulative melodrama. In an America several decades past the Civil Rights Act, where far more black families are middle class than are poor, many black students will be ready for the top schools without dragging down the bar of evaluation.

For proof, consider the University of Washington. In 1998, the year before Washington State outlawed racial preferences in a citizen referendum (also led by Connerly), the school counted 124 African-American students in its freshman class. Two years after the ban, there were 119. Before Texas banned preferences in its schools in 1996, the University of Texas enrolled 266 black freshmen. After the ban and the debut of a new system that admits the top 10 percent of every high school in the state regardless of race, the number actually bounced, to 286. (The "top 10 percent" approach has serious problems, including treating huge discrepancies in school quality as if they did not exist, but it's better than what it replaced.) If this is resegregation, bring it on.

The kind of color-blind admissions process I have outlined would likely just reshuffle the minority presence at selective schools, not reduce it. In Virginia, where racial preferences remain entrenched, black students currently make up 7.9 percent of the student body at the highly competitive University of Virginia Law School, 9.3 percent at the slightly less selective William and Mary Law School, and just 1.7 percent at the less elite, but still fine, George Mason Law School. George Mason's "diversity" deficit results from black students getting in to the more selective schools at a higher percentage than their dossiers would suggest in the absence of affirmative action. Bar preferences, and the number of black students at George Mason would rise; the overall number of blacks getting legal training in the three schools would probably remain the same.

What would be so bad about that? It's doubtful that the black students at George Mason's yearly commencement ceremony, feting their accomplishments as their parents beam beside them, worry that they will soon be on the street, selling pencils. In fact, nothing better underscores the progress made by black Americans than the prevalence in the affirmative-action camp of the bizarre notion that admission to a solid second-tier university somehow represents a tragic injustice.

Exactly this type of resorting took place after the end of preferences in California's schools. The state's flagship universities, Berkeley and UCLA, did see an initial plunge in the number of black freshmen. But minority presence rose at the same time at most state campuses. And minority admissions at the two top schools have gone up every year following the initial drop off. Having watched this whole process play out at Berkeley, I can confidently say that the black student community is far from a lonely remnant of what it was in the "good old days" of affirmative action. Berkeley still boasts a thriving black community—the same African-American student groups, the same black dorm floors, the same African-American studies and ethnic studies departments.

Moreover, the minority presence at the flagships may have taken a bigger initial hit than the ban required. Immediately after the ban, black activists at the two schools lustily proclaimed their campuses "antiblack," doubtless discouraging some black students from applying—minority applications dropped off sharply for a spell. At UC Berkeley in 1998, the minority admissions office staff actually told some black students, already accepted to the "racist" school, to enroll elsewhere. One of the motivations for writing my book *Losing the Race* was hearing a black student working in admissions casually say that she distrusted black applicants who did well enough in high school not to need preferences, since such students would not be committed to Berkeley's black community—as if it were somehow not "authentically black" to be a top student. No show lasts forever, however, and after the crowd crying "racism" had its fun and went home, minority applications have steadily climbed.

Most important of all, California's black students have started to do better now that they are going to schools that their academic background has prepared them to attend. As University of California at San Diego law professor Gail Heriot notes, before the preferences ban, 15 percent of the college's black freshmen undergraduates, compared with just 4 percent of whites, had GPAs below 2.0, which put them in academic jeopardy; only one black student had a GPA of 3.5 or better, compared with 20 percent of whites. The next year, after the outlawing of campus affirmative action, 20 percent of black freshmen reached the 3.5 or higher GPA level (compared with 22 percent of their white classmates), while black frosh with GPAs below 2.0 fell to 6 percent (about the same as all other racial groups). High freshmen dropout rates fell precipitously.

It's true that, with or without racial preferences, blacks will not make up as high a proportion of the student population at our better schools as they do of the overall population. But to worry unduly about this is ahistorical bean counting. Given the relatively short time since the nation rejected segregation, and the internal cultural factors that can hobble a group and keep it from seizing opportunities, it should surprise no one that our selective college campuses do not yet "look like America." But give it time. That's not a rhetorical statement, either: since the banning of racial preferences in California, there has been a 350 percent rise in the number of black teens taking calculus in preparation for college. Challenge people, and they respond.

Informed observers believe that the Supreme Court, in agreeing to decide two suits brought against the University of Michigan for reverse discrimination in its admissions, may be set to abolish all use of race in admissions and move the nation toward the color-blind ideal that motivated the original civil rights movement. Especially in light of the stereotypes that blacks have labored under in this country, saddling black people with eternally lowered standards is immoral. We spent too much time suffering under the hideously unjust social experiments of slavery and segregation to be subjected to further social engineering that benefits the sentiments of liberal elites instead of bettering the conditions and spirits of minorities. Unfortunately, even some conservatives remain uncomfortable with this color-blind possibility: the Bush administration's amicus brief in the case, though it views the Michigan admissions policy as an unconstitutional quota system, still contemplates school officials "taking race into account."

It's time to step up to the plate. My years on college campuses have taught me that even those willing to acknowledge the injustices of preferences in private uphold the "diversity" party line in public—something Bakke allows them to do. "John, I get where you're coming from," a genial professor once told me, "but I reserve my right to be guilty." Indeed, 25 years of Bakke show that, in practice, even a hint that race can be "a" factor in admissions will give college administrators, ever eager to Do the Right Thing, the go-ahead to continue fostering a second-tier class-within-a-class of "spunky" minorities on their campuses.

Justice Powell's Bakke opinion cited an amicus brief for "diversity" submitted by Harvard, Stanford, Columbia, and the University of Pennsylvania. The brief described how these schools had traditionally aimed to compose their classes with a mixture of "students from California, New York, and Massachusetts; city dwellers and farm boys; violinists, painters, and football players; biologists, historians, and classicists; potential stockbrokers, academics, and politicians." It's a wonderful, noble goal, this diversity—and we don't need to treat any group of citizens as lesser beings to accomplish it.

QUESTIONS: For Thinking and Writing

1. Summarize McWhorter's argument against race-based admission policies. Include in your summary his position and his supporting evidence.
2. McWhorter admits that diversity on campus adds value to a college education. What does McWhorter feel "diversity" means? How can the concept of diversity backfire? Explain.

3. Why does McWhorter feel that diversity arguments are demeaning and offensive to blacks and other minorities? Do you agree?
4. McWhorter makes his case for "color-blind" admissions. Present your own viewpoint on this issue responding specifically to McWhorter's supporting evidence and your own from outside research data and personal perspective as a college student.
5. McWhorter notes that while many admissions officers dislike the idea of race-based admissions in principle, they still believe they are necessary for a diverse campus. Assume the role of a college admissions officer and create a list of the academic standards, abilities, grades, and qualities you believe should be used to admit students to the college you currently attend. Explain why you think your standards and measures are important factors in the admissions process. Finally, explain the role race does or does not play in your admission policies.

Binge Drinking Cartoon

Brian Fairrington, *The Arizona Republic*, April 15, 2002

QUESTIONS: For Thinking and Writing

1. What is happening in this cartoon? How can you tell who the people are in the cartoon? Explain.
2. Do you think this cartoon presents a stereotype of college student life? Is it fair? Explain.
3. If you drink alcohol, how many drinks do you think is reasonable to ingest in an evening? Does it depend on the situation? Describe the different situations that influence how many drinks you have and why you believe the number you cited is a reasonable one for you.
4. Have you ever faced a dangerous situation because of alcohol or know someone who has? What role did alcohol play in the situation? Explain.
5. In response to increasingly unruly alcohol-related behavior on campus, Michigan State cut short its "welcome week," the week that allows freshman to learn about the campus before the rest of the student body arrives. Does your school have a welcome week for first-year students? What did you do during your welcome week experience? Did you drink or attend any parties? Explain.

CHARLES MURRAY

What's Wrong With Vocational School?

Are too many Americans going to college? In many European countries, at the beginning of their high-school years, students decide whether they wish to pursue a trade-based education or a professional one on a university track. Neither is better than the other; some are just right for the student, his or her career goals, and aptitude for academics. In the United States, however, over 70 percent of students go on to some form of higher education, and the vocational track for "craftsman" careers has been devalued in this country, by the general public and by employers, who are increasingly making a college degree a requirement for even entry-level office jobs. In the next essay, American Enterprise Institute scholar Charles Murray discusses how the pressure to go to college hurts less gifted students and the extremely bright ones. This essay was part of a three-part series examining education in the United States, which was published in The Wall Street Journal *the week of January 17, 2007.*

My topic yesterday was education and children in the lower half of the intelligence distribution. Today I turn to the upper half, people with IQs of 100 or higher. Today's simple truth is that far too many of them are going to four-year colleges. Begin with those barely into the top half, those with average intelligence. To have an IQ of 100 means that a tough high-school course pushes you about as far as your academic talents will take you. If you are average in math ability, you may struggle with algebra and probably fail a calculus course. If you are average in verbal skills, you often misinterpret complex text and make errors in logic.

These are not devastating shortcomings. You are smart enough to engage in any of hundreds of occupations. You can acquire more knowledge if it is presented in a format commensurate with your intellectual skills. But a genuine college education in the arts and sciences begins where your skills leave off.

In engineering and most of the natural sciences, the demarcation between high school material and college-level material is brutally obvious. If you cannot handle the math, you cannot pass the courses. In the humanities and social sciences, the demarcation is fuzzier. It is possible for someone with an IQ of 100 to sit in the lectures of Economics 1, read the textbook, and write answers in an examination book. But students who cannot follow complex arguments accurately are not really learning economics. They are taking away a mishmash of half-understood information and outright misunderstandings that probably leave them under the illusion that they know something they do not. (A depressing research literature documents one's inability to recognize one's own incompetence.) Traditionally and properly understood, a four-year college education teaches advanced analytic skills and information at a level that exceeds the intellectual capacity of most people.

There is no magic point at which a genuine college-level education becomes an option, but anything below an IQ of 110 is problematic. If you want to do well, you should have an IQ of 115 or higher. Put another way, it makes sense for only about 15 percent of the population, 25 percent if one stretches it, to get a college education. And yet more than 45 percent of recent high school graduates enroll in four-year colleges. Adjust that percentage to account for high school dropouts, and more than 40 percent of all persons in their late teens are trying to go to a four-year college—enough people to absorb everyone down through an IQ of 104.

No data that I have been able to find tell us what proportion of those students really want four years of college-level courses, but it is safe to say that few people who are intellectually unqualified yearn for the experience, any more than someone who is athletically unqualified for college varsity wants to have his shortcomings exposed at practice every day. They are in college to improve their chances of making a good living. What they really need is vocational training. But nobody will say so, because "vocational training" is second class. "College" is first class.

Large numbers of those who are intellectually qualified for college also do not yearn for four years of college-level courses. They go to college because their parents are paying for it and college is what children of their social class are supposed to do after they finish high school. They may have the ability to understand the material in Economics 1, but they do not want to. They, too, need to learn to make a living—and would do better in vocational training.

Combine those who are unqualified with those who are qualified but not interested, and some large proportion of students on today's college campuses—probably a majority of them—are looking for something that the four-year college was not designed to provide. Once there, they create a demand for practical courses, taught at an intellectual level that can be handled by someone with a mildly above-average IQ and/or mild motivation. The nation's colleges try to accommodate these new demands. But most of the practical specialties do not really require four years of training, and the best way to teach those specialties is not through a residential institution with the staff and infrastructure of a college. It amounts to a system that tries to turn out televisions on an assembly line that also makes pottery. It can be done, but it's ridiculously inefficient.

Government policy contributes to the problem by making college scholarships and loans too easy to get, but its role is ancillary. The demand for college is market-driven, because a college degree does, in fact, open up access to jobs that are closed to people without one. The fault lies in the false premium that our culture has put on a college degree.

For a few occupations, a college degree still certifies a qualification. For example, employers appropriately treat a bachelor's degree in engineering as a requirement for hiring engineers. But a bachelor's degree in a field such as sociology, psychology, economics, history, or literature certifies nothing. It is a screening device for employers. The college you got into says a lot about your ability, and that you stuck it out for four years says something about your perseverance. But the degree itself does not qualify the graduate for anything. There are better, faster, and more efficient ways for young people to acquire credentials to provide to employers.

The good news is that market-driven systems eventually adapt to reality, and signs of change are visible. One glimpse of the future is offered by the nation's two-year colleges. They are more honest than the four-year institutions about what their students want and provide courses that meet their needs more explicitly. Their time frame gives them a big advantage—two years is about right for learning many technical specialties, while four years is unnecessarily long.

Advances in technology are making the brick-and-mortar facility increasingly irrelevant. Research resources on the Internet will soon make the college library unnecessary. Lecture courses taught by first-rate professors are already available on CDs and DVDs for many subjects, and online methods to make courses interactive between professors and students are evolving. Advances in computer simulation are expanding the technical skills that can be taught without having to gather students together in a laboratory or shop. These and other developments are all still near the bottom of steep growth curves. The cost of effective training will fall for everyone who is willing to give up the trappings of a campus. As the cost of college continues to rise, the choice to give up those trappings will become easier.

A reality about the job market must eventually begin to affect the valuation of a college education: The spread of wealth at the top of American society has created an explosive increase in the demand for craftsmen. Finding a good lawyer or physician is easy. Finding a good carpenter, painter, electrician, plumber, glazier, mason—the list goes on and on—is difficult, and it is a seller's market. Journeymen craftsmen routinely make incomes in the top half of the income distribution, while master craftsmen can make six figures. They have work even in a soft economy. Their jobs cannot be outsourced to India. And the craftsman's job provides wonderful intrinsic rewards that come from mastery of a challenging skill that produces tangible results. How many white-collar jobs provide nearly as much satisfaction?

Even if forgoing college becomes economically attractive, the social cachet of a college degree remains. That will erode only when large numbers of high-status, high-income people do not have a college degree and don't care. The information technology industry is in the process of creating that class, with Bill Gates and Steve Jobs as exemplars. It will expand for the most natural of reasons: A college education need be no more important for many high-tech occupations than it is for NBA basketball players or cabinetmakers. Walk into Microsoft or Google with evidence that you are a brilliant hacker, and the job interviewer is not going to fret if you lack a college transcript. The ability to present an employer with evidence that you are good at something, without benefit of a college degree, will continue to increase, and so will the number of skills to which that evidence can be attached. Every time that happens, the false premium attached to the college degree will diminish.

Most students find college life to be lots of fun (apart from the boring classroom stuff), and that alone will keep the four-year institution overstocked for a long time. But, rightly understood, college is appropriate for a small minority of young adults—perhaps even a minority of the people who have IQs high enough that they could do college-level work if they wished. People who go to college are not better or worse people than anyone else; they are merely different in certain interests and abilities. That is the way college should be seen. There is reason to hope that eventually it will be.

QUESTIONS: For Thinking and Writing

1. Why does Murray feel that too many students are going to college? Why does he think this harms many students?
2. Is vocational school, as Murray suggests, indeed considered "second class?" What accounts for this judgment? How can this attitude hurt the United States in the long run?
3. Murray came under fire for expressing the viewpoint that we are not all equal in intelligence, so not everyone really should be going to college. He was accused of being "elitist" and of ignoring the benefits of a wider college-educated society. Does he have a point, or is he being elitist?
4. Do you think that colleges are indeed "dumbing down" curriculum to accommodate a broader range of students with lower abilities? Why or why not?
5. Murray's essay appeared as a three-part editorial series on issues connected to American education. Write your own editorial for the readership of *The Wall Street Journal* addressing Murray's argument that too many students are going to college.

Regulating Racist Speech on Campus

Charles R. Lawrence III

Muzzling Free Speech

Harvey A. Silverglate

"Congress shall make no law . . . abridging the freedom of speech, or of the press." With these simple words, the writers of the Constitution created one of the pillars of our democratic system of government—the First Amendment guarantee of every American's right to the free exchange of ideas, beliefs, and political debate. Most students support their right to express themselves without fear of government reprisal. However, over the years, questions have arisen about whether limits should be imposed on our right to free expression, when the exercise of that right imposes hardship or pain on others. What happens when the right of one person to state his or her beliefs conflicts with the rights of others to be free from verbal abuse? What happens when free expression runs counter to community and university values? At what point does the perceived degree of offensiveness warrant censorship? Are campus speech codes appropriate, or are they a violation of free speech? And who decides what is acceptable? In this chapter's Viewpoints, we look at the controversial issue of censorship and speech codes on campus. First, Charles R. Lawrence sets up the argument with an essay that first appeared in the Chronicle of Higher Education on October 25, 1989. His points are as valid today as they were almost 20 years ago, when he first penned his perspective. Then, Harvey Silverglate presents his view in an essay published in the October 2002 issue of the National Law Journal.

Regulating Racist Speech on Campus

Charles R. Lawrence III

I have spent the better part of my life as a dissenter. As a high school student, I was threatened with suspension for my refusal to participate in a civil-defense drill, and I have been a conspicuous consumer of my First Amendment liberties ever since. There are very strong reasons for protecting even racist speech. Perhaps the most important of these is that such protection reinforces our society's commitment to tolerance as a value, and that by protecting bad speech from government regulation, we will be forced to combat it as a community.

But I also have a deeply felt apprehension about the resurgence of racial violence and the corresponding rise in the incidence of verbal and symbolic assault and harassment to which blacks and other traditionally subjugated and excluded groups are subjected. I am troubled by the way the debate has been framed in response to the recent surge of racist incidents on college and university campuses and in response to some universities' attempts to regulate harassing speech. The problem has been framed as one in which the liberty of free speech is in conflict with the elimination of racism. I believe this has placed the bigot on the moral high ground and fanned the rising flames of racism.

Above all, I am troubled that we have not listened to the real victims, that we have shown so little understanding of their injury, and that we have abandoned those whose race, gender, or sexual preference continues to make them second-class citizens. It seems to me a very sad irony that the first instinct of civil libertarians has been to challenge even the smallest, most narrowly framed efforts by universities to provide black and other minority students with the protection the Constitution guarantees them.

The landmark case of *Brown* v. *Board of Education* is not a case that we normally think of as a case about speech. But *Brown* can be broadly read as articulating the principle of equal citizenship. *Brown* held that segregated schools were inherently unequal because of the *message* that segregation conveyed—that black children were an untouchable caste, unfit to go to school with white children. If we understand the necessity of eliminating the system of signs and symbols that signal the inferiority of blacks, then we should hesitate before proclaiming that all racist speech that stops short of physical violence must be defended.

University officials who have formulated policies to respond to incidents of racial harassment have been characterized in the press as "thought police," but such policies generally do nothing more than impose sanctions against intentional face-to-face insults. When racist speech takes the form of face-to-face insults, catcalls, or other assaultive speech aimed at an individual or small group of persons, it falls directly within the "fighting words" exception to First Amendment protection. The Supreme Court has held that words which "by their very utterance inflict injury or tend to incite an immediate breach of the peace" are not protected by the First Amendment.

If the purpose of the First Amendment is to foster the greatest amount of speech, racial insults disserve that purpose. Assaultive racist speech functions as a preemptive strike. The invective is experienced as a blow, not as a proffered idea, and once the blow is struck, it is unlikely that a dialogue will follow. Racial insults are particularly undeserving of First Amendment protection, because the perpetrator's intention is not to discover truth or initiate dialogue but to injure the victim. In most situations, members of minority groups realize that they are likely to lose if they respond to epithets by fighting and are forced to remain silent and submissive.

Courts have held that offensive speech may not be regulated in public forums such as streets, where the listener may avoid the speech by moving on, but the regulation of otherwise protected speech has been permitted when the speech invades the privacy of the unwilling listener's home, or when the unwilling listener cannot avoid the speech. Racist posters, fliers, and graffiti in dormitories, bathrooms, and other common living spaces would seem to clearly fall within the reasoning of these cases. Minority students should not be required to remain in their rooms in order to avoid racial assault. Minimally, they should find a safe haven in their dorms and in all other common rooms that are a part of their daily routine.

I would also argue that the university's responsibility for insuring that these students receive an equal educational opportunity provides a compelling justification for regulations that insure them safe passage in all common areas. A minority student should not have to risk becoming the target of racially assaulting speech every time he or she chooses to walk across campus. Regulating vilifying speech that cannot be anticipated or avoided would not preclude announced speeches and rallies—situations that would give minority-group members and their allies the chance to organize counter-demonstrations or avoid the speech altogether.

The most commonly advanced argument against the regulation of racist speech proceeds something like this: we recognize that minority groups suffer pain and injury as the result of racist speech, but we must allow this hate mongering for the benefit of society as a whole. Freedom of speech is the lifeblood of our democratic system. It is especially important for minorities, because often it is their only vehicle for rallying support for the redress of their grievances. It will be impossible to formulate a prohibition so precise that it will prevent the racist speech you want to suppress without catching in the same net all kinds of speech that it would be unconscionable for a democratic society to suppress.

Whenever we make such arguments, we are striking a balance on the one hand between our concern for the continued free flow of ideas and the democratic process dependent on that flow, and, on the other, our desire to further the cause of equality. There can be no meaningful discussion of how we should reconcile our commitment to equality and our commitment to free speech, until it is acknowledged that there is real harm inflicted by racist speech and that this harm is far from trivial.

To engage in a debate about the First Amendment and racist speech without a full understanding of the nature and extent of that harm is to risk making the First Amendment an instrument of domination, rather than a vehicle of liberation. We have not known the experience of victimization by racist, misogynist, and homophobic speech, nor do we equally share the burden of the societal harm it inflicts. We are often quick to say that we have heard the cry of the victims, when we have not.

The *Brown* case is again instructive, because it speaks directly to the psychic injury inflicted by racist speech by noting that the symbolic message of segregation affected "the hearts and minds" of Negro children "in a way unlikely ever to be undone." Racial epithets and harassment often cause deep emotional scarring and feelings of anxiety and fear that pervade every aspect of a victim's life.

Brown also recognized that black children did not have an equal opportunity to learn and participate in the school community, if they bore the additional burden of being subjected to the humiliation and psychic assault contained in the message of segregation. University students bear an analogous burden, when they are forced to live and work in an environment where, at any moment, they may be subjected to denigrating verbal harassment and assault. The same injury was addressed by the Supreme Court, when it held that sexual harassment that creates a hostile or abusive work environment violates the ban on sex discrimination in employment of Title VII of the Civil Rights Act of 1964.

Carefully drafted university regulations would bar the use of words as assault weapons and leave unregulated even the most heinous of ideas, when those ideas are presented at times and places and in manners that provide an opportunity for reasoned rebuttal or escape from immediate injury. The history of the development of the right to free speech has been one of carefully evaluating the importance of free expression and its effects on other important societal interests. We have drawn the line between protected and unprotected speech before without dire results. (Courts have, for example, exempted from the protection of the First Amendment obscene speech and speech that disseminates official secrets, that defames or libels another person, or that is used to form a conspiracy or monopoly.)

Blacks and other people of color are skeptical about the argument that even the most injurious speech must remain unregulated because, in an unregulated marketplace of ideas, the best ones will rise to the top and gain acceptance. Our experience tells us quite the opposite. We have seen too many good liberal politicians shy away from the issues that might brand them as being too closely allied with us.

Whenever we decide that racist speech must be tolerated because of the importance of maintaining societal tolerance for all unpopular speech, we are asking blacks and other subordinated groups to bear the burden for the good of all. We must be careful that the ease with which we strike the balance against the regulation of racist speech is in no way influenced by the fact that the cost will be borne by others. We must be certain that those who will pay that price are fairly represented in our deliberations and that they are heard.

At the core of the argument that we should resist all government regulation of speech is the ideal that the best cure for bad speech is good, that ideas that affirm equality and the worth of all individuals will ultimately prevail. This is an empty ideal unless those of us who would fight racism are vigilant and unequivocal in that fight. We must look for ways to offer assistance and support to students whose speech and political participation are chilled in a climate of racial harassment.

Civil rights lawyers might consider suing on behalf of blacks whose right to an equal education is denied by a university's failure to insure a nondiscriminatory educational climate or conditions of employment. We must embark upon the development of a First Amendment jurisprudence grounded in the reality of our history and our contemporary experience. We must think hard about how best to launch legal attacks against the most indefensible forms of hate speech. Good lawyers can create exceptions and narrow interpretations that limit the harm of hate speech without opening the floodgates of censorship.

Everyone concerned with these issues must find ways to engage actively in actions that resist and counter the racist ideas that we would have the First Amendment protect. If we fail in this, the victims of hate speech must rightly assume that we are on the oppressors' side.

Muzzling Free Speech

Harvey A. Silverglate

In the last five years, free-speech zones have become the trendiest weapon in campus administrators' war on free expression. More than 20 colleges and universities have established speech-zone systems relegating protests, demonstrations, and all other forms of student speech to a handful of places on campus. In June 2002, the University of Houston (UH) joined a growing number of colleges and universities that have turned their campuses into censorship zones, while restricting unfettered expression to a few tiny "free-speech zones."

The speech-zones movement presents a major threat to the ideals of free thought and free inquiry to which colleges and universities should be devoted. Free expression, however, means freedom to choose where and when and to whom to speak, not just what to say.

College administrators have used every trick in the book to try to limit student speech: Content-based speech codes were the weapon of choice against "offensive" speech on campuses in the early 1980s, but universities were forced to abandon these codes, after courts uniformly struck them down. Since then, administrators have used racial and sexual harassment rules to create de facto speech codes. Though these rules have had a chilling effect on campus discourse, recent court opinions finding it unconstitutional to classify as "harassment" speech that is merely offensive (but not physically threatening), reduce the utility of such rules in suppressing speech.

College speech zones are the rage, because they have not yet faced a court test. When they do, however, they will almost certainly be declared unconstitutional on public campuses. The law requires that government infringements on First Amendment rights be narrowly tailored to accomplish a specific, legitimate purpose—which speech zones are not. Public universities can restrict the "time, place, and manner of speech" to avoid disturbing, say, sleeping or studying students, but regulations aimed at forcing students to shut up or move to where they won't be heard and seen are constitutionally verboten.

Ironically, UH established its draconian new speech-zone system almost immediately after a court ruled that its previous policy was unconstitutional. The old policy allowed free expression everywhere on campus, but gave Dean William Munson authority to relegate "potentially disruptive" events to four designated areas. In March, the university allowed a large anti-abortion traveling exhibit on the main campus green. The display proved uneventful. But when a second student group, the Pro-Life Cougars, sought to bring the exhibition back for a second run in June, Munson refused permission, citing its potential disruptiveness.

The Pro-Life Cougars students sued. On June 24, 2002, the U.S. District Court for the Southern District of Texas declared Munson's actions and UH's speech policy unconstitutional. The court held that the lack of objective standards in UH's policy invited arbitrary prior restraints, and issued a preliminary injunction ordering UH to let the Cougars erect their display and barring the university from imposing restrictions on speech in the plaza.

The next day, UH's president established the new, more restrictive, zone policy, limiting free-speech events on campus to the four zones previously designated for potentially disruptive speech. Students must now register ten days in advance for even minor protests. Spontaneous demonstrations are relegated to one additional area, where amplified sound and signs mounted on sticks are prohibited. Exceptions are only at the dean's discretion.

The new policy appears to seek to avoid the unbridled-discretion problem that was fatal to its predecessor. But the administration apparently has not noted the court's warning that even a content-neutral regulation of speech in a public forum must be narrowly tailored to serve a significant government interest and must leave open ample alternative channels of communication. Simply put, there is no legitimate government interest in moving speech from the heart of campus to more peripheral areas.

Though free-speech zones are on the rise at some universities, several schools, including Penn State and the University of Wisconsin, have revoked their freshly minted zone regulations. In May 2002, speech-zone opponents convinced West Virginia University to liberalize a policy that restricted free expression to two classroom-sized areas. The school is now testing a new policy that, though it does not go far enough, lets small groups stage protests anywhere on campus, at any time, without advance permission.

It will take determined advocacy to keep speech zones from invading the rest of America's colleges and universities. But the recent successes at West Virginia University and elsewhere suggest that the censorship-zone movement may burn out as precipitously as it has caught fire. There is a growing recognition, especially by students and civil libertarians, that our entire country is a free-speech zone, and that our campuses of higher education, of all places, cannot be an exception.

QUESTIONS: For Thinking and Writing

1. What reasons does Lawrence offer for protecting racist speech from governmental restrictions? Do you agree? How are university restrictions different from those imposed by the government?
2. According to the Lawrence, how in the debate over racist language does the fight against racism conflict with the fight for free speech? What fundamental problem does Lawrence have with this conflict? Are his reasons convincing?
3. Have you ever been the victim of abusive speech—speech that victimized you because of your race, gender, religion, ethnicity, or sexual preference? Do you agree with Lawrence's argument regarding "psychic injury"? Explain.
4. Silverglate states "college administrators have used every trick in the book to try and limit student speech." What "tricks," according to the author, have they used? Why does Silverglate object to limiting student speech? Has your own campus administration employed any of the speech codes he describes?
5. Silverglate cites several universities that have employed free-speech zones, including the University of Houston, Penn State, and West Virginia University. As a class, research the arguments for and against free-speech zones as expressed in university publications available online at each of these universities. Discuss your research with the class. If your own campus has a free-speech zone, include it in your discussion.

QUESTIONS: For Further Research and Group Work

1. Write a free-speech code to be implemented at your college or university. Consider students' rights to free speech, what constitutes hate speech, and what limits can be placed on hate speech. Write a prologue to your code, explaining and supporting its tenets.
2. In a January 2003 article in *Boston Magazine*, Harvey Silverglate stated that the First Amendment should protect your right to say what you wish, but that you are not immune to what happens after that. You may be subjected to angry retorts, public shunning, and social pressure, but you should not be officially punished for your language. As a group, discuss his assertion, and write a response to Silverglate, expressing your group's conclusion on his viewpoint.
3. Working in groups, craft a college core curriculum that every student must take before graduation, regardless of their major. Select 12 courses to be taken over the 4-year time span of the average bachelor's degree. You may be general in your selection ("Western Civilization I

and II") or very specific ("Gender and Power in Modern America"). After compiling your curriculum, share your list with the class to see which courses the groups chose in common and which ones were different. Then, together as a class, narrow the list down to 12. If your college or university has a core curriculum, compare your final list to that outlined in your student handbook.

4. Debate the issue of color-blind admission policies as a class. First, your instructor should separate the class into two groups—one in favor of color-blind admissions and one against them. Working in subgroups, make a list of the pros and cons of such policies, how they can help or harm students, issues of fairness and parity, and finally, the impact on graduate admissions and professional career goals. After 20 minutes of discussion, summarize your group's position in a paragraph. A spokesperson from each group will present each group's summary in succession. Class debate should follow, addressing the summaries' points specifically.

8 CHAPTER

Race and Racism

As a nation of immigrants, the United States is comprised of many races, ethnic traditions, religions, and languages. Under a common political and legal system, we agree that we have the right to life, liberty, and the pursuit of happiness. Many of us take pride in our differences and in what makes us unique from one another. That is what makes America so special. And as Americans, we embrace, at least in theory, the principles of the Declaration of Independence—that we are all created equal. But the social reality is that our differences can pose challenges as well. Racism, the condition in which people are mistreated and oppressed because of their skin color or ethnic origin, is still a troubling social reality in America.

Racial issues in the United States began with the first Puritan settlers, who practiced forms of racism in their relationships with Native Americans. Each new immigrant group to arrive on America's shores—Irish, Italian, Chinese, German—experienced some form of racism and racial profiling, usually at the hands of the groups that came before them. As America became more ethnically blended, racism against some groups decreased and even disappeared. But racism and racial profiling in America remains a troubling reality for many ethnic groups. In this chapter, we will look at a few of the issues surrounding racial inequality and the practice of racial profiling, most specifically of African Americans and Arab Americans in the wake of September 11 and the conflict in Iraq.

ALAN JENKINS

Inequality, Race, and Remedy

It would be hopeful to believe that race is no longer a factor in poverty and that we can be a color-blind society. But America still has a legacy to overcome and to achieve. In this next essay, Alan Jenkins, executive director of The Opportunity Agenda, an organization dedicated to expanding opportunity in America, explains why we cannot ignore the past if we are to create a more hopeful future. The truth is, he explains, racial barriers still exist, and in order to overcome them, we must admit that. Can we ever become a color-blind society? Jenkins' article was first published in the April 22, 2007 issue of the American Prospect.

Our nation, at its best, pursues the ideal that what we look like and where we come from should not determine the benefits, burdens, or responsibilities that we bear in our society. Because we believe that all people are created equal in terms of rights, dignity, and the potential to achieve great things, we see inequality based on race, gender, and other social characteristics as not only unfortunate but unjust. The value of equality, democratic voice, physical and economic security, social mobility, a shared sense of responsibility for one another, and a chance to start over after misfortune or missteps—what many Americans call redemption—are the moral pillars of the American ideal of opportunity.

Many Americans of goodwill who want to reduce poverty believe that race is no longer relevant to understanding the problem, or to fashioning solutions for it. This view often reflects compassion as well as pragmatism. But we cannot solve the problem of poverty—or, indeed, be the country that we aspire to be—unless we honestly unravel the complex and continuing connection between poverty and race.

Since our country's inception, race-based barriers have hindered the fulfillment of our shared values and many of these barriers persist today. Experience shows, moreover, that reductions in poverty do not reliably reduce racial inequality, nor do they inevitably reach low-income people of color. Rising economic tides do not reliably lift all boats.

In 2000, after a decade of remarkable economic prosperity, the poverty rate among African Americans and Latinos taken together was still 2.6 times greater than that for white Americans. This disparity was stunning, yet it was the smallest difference in poverty rates between whites and others in more than three decades. And from 2001 to 2003, as the economy slowed, poverty rates for most communities of color increased more dramatically than they did for whites, widening the racial poverty gap. From 2004 to 2005, while the overall number of poor Americans declined by almost 1 million to 37 million, poverty rates for most communities of color actually increased. Reductions in poverty do not inevitably close racial poverty gaps, nor do they reach all ethnic communities equally.

Poor people of color are also increasingly more likely than whites to find themselves living in high-poverty neighborhoods with limited resources and limited options. An analysis by The Opportunity Agenda and the Poverty and Race Research Action Council found that while the percentage of Americans of all races living in high-poverty neighborhoods (those with 30 percent or more residents living in poverty) declined between 1960 and 2000, the racial gap grew considerably. Low-income Latino families were three times as likely as low-income white families to live in these neighborhoods in 1960, but 5.7 times as likely in 2000. Low-income blacks were 3.8 times more likely than poor whites to live in high-poverty neighborhoods in 1960, but 7.3 times more likely in 2000.

These numbers are troubling not because living among poor people is somehow harmful in itself, but because concentrated high-poverty communities are far more likely to be cut off from quality schools, housing, health care, affordable consumer credit, and other pathways out of poverty. And African Americans and Latinos are increasingly more likely than whites to live in those communities. Today, low-income blacks are more than three times as likely as poor whites to be in "deep poverty"—meaning below half the poverty line—while poor Latinos are more than twice as likely.

The Persistence of Discrimination

Modern and historical forces combine to keep many communities of color disconnected from networks of economic opportunity and upward mobility. Among those forces is persistent racial discrimination that, while subtler than in past decades, continues to deny opportunity to millions of Americans. Decent employment and housing are milestones on the road out of poverty. Yet these are areas in which racial discrimination stubbornly persists. While the open hostility and

"Whites Only" signs of the Jim Crow era have largely disappeared, research shows that identically qualified candidates for jobs and housing enjoy significantly different opportunities depending on their race.

In one study, researchers submitted identical resumés by mail for more than 1,300 job openings in Boston and Chicago, giving each "applicant" either a distinctively "white-sounding" or "black-sounding" name—for instance, "Brendan Baker" versus "Jamal Jones." Resumés with white-sounding names were 50 percent more likely than those with black-sounding names to receive callbacks from employers. Similar research in California found that Asian American and, especially, Arab American resumés received the least-favorable treatment compared to other groups. In recent studies in Milwaukee and New York City, meanwhile, live "tester pairs" with comparable qualifications but of differing races tested not only the effect of race on job prospects but also the impact of an apparent criminal record. In Milwaukee, whites reporting a criminal record were more likely to receive a callback from employers than were blacks without a criminal record. In New York, Latinos and African Americans without criminal records received fewer callbacks than did similarly situated whites, and at rates comparable to whites with a criminal record.

Similar patterns hamper the access of people of color to quality housing near good schools and jobs. Research by the U.S. Department of Housing and Urban Development (HUD) shows that people of color receive less information from real-estate agents, are shown fewer units, and are frequently steered away from predominantly white neighborhoods. In addition to identifying barriers facing African Americans and Latinos, this research found significant levels of discrimination against Asian Americans, and that Native American renters may face the highest discrimination rates (up to 29 percent) of all.

This kind of discrimination is largely invisible to its victims, who do not know that they have received inaccurate information or been steered away from desirable neighborhoods and jobs. But its influence on the perpetuation of poverty is nonetheless powerful.

The Present Legacy of Past Discrimination

These modern discriminatory practices often combine with historical patterns. In New Orleans, for example, as in many other cities, low-income African Americans were intentionally concentrated in segregated, low-lying neighborhoods and public-housing developments at least into the 1960s. In 2005, when Hurricane Katrina struck and the levees broke, black neighborhoods were most at risk of devastation. And when HUD announced that it would close habitable public-housing developments in New Orleans rather than clean and reopen them, it was African Americans who were primarily prevented from returning home and rebuilding. This and other failures to rebuild and invest have exacerbated poverty—already at high levels—among these New Orleanians.

In the case of Native Americans, a quarter of whom are poor, our government continues to play a more flagrant role in thwarting pathways out of poverty. Unlike other racial and ethnic groups, most Native Americans are members of sovereign tribal nations with a recognized status under our Constitution. High levels of Native American poverty derive not only from a history of wars, forced relocations, and broken treaties by the United States but also from ongoing breaches of trust—like our government's failure to account for tens of billions of dollars that it was obligated to hold in trust for Native American individuals and families. After more than a decade of litigation, and multiple findings of governmental wrongdoing, the United States is trying to settle these cases for a tiny fraction of what it owes.

The trust-fund cases, of course, are just the latest in a string of broken promises by our government. But focusing as they do on dollars and cents, they offer an important window into the economic status that Native American communities and tribes might enjoy today if the U.S. government lived up to its legal and moral obligations.

Meanwhile, the growing diversity spurred by new immigrant communities adds to the complexity of contemporary poverty. Asian American communities, for example, are culturally, linguistically, and geographically diverse, and they span a particularly broad socioeconomic spectrum.

Census figures from 2000 show that while one-third of Asian-American families have annual incomes of $75,000 or more, one-fifth have incomes of less than $25,000. While the Asian-American poverty rate mirrored that of the country as a whole, Southeast Asian communities reflected far higher levels. Among men experienced the highest poverty level (40.3 percent) of any racial group in the nation.

Race and Public Attitudes

Americans' complex attitudes and emotions about race are crucial to understanding the public discourse about poverty and the public's will to address it. Researchers such as Martin Gilens and Herman Gray have repeatedly found that the mainstream media depict poor people as people of color—primarily African Americans—at rates far higher than their actual representation in the population. And that depiction, the research finds, interacts with societal biases to erode support for antipoverty programs that could reach all poor people.

Gilens found, for instance, that while blacks represented only 29 percent of poor Americans at the time he did his research, 65 percent of poor Americans shown on television news were black. In a more detailed analysis of TV newsmagazines in particular, Gilens found a generally unflattering framing of the poor, but the presentation of poor African Americans was more negative still. The most "sympathetic" subgroups of the poor—such as the working poor and the elderly—were underrepresented on these shows, while unemployed working-age adults were overrepresented. And those disparities were greater for African Americans than for others, creating an even more unflattering (and inaccurate) picture of the black poor.

Gray similarly found that poor African Americans were depicted as especially dysfunctional and undeserving of assistance, with an emphasis on violence, poor choices, and dependency. As Gray notes, "The black underclass appears as a menace and a source of social disorganization in news accounts of black urban crime, gang violence, drug use, teenage pregnancy, riots, homelessness, and general aimlessness. In news accounts, poor blacks (and Hispanics) signify a social menace that must be contained."

Research also shows that Americans are more likely to blame the plight of poverty on poor people themselves, and less likely to support antipoverty efforts, when they perceive that the people needing help are black. These racial effects are especially pronounced when the poor person in the story is a black single mother. In one study, more than twice the number of respondents supported individual solutions (like the one that says poor people "should get a job") over societal solutions (such as increased education or social services) when the single mother was black.

This research should not be surprising. Ronald Reagan, among others, effectively used the "racialized" mental image of the African

American "welfare queen" to undermine support for antipoverty efforts. And the media face of welfare recipients has long been a black one, despite the fact that African Americans have represented a minority of the welfare population. But this research also makes clear that unpacking and disputing racial stereotypes is important to rebuilding a shared sense of responsibility for reducing poverty in all of our communities.

Removing Racial Barriers

We cannot hope to address poverty in a meaningful or lasting way without addressing race-based barriers to opportunity. The most effective solutions will take on these challenges together.

That means, for example, job-training programs that prepare low-income workers for a globalized economy, combined with antidiscrimination enforcement that ensures equal access to those programs and the jobs to which they lead. Similarly, strengthening the right to organize is important in helping low-wage workers to move out of poverty, but it must be combined with civil-rights efforts that root out the racial exclusion that has sometimes infected union locals. And it means combining comprehensive immigration reform that offers newcomers a pathway to citizenship with living wages and labor protections that root out exploitation and discourage racial hierarchy.

Another crucial step is reducing financial barriers to college by increasing the share of need-based grants over student loans and better coordinating private-sector scholarship aid—for example, funds for federal Pell Grants should be at least double current levels. But colleges should also retain the flexibility to consider racial and socioeconomic background as two factors among many, in order to promote a diverse student body (as well as diverse workers and leaders once these students graduate). And Congress should pass the DREAM Act, which would clear the path to a college degree and legal immigration status for many undocumented students who've shown academic promise and the desire to contribute to our country.

Lack of access to affordable, quality health care is a major stress on low-income families, contributing to half of the nation's personal bankruptcies. Guaranteed health care for all is critical, and it must be combined with protections against poor quality and unequal access that, research shows, affect people of color irrespective of their insurance status.

Finally, we must begin planning for opportunity in the way we design metropolitan regions, transportation systems, housing, hospitals, and schools. That means, for example, creating incentives for mixed-income neighborhoods that are well publicized and truly open to people of all races and backgrounds.

A particularly promising approach involves requiring an "opportunity impact statement" when public funds are to be used for development projects. The statement would explain, for example, whether a new highway will connect low-income communities to good jobs and schools or serve only affluent communities. It would detail where and how job opportunities would flow from the project, and whether different communities would share the burden of environmental and other effects (rather than having the project reinforce traditional patterns of inequality). It would measure not only a project's expected effect on poverty but on opportunity for all.

When we think about race and poverty in terms of the shared values and linked fate of our people, our approach to politics as well as policy begins to change. Instead of balancing a list of constituencies and identity groups, our task becomes one of moving forward together as a diverse but cohesive society, addressing through unity the forces that have historically divided us.

QUESTIONS: For Thinking and Writing

1. Jenkins opens his essay with the comment, "Our nation, at its best, pursues the ideal that what we look like and where we come from should not determine the benefits, burdens, or responsibilities that we bear in our society." What are the ideals of America? Do we believe in equality for all, at least in theory? If so, how well do we, as a society, promote the values of equality? Explain.
2. What are the connections between race and poverty in the United States? Why does Jenkins feel it is important to address these connections in order to promote a more color-blind society? Explain.
3. Jenkins observes that while "Jim Crow" signs barring African Americans from employment have disappeared, employment racism still persists. In what ways does employment racism perpetuate the cycle of poverty?
4. In addition to employment inequalities, what other forms of racism are rampant in America? Can you think of any other examples in addition to the ones Jenkins cites?

5. Jenkins describes how "attitudes and emotions about race" are often media-driven. How are issues of race presented in the media? Cite several examples of how different races are presented, and how these representations can influence public opinions in general.

DAVID BROOKS

People Like Us

From the hallowed halls of academia to the boardrooms of Fortune 500 companies, the concept of racial and social diversity is an important factor in our efforts to create a balanced, equal society. But despite efforts to promote diversity, all too often we witness "self-segregation." As David Brooks explains in this next essay, which appeared in the September 2003 issue of the Atlantic Monthly, *while we tend to pay lip service to ideals of diversity, we really prefer to associate with "people like us." Is the melting pot merely a myth?*

Maybe it's time to admit the obvious. We don't really care about diversity all that much in America, even though we talk about it a great deal. Maybe somewhere in this country there is a truly diverse neighborhood in which a black Pentecostal minister lives next to a white anti-globalization activist, who lives next to an Asian short-order cook, who lives next to a professional golfer, who lives next to a postmodern-literature professor and a cardiovascular surgeon. But I have never been to or heard of that neighborhood. Instead, what I have seen all around the country is people making strenuous efforts to group themselves with people who are basically like themselves.

Human beings are capable of drawing amazingly subtle social distinctions and then shaping their lives around them. In the Washington, D.C., area Democratic lawyers tend to live in suburban Maryland, and Republican lawyers tend to live in suburban Virginia. If you asked a Democratic lawyer to move from her $750,000 house in Bethesda, Maryland, to a $750,000 house in Great Falls, Virginia, she'd look at you as if you had just asked her to buy a pickup truck with a gun rack and to shove chewing tobacco in her kid's mouth. In Manhattan the owner of a $3 million SoHo loft would feel out of place moving into a $3 million Fifth Avenue apartment. A West Hollywood interior decorator would feel dislocated if you asked him to move to Orange County. In Georgia a barista from Athens would probably not fit in serving coffee in Americus.

It is a common complaint that every place is starting to look the same. But in the information age, the late writer James Chapin once told me, every place becomes more like itself. People are less often tied down to factories and mills, and they can search for places to live on the basis of cultural affinity. Once they find a town in which people share their values, they flock there and reinforce whatever was distinctive about the town in the first place. Once Boulder, Colorado, became known as congenial to politically progressive mountain bikers, half the politically progressive mountain bikers in the country (it seems) moved there; they made the place so culturally pure that it has become practically a parody of itself.

But people love it. Make no mistake—we are increasing our happiness by segmenting off so rigorously. We are finding places where we are comfortable and where we feel we can flourish. But the choices we make toward that end lead to the very opposite of diversity. The United States might be a diverse nation when considered as a whole, but block by block and institution by institution it is a relatively homogeneous nation.

When we use the word "diversity" today, we usually mean racial integration. But even here our good intentions seem to have run into the brick wall of human nature. Over the past generation, reformers have tried heroically, and in many cases successfully, to end housing discrimination. But recent patterns aren't encouraging: according to an analysis of the 2000 census data, the 1990s saw only a slight increase in the racial integration of neighborhoods in the United States. The number of middle-class and upper-middle-class African-American families is rising, but for whatever reasons—racism, psychological comfort—these families tend to congregate in predominantly black neighborhoods.

In fact, evidence suggests that some neighborhoods become more segregated over time. New suburbs in Arizona and Nevada, for example, start out reasonably well integrated. These neighborhoods don't yet have reputations, so people choose their houses for other, mostly economic reasons. But as neighborhoods age, they develop personalities (that's where the Asians live, and that's where the Hispanics live), and segmentation occurs. It could be that in a few years, the new suburbs in the Southwest will be nearly as segregated as the established ones in the Northeast and the Midwest.

Even though race and ethnicity run deep in American society, we should in theory be able to find areas that are at least culturally diverse.

But here, too, people show few signs of being truly interested in building diverse communities. If you run a retail company and you're thinking of opening new stores, you can choose among dozens of consulting firms that are quite effective at locating your potential customers. They can do this because people with similar tastes and preferences tend to congregate by zip code.

The most famous of these precision marketing firms is Claritas, which breaks down the U.S. population into 62 psycho-demographic clusters, based on such factors as how much money people make, what they like to read and watch, and what products they have bought in the past. For example, the "suburban sprawl" cluster is composed of young families making about $41,000 a year and living in fast-growing places such as Burnsville, Minnesota, and Bensalem, Pennsylvania. These people are almost twice as likely as other Americans to have three-way calling. They are two and a half times as likely to buy Light n' Lively Kid Yogurt. Members of the "towns and gowns" cluster are recent college graduates in places such as Berkeley, California, and Gainesville, Florida. They are big consumers of Dove Bars and *Saturday Night Live.* They tend to drive small foreign cars and read *Rolling Stone* and *Scientific American.*

Looking through the market research, one can sometimes be amazed by how efficiently people cluster—and by how predictable we all are. If you wanted to sell imported wine, obviously you would have to find places where rich people live. But did you know that the 16 counties with the greatest proportion of imported-wine drinkers are all in the same three metropolitan areas (New York, San Francisco, and Washington, D.C.)? If you tried to open a motor-home dealership in Montgomery County, Pennsylvania, you'd probably go broke, because people in this ring of the Philadelphia suburbs think RVs are kind of uncool. But if you traveled just a short way north, to Monroe County, Pennsylvania, you would find yourself in the fifth motor-home-friendliest county in America.

Geography is not the only way we find ourselves divided from people unlike us. Some of us watch *Fox News*, while others listen to NPR. Some like David Letterman, and others—typically in less urban neighborhoods—like Jay Leno. Some go to charismatic churches; some go to mainstream churches. Americans tend more and more often to marry people with education levels similar to their own, and to befriend people with backgrounds similar to their own.

My favorite illustration of this latter pattern comes from the first, noncontroversial chapter of *The Bell Curve.* Think of your 12 closest friends, Richard J. Herrnstein and Charles Murray write. If you had chosen them randomly from the American population, the odds that half of your 12 closest friends would be college graduates would be six in a thousand. The odds that half of the 12 would have advanced degrees would be less than one in a million. Have any of your 12 closest friends graduated from Harvard, Stanford, Yale, Princeton, Caltech, MIT, Duke, Dartmouth, Cornell, Columbia, Chicago, or Brown? If you chose your friends randomly from the American population, the odds against your having four or more friends from those schools would be more than a billion to one.

Many of us live in absurdly unlikely groupings, because we have organized our lives that way.

It's striking that the institutions that talk the most about diversity often practice it the least. For example, no group of people sings the diversity anthem more frequently and fervently than administrators at just such elite universities. But elite universities are amazingly undiverse in their values, politics, and mores. Professors in particular are drawn from a rather narrow segment of the population. If faculties reflected the general population, 32 percent of professors would be registered Democrats and 31 percent would be registered Republicans. Forty percent would be evangelical Christians. But a recent study of several universities by the conservative Center for the Study of Popular Culture and the American Enterprise Institute found that roughly 90 percent of those professors in the arts and sciences who had registered with a political party had registered Democratic. Fifty-seven professors at Brown were found on the voter-registration rolls. Of those, 44 were Democrats. Of the 42 professors in the English, history, sociology, and political science departments, all were Democrats. The results at Harvard, Penn State, Maryland, and the University of California at Santa Barbara were similar to the results at Brown.

What we are looking at here is human nature. People want to be around others who are roughly like themselves. That's called community. It probably would be psychologically difficult for most Brown professors to share an office with someone who was pro-life, a member of the National Rifle Association, or an evangelical Christian. It's likely that hiring committees would subtly—even unconsciously—screen out any such people they encountered. Republicans and evangelical Christians have sensed that they are not welcome at places like Brown, so they don't even consider working there. In fact, any registered Republican who contemplates a career in academia these days is both a hero and a fool. So, in a semi-self-selective pattern, brainy people with generally liberal social mores flow to academia, and brainy people with generally conservative mores flow elsewhere.

The dream of diversity is like the dream of equality. Both are based on ideals we celebrate even as we undermine them daily. (How many times have you seen someone renounce a high-paying job or pull his child from an elite college on the grounds that these things are bad for equality?) On the one hand, the situation is appalling. It is appalling that Americans know so little about one another. It is appalling that many of us are so narrow-minded that we can't tolerate a few people with ideas significantly different from our own. It's appalling that evangelical Christians are practically absent from entire professions, such as academia, the media, and filmmaking. It's appalling that people should be content to cut themselves off from everyone unlike themselves.

The segmentation of society means that often we don't even have arguments across the political divide. Within their little validating communities, liberals and conservatives circulate half-truths about the supposed awfulness of the other side. These distortions are believed because it feels good to believe them.

On the other hand, there are limits to how diverse any community can or should be. I've come to think that it is not useful to try to hammer diversity into every neighborhood and institution in the United States. Sure, Augusta National should probably admit women, and university sociology departments should probably hire a conservative or two. It would be nice if all neighborhoods had a good mixture of ethnicities. But human nature being what it is, most places and institutions are going to remain culturally homogeneous.

It's probably better to think about diverse lives, not diverse institutions. Human beings, if they are to live well, will have to move through a series of institutions and environments, which may be individually homogeneous but, taken together, will offer diverse experiences. It might also be a good idea to make national service a rite of passage for young people in this country: it would take them out of their narrow neighborhood segment and thrust them in with people unlike themselves. Finally, it's probably important for adults to get out of their own familiar circles. If you live in a coastal, socially liberal neighborhood, maybe you should take out a subscription to *The Door*, the evangelical humor magazine; or maybe you should visit Branson, Missouri. Maybe you should stop in at a megachurch. Sure, it would be superficial familiarity, but it beats the iron curtains that now separate the nation's various cultural zones.

Look around at your daily life. Are you really in touch with the broad diversity of American life? Do you care?

QUESTIONS: For Thinking and Writing

1. When you were growing up, with whom did your parents socialize? Where did they live, and what social functions were they likely to attend? Now that you are an adult, with whom do you chose to socialize? What is the demographic anatomy of your social group? Is it influenced by race and ethnicity or by common interests? Explain.
2. What does Brooks mean when he says, "Human beings are capable of drawing amazingly subtle social distinctions and then shaping their lives around them"? What examples does he give of such distinctions? Can you think of any subtle distinctions in your own life that influence where you live and with whom you choose to associate? Explain.
3. What is "cultural affinity"? How does it influence the social and cultural values of a particular area? How is it reinforced, and how can it break down? Explain.
4. When we refer to the word "diversity," what do we usually mean? What types of diversity are identified by the author? What factors tend to influence people to find others like them?
5. Describe the neighborhood in which you currently live. How does it connect to the points Brooks makes in his essay? (A dormitory can be considered a "neighborhood.") Consider also in your narrative the reasons why you chose the college you now attend and the social groups with which you associate. Draw connections between your own "cultural cluster" and Brooks's observations on diversity in practice.

JORDAN LITE

Please Ask Me, "Who", Not "What", I Am

As a nation comprised of every nationality and ethnicity, we frequently seek to classify people by "what" they are—Asian, German, French—it seems everyone has to have a label. In the next piece, Jordan Lite, a young woman who describes herself as "unclassifiable," asks why casual acquaintances seem to think it is permissible to ask about her ethnic background. As she explains, her race isn't obvious, and Lite wonders why it should matter to people she's just met. Her editorial appeared on the "My View" column of Newsweek *magazine in July 2001.*

I've been thinking a lot about a *Seinfeld* episode where Elaine is dating this guy and it's driving her nuts, because she doesn't know "what" he is. They ultimately discover that neither is exotic enough for the other, and they're so disappointed that they stop seeing each other.

It's the story of my life these days. Each new guy I meet, it seems, is fascinated by my ostensible failure to fall into an obvious racial category. Last year we could opt out of defining ourselves to the Census Bureau, but that option doesn't seem to have carried over into real life. I've lost track of how many flirty men have asked me what I am.

The first time, I was in Iowa and snobbishly dismissed the inquiry as rural provincialism. Then it happened again while I was on a date in San Francisco, a city that prides itself on its enlightenment.

Isn't it rude to ask "what" someone is when you've just met? Common courtesy would suggest so. But many people seem to feel uncomfortable if they can't immediately determine a new person's racial or ethnic background.

Of course, I've mused over "what" a stranger might be. But it's never occurred to me that asking "What are you?" of someone I've just met would elicit anything particularly revealing about him. I ask questions, but not that one.

So when a potential boyfriend asks me "What are you?" I feel like he wants to instantly categorize me. If he'd only let the answer come out naturally, he'd get a much better sense of what I'm about.

Perhaps acknowledging explicitly that race and ethnicity play a role in determining who we are is just being honest. But I'm not sure that such directness is always well intended. After I grouchily retorted "What do you mean, 'What am I?' " to one rather bewildered date, he told me his dad was African American and his mom Japanese, and that he ruminated all the time over how to reconcile such disparate influences. I realized then that he believed my being "different" would magically confer upon me an understanding of what it was like to be like him.

If you're looking for your soulmate, maybe it's only natural to want a persona who has shared your experience. But for some people, "What are you?" is just a line. "You're exotic-looking," a man at a party explained when I asked him why he wanted to know. In retrospect, I think he probably meant his remark as a compliment. As a Hispanic friend pointed out, when all things Latin become the new craze, it's trendy to be exotic. But if someone wants to get to know me, I wish he would at least pretend it's not because of my looks.

Still, this guy's willingness to discuss my discomfort was eye-opening. He told me that he was part Korean, part white. Growing up in the Pacific Northwest, he wasn't the only biracial kid on the block. One could acknowledge race, he said, and still be casual about it.

Although I spent my childhood in a town lauded for its racial diversity, discussing race doesn't often feel easy to me. Maybe my Japanese classmate in the first grade could snack on seaweed without being hassled, but I can readily recall being 11 years old and watching a local TV news report about a pack of white boys who beat, then chased a terrified black teen onto a highway, where he was struck by a car and killed. The violence on TV silenced me. It seemed better not to risk asking questions that might offend.

Years after we graduated from our private high school, one of my good friends told me how out of place she felt as one of the few black students. Her guardedness had kept me from probing; but there's a part of me that wonders if talking with her then about her unease at school would have made me more comfortable now, when people ask me about my place in the world.

But as it is, I resent being pressed to explain myself upfront, as if telling a prospective date my ethnicity eliminates his need to participate in a real conversation with me. "What are you?" I am asked, but the background check he's conducting won't show whether we share real interests that would bring us together in a genuine give-and-take.

In a way, I enjoy being unclassifiable. Though there are people who try to peg me to a particular ethnic stereotype, I like to think others take my ambiguous appearance as an opportunity to focus on who I am as a person. So I haven't figured out why being myself should kill any chance of a relationship. Not long ago, a man asked me about my background when we met for a drink.

"Just a Jewish girl from New Jersey," I answered truthfully.

I never heard from him again.

QUESTIONS: For Thinking and Writing

1. Why do Americans seem so keen on knowing the details of ethnicity and race?
2. Lite comments that the men she dates keep trying to find out "what" she is because she looks "exotic." What do you think she means? What is an "exotic" look? Against what standard is it compared?
3. Lite notes that although the census bureau considers revealing one's racial background optional, this latitude is often not afforded in social interaction. Is it important for you to know someone's ethnic background? Is it important to your identity to share your own background with others? Explain.
4. How did Lite's experiences as a child influence her "silence"? Is her reaction justifiable considering the circumstances? Is it safer to guard your ethnic background? Explain.
5. Lite provides a personal perspective on the ways people identify themselves by race and the ways others try to identify them. Write an essay about what is important to your own sense of identity. Is race an important factor? What about other factors, such as gender, age, religion, or education. In your opinion, on what criteria do the people you meet judge you? What do you want them to judge you by?

DON TERRY

Getting Under My Skin

Depending on who wants to know, the author of the next essay could be white, black, both, and neither. Why it matters at all is another question. New York Times *reporter Don Terry, the offspring of a white mother and a black father, describes his personal struggle to be "an integrated man in a segregated world." His personal narrative appeared as part of a series of articles on race and ethnicity run by the* New York Times *in July of 2000.*

When I was a kid growing up in Chicago, I used to do anything I could to put off going to bed. One of my favorite delaying tactics was to engage my mother in a discussion about the important questions of the day, questions my friends and I had debated in the backyards of our neighborhood that afternoon—like, who did God root for, the Cubs or the White Sox? (The correct answer was, and still is, the White Sox.)

Then one night I remember asking my mother something I had been wondering for a long time. "Mom," I asked, "What am I?"

"You're my darling Donny," she said.

"I know. But what else am I?"

"You're a precious little boy who someday will grow up to be a wonderful, handsome man."

"What I mean is, you're white and Dad's black, so what does that make me?"

"Oh, I see," she said. "Well, you're half-black and you're half-white, so you're the best of both worlds."

The next day, I told my friends that I was neither black nor white. "I'm the best of both worlds," I announced proudly.

"Man, you're crazy," one of the backyard boys said. "You're not even the best of your family. Your sister is. That girl is fine."

For much of my life, I've tried to believe my mother. Having grown up in a family of blacks and whites, I'd long thought I saw race more clearly than most people. I appreciated being able to get close to both worlds, something few ever do. It was like having a secret knowledge.

And yet I've also known from an early age that things were more complicated than my mother made them out to be. Our country, from its very beginnings, has been obsessed with determining who is white and who is black. Our history has been shaped by that disheartening question. To be both black and white, then, is to do nothing less than confound national consciousness.

My mother denies it, but it has also sometimes confounded our family. For as my mother was answering my bedtime question, my brothers, David and Robert, her children from an earlier marriage, were going to sleep in a house 15 miles away. My father was black. David and Robert's was white. They lived with my grandmother in an all-white neighborhood. I lived with my mother and my younger sister, Diane, in Hyde Park, a mixed neighborhood on the South Side of Chicago. We shared a loving parent, but we lived in separate Americas. We have spent most of our lives trying to come together.

My father, Bill Terry, was born in Covington, Kentucky, in 1921, the grandson of slaves. In his youth, he was a professional boxer. Later, he went to work as a bodyguard for the unions in Chicago, cracking scab heads. He was one black man who was not at all shy about standing up to authority. In his late thirties, he became an actor. He was good at it, too. My mother told me years later that when my father walked onto a stage to deliver his lines in *The Death of Bessie Smith*, the audience gasped. "He had presence," my mother said. "Incredible presence."

He was a lifelong integrationist, but the nonviolent civil rights movement was not for him. He could not understand how protesters could allow themselves to be roughed up and spat on at sit-ins and not defend themselves. Bill Terry didn't turn the other cheek; he threw the other fist.

My mother, Jeanne Katherine Ober, was born in 1918 and was reared on a dairy farm outside the village of Greenwood, Illinois. She was sent to high school in Chicago and then, at 25, she returned home to marry the son of a wealthy farmer. It was a rocky union: her husband drank too much, and after eight years of marriage, my mother left, taking her two sons to Chicago—David was 8, Robert was 2. There, she opened a nursery school and became involved in civil rights work through her Unitarian church. Until then, she had never personally known a black person.

My parents met in 1956, at a party of racially mixed hipsters. He was 35; she was 38. As my mother tells it, she had been eyeing my father for much of the evening. He was the center of attention, with his boxer's grace and a smile that could light up the darkest corners of the room. Before long, my father asked my mother to dance. At 6 feet 2 inches, he towered over her. Soon, my parents were living together—along with David and Robert—in my mother's four-bedroom Colonial in Evanston, a Chicago suburb. Ten months after they met, I was born.

I was 6 months old when my father decided he wanted to sell the house and move to California. When my mother's mother heard about the plan, she had a fit. My grandmother said the boys needed stability and insisted they live with her and her second husband, Gerhard Raven.

My staying with Grandpa Raven was not an option. On the day Grandpa Raven found out my mother was carrying a black man's baby, he got uncharacteristically drunk. My grandmother told him about the pregnancy at a restaurant, because she felt that perhaps if she explained it in a public place, he might not explode. When they got home, Gerhard poured himself a drink and took it outside to the front porch. He sat on the cement steps muttering about the "goddamn niggers."

When we left for California, the plan was for my parents to send for my brothers once we got settled. But "instead of getting settled," my mother said, "we got poor." We quickly ran out of money. My father lost his landscaping job and stopped looking for work. Less than a year after arriving in L.A., he hopped into our car and disappeared without saying goodbye.

My mother was desperate. She used her last few dollars to buy a plane ticket to get the two of us back to Chicago, where she knew my father was headed. We arrived around Christmas with nowhere to go. My grandmother made it clear that we were not welcome at her house. We spent the holiday sleeping in the home of a black friend of my mother's. "I was disowned," my mother said recently, when I asked her about those days.

"Was it because of me?" I asked, sounding to myself like a little boy again. "Was it because I was black?"

"No." my mother said. "No, it had nothing to do with you. My mother was mad at me for going through the money."

I was surprised at how relieved I felt. I wasn't sure that I believed her, though I desperately wanted to. One of the nightmares of race is that it's sometimes hard to distinguish between cruelties—hard to know what is racism and what is the simple human infliction of pain.

A white friend of my mother's from the civil rights movement allowed us to move into his roach-infested tenement on the edge of Hyde Park. A few weeks after we got settled, my father reappeared and my parents reconciled. We were a family again—except that my brothers continued to live with my grandmother and Gerhard.

A year later, in 1959, my parents had a daughter, Diane. I remember how happy I was that we were all together. It was especially great to have my father around. If I bugged him enough, he would put down his paper and, like his hero, Paul Robeson, sing *Ol' Man River* for me. On hot summer evenings, when it seemed the whole neighborhood was out, my father would scoop me up in his arms and run with me through the warm evening air. I was home. My dad was with me; it was heaven.

Hyde Park itself played a major role in my happiness. The neighborhood, which is home to the University of Chicago, had been integrated since the late 1940s, despite the early resistance of the university. By the time I came along, having a black father and a white mother was common in Hyde Park. In fact, there were so many biracial children running around the neighborhood when I was a kid that it was almost hip to be "mixed," as we called ourselves then. It was so hip that some people who weren't pretended that they were. Sophia, for example, was white, but she told everyone that her father, who was from the Soviet Union, was a "black Russian—you know, like the drink," she said. Since she was only trying to fit in, we forgave her lies.

Most of the mixed kids in Hyde Park were pure-blooded mulattos, so to speak. There were Bob, Michael, Rebecca, Cindy, the Twins, and many others. All of them had black fathers and white mothers. With so many kids who looked like me and with so many parents who looked like mine, it was easy to feel completely comfortable saying I was simply half and half. My memory is one of togetherness.

That's not to say that even in this utopia the power of race was entirely absent from our lives. When I was a boy, my father would perform a ritual. He'd plop his long brown arm down on a tabletop and ask me if I could see the red tint in his skin. "See there," he'd say. "That's the Indian blood in me. You have it, too. All the Terrys do. We're a quarter Cherokee."

I'd carefully inspect his arm, turning it over in the light, but all I could ever see was the brown skin of a black man. I thought it was a strange game. He did not look like an Indian. His skin was brown. There was nothing red about him.

There was nothing red about me either. My complexion is the color of sand. The texture of my hair is somewhere between kinky and curly. I have my father's full lips, and my nose and thick eyebrows come from my mother. When I look in the mirror, it is easy for me to see Europe and Africa dancing across my face like lovers.

Other people, however, aren't sure what they see. When they ask, "What's your nationality?" I often suspect that they really mean: are you on our side or their side? Can we trust you, Brother? Are you dangerous, Nigger? I'm not sure my answer can ever really change the interaction. These questions, these loyalty oaths, have followed me most of my life.

In 1962, our world changed. My parents got into a vicious argument. My father had been out carousing and my mother was fed up with him drinking up what little money we had. In a flash, my father had his big hands wrapped around my mother's throat, squeezing as hard as he could, banging her head against the wall. It sounded like a thunderstorm. I was terrified. I had heard my father yell before, but he had never picked my mother up by her throat and screamed into her face, "Bitch!"

I had no idea what to do, so I threw myself at his tree trunk of a leg and tried to bite him. Whenever I think of that night, my father transforms, in my child's memory, into one of those scary talking trees in *The Wizard of Oz*. "Daddy!" I screamed. "Please stop hurting Mama. Please, Daddy. Please."

He would not stop. I bit him again. He banged her head some more. My cousin Junior, who was a grown man, but not nearly as grown as my father, somehow persuaded him to stop, and my mother slumped to the floor, holding her throat and looking almost as scared as I was.

In a few minutes, the police seemed to fill up the apartment with their rough voices and the sound of their clubs slapping against their leather gun belts and holsters. They yelled at my father to turn around and to put his hands behind his back so they could put the handcuffs on. I was confused. I didn't know what was happening. After all, the only time I really saw my father with his hands behind his back was when he brought me candy from the corner store. He would make me guess which hand held the sweets.

Then the police took him down the stairs, and I remember being scared all over again. I begged them not to take my father away, but they never turned back.

After that, my parents separated for good. My father moved to New York City to pursue his acting career. My mother was left with two children in a crumbling apartment. Sometimes my mother had to choose between buying food for us or paying the utility bills. Once, when the electricity was cut off, my sister and I snaked an extension cord under our front door and plugged it into a socket in the building's hall so we could have a lamp to do homework. We went on public assistance.

The only salvation was that, bit by bit, we started to see my grandmother and brothers again. Of course, we could only visit my grandmother's yellow brick bungalow on the far North Side of Chicago when Grandpa Raven was at work or out of town on one of his fishing trips. Grandpa Raven had a bad heart. My grandmother was afraid that the stress of seeing his stepdaughter and her black children would kill him. So we made sneak visits.

To me, my brothers seemed rich. There was a push-button television console in the living room, a new Dodge in the garage and a freezer stuffed with ice cream bars in the basement. My grandmother, whom we called Nana, would also sneak my brothers down to Hyde Park, reminding them, "Don't tell Grandpa Raven."

Gerhard Raven died when I was 8. His heart finally gave out. But I can sleep easy that the sight of a black child in his family was not what killed him. He died never having laid eyes on me.

As far I was concerned, Grandpa Raven was an unrepentant racist; to my brothers, however, the man who took them fishing couldn't have been a better surrogate grandfather. "He was better than a father," David said. "He was a great guy. He was not a man motivated by prejudice." My brother even had an explanation for the drunken rantings on the steps that day: "Rather than blame Mother," he said, "he blamed 'the niggers.' "

In my view, David is just as blinded by his love for Grandpa Raven as I am by my hate. I tell myself that Gerhard is racist evil incarnate. In my heart, though, I know there is more to it than that. The truth is a child's truth: I had wanted Gerhard to be my grandfather, too.

After Gerhard's death, we visited my grandmother every other weekend, making up for lost years. One night, I stayed over at Nana's. When it came time for my bath, I hopped into the tub, pretending to recreate the moon landing, which had just taken place. I had one foot in when Nana called from the living room, "Remember, Donny, just because your skin is darker doesn't mean I can't see the dirt, so scrub hard."

Nana didn't mean to hurt my feelings, but she did. Yet I never thought of her as prejudiced. She was an elderly white woman, trying to make her way in a changing world. She never said "nigger." She said "negro." She tried to treat everyone fairly. She called me "Darling" and "Honey Bunch." She made sure there were always plenty of big chocolate chips in the pantry. I loved her dearly and she loved me. Without her, we would have sunk completely into poverty.

Biracial though I was, my first real memory of being called "nigger" was the same cruel rite of passage it has been for black children the country over. I was 7, and I was playing football with a group of white kids in a suburb 25 long miles from Hyde Park. A boy, about my age, saw me in a neighbor's yard and started jumping up and down. He pointed at me excitedly as he chanted: "Nigger. Nigger. Nigger."

I was shocked. I wasn't a nigger. My mother was white. Couldn't he see her standing there, a few feet away? He had heard me call her mom at least a half-dozen times: "Mom, I'm having too much fun. Mom, please, can we stay a little longer, so I can play with my new friends?" Couldn't he tell I was only half-black? He could have easily called me whitey, honky, or cracker. Why didn't he do that? I had just as much white blood in me as black. And even if I was all black, why was he calling me names?

I tried to go after the boy, but my mother pulled me back. Then she did something that shocked me—and filled me with joy. From 10 feet away, she threw a plastic cup at the kid, hitting him in the head and sending him running down the street, calling for his mother.

A few years after the football game, I was walking down the street with a white friend. A well-dressed member of the Nation of Islam asked me if I wanted to buy a copy of *Muhammad Speaks*, the group's newspaper. "No thanks," I said.

"Come on, brother, help your people out."

"No thanks."

"Man, you just want to be with Europeans," the Muslim said bitterly, pointing his paper at my friend.

"My mother is a European," I said.

"Brother, I'm sorry for you," the Muslim shot back.

Other moments also made it clear that a mixed family seemed foreign to the eyes of America. In the summer of 1972, when I was 15, my brother David, who collects old Packards, took me to Nebraska to pick up a 1956 Patrician. I was excited—it was my first out-of-town trip with one of my brothers. At the car owner's house, David introduced me to a white man in white shoes. He leaned against a white picket fence.

"This is my little brother, Donny," he said. The man and I shook hands. Then he stared at me. I had a huge Afro; David's straight brown hair was cut Young Republican short. The man winked at David. "You mean you work together?" he asked.

"No," David said. "I mean this is my brother."

"Oh, I get what you're saying," the man said. "The Bible says we are all brothers under the skin. It's good to see people taking the word of God to heart."

What a fool, I thought to myself then. Today I know: as a person of mixed race, it's the norm to have your closest relationships questioned at every turn.

Until I went to college, racial difference stood out for me precisely because it was the exception to the rule. In college, it became a defining force in my life.

It didn't start that way. In 1975, when I discovered Oberlin College, I was confident I had found a place where I could be my mixed-race self.

As a stop on the underground railroad, Oberlin had a special reputation for enlightened race relations. It was the school's brochure that sold me, though. Featured prominently was a picture of two baseball players conferring on the mound. One player was white with a long ponytail, the other black with an Afro. It looked like home.

But at the start of freshman year, I was startled to see a very different picture. When I walked into the dining room, black students were sitting together at a group of tables in the middle of the room; white students were eating together at tables along the windows. At football and basketball games, black fans usually sat with blacks, whites with whites. The intramural sports teams were rarely mixed.

For a while, I tried to recreate Hyde Park at Oberlin. I hung out with a mixed group of friends and my intramural teams always included white guys and black guys—and slow guys of every color. I decided not to join the African Heritage dorm. But even on this supposedly liberal campus, trying to live integrated was an uphill battle.

A black student asked me once, "My man, where's the mail room?"

"See that brother over there?" I said, pointing across the nearly empty room.

"What brother?"

"That one," I said. "That blond dude."

"Man, that's no brother," he said. "That's a white boy. What's wrong with you?"

What was wrong with me? I wasn't split in two—the world was. And yet I was the one expected to adjust. Being away from Hyde Park was a shock to my racial system. I felt even more out of step with most white students. For the first time, I was exposed to white people who had not known black people as friends, neighbors, or even classmates.

One night, I was visiting a white girl and her white roommate in their dorm. The door was open and we were just talking. Another black student was also there, flirting with the roommate. I was just about to leave when a white girl walking down the hall passed the open door and stuck her head in. She looked disgusted. "What's this," she asked, "a soul-brother session?" I was stunned. What did race have to do with anything? We were just two guys rapping to two girls and not getting anywhere. The girl I was visiting looked embarrassed. I wasn't sure if she was embarrassed about her rude neighbor—or that her rude neighbor had "caught" a couple of brothers in her room.

Fed up, I embraced blackness—as a shield and a cause. I signed up for a course on black nationalism. The decision was one of the most important developments of my life. Black studies saved me. It gave me a sense of discovery both academically and personally. Black studies helped me find an identity. As important, it helped me for the first time to understand my father's anger.

The more I learned the more I began to realize the struggles a black person born in 1921 had to go through just to survive. Once, after reading about the brutality of the race riots following the First World War, I had to walk around the library to cool off. That was my father's welcome to life. I didn't want to run into any of my white friends that afternoon. I didn't know what I might say to them.

At last, I felt in touch with my rage that race, even at my "progressive" college, mattered so much; that I could not completely be who I was, Don Terry, an integrated man, with a white mother and a black father; that I would repeatedly be lumped in a broad racial category—black—and treated like a caricature instead of the complicated individual I knew myself to be.

It was exhausting and maddening, being constantly judged by people who thought they knew so much about me solely because of the color of my skin, when in fact they knew nothing at all. I seemed to be the only one to understand that the Don Terry who went to campus rallies to protest the school's investments in South Africa could, at the end of the day, relax to the Rolling Stones. Disgusted by the world's refusal to see me as mixed and individual, I chose "blackness."

My decision, I've come to believe, had as much to do with anger as anything else. I started using the term "white boy," something I had never done in my life. It felt liberating at first, like standing up to a bully. But I felt guilt when I went home to Hyde Park and spent time with my family and old friends. I was afraid I was becoming a racist.

One afternoon, I was driving my mother's tiny Volkswagen. She was sitting in the passenger seat. One of my best friends, Danny Gnatz, a white guy with hair down past his shoulders, was in back. We were talking and laughing when a fat white man, driving a big American car, suddenly cut in front of me. We nearly collided. I slammed on the brakes, glared out the window, and shouted, "You stupid white son of a bitch."

As soon as I said it, I felt like jumping out of the car and running away in shame. At first, my mother and Danny pretended that they had not heard. What was going on with me? What did race have to do with it? "I'm sorry, you guys," I said. "That's okay, Donny," my mother said, patting my arm. Danny slapped me on the back of the head, signaling that everything was all right. But we drove a long way in silence.

The incident in the car caused me to question my behavior, but not my identity. When I returned to Oberlin, I enrolled in more black studies courses and became even more involved in the anti-apartheid movement. I left Oberlin a thoroughly black man.

After college, I went into journalism, hoping to do good in the world, as my parents had tried to do. My first job was at the *Chicago Defender*, a small and struggling but historically significant black newspaper. I then went on to work for a number of larger papers in the Midwest before coming to the *New York Times* in 1988.

In just about every one of these jobs, my reputation was built as much around my race as my journalism; I was the black man with a big mouth, ready to get loud at the slightest racial slight—the brother with a boulder on his shoulder. An editor at the *Chicago Tribune*, where I used to work, called me the most contentious young reporter he'd ever met.

Once, at the *Times*, as I was finishing a crime piece, an editor came up to me and asked whether the arrested man, whom the police had roughed up, had a criminal record. I put it right back to him: how come you're not asking me if the cop has a record of brutality complaints? In short, I was the one who could always be counted on to ask the editors why our stories on welfare seemed to focus on black people, when more whites received public assistance.

And yet. And yet even as a "black man," I remained confusing to the world around me, including the black world. One weekend, after I had joined the *Times*, I brought home a girlfriend—a talented black woman, a poet, and fellow journalist. I took her to meet my brother David. His young daughter, Julie, was wild that afternoon, running around the house, jumping on the furniture and singing *Heartbreak Hotel* over and over.

Afterward my girlfriend, rubbing her temples with both hands, told me, "That Julie is a white brat." I was startled by how much those words hurt. Why couldn't Julie just be a brat? She was a little kid. I used to shoot arrows down the hall of our apartment; my brother Robert loved to run barefoot through the snow. In my family the kids, black and white, are wild. Not long after that, my girlfriend and I broke up. Julie may have been a brat, but not a white brat.

I like to joke that my mother had four children, if you don't count any of the men in her life. David is a successful stockbroker. Robert is an artist and boat captain. My sister, Diane, has spent the past 22 years battling schizophrenia. Diane has a daughter, Wakara, who was reared mostly by my mother and me, and who graduated from Oberlin in May. When she accepted her diploma, David was there, just as he has been for every one of her graduations—and every one of mine.

Still, though we are adults now in a more enlightened time, race can appear like a ghost, disrupting the life of our family. A few years ago, I was at David's house. It was a cold Chicago night, yet inside, with flames crackling, we felt wonderfully warm. David was mixing drinks. Julie, then 12, announced to us that she had received an A on her seventh-grade social studies assignment. "Would you like to see my project, Uncle Donny?" she asked me.

Using old photographs, Julie had laid out 100 years of the family's history, culminating in the well-kept suburb where she and her family now lived. She handed me the three-ring notebook. Under a photograph of my mother on a pony, the caption read, "This is a picture of my Grandma Jeanne when she was 12 years old on the family farm in Greenwood, Illinois." A few pages and decades later the text reported: "This is a picture of my Uncle Robert in the sixties. As you can see, he was a hippie." There were pictures and words about almost everyone in the family, including Julie's dog, Buddy, and her cat, Clipper. There were pictures of everyone, except for Aunt Diane, Cousin Wakara, and Uncle Donny, the black members of the family.

I could not believe that we had been left out. Then I figured I must have gone through the pictures too fast. Or maybe, I thought, putting down my glass, it was the drink. So I went through the book a second time, searching for our pictures, or at least a few words about us. "I'm not in this," I said, closing the book and handing it back to Julie. "What's up with that?" There was only awkward silence.

Though I tried to let the incident go, I found myself one day raising it with David's son, Noah, who had just returned from the Navy. Noah listened to the story, and then told me one of his own. He was showing his photo album to a black shipmate. When the sailor turned to pictures of Wakara and me, Noah said: "The guy was happy. He patted me on the back. He said, 'We don't have to worry about Noah. He's part black.' "

My nephew paused. "I told him I'm not part black," he said. "It didn't matter to him. He was still happy." And so was I.

My brother Robert lives in a small city in Washington State, largely isolated from the rest of the family. It is clear, too, that he has isolated himself from memories of our childhood. His distance—both geographic and emotional—is understandable, for he bears the wounds of an 8-year-old who was left behind by his mother. When I asked Robert questions about the past, he repeatedly said he did not remember and that I should ask David. But one afternoon, as we drove through his town, he slowly began to open up.

Robert does not think he harbors any ill will toward black people because of Bill Terry's role in dividing our family. But I'm not so sure. "You could say," Robert said, "that a black person came in and tore up the family." He didn't say, "You could say another man came in and. . . ."

"You could blame Bill for destroying the family," he went on, negotiating the road's curves. "But I don't think that has rubbed off on me as being a racist. I don't think it's affected me in a negative way. You can see it affecting someone like Grandpa Raven, though," he continued. "He had a little bit about him that was kind of Aryan. People build up these barriers and it's hard for them to climb over them."

We headed toward the town's waterfront, and the more Robert talked, the more I worked to hide my anger and my hurt—and to remember his. "Mother," he said, "seemed to develop a propensity for black men."

I simmered. What did it matter that Mom had black boyfriends? She lived on the South Side of Chicago and was involved in the civil rights movement. There were a lot of black men around. If she had white boyfriends instead, would Robert say that she had developed a propensity for white men?

It began to rain, and we passed a couple of young Latino men standing on a corner. Robert glanced at them and said his town wasn't the same anymore. More and more people who looked like gang members seemed to be showing up, many of them Latino. "I get upset with the country changing so much," he said.

Jesus, I thought to myself. What the hell does that mean? If Robert had been any other white man talking about the "good ol' days" and the changing country, if I had been interviewing Robert as a reporter on assignment, I would have been convinced I'd found a racist. But even in the midst of my anger, I kept forcing myself to try to believe that Robert was not a racist. He was my big brother, a star athlete, the guy I wanted to impress when I was a kid.

No matter what, I was willing to give him the benefit of the doubt, something I realized I do not often do for most white people. "I don't think I'm a racist," Robert said, making me think he had read my mind. "But maybe I am. I hope not."

If Robert and I were struggling with race—after all, in heavy traffic, I occasionally mumble about bad-driving white boys—his 8-year-old son, Henry, was not. One day, Robert, Henry and I drove up to Vancouver, Canada. We spent a wonderful afternoon going to museums and eating fish and chips. In the evening, we headed home, with Robert driving and Henry and me sitting in the back. At the border, Robert pulled into the line of cars waiting to go into the United States. From the back seat, I could see the American border guard, a young black man, wave several cars through with hardly a word. When it was our turn, however, he walked slowly around our car, peering into the windows. Something was suspicious about us.

"Where are you going?" he asked Robert.

"We're going home," Robert said.

"Who's that in the back seat?" the guard asked, pointing at me.

"That's my brother."

"Your brother?"

"Yeah," Robert said. "We're half brothers." I cringed at the word "half." The guard looked at me again. He was on the verge of asking another question, when Henry leaned across my lap and, poking his head out the window, said, "He's my Uncle Donny, and we love him."

The young American still looked suspicious, but he stepped aside and waved us on our way home.

Perhaps, I thought, that's the best we can hope to do—to insist upon our allegiance to one another, our brotherhood across the divide—and try to go home.

And my parents? My mother went back to college when she was in her forties and has been a schoolteacher ever since. At 82, she teaches history and conflict resolution at an alternative school, Sullivan House, on the South Side of Chicago.

Not long ago, I tried to ask her why she didn't bring David and Robert with us to California. It was a gentle summer day and we were in a small Catholic cemetery near her hometown. My mother sat in the grass next to her mother's grave. She was hugging her knees to her chest. Her back was turned to me. She was crying.

We had been to the cemetery many times over the years, but I could not remember my mother crying before. The tears were my fault.

I was asking her questions. The child in me wanted to know what she was thinking when she left my brothers behind. Didn't she see the harm it would do to us all? But all she answered was: "I was at my wits' end in those days. Everything was falling apart."

She paused. "We had no money. I guess I just thought the boys were living with Nana and Gerhard, and they were better off."

Leave her be, I told myself, as I looked out over the graves of my ancestors. What good can come from dredging up painful memories?

My father died of cancer in 1998 in New York City at age 76. I hadn't seen him for two years, though I had kept track of his acting career, which included a role in *Forrest Gump*. A group of my father's friends arranged a memorial to be held in his apartment building—though I finally could not bear to go to the service, all those years late. My grief and anger over his abandonment was still strong. A friend brought me a videotape of the service.

I was pleased to see a parade of mourners of all colors walk to the front of the room and say kind things about my father. They said he had stopped drinking, that he had found peace with God, that he had become like a grandfather to some of the children in the building. It was the kind of integrated gathering he had fought for and loved.

One speaker was a stylishly dressed white man in his late sixties. He said he and my father had spent a lot of time talking about my father's childhood. The man started choking up and walked away.

The man, it turned out, was a psychologist my father had started seeing when he was 70. A few months after watching the tape, I called him. We talked about the fact that Bill had fathered seven children with four different women—three white, one black. With the obvious exception of my sister, I barely know any of them. "He was repeatedly touching on the issue of white women as if he were trying to make rational in somebody else's eyes how he had lived his life," the therapist said. "He couldn't see it as accidental that he had a succession of nonblack women in his life who gave birth to his children."

The therapist said that my father wanted to have racially mixed children in part to prove himself to his mother. As a boy he had been passed from relative to relative and was never really sure of who his father was. Bill also told the therapist that his mother had been disappointed that his skin was a dark shade. By having lighter, mixed-race children, he was saying, the therapist concluded: " 'Look at these beautiful children I've produced.' It was a search for approval."

I believe that chasing white women was more than that for my father. It was about fighting back against pre-civil rights America. One thing that my father liked about white women, he told his therapist, was the fact that seeing them on his thick brown arm drove white men crazy. It reminded me of something my father had told me once: "I took my wife anywhere I wanted to go. I'm a man."

The day after my father died, I wandered through his apartment. I ran my hands over his books, his saxophone, and the photograph on the wall of his hero, Paul Robeson, dressed as Othello. My father's love for Robeson was one of the few uncomplicated joys we shared. After my father died, all I wanted was that picture.

I took the picture down and hugged it. Then I peeked into my father's closet and slipped on his too-big-for-me leather jacket, knotting the belt tightly like a little boy playing Daddy. I took a series of deep breaths and inhaled the aroma of his pipes, lifting them to my nose from the carousel on the coffee table.

Then, from under his bed, I pulled a small strongbox with a broken lock. It was full of documents. One was a copy of my birth certificate. I was surprised and touched that he had it. Then I noticed what he had done to it. On lines 8 and 13 of the document, the clerk's office for Cook County, Illinois, had recorded that my father was "Negro" and my mother "Caucasian." My father, however, had a different idea. Using dark blue ink, he had crossed out the references to race on my birth certificate, leaving just "father" and "mother."

On paper, at least, he tried to give me a gift that could not be fully realized in his life: the gift of family that transcends divisions of race.

On paper, it was that simple.

QUESTIONS: For Thinking and Writing

1. Terry notes that "having grown up in a family of blacks and whites, I'd long thought I saw race more clearly than most people." Based on this essay, do you think he is correct?
2. Terry observes that the United States, from its "very beginnings, has been obsessed with determining who is white and who is black." What does he mean? How does Terry's story support this observation. Can your relate any stories of your own that support this viewpoint?
3. As Jordan Lite does in her essay, Terry comments that people want to know "what" he is. Terry believes that they ask because they want to

know "are you on our side or their side?" How does this assessment differ from Lite's?

4. Have you ever anticipated or expected that you might be mistreated due to your race, age, or gender? If so, describe the situation and its outcome.
5. Terry notes in several places in his essay anxiety over how he looks and the reaction of others. Confusion over "what" he is and "what side" he is on adds to his struggle with personal identity. Consider the connection between how others "see" you and how you perceive yourself. Critically analyze how your physical appearance may be interpreted by others.

VIEWPOINTS

You Have the Right to Remain a Target of Racial Profiling

Eugene Robinson

The Racial Profiling Myth Lives On

Steve Chapman

Racial profiling is the practice by law enforcement of considering race as an indicator of the likelihood of criminal behavior. Based on statistical assumptions, racial profiling presumes that certain groups of people are more likely to commit, or not commit, certain crimes. The Supreme Court officially upheld the constitutionality of this practice, as long as race is only one of several factors leading to the detainment or arrest of an individual.

"Driving while black" is an expression used to describe the phenomenon in which African Americans are pulled over for traffic violations more often than whites and people of other races. Almost a decade ago, a U.S. Department of Justice investigation of the New Jersey State Police revealed that racial profiling—the practice of stopping people suspected of criminal activity based on race—was indeed a problem in that state. A Gallup poll taken a year later in 1999 reported that over half of those polled believed that the police were actively engaged in the practice of racial profiling, and 81 percent said that they disapproved of the practice. Reacting to pressure from victims groups, the public, and the ACLU, over 20 states have passed legislation prohibiting racial profiling. In February 2001, during an address to a joint session of Congress, President George W. Bush said of racial profiling, "It's wrong and we will end it in America." Yet, despite efforts of law enforcement agencies to prove otherwise, many people believe that racial profiling for African Americans is still a problem on the nation's highways.

The next two essays present different viewpoints on racial profiling and "driving while black." Eugene Robinson reports in the May 1, 2007 edition of the

Seattle Times *that the problem still exists. Steve Chapman, drawing from the same data, challenges this view in an essay published by* Reason *magazine on May 7, 2007.*

You Have the Right to Remain a Target of Racial Profiling

Eugene Robinson

This just in: Driving while black is still unsafe at any speed, even zero miles per hour. The same goes for driving while brown.

The Federal Bureau of Justice Statistics released a report Sunday showing that white, African-American, and Hispanic drivers are equally likely to be pulled over by police for an alleged traffic offense. In 2005, the year covered by the study, black drivers were actually less likely—by a tiny margin—to be stopped by police than drivers belonging to the other groups. You might be tempted to conclude that the constitutional imperative of equal protection had finally been extended to America's streets and highways.

But you would be wrong. The study reports that African-American and Hispanic drivers who are stopped by police are more than twice as likely as whites to be subjected to a search. Specifically, police searched only 3.6 percent of white drivers pulled over in a traffic stop, while they searched 9.5 percent of African Americans who obeyed the flashing lights and 8.8 percent of Hispanics.

The report says the "apparent disparities" between racial groups "do not constitute proof that police treat people differently along demographic lines," since there could be "countless other factors and circumstances" that go into the decision of whom to spread eagle on the hood.

All right, those figures alone might not constitute "proof" of bias that would convince a jury beyond a reasonable doubt. They are pretty compelling, though, especially when you also consider that black and Hispanic drivers are much more likely to experience "police use of force" than whites.

And besides, the following paragraph in the report pretty effectively demolishes that "move along, folks, nothing to see here" disclaimer about bias:

"Police actions taken during a traffic stop were not uniform across racial and ethnic categories. Black drivers (4.5 percent) were twice as likely as white drivers (2.1 percent) to be arrested during a traffic stop, while Hispanic drivers (65 percent) were more likely than white (56.2 percent) or black (55.8 percent) drivers to receive a ticket.

In addition, whites (9.7 percent) were more likely than Hispanics (5.9 percent) to receive a written warning, while whites (18.6 percent) were more likely than blacks (13.7 percent) to be verbally warned by police."

African Americans have been putting up with the "driving while black" thing for so long that we've become somewhat cynical. For example, nearly three-quarters of whites and Hispanics who were pulled over for allegedly running a red light or a stop sign were willing to concede that they had been caught dead to rights, while nearly half of African Americans in that situation believed they had committed no infraction. About 90 percent of white drivers detained for some sort of vehicle defect, such as a busted taillight, thought the stop was legitimate, as opposed to 67 percent of black drivers.

Think that's just paranoia? Then try to reconcile the counterintuitive fact that while blacks are much more likely than whites to be arrested in a traffic stop, they are also more likely to be released with no enforcement action, not even a warning. This looks to me like powerful evidence that racial profiling is alive and well. It suggests there was no good reason to stop those people.

"About one in ten searches during a traffic stop uncovered evidence of a possible crime," the report says. What could be wrong with that? Isn't that what police should be doing—enforcing the nation's laws, capturing criminals, making law-abiding Americans that much safer?

Of course that's what we pay our police officers to do, but not selectively. Whites, too, drive around with drugs, illegal weapons, open containers of alcohol, or other contraband in their cars. The numbers in the report suggest that if white drivers stopped by police were searched at the same rate as blacks or Hispanics, police would uncover evidence of tens of thousands of additional crimes each year, doubtless putting thousands of dangerous people behind bars.

But, of course, we don't want a society in which everybody is being patted down by police officers all the time. We don't want a society in which people have to stand by the side of the road, fuming, while police arbitrarily rummage through the stuff in their cars—shopping bags, children's toys, McDonald's wrappers—on the off chance of finding something illegal.

If you're black or brown, though, may I see your license and registration, please?

The Racial Profiling Myth Lives On

Steve Chapman

We've all heard of the offense of "driving while black." But not everyone has heard the good news: It doesn't exist anymore. According to an authoritative report, black motorists are no more likely than whites to be pulled over by police. So how has that study been greeted? As proof that police racism is still a powerful force.

It's a widely accepted article of faith that cops systematically engage in racial profiling against dark-complexioned folks. Yet this is the second consecutive survey from the Federal Bureau of Justice Statistics—using information supplied not by police but by citizens—that finds law enforcement to be admirably color-blind when it comes to routine traffic enforcement. Not a puny achievement, but one that was overlooked by people straining to find lingering discrimination.

The complaint is that though they get stopped at the same rate as whites, minority motorists are more likely to get unfavorable treatment during the stop. According to BJS, 3.6 percent of whites are searched, compared with 9.5 percent of blacks and 8.8 percent of Latinos. African Americans are more likely to have force used against them and to be arrested. And they more often feel their treatment is unwarranted.

What can we make of these figures? Not what is claimed by critics, like those at the American Civil Liberties Union, which labeled the disparities "disturbing," and columnist Eugene Robinson of the *Washington Post*, who detected "powerful evidence that racial profiling is alive and well." Some people get their exercise jumping to conclusions.

The researchers at BJS tried to discourage snap judgments. "The apparent disparities documented in this report do not constitute proof that police treat people differently along demographic lines," they warn. "Any of these disparities might be explained by countless other factors and circumstances that were not taken into account in the analysis."

Plenty of other elements could generate these divergent patterns. Why would black drivers be arrested more often? Maybe because African Americans commit crimes at a far higher rate and are convicted of felonies at a far higher rate. In 2005, for instance, blacks were nearly seven times more likely to be in prison than whites.

Those disparities are bound to affect the outcome of traffic stops. Most blacks, like most whites, are not crooks. But since the average black driver is statistically more likely to be a criminal than the average white driver, he's more likely to have an outstanding arrest warrant, which the police would find when running a computer check of his license. A computer check that turns up a long rap sheet will probably induce the patrol officer to ask for a look inside the trunk.

A motorist of felonious habits is also more likely to have illegal guns or drugs on board. If the contraband is visible to a traffic cop, or if it shows up in a search, the driver can expect to be arrested. Not to mention that the vehicle itself may turn out to be stolen.

Given the racial gap in crime rates, it would be a shock if traffic stops didn't generate more searches and arrests of blacks than whites. Even in a world where cops are completely free of racial prejudice, that is exactly what you would expect. There is a similar difference, after all, between the sexes—males are nearly twice as likely as females to be arrested during a stop. Is that because cops are sexists? No, it's because men commit more crimes.

Trying to find "compelling" evidence of racism in this data is a fruitless task. Robinson makes much of the fact that blacks who are stopped are more likely to be sent on their way without any corrective action, even an oral warning. That, he says, "suggests there was no good reason to stop these people." Or it might suggest that cops cut African-American motorists a bit more slack on petty issues, perhaps in the hope of improving their reputation.

Whatever they do, the cops can't win. Blacks don't get stopped more often? Big deal. Blacks have higher arrest rates? Proof of racism. More blacks are let off without a warning? More proof of racism.

And if fewer blacks were let off without a warning? I'll let you guess how that would be interpreted.

QUESTIONS: For Thinking and Writing

1. Robinson observes, "You might be tempted to conclude that the constitutional imperative of equal protection had finally been extended to America's streets and highways." Why, if statistics indicate that black drivers are being pulled over less often, does he feel that racial profiling is still a problem?
2. Robinson quotes the report, "Police actions taken during a traffic stop were not uniform across racial and ethnic categories. Black drivers (4.5 percent) were twice as likely as white drivers (2.1 percent) to be arrested during a traffic stop." Does this information reinforce his points about profiling? What explanation does Chapman offer for this phenomenon? Explain.
3. How have years of racial profiling jaded black motorists? If black drivers think they have been pulled over due to racial profiling, even if they have committed a traffic violation, how do police overcome the perception? Can it be addressed?
4. Evaluate Robinson's observation that because blacks are often released with no enforcement action, the reason is "racial profiling is alive and well. It suggests there was no good reason to stop those people." Does he have a point? Why does Chapman take issue with Robinson's conclusion? Explain.
5. Robinson notes that years of racial profiling have made blacks "cynical." Has racial profiling influenced your perception of law enforcement and the justice system? Why or why not?

AMERICAN CIVIL LIBERTIES UNION, FLORIDA CHAPTER

Which Man Looks Guilty?

Since its inception in 1920, the nonprofit, nonpartisan American Civil Liberties Union (ACLU) has grown from a small group of activists to an

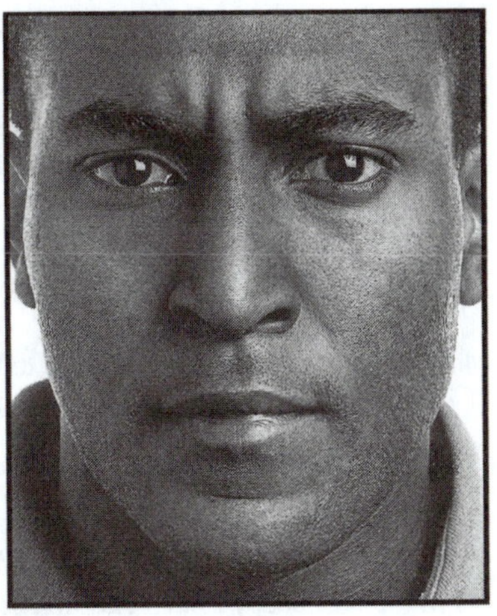

Which man looks guilty? If you picked the man on the right, you're wrong. Wrong for judging a person based upon the color of their skin. Because if you look closely, you'll see that they're the same man. Unfortunately, racial stereotyping like this happens everyday. On America's highways, police stop drivers based on their skin color rather than for the way they are driving. For example, in Florida 80% of those stopped and searched were black and Hispanic, while they constituted only 5% of all drivers. These humiliating and illegal searches are violations of the Constitution and must be fought. Help us defend your rights. Support the ACLU. www.aclu.org **american civil liberties union**

organization of nearly 400,000 members with offices in almost every state. The ACLU's mission is to fight civil liberties violations wherever and whenever they occur. It is also active in national and state government arenas, and is dedicated to upholding the Bill of Rights. This ad addressing racial profiling appeared as part of the ACLU of Florida's Racial Profiling campaign in 2002.

QUESTIONS: For Thinking and Writing

1. At first glance, did you think the men in the photos were two different people? At what point did you realize they were the same person?
2. Did you seriously consider the question posed by the ad, "Which man looks guilty?" If so, which one did you chose? Was race a factor? Why or why not?
3. What point is this ad trying to make? How effective is this ad at getting its message across?
4. How important is the audience to the effectiveness of this ad? Where would you expect to see it? Where would it work, and where would it carry less impact? Explain.

QUESTIONS: For Further Research and Group Work

1. In the first essay in this chapter, Jenkins charges that the media, especially television, contributes to racism by presenting groups of people differently. With the help of *TV Guide* or another television guide, make a list of programs on prime-time television—beginning at 8:00 PM and ending at 11:00 PM—and describe the characters in terms of race and ethnicity as detailed in this essay. For example, are African Americans more likely to be portrayed as dysfunctional or poor? Based on your review of the prime-time lineup, discuss how television may contribute to racial stereotypes. Alternatively, if your data reveals no or little racism, make a note of that as well. Share the results of your group discussion with the class.
2. David Brooks observes that many neighborhoods have failed to be truly racially integrated "for whatever reasons." Interview a diverse group of students about where they grew up. Name the region, state, city or town, and even neighborhood, and ask those you survey to describe its demographic profile, including social, intellectual, professional, and economic aspects. Ask the people you interview for their impressions on why their family lived where they did and the cultural influences they experienced. Prepare a report on your findings. What did you discover about demographic clustering? What might it mean for diversity efforts in the next 20 years?
3. Working in small groups, discuss how ethnic and racial differences divide and unite us as a nation. According to the report *Changing America* by the President's Initiative on Race, the gaps among races and ethnic groups in the areas of education, jobs, economic status, health, housing, and criminal justice are substantial. Access this report at http://www.access.gpo.gov/eop/ca/pdfs/toc.pdf. Choose one subject area from its table of contents, and read through that chapter

and charts. Then, summarize what you have learned about the differences among racial and ethnic groups, and discuss how you think these disparities affect our chances of creating a society in which all Americans can participate equally.

4. Jordan Lite wonders why it is so important that the people she meets know "what" she is. As a nation of peoples from many countries and cultures, it is a question many Americans want to ask. As a class, answer this question in your own words, "introducing" yourself to the rest of the class. Then, as a class, discuss what we do with this information. How does the answer define us to others? What are others likely to think, and why?
5. Don Terry describes the internal conflict he faces every day as he navigates the "two worlds" of his family. Part of his method for dealing with this is through storytelling and sharing his experiences with others. Explore the psychology at work here. Describe how your own identity—including your racial identity—was shaped in childhood, and how that identity impacts the student you are now and the person you hope to become after graduation.
6. Read the Racial Profiling Fact Sheet posted by the ACLU at http://www.aclu.org/racialjustice/racialprofiling and the one listed at the U.S. Department of Justice at http://www.usdoj.gov/opa/pr/2003/June/racial_profiling_fact_sheet.pdf. Review both fact sheets in their entirety and discuss them as a class. What is the government's official position on racial profiling? What exceptions do they make concerning racial profiling, and why? Identify any areas of the document that you find questionable or particularly compelling, and share them with the rest of the class as part of a larger discussion of this document.
7. Visit the Federal Bureau of Justice Statistics and review the latest data on racial profiling and traffic violations. Based on the data, write your own opinion piece on what the data reveals.

9 CHAPTER

The Immigration Debate

THE UNITED STATES OF AMERICA IS A UNION PREDICATED on similar moral values, political and economic self-interest, a common legal system, and a democratic form of government. While we have much in common, we are also a nation of immigrants—people of different ethnic backgrounds, religions, traditions, languages, and cultures. We are a nation whose motto, *e pluribus unum* ("one out of many") bespeaks a pride in its multicultural heritage. But we are also a nation divided by race and ethnicity. We may glorify the memory of our own immigrant ancestors, but do not always welcome with open arms new waves of immigrants. The essays in this unit explore current issues connected with immigration reform, especially as it relates to immigrants coming from Mexico and South America.

Most of the arguments regarding the issue of immigration focus on illegal aliens circumventing U.S. laws. Some critics argue that immigrants themselves have changed—that the current wave of newcomers is different from waves of the past, that this group refuses to assimilate, threatens the American way of life, and expects free handouts. Immigration advocates counter that all immigrant groups resist integration to a certain extent at first, and then assimilate into mainstream culture. They also contend that immigrants promote diversity, revitalize the workforce, and are good for the economy overall. With such diverse perspectives and positions, the issue can be challenging to navigate.

Although America has been a multiethnic and multiracial society since its founding, in the last few decades, different groups of Americans have reasserted their ethnic and racial identities. While this attention to native roots has created greater tolerance and celebration of differences, it has also challenged our definition of ourselves as Americans. Furthermore, immigration compels us to think about how to balance ethnic heritage and identity and how we fit into broader American culture. Are we no longer the "great melting pot" that is often extolled in the history books? Do we need to rethink our definitions of cultural "melting"?

GREGORY RODRIGUEZ

Forging a New Vision of America's Melting Pot

Mexican Americans now comprise the largest immigrant population in American history, and they are poised to become America's largest minority group. Influences of Latino culture pervade mainstream American culture, from style and architecture to art and music. One Californian historian has commented, "the Latinization of America is so profound that no one really sees it." In the next piece, Gregory Rodriguez, a senior fellow at the New America Foundation, explains in his article, first published in the New York Times *on February 11, 2001, how this group will change how the nation views itself in the next century.*

While visiting Ellis Island at the turn of the twentieth century, Henry James wondered how the sweeping tide of immigrants would ultimately affect "the idea of" America. Comparing the incorporation of foreigners to sword- and fire-swallowing feats at a circus, James reflected on what it meant for America to share its patrimony with those "inconceivable aliens."

Yet throughout American history, immigrants and minority groups, seeking to make room for themselves, have broadened the definition of America. Minority experiences have acted as a powerful force in the creation of America's self-image.

For the first half of the twentieth century, Jews were the paradigmatic American minority by which all other minority experiences were understood. In the second half, African Americans, the descendants of a forced migration, set the standard for a racial debate that altered the nation's vision of itself. Now, with Hispanics poised to become the largest minority group, Mexican Americans—who make up two-thirds of all Latinos in the United States—could change how the nation sees itself in the twenty-first century.

Their unique perspectives on racial and cultural synthesis may fundamentally alter the nation's attitudes, for they are the second largest immigrant group in American history—the largest when including illegal immigrants. Mexicans, themselves the product of the clash between the Old and New Worlds, could shift this country's often divisive "us versus them" racial dialogue.

A Census Bureau study released in January of 2001 found that about 10 percent of United States residents are foreign-born, midway between the high of 15 percent at the turn of the twentieth century and the low of 5 percent in 1970. And Mexicans are by far today's biggest immigrant group. As such, they are the most likely to leave a permanent imprint on the culture.

For instead of simply adding one more color to the multicultural rainbow, Mexican Americans may help forge a unifying vision. With a history that reveals an ability to accept racial and cultural ambiguity, Mexican Americans could broaden the definition of America unlike any earlier immigrants.

The early twentieth-century debate about the "melting pot" evolved as Jewish writers envisioned an America that might better accommodate Jews. Their historic experience as a minority prompted them to take the lead in re-imagining America for an entire wave of immigrants. The playwright Israel Zangwill, in a 1908 drama about a Jewish immigrant rejecting his faith's prohibition against intermarriage, developed the optimistic American civic faith that a fusion of ethnicities will create a stronger nation. For Zangwill, the United States was both a safe harbor and a crucible that melted Old World ethnics into a distinctly new American culture.

But by the 1960s, America's exclusion of African Americans from the mainstream forged a new vision based on multiculturalism. Though it encompassed other minority groups, including women and gays, blacks gave the multicultural movement its key moral impetus. The civil rights movement had begun by advocating racial integration, but by the late 1960s its message had fused with a reemergent black separatism that fueled the nascent multicultural movement.

Multiculturalism—the ideology that promotes the coexistence of separate but equal cultures—essentially rejects assimilation and considers the melting-pot concept an unwelcome imposition of the dominant culture. Race became the prism through which all social issues were perceived.

But because their past and present is characterized by a continual synthesis, a blending of the Spanish and indigenous cultures, Mexican Americans could project their own melting pot vision onto America, one that includes mixing race as well as ethnicity. Rather than upholding the segregated notion of a country divided by mutually exclusive groups, Mexican Americans might use their experience to imagine an America in which racial, ethnic, and cultural groups collide to create new ways of being American.

It was never clear where Mexican Americans belonged on the American racial scale. In 1896, two white politicians in Texas grew worried that more Mexican immigrants would naturalize and vote. They filed suit against a Mexican-born citizenship applicant, Ricardo Rodriguez, because he was not white, and so, like Asians and American Indians, not eligible to become a citizen. Citing the Treaty of Guadalupe Hidalgo, in which citizenship was granted to Mexicans in the conquered region of the Southwest after 1848, the court rejected the suit on the grounds that Mr. Rodriguez's national origins qualified him for citizenship regardless of his racial background.

In the 1920 census, Mexicans were counted as whites. Ten years later, they were reassigned to a separate Mexican "racial" category, though in 1950 they were white again. Mexican Americans and Hispanics as a whole are commonly viewed as a mutually exclusive racial, linguistic, and cultural category in a country of competing minorities. But Mexican Americans do not share the overarching ethnic narrative of Jews or the shared history of suffering that has united African Americans. For all the discrimination and segregation Mexican Americans suffered in the region, the Southwest was never the Deep South. In any case, as the memoirist John Phillip Santos wrote recently, "Mexicans are to forgetting what the Jews are to remembering."

By the late 1990s, both the largely ethnic-Mexican Hispanic Congressional Caucus and the powerful California Latino Legislative Caucus had adopted "Latino issues are American issues" as their mantra. Mexican Americans are using their growing political power to enter the American mainstream, not to distance themselves from it. The new chairman of the Hispanic Congressional Caucus, Representative Silvestre Reyes, Democrat of Texas, was once a high-ranking Border Patrol official and the architect of Operation Hold the Line, the labor-intensive strategy to stem illegal immigration along the West Texas border.

Perhaps assuming that Mexicans would (or should) follow the organizational model of Jews or African Americans, East Coast-based foundations contributed to the founding of national ethnic-Mexican institutions. The New York-based Ford Foundation was instrumental in creating three of the most visible national Mexican-American organizations—all modeled after similar black organizations.

But with the exception of some scattered homegrown social service organizations and political groups, Mexican Americans have developed little parallel ethnic infrastructure. One national survey has shown that Mexican Americans are far more likely to join a nonethnic civic group than a Hispanic organization. There is no private Mexican-American college similar to Yeshiva University or Morehouse College. In Los Angeles, which has the largest Mexican population in the country, there is no ethnic-Mexican hospital, cemetery, or broad-based charity organization. Nor does Los Angeles have an English-language newspaper for Mexican Americans similar to the black Amsterdam News and the Jewish Forward in New York.

Though the Spanish-language media is often referred to as the "Hispanic media," it generally serves first generation immigrants and not their English-dominant children and grandchildren.

In the late 1920s, Representative John C. Box of Texas warned his colleagues on the House Immigration and Naturalization Committee that the continued influx of Mexican immigrants could lead to the "distressing process of mongrelization" in America. He argued that because Mexicans were the products of mixing among whites, Indians, and sometimes blacks, they had a casual attitude toward interracial unions and were likely to mix freely with other races in the United States.

His vitriol notwithstanding, Mr. Box was right about Mexicans not keeping to themselves. Apart from the cultural isolation of immigrants, subsequent generations are oriented toward the American mainstream. But because Mexican identity has always been more fluid and comfortable with hybridity, assimilation has not been an either/or proposition. For example, Mexican Americans never had to overcome a cultural proscription against intermarriage. Just as widespread Mexican-Anglo intermarriage helped meld cultures in the nineteenth-century Southwest, so it does today. In fact, two-thirds of intermarriages in California involve a Latino partner.

According to James P. Smith, an economist and immigration scholar at the Rand Corporation, by 2050 more than 40 percent of United States Hispanics will be able to claim multiple ancestries. "Through this process of blending by marriage in the United States," he says, "Latino identity becomes something even more nuanced."

The fact that people of mixed ancestry came to form a greater proportion of the population of Latin America than in Anglo America is the clearest sign of the difference between the two outlooks on race. Mexican Americans bring the New World notion encompassed by the word *mestizaje*, or racial and cultural synthesis, to their American experience. In 1925, the romantic Mexican philosopher Jose Vasconcelos wrote that the Latin American *mestizo* heralds a new postracialist era in human development. More recently, the preeminent Mexican-American essayist Richard Rodriguez stated, "The essential beauty and mystery of the color brown is that it is a mixture of different colors."

"Something big happens here at the border that sort of mushes everything together," says Maria Eugenia Guerra, publisher of LareDos, an alternative monthly magazine in Laredo, Texas, a city that has been a majority Latino since its founding in 1755. As political and economic power continues to shift westward, Mexican Americans will increasingly inject this mestizo vision onto American culture. "The Latinization of America is so profound that no one really sees it," asserts Kevin Starr, the leading historian of California, who is writing a multivolume history of the state. The process of they becoming us will ultimately force us to reconsider the very definition of who we are.

QUESTIONS: For Thinking and Writing

1. Think about your own family's experience in the United States. Did it take them long to be accepted? Did they assimilate quickly, or did it require generations to complete? Or is the processes of assimilation still a daily reality for your family? Explain.
2. What is the "idea" of America? How have immigrants and minority groups broadened the definition of America? Does the term *melting pot* seem appropriate? Why or why not?

3. What influence does Rodriguez foresee Mexican Americans having on national identity in the twenty-first century? Explain.
4. Respond to Rodriguez's statement that as the second largest immigrant population, Mexican Americans could "shift the country's often divisive 'us verses them' racial dialogue." What does he mean? Who is "us," and who is "them"?
5. According to the author, how could Mexican Americans' legacy of "mixed ancestry" in turn influence America's melting pot?
6. In what ways are Mexican Americans different from other immigrant populations? How could this difference ultimately provide them with more political and social power? Explain.

VICTOR DAVIS HANSON

Do We Want Mexifornia?

The flood of illegal immigration into California raises urgent questions that the whole nation must face. Unlike most past immigrant groups, many Mexicans and other Latinos who arrive in U.S. cities and towns are resisting assimilation and mainstream U.S. culture and even the English language. Now representing the largest immigrant population in modern America, the sheer numbers of Mexican and Latino immigrants—especially in California—are influencing American culture in an unprecedented way. What are the consequences of this huge migration from Mexico? How is it changing California? With its huge Mexican population, is the golden state turning into "Mexifornia"? This essay first appeared in City Journal's *Spring 2002 issue.*

Thousands arrive illegally from Mexico into California each year—and the state is now home to fully 40 percent of America's immigrants, legal and illegal. They come in such numbers because a tacit alliance of Right and Left has created an open-borders policy, aimed at keeping wage labor cheap and social problems ever fresh, so that the ministrations of Chicano studies professors, La Raza activists, and all the other self-appointed defenders of group causes will never be unneeded. The tragedy is that though illegal aliens come here hoping to succeed, most get no preparation for California's competitive culture. Instead, their activist shepherds herd them into ethnic enclaves, where inexorably they congeal into an underclass. The concept of multiculturalism is the force-multiplier that produces this result: it transforms a stubborn problem of assimilation into a social calamity.

Given hard feelings over recent ballot initiatives that curtailed not only aid to illegals but also affirmative action and bilingual education, unlawful immigration has become the third rail of California politics. Even to discuss the issue can earn politicians the cheap slander of "racist" or "nativist." Tensions abound even within families. One of my siblings is married to a Mexican American; another has two stepchildren whose father was an illegal alien from Mexico; I have a prospective son-in-law whose parents crossed the border. Yet we all disagree at different times whether open borders are California's hope or its bane.

And why not? Californians cannot even obtain accurate numbers of how many of the state's more than ten million Hispanic residents have arrived here from Mexico unlawfully in the last two decades. No one believes the government's old insistence on a mere six million illegal residents nationwide; the real figure may be twice that. The U.S. Hispanic population—of which over 70 percent are from Mexico—grew 53 percent during the 1980s, and then rose another 27 percent to a total of 30 million between 1990 and 1996. At present rates of births and immigration, by 2050 there will be 97 million Hispanics, one-quarter of the American population.

Nor is there agreement on the economic effects of the influx. Liberal economists swear that legal immigrants to America bring in $25 billion in net revenue annually. More skeptical statisticians using different models conclude that aliens cost the United States over $40 billion a year, and that here in California, each illegal immigrant will take $50,000 in services from the state beyond what he will contribute in taxes during his lifetime. Other studies suggest that the average California household must contribute at least $1,200 each year to subsidize the deficit between what immigrants cost in services and pay in taxes.

The irony, of course, is that the present immigration crisis was not what any Californian had anticipated. Along with the cheap labor that the tax-conscious Right wanted, it got thousands of unassimilated others, who eventually flooded into the state's near-bankrupt entitlement industry and filled its newly built prisons: California is $12 billion in the red this year and nearly one-quarter of its inmates are aliens from Mexico (while nearly a third of all drug-trafficking arrests involve illegal aliens). The pro-labor Left found that the industrious new arrivals whom it championed eroded the wages of its own domestic low-wage constituencies—the Labor Department attributes 50 percent of real wage declines to the influx of cheap immigrant labor. And while the

Democrats think the illegals will eventually turn into liberal voters, the actual Hispanic vote so far remains just a small fraction of the eligible Mexican-American pool: of the 14,173 residents of the central California town of Hanford who identified themselves as Latino (34 percent of the town's population), for example, only 770 are registered to vote.

My sleepy hometown of Selma, California, is in the dead center of all this. The once rural San Joaquin Valley community has grown from 7,000 to nearly 20,000 in a mere two decades, as a result of mostly illegal immigration from Mexico. Selma is now somewhere between 60 and 90 percent Hispanic. How many are U.S. citizens is either not known or not publicly disclosed: but of all those admitted legally from Mexico to the United States since 1982, only 20 percent had become citizens by 1997. Some local schools, like the one I went to two miles from our farm, are 90 percent first-generation Mexican immigrants. At the service station a mile away, I rarely hear English spoken; almost every car that pulls in displays a Mexican flag decal pasted somewhere.

To contrast the Selma I live in today with the Selma I grew up in will doubtless seem hopelessly nostalgic. But the point of the contrast is not merely that 40 years ago our community was only 40 or 50 percent Mexican, but rather that the immigrants then were mostly here legally. Crime was far rarer: the hit-and-run accidents, auto theft, drug manufacturing and sale, murders, rapes, and armed robberies that are now customary were then nearly nonexistent. Fights that now end in semiautomatic-weapon fire were settled with knives then.

I used to worry over the theft of a tractor battery. Yet in the last decade, I have run off at gunpoint three gang members trying to force their way into our house at 3 AM. Last year, four patrol cars—accompanied by a helicopter whirling overhead—chased drug dealers in hot pursuit through our driveway. One suspect escaped and turned up two hours later, hiding behind a hedge on our lawn, vainly seeking sanctuary from a sure prison term. When a carload of thieves tried to steal oranges from our yard, I soon found myself outmanned and outgunned—and decided that 100 pounds of pilfered fruit is not worth your life.

It is a schizophrenic existence, living at illegal immigration's intersection. Each week I pick up trash, dirty diapers, even sofas and old beds dumped in our orchard by illegal aliens—only to call a Mexican-American sheriff who empathizes when I show him the evidence of Spanish names and addresses on bills and letters scattered among the trash. So far I have caught more than 15 illegal dumpers, all Mexican, in the act. In the last 20 years, four cars piloted by intoxicated illegal aliens have veered off the road into our vineyard, causing thousands of dollars in unrecompensed damage. The drivers simply limped away and disappeared. The police sighed, "No license, no insurance, no registration" ("the three noes"), and towed out their cars.

Yet I also walk through vineyards at 7 AM in the fog and see whole families from Mexico, hard at work in the cold—while the native-born unemployed of all races will not—and cannot—prune a single vine. By natural selection, we are getting some of the most intelligent and industrious people in the world, people who have the courage to cross the border, the tenacity to stay—and, if not assimilated, the potential to cost the state far, far more than they can contribute.

We know what caused the tidal waves of immigration of the last three decades. While Mexico's economy has been in a state of chronic collapse, California has needed workers of a certain type—muscular, uneducated, and industrious—to cut our lawns, harvest fruit, cook and serve meals, babysit kids, build homes, clean offices, and make beds in motels and nursing homes. The poor from Armenia, Japan, China, the Azores, and Oklahoma had all begun their odysseys of success in California doing just these menial tasks, albeit in far smaller numbers. But despite mechanization, California today demands more, not less, stoop work than 30 years ago, because of the state's radically changed attitudes and newly affluent lifestyle.

When I was 10 in 1963, all suburbanites mowed their own lawns—many with push mowers. Now almost everyone hires the job out. Nannies for toddlers and grannies, unheard-of then, are now ubiquitous from Visalia to Palos Verdes. Rural schools used to begin in mid September to ensure that we natives could pick grapes to earn our school clothes and shoes. Today not a single student in California would do such hot, dirty work, now considered demeaning. With demand for such workers high, and the supply of native-born citizens willing to do it low, Mexico came to the rescue of California.

There is a well-known cycle in California immigration. Young people between ages 15 and 30 arrive here illegally and, for a while, stay single. Over decades, many live hard and toil at menial jobs, earning perhaps $8 an hour, usually paid in cash, which is a bargain for everyone involved. Without state, federal, and payroll taxes, the worker earns the equivalent of a gross $10-an-hour rate, while the employer saves

30 percent in payroll contributions, audits, and paperwork—even as such cash payments force other Americans and legal immigrants to pay steeper taxes, in part to cover those who don't pay. The immigrants work hard until their joints stiffen and their backs give out. By then their families are large. Their English stays perpetually poor; their education is still nonexistent, even as their IDs remain fraudulent.

Now, $8 per hour in California, rather than per week in Mexico, no longer seems such a bonanza, and they use their counterfeit documentation to get onto workers compensation, unemployment insurance, and state assistance to garner what their weary bodies can no longer earn. Meanwhile, they romanticize a distant Mexico while chastising an ever-present America. And the second generation has learned how to live, spend, and consume as Americans, but not, like their fathers, to work and save as Mexicans. If rising crime rates, gang activity, and illegitimacy are any indication, many now resent, rather than sacrifice to escape, their poverty. And the rates are rising fast: for example, while 37 percent of all births to Hispanic immigrants are illegitimate, the illegitimacy rate among American-born Mexican mothers is 48 percent.

Census data show us that median household income by the mid 1990s had risen for a decade for all groups, except for the nation's Hispanics, whose incomes dropped 5.1 percent. Although recent immigrants from Mexico and their U.S.-born children under 18 now officially make up only 4.2 percent of America's population, they represent 10.2 percent of our poor. When you add in longtime residents, Hispanics account for 24 percent of America's impoverished, up 8 percentage points since 1985. The true causes of such checkered progress—continual and massive illegal immigration of cheap labor that drives down wages for working Hispanics here; failure to learn English; the collapse of the once strong Hispanic family due to federal entitlement; soaring birthrates among a demoralized underclass; an intellectual elite that downplays social pathology, claims perpetual racism, and seeks constant government largesse and entitlement; and years of bilingual education that ensure dependency upon a demagogic leadership—are rarely mentioned.

They cannot be mentioned. To do so would be to suggest that the billions of public dollars spent on social redress did more to harm Hispanics than did all the racists in America. Moreover, we wish to maintain cordial relations with Mexico—but in many ways, no government in the last 50 years has been more hostile. Mexico's policy for a half-century has been the deliberate and illegal export of millions of its poorest citizens to the United States, which is expected to educate, employ, and protect them in ways not possible at home. Only that way has the chronically corrupt Mexican government avoided a revolution, as its exploited underclass from Oaxaca or the small hamlets of the Sierra Madre Mountains headed north, rather than marching en masse on Mexico City. Only that way can billions of earned foreign currency be sent home to prop up a bankrupt economy; only that way, for the first time in his life, can a poor Mixtec from Michoacan find an advocate for his health and safety from the Mexican consulate—once he is safely ensconced far north of the border.

You can leave Selma and be across the border in about 6 hours. That proximity in terms of immigration is paradoxical. The richest economy in the world is only a stone's throw from one of the most backward. The illegal alien leaves his pueblo in Yucatán, where cattle starve for adequate fodder, and in a day can be processed through familial connections to begin mowing and bagging fescue grass in the most leisured and affluent suburbs in Los Angeles.

Mexican Americans never experience the physical or psychological amputation from the mother country that most other immigrants to California found, after thousands of miles of seawater cut the old country clean off and relegated it to the romance of memory. But the Mexican immigrant can easily recross the Rio Grande by a drive over a short bridge. A limited annual visit or a family reunion nourishes enough nostalgia for Mexico to war with the creation of a truly American identity.

For Mexican immigrants, the idea of Mexico has shifted from a liability to an important benchmark of ethnic pride in the last two decades. A visiting Mexican soccer club playing almost any American team will find in our local fans a home-crowd advantage—despite being a thousand miles from home. Mexicans in California turn out to vote in booths set up in California for local and national candidates in Mexico, who come up to campaign in Fresno every year—and often learn to their dismay that California's Mexicans are among the sternest critics of Mexico City's endemic government corruption.

Instead of growing more distant, a romanticized Mexico stays close to the heart of the new arrival and turns into a roadblock on his journey to becoming an American. Many immigrants die as Mexicans in

California, never seeking to become citizens. A columnist for our local paper recently described their suspension between two worlds: "*Pensaban que se iban a ir patria*" ("They thought they would go back"). Aside from our own self-interest in having our residents accept the responsibilities of full citizenship, it is entirely in the material interest of aliens to integrate and assimilate as quickly as possible into the general culture of California: they will eat better and have nicer houses and more secure futures for their children in California if they become Americans, rather than permanent Mexican aliens.

Some sociologists and journalists assure us that retaining this cultural umbilical cord is not injurious. Instead, we are creating a unique regional culture that is neither Mexican nor American, but an amorphous, fluid society that is the dividend on our multicultural investment. This Calexico or Mexifornia will not be a bad thing at all but something, if not advantageous, at least inevitable. So we allow illegal aliens to obtain California driver's licenses—the foundation of all other means of legal identification—and to pay reduced in-state tuition at the University of California, thereby providing several thousand dollars in discounts not available to American citizens from out of state. Whether you break the law to reach California or immigrate legally, it makes little difference in how you drive, send your kids to college, or draw on the public services of the state.

These pundits hope privately, of course—though they do not say so publicly—that this new regional civilization will resemble San Diego more than Tijuana. And in truth, no immigrant, despite his grandiose boasts, wants to return to Mexico or anything like it, to be a Mexican in Mexico, rather than in California.

And here we come to the heart of our immigration problem. It is not that our state is too crowded per se: Japan, after all, feeds, clothes, and educates three times as many as we Californians do, without our natural wealth or open spaces. The real problem is that, while it has always been easier for people who emigrate to keep their own culture, rather than join the majority, for the first time in our state's (and nation's) history, the majority feels it is easier to let them do it.

Rarely now do Californians express a confidence in our national culture or a willingness to defend the larger values of Western civilization. The result is that our public schools are either apathetic about, or outright hostile to, the Western paradigm—even as millions from the south risk their lives to enjoy what we so often smugly dismiss. We do not teach immigrant or native-born children that free association, free speech, free inquiry, and the material prosperity that springs from the sanctity of private property and free markets are the essential elements that preserve the dignity of the individual that we enjoy. Our elites do not understand just how rare consensual government is in the history of civilization, and therefore they wrongly think that they can instill confidence by praising the other, less successful, cultures that aliens are escaping from, rather than explaining the dynamism and morality of the civilization that they have voted for with their feet.

Our schools, through multiculturalism, cultural relativism, and a therapeutic curriculum, often promote the very tribalism, statism, and group rather than individual interests that our new immigrants are fleeing from. If taken to heart, such ideas lead our new arrivals to abject failure in California. Moreover, if we were to entertain attitudes toward women that exist in Mexico, emulate its approach to religious diversity, copy the Mexican constitution, court system, schools, universities, tax code, bureaucracy, energy industry, or power grid, then millions of Mexicans quite simply would stay put where they are. Indeed, even the most pro-Mexico Mexican native in America never chooses to forgo the Western emergency room for the herbalist and exorcist in times of acute sickness or gunshot trauma. He does not complain that the American middle class is too large, the water too clean, the gasoline not adulterated, the food too abundant and noninfectious. Nor does he lament the absence of uniformed machine-gun-carrying soldiers on his block. Illegal aliens clamor for reduced tuition for their offspring at supposedly biased U.C. campuses, not native fellowships for them to enroll in Mexican universities. I often suggest to teachers who tell aliens that our culture is racist, exploitative, and sexist that they should live in Mexico themselves to fathom why millions are dying to obtain what they so casually dismiss.

The sheer numbers of new immigrants presented a golden opportunity for the demagogue. And sure enough, at times of racial tension, you can see brazen agitators on the street with bullhorns and picket signs. Some are organized by MEChA (*Movimiento Estudiantil Chicano de Aztlan*)—one of whose mottoes once was: "For our race, everything; for those outside our race, nothing." Sometimes the provocateur shows up at a local school, after a Chicano gang has kicked to near death a (Mexican-American) school guard and consequently been expelled. With megaphone—and with the 6 o'clock news cameras rolling—he screams about "targeting La Raza" and "keeping the brown down." "There is only one gang who murders in Fresno," he announces at his poorly attended press conference, "and they wear police blue."

The brawling provocateur is as old as America itself, and today's California demagogue harks back to the urban ward bosses of old. More than a century too late, he shares their nineteenth-century vision of enormous ethnic blocs, entirely unassimilated, with tough ramrods like himself at their head—but with the added advantage that his Mexican immigrant constituency in the new age of multiculturalism might be permanent rather than destined to assimilate. His chief fear, I think, is that immigration may slow down; that millions may read and write excellent English; that his brother or sister—or he himself—may marry the white or Asian other; that a Mexican middle class might emerge in private enterprise outside of government entitlement and civil service; that the Mexican propensity for duty, family, and self-sacrifice might yet make him obsolete; that we all might integrate and forget about race; that he will not be needed and thus not have to be bargained off.

Other opportunists—for some reason, more often Spanish than native American—are the products of Chicano, Latino, La Raza ("The Race"), or Hispanic studies programs at universities. (Could we ever tolerate any other university program or national organization dubbed "The Race"?) They are the well-meaning Latino elites who have suddenly reverted from Alex to Alejandro and have never met an "r" they won't trill. These self-appointed leaders are professed tribalists—who do not wish to live within the tribe. They may make speeches and films about gang violence and teen pregnancy, but they never really tell us why these endemic problems came into being and how they can be prevented. They leave cause and effect unspoken, allege racism and victimization, not a failure to learn English and accept a common culture—and then they go home in SUVs to upscale suburban homes well apart from the unassimilated barrios they claim to represent.

This state, like the country at large, was a raw experiment, a multiracial society united by a common language, culture, and law. But that subjugation of race to culture is forever a fragile creation, not a natural entity. Each day it can erode. A single fool can undo the work of decades and so allow small people to feel one with those of like tongue and skin color, not united by shared ideals and values. Thus, each time a university president, a politician on the make, or a would-be muckraking journalist chooses the easy path of separatism, he, like the white chauvinists of the past, does his own little part in turning us into Rwanda or Kosovo. The wrong message at the top eventually filters down to the newly arrived and helps determine whether they succeed or fail in the no-nonsense arena of America.

How did the old assimilationist model work? Brutally and effectively. In our grammar schools during the 1950s and 1960s, no Spanish was to be spoken on the playground—officially at least. Groups of four and larger were not allowed to congregate at recess. When we were caught fighting, nontraditional kicking instead of the accepted punching earned four, rather than two, spankings. A rather tough Americanism in class was rammed down our throats—biographies of Teddy Roosevelt, stories about Lou Gehrig, a repertory of a dozen or so patriotic songs, recitations from Longfellow, and demonstrations of how to fold the flag. "Manners" and "civics" were taught each week, with weird lessons about not appearing "loud" in public or wearing glittery or showy clothes, and especially not staring down strangers or giving people the "hard look" with the intent of "being unpleasant." Our teachers were at times insufferable in their condescension as they disclosed the formula for "making it in America"—but make it in America the vast majority of these immigrants did.

Apparently, these rather unsophisticated teachers thought that learning to master English and acquiring the rudiments of math, American literature, and national culture were more valuable to the immigrant than were racial studies, Chicano dance, and other popular courses now au courant and designed to instill ethnic pride. As I can best fathom it some 40 years later, their egalitarian aim was to create a mass of students who would reach high school with equal chances of success. And so they gave us detention for silly things like mispronouncing names and other felonies like chewing gum, handing our papers in without our names written on the upper-right-hand corner, and wearing Frisco baggy pants.

Most of the kids I saw each day then—just as most of the adults I see daily now around the same farm—were from Mexico. Skin color and national origin were quite out in the open. We five Anglos in our class of 40 at our rural elementary school were labeled "white boys" and "gringos"; in turn, we knew the majority as "Mexicans," their parents more respectfully as "Mexican Americans." Most fights, however, were not racial. We in the white minority fought beside and against Mexican Americans; the great dividing line of most rumbles was whether you were born in Selma or Fresno. We had our fringe racists, of course: Mr. Martinez, the fourth-grade teacher, told me in 1963 that "whitey was through in California," even as Mrs. Wilson, a Texas native, complimented those in the art class who were "lighter than most from Mexico." There was nothing of the contemporary multicultural model—no bilingual aides, written and spoken communication with parents in Spanish, textbooks highlighting the Aztecs and the theft of northern Mexico, or federally funded counselors to remind students that "the borders crossed us, not we the borders." Excused absences for catechism classes at the Catholic church emptied our classrooms, giving us five Anglo Protestants a much-welcomed three-hour recess. We all suffered fish sticks on Friday, the public school's concession to the vast Catholic majority.

That elementary school is still two miles away, but whereas 40 years ago it turned out educated and confident Americans, its graduates who enter high school now have among the lowest literacy levels and most dismal math skills in the state. The lucky ones who go on to college generally end up in the California State University system's remedial classes. Yet just reaching those remedial programs is a great achievement in itself. In 1996, the high school graduation rate of California's Hispanics—both native and foreign-born—was only 61 percent. And of those still in high school by their senior year, only 50 percent of Hispanic students met "basic" standards of twelfth-grade math—compared with 80 percent of whites. A mere 6 percent tested "proficient." That means that, out of every 100 Hispanics who now enter California high schools, 40 will drop out. And of the remaining 60, fewer than four will matriculate prepared for any serious college-level courses in mathematics. Only 7 percent of all Mexican Americans currently hold a B.A. In short, this is a national tragedy.

Yet few of the Mexican-American friends I grew up with speak fluent Spanish anymore, regardless of whether they finished college. Completing eighth grade then provided a far better education than finishing high school does now. All of them are well informed and can read, write, compute, and understand the basic tenets of the culture they have helped to build and maintain—and which they most certainly think is far superior to Mexico's. Their children know only a few words of Spanish—by contrast with the present 65 percent of all Hispanic foreign-born in the United States who now speak only "limited English." Most of my generation have become insurance salesmen, mechanics, contractors, teachers, civil servants, occasionally wealthy businessmen and high-government bureaucrats—in other words, the present-day future of California. There are no Mexican flags on their cars, which more likely sport decals like "Proud Parent of a Lincoln School Honors Student" or "Semper Fi." About half, it seems to me, are not married to Mexican Americans.

Most vote as conservative Democrats, are probably antiabortion, and perhaps even support the death penalty. Some joined and prospered in the Marines; others run the Lions and Kiwanis. They are sensitive to occasional news of ethnic prejudice yet display little affinity for the La Raza industry. In their daily lives, they are more worried about gangs and Mexican crime than white racism; most are ambivalent about having thousands of new illegal aliens arrive into their small towns from central Mexico. A few seem to be conscious of race only when the father is Anglo, the mother Mexican: affirmative action, they believe, takes a dimmer view of a Justin Smith who is half-Mexican than a Justin Martinez. Their loss of indigenous culture is sad, perhaps—but no sadder than my own failure to speak Swedish, put cow-horn helmets on my wall, care much about Leif Eriksson, defend Swedish duplicity in World War II, or buy Volvos and Electrolux vacuums out of ethnic pride.

I often think that if I did not particularly like my Mexican-American students (who make up the majority of my classics classes), and if I wanted them to fail, I would not continue to teach them Latin (much less Greek), English composition, or Western history and culture. Nor would I insist on essays free of grammatical error or demand oral reports that employ classical rhetorical tropes.

No, if I did not like them or did not wish to live among thousands of illegal and legal immigrants and wish them married into my family, I would keep them distant by teaching them therapy, letting them speak poor English—or no English at all—and insisting on the superiority of the Mexican culture that they or their parents had fled. If I did not like my students and wished them to remain in the fields—or when they were employed in the office to be snickered at behind closed doors by their white benefactors—I would move from the west side of Selma to an exclusive white suburb in north Fresno, and then as penance teach them during the day about the glory of the Aztecs, the need for government entitlement, and the idea that grammar is but a "construct." I would insist that white racism and capitalist brutality alone explain Mexican-American crime rates, and I would explain why they need someone like me to champion their cause to the wealthy and educated. If I really wished to be distant from my students, I would insist that they attend our university's separate Hispanic graduation assemblies to remind them that they are intrinsically different from, rather than inherently equal to, me. I would be more like the sensitive teachers who teach today than the insensitive ones who once taught me.

So I have made my choice on the great question that California must decide: whether we will remain multiracial or become America's first truly multicultural state. For our future, will we all return to an imperfect, insensitive, but honest assimilationist past that nevertheless worked, or stay with the utopian and deceitful multiculturalist present that is clearly failing? Unchecked illegal immigration and multiculturalism are a lethal mix. California—if it is to stay as California—might have coped with one or even the other, but surely not both at once.

QUESTIONS: For Thinking and Writing

1. What does *assimilation* mean to you? In this essay, Hanson notes that the current generation of immigrants is fighting assimilation. What does he think this means for the long-term well-being of this immigrant group and the Californian population as a whole?
2. What is Hanson's argument? List the different elements of his argument and how he supports each primary point. What must his readers know about the issue and topic in order to understand his discussion?
3. What, according to the author, could be the consequences of sustained Mexican immigration if current trends continue? Explain.
4. Why does Hanson contrast the Selma he grew up in to the Selma he lives in now? What does this contrast reveal about immigration in this area today? How is his childhood home different from the town today? How are the immigrants themselves different? Explain.
5. Are there particular traditions, practices, and behaviors that we expect new immigrants to adopt when they arrive in the United States? If so, what are they? Write an essay describing the things you think new immigrants should be willing to do in order to live in the United States.

DAVID M. KENNEDY

Can We Still Afford to Be a Nation of Immigrants?

The United States has always recognized that it is a nation largely comprised of immigrants. And while each new immigrant group was rarely welcomed with open arms, their diverse backgrounds, languages, and traditions gradually mixed with mainstream American culture. In time, the richness of our diverse history became a source of pride and celebration. Comparing yesterday's immigration with today's, however, historian David M. Kennedy is struck by the unprecedented nature of our present immigrant situation. Are immigrants today very different from the people who arrived in the United States a century ago? Has immigration changed so much that we can no longer be a "nation of immigrants"? Kennedy's essay appeared in the November 1996 issue of the Atlantic Monthly.

The question in my title implies a premise: that historically the United States has well afforded to be a nation of immigrants—indeed, has benefited handsomely from its good fortune as an immigrant destination. That proposition was once so deeply embedded in our national mythology as to be axiomatic. More than a century ago, for example, in the proclamation that made Thanksgiving Day a national holiday, Abraham Lincoln gave thanks to God for having "largely augmented our free population by emancipation and by immigration."

Lincoln spoke those words when there were but 34 million Americans and half a continent remained to be settled. Today, however, the United States is a nation of some 264 million souls on a continent developed beyond Lincoln's imagination. It is also a nation experiencing immigration on a scale never before seen. In the past three decades, since the passage of the Immigration and Nationality Act Amendments of 1965, the first major revision in American immigration statutes since the historic closure of immigration in the 1920s, some 20 million immigrants have entered the United States. To put those numbers in perspective: prior to 1965 the period of heaviest immigration to the United States was the quarter century preceding the First World War, when some 17 million people entered the country—roughly half the total number of Europeans who migrated to the United States in the century after 1820 (along with several hundred thousand Asians). The last prewar census, in 1910, counted about 13.5 million foreign-born people in the American population, in contrast to about 22.5 million in 1994. Historians know a great deal about those earlier immigrants—why they came, how they ended up, what their impact was on the America of their day. Whether America's historical experience with immigration provides a useful guide to thinking about the present case is the principal question I want to address. I want not only to explore the substantive issue of immigration but also to test the proposition that the discipline of history has some value as a way of knowing and thinking about the world.

With respect to immigration itself, I intend to explore two sets of questions:

Why did people migrate to America in the past, and what were the consequences, for them and for American society, once they landed?

Why are people migrating to America today, and what might be the consequences, for them and for American society, of their presence in such numbers?

A generation or two ago upbeat answers to the first pair of questions so pervaded the culture that they cropped up in the most exotic places—in Tunisia, for example, on July 9, 1943. The occasion was the eve of the invasion of Sicily, and General George S. Patton Jr. was addressing his troops, who were about to embark for the battle. He urged, "When we land, we will meet German and Italian soldiers whom it is our honor and privilege to attack and destroy. Many of you have in your veins German and Italian blood, but remember that these ancestors of yours so loved freedom that they gave up home and country to cross the ocean in search of liberty. The ancestors of the people we shall kill lacked the courage to make such a sacrifice and continued as slaves."

In his own inimitable idiom, Patton was invoking what for most Americans was—and still is—the standard explanation of who their immigrant forebears were, why they left their old countries, and what was their effect on American society. In this explanation, immigrants were the main chance-seeking and most energetic, entrepreneurial, and freedom-loving members of their Old World societies. They were drawn out of Europe by the irresistible magnet of American opportunity and liberty, and their galvanizing influence on American society made this country the greatest in the world.

A radically different explanation of immigration has also historically been at work in the American mind. As the noted social scientist Edward Alsworth Ross put it in 1914:

> *Observe immigrants not as they come travel-wan up the gangplank, nor as they issue toil-begrimed from pit's mouth or mill-gate, but in their gatherings, washed, combed, and in their Sunday best. . . . [They] are hirsute, low-browed, big-faced persons of obviously low mentality. . . . They simply look out of place in black clothes and stiff collar, since clearly they belong in skins, in wattled huts at the close of the Great Ice Age. These oxlike men are descendants of those who always stayed behind.*

Ross was describing in these invidious terms what he and his turn-of-the-century contemporaries called the "new" immigrants—new because they came predominantly from eastern and southern Europe, as distinct from the "old," early-and-mid-nineteenth-century immigrants, who had come mainly from northern and western Europe. Ironically, Ross was also talking about the parents of those very troops (at least the Italian-American troops) whom Patton addressed in 1943.

Between those two poles of explanation, American views of immigration have oscillated. On the one hand, as Patton reminds us, immigrants were judged to be noble souls, tugged by the lodestone of American opportunity, whose talents and genius and love of liberty account for the magnificent American character. On the other hand, as in Ross's view, especially if they had the misfortune to arrive on a more recent boat, immigrants were thought to be degraded, freeloading louts, a blight on the national character and a drain on the economy—the kind of people described all too literally, so the argument goes, by Emma Lazarus's famous inscription on the base of the Statue of Liberty: "your tired, your poor . . . the wretched refuse of your teeming shore."

Yet for all their differences, the two views have several things in common. Both explain immigration in terms of the moral character of immigrants. Both understand immigration as a matter of individual choice. And both implicitly invoke the American magnet as the irresistible force that put people in motion, drawing them either to opportunity or to dependency.

Those concepts do not bear close analysis as adequate explanations for the movement of some 35 million human beings over the course of a century. This was a historical phenomenon too huge and too specific in time to be sufficiently accounted for by summing 35 million decisions supposedly stimulated by the suddenly irresistible gravitational attraction of a far-off continent.

The Push of Europe

For the first three centuries or so after the European discovery of the New World, the principal source of immigrants to the two American continents and the Caribbean was not Europe but Africa. Only in the early nineteenth century did the accumulated total of European settlers in the New World exceed the approximately ten million Africans who had made the trans-Atlantic voyage in the years since 1492. To explain the African diaspora by citing entrepreneurial instincts, the love of democracy, or the freely chosen decisions of migrants to follow the lodestar of American promise would be a mockery. Clearly, the involuntary movement of those ten million Africans is best explained not in terms of their individual characters and choices but in terms of the catastrophically disruptive expansion of large-scale plantation agriculture and its accursed corollary, large-scale commercial slavery.

A comparable—though, to be sure, not identical—element of involuntariness characterized emigration from nineteenth-century Europe. Any generalization about what prompted a phenomenon as long-lived and complicated as the great European migration must, of course, be subject to many qualifications. All discussions of the migration process recognize both push and pull factors. But at bottom, the evidence convincingly supports the argument that disruption is essential to the movement of people on such a scale. And, as in the African case, the best, most comprehensive explanation for a process that eventually put some 35 million people in motion is to be found in two convulsively disruptive developments that lay far beyond the control of individual Europeans. Those developments had their historical dynamic within the context of European, not American, history.

The first of these needs little elaboration. It was, quite simply, population growth. In the nineteenth century, the population of Europe more than doubled, from some 200 million to more than 400 million, even after about 70 million people had left Europe altogether. (Only half of these, it should be noted, went to the United States—one among many clues that the American-magnet explanation is inadequate.) That population boom was the indispensable precondition for

Europe to export people on the scale that it did. And the boom owed little to American stimulus; rather, it was a product of aspects of European historical evolution, especially improvements in diet, sanitation, and disease control.

The second development was more complex, but we know it by a familiar name: the Industrial Revolution. It includes the closely associated revolution in agricultural productivity. Wherever it occurred, the Industrial Revolution shook people loose from traditional ways of life. It made factory workers out of artisans and, even more dramatically, turned millions of rural farmers into urban wage-laborers. Most of those migrants from countryside to city, from agriculture to industry, remained within their country of origin, or at least within Europe. But in the early stages of industrialization, the movement of people, like the investment of capital during the unbridled early days of industrialism, was often more than what the market could bear. In time most European societies reached a kind of equilibrium, absorbing their own workers into their own wage markets. But in the typical transitional phase, some workers who had left artisanal or agricultural employments could not be reabsorbed domestically in European cities. They thus migrated overseas.

The large, scholarly literature documenting this process might be summarized as follows: Imagine a map of Europe. Across this map a time line traces the evolution of the Industrial Revolution. From a point in the British Isles in the late eighteenth century, the line crosses to the Low Countries and Germany in the early and mid nineteenth century and to eastern and southern Europe in the late nineteenth and early twentieth centuries. Across the same map, a second line traces the chronological evolution of migration to the United States. As it happens, the two lines are almost precisely congruent—migration came principally from the British Isles in the eighteenth and early nineteenth centuries, then mainly from Germany, and finally from the great watersheds of the Vistula and the Danube and the mountain ranges of the Apennines and Carpathians to the south and east.

The congruence of those lines is not coincidental. Industrialization, in this view, is the root cause and the most powerful single variable explaining the timing, the scale, the geographic evolution, and the composition of the great European migration.

For another perspective on the importance of understanding the European migration from a European point of view, consider the lyrics of a nineteenth-century Italian folk song called *The Wives of the Americans.* In this case, the "Americans" were men who had gone off to America and left their wives behind in Italy—specifically, the southern region of Campania. In fact, men, young men in particular, predominated in the nineteenth-century migratory stream, and their predominance constitutes a reliable indicator of their purposes. Many of them never intended to settle permanently elsewhere but hoped to work abroad for a time and eventually return to the old country. Repatriation rates for European immigrants averaged nearly 40 percent. Only the Jews and the Irish did not go home again in significant numbers. For some later, "new" immigrant groups, especially from the southern Danube regions, repatriation rates ran as high as 80 percent.

The song describes the wives of the Americans going to church and praying, "Send money, my husband. Send more money. The money you sent earlier I have already spent. I spent it on my lover. I spent it with pleasure. Send more money, you *cornuto fottuto* [damnable cuckold]." Those lyrics conjure an image of immigration quite different from the one General Patton urged on his Italian-American troops in 1943. Together with the figures on repatriation, they offer a strong corrective to uncritical reliance on the American-magnet explanation for the past century's European migration.

The Immigrants in America

What happened to European immigrants, and to American society, once they arrived? Much historical inquiry on this point focuses on immigrant hardship and on recurrent episodes of nativism, anti-Semitism, anti-Catholicism, and anti-foreign-radicalism, from the Know-Nothing movement of the 1850s to the American Protective Association of the late nineteenth century and the revived Ku Klux Klan of the early twentieth century, culminating in the highly restrictive immigration legislation of the 1920s. Those are important elements in the history of American immigration, and we would forget them at our peril. But getting the question right is the most challenging part of any historical investigation, and there is an analytically richer question to be asked than, why did immigrants meet sometimes nasty difficulties?

An even more intriguing question is, how did tens of millions of newcomers manage to accommodate themselves to America, and America to them, without more social disruption? How can we explain this society's relative success—and success I believe it was—in making space so rapidly for so many people?

The explanation is surely not wise social policy. Beyond minimal monitoring at the ports of entry, no public policy addressed the condition of immigrants once they were cleared off Castle Garden or Ellis Island. But three specific historical circumstances, taken together, go a long way toward composing an answer to the question.

First, somewhat surprisingly, for all their numbers, immigrants—even the 17 million who arrived from 1890 to 1914—never made up a very large component of the already enormous society that was turn-of-the-century America. The census of 1910 records the highest percentage of foreign-born people ever resident in the United States: 14.7 percent. Now, 14.7 percent is not a trivial proportion, but it is a decided minority, and relative to other societies that have received large numbers of immigrants, a small minority. The comparable figures in Australia and Canada at approximately the same time were 17 percent and more than 20 percent, and even higher in Argentina. So here is one circumstance accounting for the relative lack of social conflict surrounding immigration a century ago: at any given moment immigrants were a relatively small presence in the larger society.

A second circumstance was economic. Immigrants supplied the labor that a growing economy urgently demanded. What is more, economic growth allowed the accommodation of newcomers without forcing thorny questions of redistribution—always the occasion for social contest and upheaval. Here, as so often in American history, especially during the period of heavy immigration before the First World War, economic growth worked as a preemptive solution to potential social conflict.

The third circumstance was more complicated than sheer numbers or economic growth. I call this circumstance "pluralism"—by which I mean simply that the European immigrant stream was remarkably variegated in its cultural, religious, national, and linguistic origins. These many subcurrents also distributed themselves over an enormous geographic region—virtually the entire northeastern quadrant of the United States—and through several political jurisdictions. By the 1920s immigrants were distributed widely across the great industrial belt that stretched from New England through New York, New Jersey, Pennsylvania, and beyond: Ohio, Indiana, Illinois, Michigan, Wisconsin, and Minnesota. The states with the most immigrants, not incidentally, also had per capita incomes higher than the national average—an important fact pertinent to understanding the relationship between immigration and economic vitality.

The varied composition and broad dispersal of the immigrant stream carried certain crucial implications, one being that no immigrant group could realistically aspire to preserve its Old World culture intact for more than a few generations at best. To be sure, many groups made strenuous efforts to do just that. Legend to the contrary, last century's immigrants did not cast their Old World habits and languages overboard before their ship steamed into New York Harbor. In fact, many groups heroically exerted themselves to sustain their religions, tongues, and ways of life. The Catholic school system, which for a generation or two in some American cities educated nearly as many students as the public school system, eloquently testified to the commitment of some immigrant communities to resist assimilation. But circumstances weighed heavily against the success of such efforts. The virtual extinction of the parochial school system in the past generation—the empty schools and dilapidated parish buildings that litter the inner cores of the old immigrant cities—bears mute witness both to the ambition and to the ultimate failure of those efforts to maintain cultural distinctiveness.

A second and no less important implication of pluralism was that neither any single immigrant group nor immigrants as a whole could realistically mount any kind of effective challenge to the existing society's way of doing things. No single group had sufficient weight in any jurisdiction larger than a municipality to dictate a new political order. And there was little likelihood that Polish Jews and Italian Catholics and Orthodox Greeks could find a common language, much less common ground for political action.

To recapitulate: The most comprehensive explanation of the causes of immigration a century ago is to be found in the disruptions visited on European society by population growth and the Industrial Revolution. The United States was, to use the language of the law, the incidental beneficiary of that upheaval. The swelling immigrant neighborhoods in turn-of-the-century American cities were, in effect, byproducts of the urbanization of Europe. And once landed in America, immigrants accommodated themselves to the larger society—not always easily assimilating, but at least working out a modus vivendi—without the kinds of conflicts that have afflicted other multinational societies. That mostly peaceful process of accommodation came about because of the relatively small numbers of immigrants at any given time, because of the health of the economy, and because of the constraints on alternatives to accommodation inherent in the plural and dispersed character of the immigrant stream.

Having lit this little lamp of historical learning, I would like to carry it forward and see if it can illuminate the present.

Today's Immigration

The biggest apparent novelty in current immigration is its source, or sources. Well over half of the immigration of the past 30 years has come from just seven countries: Mexico, the Philippines, China (I am including Taiwan), Vietnam, Korea, India, and the Dominican Republic.

Not a single European country is on that list. Here, it would seem, is something new under the historical sun. Europe has dried up as a source of immigration and been replaced by new sources in Latin America and Asia.

And yet if we remember what caused the great European migration, the novelty of the current immigration stream is significantly diminished. Though particular circumstances vary, most of the countries now sending large numbers of immigrants to the United States are undergoing the same convulsive demographic and economic disruptions that made migrants out of so many nineteenth-century Europeans: population growth and the relatively early stages of their own industrial revolutions.

Mexico, by far the leading supplier of immigrants to the United States, conforms precisely to that pattern. Since the Second World War, the Mexican population has more than tripled—a rate of growth that recollects, indeed exceeds, that of nineteenth-century Europe. And as in Europe a century ago, population explosion has touched off heavy internal migration from rural to urban areas. By some reckonings, Mexico City has become the largest city in the world, with 20 million inhabitants and an in-migration from the Mexican countryside estimated at a thousand people a day.

Also since the Second World War, the Mexican economy, despite periodic problems, has grown at double the average rate of the U.S. economy. Rapid industrialization has been accompanied by the swift and widespread commercialization of Mexican agriculture. A Mexican "green revolution," flowing from improvements in mechanical processing, fertilizers, and insecticides, has in fact exacerbated the usual disruptions attendant on rapid industrialization: depopulation of the countryside, urban in-migration, and movement across the national border. But as in nineteenth-century Europe, most of the movement has been within Mexico itself. Since 1970 some five million Mexicans have entered the United States to stay; probably more than ten million have moved to Mexico City alone.

Thus we are in the presence of a familiar historical phenomenon, impelled by developments that are for all practical purposes identical to those that ignited the great European migration of a century ago.

What Does the Future Hold?

If the causes of present-day immigration are familiar, what will be the consequences for today's immigrants and tomorrow's America?

I have suggested that three historical circumstances eased the accommodation between immigrants and the American society of a century ago—the relatively small number of immigrants present at any given time, the needs and vitality of the economy, and the plural and distributed character of the immigrant stream. How do those factors weigh in an analysis of immigration today?

With respect to numbers, the historical comparison gives a basis for confidence that the answer to our original question, can we still afford to be a nation of immigrants, is yes. The U.S. Census Bureau reports that as of 1994, foreign-born people represented 8.7 percent of the American population, or just a bit more than half the proportion they made up in the census of 1910. (Comparable recent numbers for Canada and Australia, incidentally, are approximately 16 percent and 22 percent.) So, with reference to both American historical experience and contemporary experience in other countries, the relative incidence of current immigration to the United States is rather modest. Surely the United States at the end of the twentieth century is resourceful enough to deal with an immigrant inflow proportionally half what American society managed to deal with quite successfully in the early years of this century.

With reference to the needs and vitality of the economy, the historical comparison is more complicated. Economic theory suggests that immigration is a bargain for any receiving society, because it augments the labor supply, one of the three principal factors of production (along with land and capital), essentially free of cost. The sending society bears the burden of feeding and raising a worker to the age when he or she can enter the labor market. If at that point, the person emigrates and finds productive employment elsewhere, the source society has in effect subsidized the economy of the host society. That scenario essentially describes the historical American case, in which fresh supplies of immigrant labor underwrote the nation's phenomenal industrial surge in the half-century after the Civil War.

The theory is subject to many qualifications. Unskilled immigrant workers may indeed increase gross economic output, as they did from the Pittsburgh blast furnaces to the Chicago packinghouses a century ago, and as they do today in garment shops and electronic assembly plants from Los Angeles to Houston. But as productivity has become more dependent on knowledge and skill, the net value of unskilled immigrant labor has decreased, a point that informs much of the current case for restricting immigration. Yet it is important to note that argument on this point turns on the relative contribution of low-skill workers to overall output; the theory is still unimpeachable in its insistence on the absolute value of an additional worker, from whatever source, immigrant or native. Nevertheless, large numbers of unskilled immigrants may in the long run retard still higher potential outputs, because the inexpensive labor supply that they provide diminishes incentives to substitute capital and improved technology for labor, and thus inhibits productivity gains. On the other hand, just to complicate the calculation further, insofar as the host society continues to need a certain amount of low-skill work done, the availability of unskilled immigrants may increase the economy's overall efficiency by freeing significant numbers of better-educated native workers to pursue higher-productivity employment. And overhanging all this part of the immigration debate is the question of whose ox is gored. Low-skill immigrants may benefit the economy as a whole, but may at the same time impose substantial hardships on the low-skill native workers with whom they are in direct competition for jobs and wages.

Of course, the theory that immigration subsidizes the host economy is true only insofar as the immigrant in question is indeed a worker, a positive contributor to the productive apparatus of the destination society. Even the crude, American immigration-control system of the nineteenth century recognized that fact, when it barred people likely to become social dependents, such as the chronically ill or known criminals.

The issue of dependency is particularly vexatious in the United States today for two reasons. First, the 1965 legislation contained generous clauses providing for "family reunification," under the terms of which a significant portion of current immigrants are admitted not as workers but as the spouses, children, parents, and siblings of citizens or legally resident aliens. In 1993, a typical year, fewer than 20 percent of immigrants entered under "employment-based" criteria.

Because of family-reunification provisions, the current immigrant population differs from previous immigrant groups in at least two ways: it is no longer predominantly male and, even more strikingly, it is older. The percentage of immigrants over 65 exceeds the percentage of natives in that age group, and immigrants over 65 are two-and-a-half times as likely as natives to be dependent on Supplemental Security Income, the principal federal program making cash payments to the indigent elderly. Newspaper accounts suggest that some families have brought their relatives here under the family-reunification provisions in the law expressly for the purpose of gaining access to SSI. Thus it appears that the availability of welfare programs—programs that did not exist a century ago—has combined with the family-reunification provisions to create new incentives for immigration that complicate comparisons of the economics of immigration today with that in the nineteenth century.

But on balance, though today's low-skill immigrants may not contribute as weightily to the economy as did their European counterparts a hundred years ago, and though some do indeed end up dependent on public assistance, as a group they make a positive economic contribution nevertheless. It is no accident that today's immigrants are concentrated in the richest states, among them California (home to fully one-third of the country's immigrant population), just as those of the 1920s were. And just as in that earlier era, immigrants are not parasitic on the "native" economy but productive participants in it. The principal motivation for immigration remains what it was in the past: the search for productive employment. Most immigrants come in search of work, and most find it. Among working-age males, immigrant labor-force-participation rates and unemployment rates are statistically indistinguishable from those for native workers. The ancient wisdom still holds: *Ubi est pane, ibi est patria* ("Where there is bread, there is my country"). Not simply geography but also that powerful economic logic explains why Mexico is the principal contributor of immigrants to the United States today: the income gap between the United States and Mexico is the largest between any two contiguous countries in the world.

One study, by the Stanford economist Clark W. Reynolds, estimated the future labor-market characteristics and prospects for economic growth in Mexico and the United States. For Mexico to absorb all the new potential entrants into its own labor markets, Reynolds concluded, its economy would have to grow at the improbably high rate of some 7 percent a year. The United States, in contrast, if its economy is to grow at a rate of 3 percent a year, must find somewhere between 5 million and 15 million more workers than can be supplied by domestic sources. Reynolds's conclusion was obvious: Mexico and the United States need each other, the one to ease pressure on its employment markets, the other to find sufficient labor to sustain acceptable levels of economic growth. If Reynolds is right, the question with which I began, can we still afford to be a nation of immigrants, may be wrongly put. The proper question may be, can we afford not to be?

The Reconquista

But if economic necessity requires that the United States be a nation of immigrants into the indefinite future, as it has been for so much of its past, some important questions remain. Neither men nor societies live by bread alone, and present-day immigration raises historically unprecedented issues in the cultural and political realms.

Pluralism—the variety and dispersal of the immigrant stream—made it easier for millions of European immigrants to accommodate themselves to American society. Today, however, one large immigrant stream is flowing into a defined region from a single cultural, linguistic, religious, and national source: Mexico. Mexican immigration is concentrated heavily in the Southwest, particularly in the two largest and most economically and politically influential states—California and Texas. Hispanics, including Central and South Americans but predominantly Mexicans, today compose 28 percent of the population of Texas and about 31 percent of the population of California. More than a million Texans and more than three million Californians were born in Mexico. California alone holds nearly half of the Hispanic population, and well over half of the Mexican-origin population, of the entire country.

This Hispanicization of the American Southwest is sometimes called the *Reconquista*, a poetic reminder that the territory in question was, after all, incorporated into the United States in the first place by force of arms, in the Mexican War of the 1840s. There is a certain charm in this turn of the wheel of history, with its reminder that in the long term, the drama of armed conquest may be less consequential than the prosaic effects of human migration and birth rates and wage differentials. But the sobering fact is that the United States has had no experience comparable to what is now taking shape in the Southwest.

Mexican Americans will have open to them possibilities closed to previous immigrant groups. They will have sufficient coherence and critical mass in a defined region so that, if they choose, they can preserve their distinctive culture indefinitely. They could also eventually undertake to do what no previous immigrant group could have dreamed of doing: challenge the existing cultural, political, legal, commercial, and educational systems to change fundamentally not only the language but also the very institutions in which they do business. They could even precipitate a debate over a "special relationship" with Mexico that would make the controversy over the North American Free Trade Agreement look like a college bull session. In the process, Americans could be pitched into a soul-searching redefinition of fundamental ideas, such as the meaning of citizenship and national identity.

All prognostications about these possibilities are complicated by another circumstance that has no precedent in American immigration history: the region of Mexican immigrant settlement in the southwestern United States is contiguous with Mexico itself. That proximity may continuously replenish the immigrant community, sustaining its distinctiveness and encouraging its assertiveness. Alternatively, the nearness of Mexico may weaken the community's coherence and limit its political and cultural clout by chronically attenuating its members' permanence in the United States, as the accessibility of the mother country makes for a kind of perpetual repatriation process.

In any case, there is no precedent in American history for these possibilities. No previous immigrant group had the size and concentration and easy access to its original culture that the Mexican immigrant group in the Southwest has today. If we seek historical guidance, the closest example we have to hand is in the diagonally opposite corner of the North American continent, in Quebec. The possibility looms that in the next generation or so, we will see a kind of Chicano Quebec take shape in the American Southwest, as a group emerges with strong cultural cohesiveness and sufficient economic and political strength to insist on changes in the overall society's ways of organizing itself and conducting its affairs.

Public debate over immigration has already registered this prospect, however faintly. How else to explain the drive in Congress, and in several states, to make English the "official" language for conducting civil business? In previous eras no such legislative muscle was thought necessary to expedite the process of immigrant acculturation, because alternatives to eventual acculturation were simply unimaginable. Less certain now that the traditional incentives are likely to do the work of assimilation, we seem bent on trying a ukase—a ham-handed and provocative device that may prove to be the opening chapter of a script for prolonged cultural warfare. Surely our goal should be to help our newest immigrants, those from Mexico especially, to become as well integrated in the larger American society as were those European "new" immigrants whom E. A. Ross scorned but whose children's patriotism George Patton could take for granted. To reach that goal, we will have to be not only more clever than our ancestors were but also less confrontational, more generous, and more welcoming than our current anxieties sometimes incline us to be.

The present may echo the past, but will not replicate it. Yet the fact that events have moved us into *terra nova et incognita* does not mean that history is useless as a way of coming to grips with our situation. To the contrary, the only way we can know with certainty as we move along time's path that we have come to a genuinely new place is to know something of where we have been. "What's new in the starry sky, dear Argelander?" Kaiser Wilhelm I is said to have asked his state astronomer, to which Argelander replied, "And does Your Majesty already know the old?" Knowing the old is the project of historical scholarship, and only that knowledge can reliably point us toward the new. As Lincoln also said, "As our case is new, so we must think anew, and act anew. We must disenthrall ourselves, and then we shall save our country."

QUESTIONS: For Thinking and Writing

1. How does Kennedy use American history to support his argument? Is it an effective way to bolster his argument? Could history also be used to discredit his points? Explain.

2. Kennedy notes that critics lament that today's immigrants resist assimilation. He adds that past immigrant groups did exactly the same thing, but that over time, assimilation was impossible to resist. Respond to this observation with your own viewpoint. How important is assimilation?
3. What two questions does Kennedy set out to explore in his essay, and how do these questions help answer the question he poses in his title?
4. Kennedy traces historical trends to draw conclusions to support his argument. What trends does he determine drove the first wave of immigration to the United States? How is the current wave of immigration similar to or different from the first? Explain.
5. Kennedy notes that when we think of our immigrant forebears, we tend to romanticize them as noble and courageous. How do our memories of our ancestors compare to how we feel about current immigrant populations?

Anti-Immigration Rally

In the photo below, a woman wears an anti-immigration sticker on her back as she listens to a speaker at a rally on the steps of the state capitol building on April 17, 2006, in Atlanta, Georgia. About 300 people gathered to protest illegal immigration, especially in the state of Georgia, which has a rapidly growing population of illegal immigrants. Shortly afterward, Georgia Governor Sonny Perdue signed the Georgia Security and Immigration Compliance Act (SB529) into law. The organization cited at the bottom of the sticker is named for a teenage boy who was killed in a car accident by an illegal alien in Georgia.

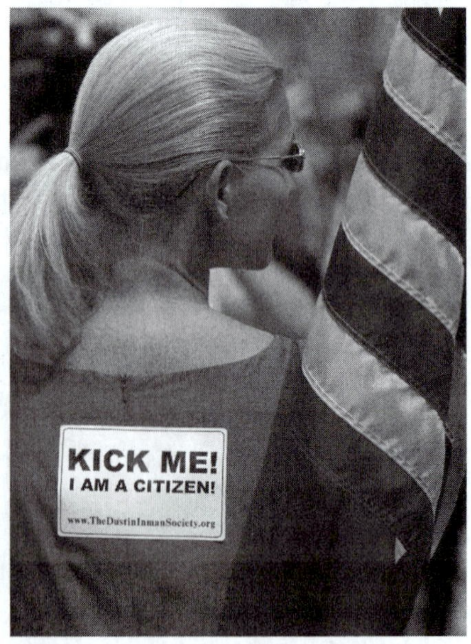

(Photo by Barry Williams/Getty Images)

QUESTIONS: For Thinking and Writing

1. What does the sticker on the woman's back mean? What sentiment is it trying to convey?
2. One objection against illegal immigration is that immigrants enjoy financial and medical benefits at the expense of U.S. taxpayers. Research this issue in greater depth.
3. Research the act Governor Purdue signed in to law, the Georgia Security and Immigration Compliance Act, online. Try the Governor's office Web site at http://www.gov.state.ga.us/press/2006/press1114.shtml. What does the law protect? What do you think of the law? Should other states adopt similar legislation? Why or why not?

TOMÁS R. JIMÉNEZ

The Next Americans

*An often-cited concern critics of immigration make is that too many foreigners threaten the American way of life and our national identity. By refusing to assimilate and demanding multicultural acceptance in government and in the classroom, immigrants are forcing Americans to be more like them, instead of the other way around. A June 2006 NBC/*Wall Street Journal *poll found the public evenly divided on the fundamental question of whether immigration helps or hurts the country, with 44 percent saying it helps and 45 percent saying it hurts the United States. Are immigrants changing America's identity? Are they likely to hurt or help America in the long run? In the next article, sociology professor Tomás R. Jiménez explains why he thinks immigrants do not destroy our national identity, they renew it. This article first appeared in the* L.A. Times *on May 27, 2007.*

Behind the outcry over the controversial immigration reform legislation making its way through the Senate lies an unsettling question for many Americans. Should the bill become a reality, an estimated 12 million unauthorized immigrants, the vast majority of whom are Latino, would become eligible for citizenship immediately, and opportunities for millions of others to follow them would be created. What effect will these permanently settled immigrants have on American identity?

Some critics of the legislation are already arguing that inviting millions of immigrants to stay permanently in the United States and become citizens will hasten the fading of a cohesive nation. They say that immigrants may become more interwoven into the fabric of the United States, but the ethnic patches to which they bind their identities will remain all too distinguishable from the rest of the American quilt.

How immigrants and their descendants see themselves will change over time, and they will simultaneously transform many aspects of what it means to be an American. This is undoubtedly an uncomfortable process, fraught with tension between newcomers and established Americans that can occasionally become explosive. But the real issue is whether the United States can provide opportunities for upward mobility so that immigrants can, in turn, fortify what is most essential to our nation's identity.

History is instructive on whether immigrants will create a messy patchwork of ethnicities in the United States. About a century ago, a tide of southern and eastern European immigrants arriving on our shores raised fears similar to those we hear today. Then, as now, Americans worried that the newcomers were destroying American identity. Many were certain that Catholic immigrants would help the pope rule the United States from Rome, and that immigrant anarchists would destroy American democracy. Some eugenicists thought that the dark-skinned immigrants from southern Europe would contaminate the American gene pool.

None of this came to pass, of course. The pope has no political say in American affairs, the United States is still a capitalist democracy, and there is nothing wrong with the American gene pool. The fact that these fears never materialized is often cited as proof that European-origin immigrants and their descendants successfully assimilated into an American societal monolith.

However, as sociologists Richard Alba and Victor Nee point out, much of the American identity as we know it today was shaped by previous waves of immigrants. For instance, they note that the Christian tradition of the Christmas tree and the leisure Sunday made their way into the American mainstream, because German immigrants and their descendants brought these traditions with them. Where religion was concerned, Protestantism was the clear marker of the nonsecular mainstream. But because of the assimilation of millions of Jews and Catholics, we today commonly refer to an American "Judeo-Christian tradition," a far more encompassing notion of American religious identity than the one envisioned in the past.

Immigrants are also redefining American identity today, though there are differences. For one, assimilation no longer exclusively means shedding all remnants of ethnicity and adopting a way of life largely identified with Anglo Protestants. For instance, it was not at all uncommon in the early twentieth century for teachers to give young immigrant pupils a stern rap across their knuckles for speaking their parents' mother tongue in school. By contrast, multiculturalism and the value of diversity are now widely adopted.

Although some see this as undercutting a cohesive United States, we nonetheless regularly celebrate, even if sometimes superficially, the various ethnic strands in our multicultural nation. Education, business, and political leaders tout the virtues of diversity, and the world of commerce affirms ethnic identity through ethnically oriented marketing aimed at selling everything from laundry detergent to *quinceañera* celebration packages at Disneyland.

These differences from the past have not—and are not—reversing the course of assimilation, even if they have given it a new tone. There are notable signs that immigrants and their children are already adopting features of American identity as their own. Consider, for instance, language, a central front in debates over assimilation. The growth of non-English-speaking immigrant populations, particularly those that speak Spanish, and the explosive rise in commercial services and media that cater to them have led commentators such as Pat Buchanan to pronounce the coming of a polyglot society. But nothing appears to be further from the truth.

Even in Los Angeles County, where 36 percent of the population is foreign-born and more than half speak a language other than English at home, English is not losing out in the long run. According to a recent study by social scientists Rubén Rumbaut, Douglas Massey, and Frank Bean, published in the *Population and Development Review*, the use of non-English languages virtually disappears among nearly all U.S.-born children of immigrants in the county. Spanish shows more staying power among the U.S.-born children and grandchildren of Mexican immigrants, which is not surprising, given that the size of the Spanish-speaking population provides near-ubiquitous access to the language. But the survival of Spanish among U.S.-born descendants of Mexican immigrants does not come at the expense of their ability to speak English and, more strikingly, English overwhelms Spanish-language use among the grandchildren of these immigrants.

An equally telling sign of how much immigrants and their children are becoming "American" is how different they have become from those in their ethnic homelands. Virtually all of today's immigrants stay connected to their countries of origin. They send money to family members who remain behind. Relatively inexpensive air, rail, and bus travel and the availability of cheap telecommunication and e-mail enable them stay in constant contact, and dual citizenship allows their political voices to be heard from abroad. These enduring ties might lead to the conclusion that continuity between here and there threatens loyalty to the Stars and Stripes.

But ask any immigrant or their children about a recent visit to their country of origin, and they are likely to tell you how American they felt. The family and friends they visit quickly recognize the prodigal children's tastes for American styles, their American accents, and their declining cultural familiarity with life in the ethnic homeland—all telltale signs that they've Americanized. As sociologist David Fitzgerald puts it, their assimilation into American society entails a good deal of "dissimilation" from the countries the immigrants left behind.

American identity is absorbing something quite significant from immigrants and being changed by them. Language, food, entertainment, and holiday traditions are palpable aspects of American culture on which immigrants today, as in the past, are leaving their mark. Our everyday lexicon is sprinkled with Spanish words. We are now just as likely to grab a burrito as a burger. Hip-hop is tinged with South Asian rhythms. And Chinese New Year and Cinco de Mayo are taking their places alongside St. Patrick's Day as widely celebrated American ethnic holidays.

But these are not the changes to American identity that matter most. At its core, American identity is a shared belief in the United States as a land of opportunity—a place where those who work hard and display individual effort realize their ambitions. Today's immigrants, including the estimated 12 million that may soon become authorized, have the potential to fortify the idea of the United States as a land of opportunity. Their willingness to risk their lives to come here, and the backbreaking work many of them do, attest to their ambition.

But their capacity to refresh what is essential to American identity depends a great deal on our ability to stay true to its essence—to be a land of opportunity. This means that we should be, above all, concerned that the rungs on the ladder of economic mobility are sturdy and closely spaced.

If we are going to take on the formidable challenge of further integrating 12 million mostly poor immigrants, we have to provide better public schools, a more affordable college education, healthcare, and jobs that offer a decent wage and benefits so that they and their children are able to rejuvenate the American dream. The real threat is not that immigrants will fail to buy into what's essential to American identity, but that we will fall short in providing them the tools to do so.

QUESTIONS: For Thinking and Writing

1. Why does the prospect of 12 million Latino immigrants becoming citizens make so many people nervous? Do you think racism is a factor? What if 12 million Danish immigrants or 12 million Italian immigrants were at issue? Do you think critics of immigration would voice the same concerns? What if the 12 million immigrants were not poor? Explain.
2. What is the "American identity" so often referred to by critics of large-scale immigration?
3. Jiménez notes that throughout American history, citizens have feared that the next wave of immigrants would change America for the worse. What really happened? Can history inform what we can expect in the future?
4. Jiménez states that "virtually all of today's immigrants stay connected to their countries of origin." Are you in contact with family members living outside the United States? If so, describe your relationship.
5. Some Americans fear that the close connections between today's immigrant populations and their countries of origin threaten their loyalty to the United States and their commitment to American culture and society. What answer does Jiménez provide to this issue? Do you agree with his argument? Why or why not? How might other authors in this section respond, such as Kennedy or Hanson?

VIEWPOINTS

A Nation Divided by One Language

James Crawford

My Spanish Standoff

Gabriella Kuntz

The question of whether the United States should have an official language is highly controversial. On one side is the fear that racism and xenophobia motivate the English-only movement. The English-only movement is particularly troubling for many Spanish-speaking areas of the country, such as California, the Southwest, and Florida. Latino opponents to the movement fear that laws forbid-

ding the use of Spanish on voting ballots, in marriage ceremonies, and in the classroom would only further violate their civil liberties. On the other side of the argument, English-only proponents insist that linguistic divisions prevent national unity, isolate ethnic groups, and reinforce the economic disparagement between the haves and the have-nots. They are quick to point out that bilingual programs in other countries such as Canada and Belgium have only led to unrest. Furthermore, they argue that laws providing bilingual education, such as in California, provide little inducement for non-English speakers to participate in mainstream American culture, preventing them from pursuing higher education and professional employment. In the first article, published in the March 8, 2001 edition of the British newspaper the Guardian, *bilingual education specialist James Crawford explains that overturning bilingual education programs has less to do with helping children and more to do with the political and cultural fears of its opponents. His essay is followed by an essay by Peru-born immigrant Gabriella Kuntz, who explains in a May 4, 2004, article appearing in* Newsweek *why she chose not to teach her children Spanish or to allow the language to be spoken in the home. In her opinion, English is the language of opportunity, power, and acceptance. Witnessing firsthand the differences between how English-speaking and Spanish-speaking people were treated, she decided to make English the only language spoken in her home, with some surprising reactions from her children.*

A Nation Divided by One Language

James Crawford

"If you live in America, you need to speak English." According to a *Los Angeles Times* poll, that was how three out of four voters explained their support for Proposition 227, the ballot initiative that dismantled bilingual education in California. Many Arizonans cited the same reason for passing a similar measure (Proposition 203) [in 2000].

Ambiguous as it is, this rationale offers some clues about the way Americans think about language. No doubt for some the statement has a patriotic subtext: one flag, one language. Rejecting bilingual education was a way to "send a message" that, in the United States, English and only English is appropriate for use in the public square.

Other voters merely seemed intent on restating the obvious. English is so dominant in the United States that non-English speakers are at a huge disadvantage. Thus schools must not fail to teach English to children from minority language backgrounds. Students' life chances will depend to a large extent on the level of English literacy skills they achieve.

Immigrants have generally understood these truths more keenly than anyone, and behaved accordingly. As the linguist Elnar Haugen observes, "America's profusion of tongues has made her a modern Babel, but a Babel in reverse."

There is no reason to think the historic pattern has changed. Although the number of minority language speakers has grown dramatically in recent years, thanks to a liberalization of immigration laws in 1965, so has their rate of acculturation. Census figures confirm the paradox. While one in seven U.S. residents now speaks a language other than English at home, bilingualism is also on the rise. A century ago the proportion of non-English speakers was nearly five times as large. As the population becomes increasingly diverse, newcomers seem to be acquiring the national language more rapidly than ever before.

The political problem is that many Americans have trouble believing all this. One conservative organization claims: "Tragically, many immigrants these days refuse to learn English! They never become productive members of society. They remain stuck in a linguistic and economic ghetto, many living off welfare and costing working Americans millions of tax dollars every year."

Such perceptions are not uncommon. Perhaps this is because Americans who came of age before the 1970s had little experience of linguistic diversity. Growing up in a period of tight immigration quotas, they seldom encountered anyone speaking a language other than English, except foreign tourists.

So today, when Spanish and Vietnamese are heard routinely in public and when bilingual government services in Tagalog and Gujarati are not unknown, some Americans conclude that the hegemony of English is threatened, and perhaps their "way of life" as well. Suddenly they are endorsing coercive measures, as suggested by the U.S. English lobby, to "defend our common language." An English-only movement based on these premises came to prominence in the eighties. Thus far it has succeeded in legislating English as the official language of 23 states, although such declarations have been primarily symbolic, with few legal effects as yet.

The campaign's ideological effects have been more significant. In particular, English-only agitation has made bilingual schooling a lightning rod for political attacks from people concerned about immigration policy, cultural change, and the expansion of minority rights. Debating the best way to teach English to children becomes a form of shadowboxing that has less to do with pedagogical issues than with questions of social status and political power.

It does not help that the pedagogical issues are so poorly understood. Monolinguals tend to regard language learning as a zero-sum game. Any use of children's mother tongue for instruction, the assumption goes, is a diversion from English acquisition. Thus assigning English learners to bilingual classrooms would seem to delay their education.

Research has shown that precisely the opposite is true. Far from a waste of learning time, native-language lessons support the process of acquiring a second language while keeping students from falling behind in other subjects.

Stephen Krashen, of the University of Southern California, has documented the "transfer" of literacy skills and academic knowledge between various languages even when alphabets differ substantially. "We learn to read by reading, by making sense of what we see on the page," Krashen explains. Thus "it will be much easier to learn to read in a language we already understand." And literacy need not be relearned as additional languages are acquired. "Once you can read, you can read."

Other studies confirm that by the time children leave well-structured bilingual programs, typically after 4 to 5 years, they are outperforming their counterparts in nonbilingual programs, and in some cases students from native-English backgrounds as well. Yet such success stories remain poorly publicized. Until recently bilingual educators have done little to explain their methods and goals, while the U.S. media have become increasingly skeptical. "If all I knew about bilingual education was what I read in the newspapers," says Krashen, "I'd vote against it, too."

Mixed messages have compounded the public relations problem. Bilingual education, which began as an effort to guarantee equal educational opportunities, is increasingly promoted as a form of multicultural enrichment. To counter the English-only mentality, advocates have coined the slogan "English Plus". They argue that the U.S. remains an underdeveloped country where language skills are concerned. In a global economy, more multilingualism, not less, would clearly advance the national interest.

Some English-speaking parents have been receptive to the "bilingual is beautiful" pitch. Over the past decade, a growing number have enrolled their children in "dual immersion" classrooms alongside minority children learning English. Yet despite excellent reports on this method of cultivating fluency in two languages, no more than 20,000 English-background students are participating. Compare that with the 300,000 Canadian anglophones in French immersion programs, in a country with one-tenth the population of the United States.

By and large, English Plus appeals primarily to language educators and ethnic leaders—that is, to those who already value bilingual skills. Other Americans remain suspicious of the "plus." Most harbor the false impression that bilingual education is primarily about maintaining Hispanic culture. Knowing a foreign language is wonderful, they say, but shouldn't English come first? The U.S. language policy debate rarely seems to get past that question.

My Spanish Standoff

Gabriella Kuntz

Once again my 17-year-old daughter comes home from a foreign-language fair at her high school and accusingly tells me about the pluses of being able to speak two languages. Speaker after speaker has extolled the virtues of becoming fluent in another language. My daughter is frustrated by the fact that I'm bilingual and have purposely declined to teach her to speak Spanish, my native tongue. She is not the only one who has wondered why my children don't speak Spanish. Over the years, friends, acquaintances, and family have asked me the same question. Teachers have asked my children. My family, of course, has been more judgmental.

I was born in Lima, Peru, and came to the United States for the first time in the early fifties, when I was 6 years old. At the parochial school my sister and I attended in Hollywood, California, there were only three Hispanic families at the time. I don't know when or how I learned English. I guess it was a matter of survival. My teacher spoke no Spanish. Neither did my classmates. All I can say is that at some point, I no longer needed to translate. When I spoke in English, I thought in English, and when I spoke in Spanish, I thought in Spanish. I also learned about peanut-butter-and-jelly sandwiches, Halloween, and Girl Scouts.

We went to a high school in Burbank. Again, there were few Hispanic students at the time. My sister and I spoke English without an "accent." This pleased my father no end. He would beam with pleasure when teachers, meeting him and my mother for the first time and hearing their labored English, would comment that they had no idea English was not our native tongue.

My brother was born in Los Angeles in 1959, and we would speak both English and Spanish to him. When he began to talk, he would point to an object and say its name in both languages. He was, in effect, a walking, talking English-Spanish dictionary. I have often wondered how his English would have turned out, but circumstances beyond our control prevented it.

Because of political changes in Peru in the early sixties (my father being a diplomat), we had to return to Peru. Although we had no formal schooling in Spanish, we were able to communicate in the language. I was thankful my parents had insisted that we speak Spanish at home. At first our relatives said that we spoke Spanish with a slight accent. But over time the accent disappeared, and we became immersed in the culture, our culture. My brother began his schooling in Peru, and even though he attended a school in which English was taught, he speaks the language with an accent. I find that ironic, because he was the one born in the United States, and my sister and I are the naturalized citizens.

In 1972 I fell in love and married an American who had been living in Peru for a number of years. Our first son was born there, but when he was 6 months old, we came back to the States. My husband was going to get his doctorate at a university in Texas.

It was in Texas that, for the first time, I lived in a community with many Hispanics in the United States. I encountered them at the grocery store, the laundry, the mall, church. I also began to see how the Anglos in the community treated them. Of course, I don't mean all, but enough to make me feel uncomfortable. Because I'm dark and have dark eyes and hair, I personally experienced that look, that unspoken and spoken word expressing prejudice. If I entered a department store, one of two things was likely to happen: Either I was ignored, or I was followed closely by the salesperson. The garments I took into the changing room were carefully counted. My check at the grocery store took more scrutiny than an Anglo's. My children were complimented on how "clean" they were instead of how cute. Somehow, all Hispanics seemed to be lumped into the category of illegal immigrants, notwithstanding that many Hispanic families have lived for generations in Texas and other Southwestern states.

To be fair, I also noticed that the Latinos lived in their own enclaves, attended their own churches, and many of them spoke English with an accent. And with their roots firmly established in the United States, their Spanish was not perfect either.

It was the fact that they spoke neither language well and the prejudice I experienced that prompted my husband and me to decide that English, and English only, would be spoken in our house. By this time my second dark-haired, dark-eyed son had been born, and we did not want to take a chance that if I spoke Spanish to them, somehow their English would be compromised. In other words, they would have an accent. I had learned to speak English without one, but I wasn't sure they would.

When our eldest daughter was born in 1980, we were living in southeast Missouri. Again, we decided on an English-only policy. If our children were going to live in the United States, then their English should be beyond reproach. Of course, by eliminating Spanish we have also eliminated part of their heritage. Am I sorry? About the culture, yes; about the language, no. In the Missouri Legislature, there are bills pending for some sort of English-only law. I recently read an article in a national magazine about the Ozarks, where some of the townspeople are concerned about the number of Hispanics who have come to work in poultry plants there. It seemed to me that their "concerns" were actually prejudice. There is a definite creeping in of anti-Hispanic sentiment in this country. Even my daughter, yes, the one who is upset over not being bilingual, admits to hearing "Hispanic jokes" said in front of her at school. You see, many don't realize, despite her looks, that she's a minority. I want to believe that her flawless English is a contributing factor.

Last summer I took my 10-year-old daughter to visit my brother, who is working in Mexico City. She picked up a few phrases and words with the facility that only the very young can. I just might teach her Spanish. You see, she is fair with light brown hair and blue eyes.

QUESTIONS: For Thinking and Writing

1. Crawford states that the argument "If you live in America, you need to speak English" offers some clues about the way Americans think about

language. What clues does he think this attitude reveals about language? Explain.

2. Besides ethnic prejudice, what other reasons does Kuntz cite supporting her decision to speak only one language to her children?
3. In what ways does Kuntz experience prejudice as it is connected to her ethnic background? Is this prejudice linked to her speaking Spanish? In light of the ways she experiences intolerance and suspicion based on her ethnic heritage, why is it ironic that she bans the Spanish language from her home?
4. What is the opinion of Kuntz's children regarding her "English-only" decision? Why does her 17-year-old daughter "accusingly" tell her mother of the benefits of speaking a second language? Why is Kuntz considering teaching her 10-year-old daughter Spanish? Explain.
5. Write an essay supporting or opposing an amendment to the U.S. Constitution making English the official language.

QUESTIONS: For Further Research and Group Work

1. Discuss what *traditional American* and *American mainstream society* mean. If you were to define these terms for a foreign visitor, what would you say? Prepare your definition individually, and then discuss this question as a group to refine and expand the definition.
2. Estimates report that between 400,000 and one million undocumented migrants try to slip across the 2,000-mile (3,200-km) U.S.-Mexico border annually. In 2005, over 1.2 million illegal immigrants were apprehended by the Border Patrol. The Border Patrol itself admits a certain impotence in the situation, estimating that they catch only about one out of every four illegal border crossers. Solutions span from opening the borders and broadening immigration quotas to building walls and deporting entire families. As a group, discuss border issues. Should the United States build a wall? Should immigration laws be relaxed? Who decides?
3. Interview several people who either immigrated to the United States or are in the country as legal residents (with student visas, etc.). Ask them to discuss their experience in the United States as a foreigner coming to live in this country. Were they welcomed? Did they find a community to support them?
4. At the end of his essay, Jiménez provides a list of things the United States must do if it is to successfully integrate its 12 million illegal, mostly poor immigrants. Discuss this list as a group, and evaluate how it would be implemented. What are the economic and social costs of implementing such a list? Is it easy to say, but hard to do? Is the list

missing anything you think is important? After you discuss the issue with your group, write an essay on your conclusions and concerns.

5. An argument in favor of bilingual education is that mother-tongue instruction increases cultural and ethnic pride in the heritage of the mother country, so immigrant children are allowed to take pride in their home culture, while learning in their native tongue. Research this issue further online and present your view. What are the pros and cons of preserving mother-tongues? Explain.

photo credits

p. 36: National Eating Disorders Association, www.NationalEatingDisorders.org, 1-800-931-2237

p. 99, top: The Advertising Archives

p. 99, bottom: The Advertising Archives

p. 100, top: The Advertising Archives

p. 100, bottom: Girl Scouts of America

p. 136: The Quad City Times

p. 169: Center for SCREEN-TIME Awareness

p. 199: Richard Primack (2)

p. 219: © The New Yorker Collection 2002 David Sipress from cartoonbank.com. All Rights Reserved.

p. 266: Brian Farrigton/Cagle Cartoons

p. 317: Courtesy of DeVito/Verdi and the ACLU

p. 354: Barry Williams/Getty Images

credits

The American Academy of Pediatrics. "AAP Discourages Television for Very Young Children," from AAP press release, August 2, 1999. Fair use reprint.

Lyz Baranowski. "Girls, We Really Are Our Own Worst Enemies," from *The Gustavian Weekly*, May 2, 2003. Reprinted with the permission of the author.

David Brooks. "The Year of Domesticity," from the *New York Times*, January 1, 2006. Reprinted with permission.

David Brooks. "People Like Us," From the *Atlantic Monthly*, September 2003. Reprinted with permission of the author.

Margaret A. Somerville. "The Case Against Same-Sex Marriage." Excerpt from *A Brief Submitted* to *The Standing Committee on Justice and Human Rights*, April 29, 2003. Reprinted by permission of the author.

Steve Chapman. "The Racial Profiling Myth Lives On," from *Reason Online*, May 7, 2007. Reprinted by permission.

John Cloud. "Never Too Buff" *TIME* Magazine, April 24, 2000. Copyright © TIME Inc. Reprinted by permission.

Stephanie Coontz. "For Better, For Worse," The *Washington Post*, May 1, 2005. Reprinted with permission of the author.

James Crawford. "A Nation Divided By One Language," from *The Guardian*, March 8, 2001. Reprinted by permission of the author.

Betty G. Farrell. "Family: Idea, Institution, and Controversy." Reprinted by permission of Westview Press, a member of Perseus Books Group.

Garance Franke-Ruta, "The Natural Beauty Myth," *The Wall Street Journal*, December 15, 2006. Copyright © *The Wall Street Journal*. Reprinted with permission.

Ellen Goodman. "No Change in Political Climate." Copyright © 2007, The Washington Post Writers Group. Reprinted with Permission.

Al Gore. "Global Warming is an Immediate Crisis." This was presented in a speech to the New York University School of Law on September 18, 2006. Reprinted with permission.

Victor Davis Hanson. "Do We Want Mexifornia?" from *City Journal*, Spring 2002. Reprinted by permission.

Jeffrey Hart. "How to Get a College Education," from The National Review, September 29, 1996. Copyright © 1996 by National Review, Inc, 215 Lexington Avenue, New York, NY 10016, Reprinted by permission.

Heather Havrilesky. "Three Cheers for Reality TV," *Salon* magazine, September 13, 2004. This article first appeared in Salon.com, at http://www.salon.com. An online version remains in the Salon archives. Reprinted with permission.

Linda Hirshman. "Homeward Bound," from *The American Prospect*, Volume 16, Number 12: November 21, 2005. The American Prospect, 2000 L Street NW, Suite 171, Washington, DC 20036. All rights reserved. Reprinted with permission from the author.

Niranjana Iyer, "Weight of the World," *Smithsonian Magazine*, August 2006. Reprinted with permission of the author.

Allen Jenkins, "Inequality, Race and Remedy," from *The American Prospect*, Volume 18, Number 5: May 4, 2007. The American Prospect, 2000 L Street NW, Suite 717, Washington, DC 20036. All rights reserved Reprinted with permission.

Tomas R. Jimenez. "The Next Americans," the *Los Angeles Times*, May 27, 2007. Reprinted with permission of the author.

Lindsay Johns. "In Search of Notorious PhDs," from *New Black Magazine*, Spring 2007. Reprinted with permission of the author.

Liz Jones. "What I Think of the Fashion World," You Magazine, April 15, 2001. Copyright © You Magazine. Reprinted with permission.

Madeleine Begun Kane. "My Most Attractive Adversary," *PopPolitics*, December 2000. Reprinted with permission of the author.

Jason Kelly. "The Great TV Debate." Originally appeared in *PopPolitics*, December 5, 2001. Reprinted by permission of the author.

David M. Kennedy. "Can We Still Afford to Be a Nation of Immigrants?" from *The Atlantic Monthly*, November 1996. Reprinted with permission from the author.

Gabriella Kuntz. "My Spanish Standoff," from *Newsweek*, May 4, 1998. Reprinted by permission.

Charles R. Lawrence III. "Regulating Racist Speech on Campus," from

The Chronicle of Higher Education, October 25, 1989. Reprinted with permission of the author.

Catherine Lawson. "Why Do We Get to Laugh at Fat Guys?" Copyright © 2007. Reprinted with permission of the author.

Richard S. Lindzen. "Don't Believe the Hype," *The Wall Street Journal*, July 2, 2006. Reprinted with permission of the author.

Jordan Lite. "Please Ask 'Who,' Not 'What' I Am," from *Newsweek*, July 16, 2001. Copyright © 2001 Newsweek, Inc. All rights reserved. Reprinted by permission.

William Lutz. "With These Words I Can Sell You Anything," from *Doublespeak* by William Lutz. Copyright © 1989 by Blond Bear, Inc. Reprinted by permission of the author.

Scott McKeen. "Slimming Couture," the *Edmonton Journal*, December 9, 1999. Copyright © 1999 the *Edmonton Journal*. Reprinted with permission.

John H. McWhorter. "Who Should Get into College?" from *City Journal*, Spring 2003. Reprinted with permission.

Charles Murray. "What's Wrong With Vocational School?" from *The Wall Street Journal*, January 17, 2007. Reprinted with permission of the author.

Andrew O'Hehir. "The Myth of Media Violence," March 17, 2005. This article first appeared in Salon.com, at http://www.salon. com. An online version remains in the Salon archives. Reprinted with permission.

Charles O'Neill. "The Language of Advertising." Reprinted by permission of the author.

Peggy Orenstein. "What's Wrong With Cinderella," the *New York Times Magazine*, December 24, 2006. Reprinted with permission of the author.

Pew Research Center for the People and the Press. "Global Warming: A Divide on Causes and Solutions," released on January 24, 2007.

David Popenoe & Barbara Dafoe Whitehead, "The Cultural Devaluation of Child-Rearing," excerpted from the essay "Life Without Children," 2006, The National Marriage Project, © 2006, Rutgers, The State University of New Jersey. Reprinted by permission.

Dennis Prager. "On Comparing Global Warming Denial to Holocaust Denial," from Townhall.com, February 19, 2007. Reprinted with permission.

Eugene Robinson. "You Have the Right to Remain a Target of Racial Profiling," from the *Seattle Times*, May 1, 2007. Reprinted by permission.

Gregory Rodriguez. "Forging a New Melting Pot," from the *New*

York Times, February 11, 2001. Reprinted by permission.

Douglas Rushkoff, "Which One of These Sneakers is Me?" the *London Times*, April 30, 2000. Reprinted with permission of the author.

Robert J. Samuelson. "Shop 'til We Drop?" *The Wilson Quarterly*, Winter 2004. Copyright © The Wilson Quarterly. Reprinted with permission of the author.

Jane Rosenzweig. "Can Television Improve Us?" The American Prospect, Volume 10, Number 45: July 01, 1999. *The American Prospect*, 2000 L Street NW, Suite 717, Washington, DC 20036. Reprinted with permission, all rights reserved.

Scott Russell Sanders. "The Men We Carry in Our Minds," Copyright © 1984 by Scott Russell Sanders; *Milkweed Chronicle*; from *The Paradise of Bombs*. Reprinted by permission of the author and the author's agents, the Virginia Kidd Agency, Inc.

Alicia C. Shepard. "A's for Everyone!" from *The Washington Post*, June 5, 2005. Copyright © 2005, The Washington Post Writers Group. Reprinted with permission.

Harvey A. Silvergate and Joshua Gewolb. "Muzzling Free Speech," from the September 30, 2002 edition of *The National Law Journal*. © 2002 ALM Properties, Inc. All rights reserved.

Andrew Sullivan. "Why the 'M' Word Matters to Me." *TIME* Magazine, February 8, 2004. Reprinted by permission of the author.

Don Terry. "Getting Under My Skin," from the *New York Times*, July 16, 2000. Copyright © The New York Times, Inc. Reprinted by permission.

James B. Twitchell. "Lux Populi," *The Wilson Quarterly*, Winter 2007. Reprinted with permission of the author.

Alisa Valdes. "My Hips, My Caderas," from the *Los Angeles Times*, April 24, 2000. Copyright © 2000. Reprinted by permission of Tribune Media Services Reprints.

James Q. Wilson. "The Decline of Marriage," from "Why We Don't Marry," which originally appeared in The *City Journal*, Winter 2002. Copyright © 2002, The City Journal. Reprinted with permission.

index

Additional Titles of Interest

Note to Instructors: Any of these Penguin-Putnam, Inc., titles can be packaged with this book at a special discount. Contact your local Allyn & Bacon/Longman sales representative for details on how to create a Penguin-Putnam, Inc., Value Package.

Allison, *Bastard Out of Carolina*

Alvarez, *How the Garcia Girls Lost Their Accents*

Augustine, *The Confessions of St. Augustine*

Austen, *Persuasion*

Austen, *Pride and Prejudice*

Austen, *Sense and Sensibility*

Bloom, *Shakespeare: The Invention of the Human*

C. Brontë, *Jane Eyre*

E. Brontë, *Wuthering Heights*

Burke, *Reflections on the Revolution in France*

Cather, *My Ántonia*

Cather, *O Pioneers!*

Cellini, *The Autobiography of Benvenuto Cellini*

Chapman, *Black Voices*

Chesnutt, *The Marrow of Tradition*

Chopin, *The Awakening and Selected Stories*

Conrad, *Heart of Darkness*

Conrad, *Nostromo*

Coraghessan-Boyle, *The Tortilla Curtain*

Defoe, *Robinson Crusoe*

Descartes, *Discourse on Method and The Meditations*

Descartes, *Meditations and Other Metaphysical Writings*

de Tocqueville, *Democracy in America*

Dickens, *Hard Times*

Douglass, *Narrative of the Life of Frederick Douglass*

Dubois, *The Souls of Black Folk*

Equiano, *The Interesting Narrative and Other Writings*

Gore, *Earth in the Balance*

Grossman, *Electronic Republic*

Hawthorne, *The Scarlet Letter*

Hutner, *Immigrant Voices*

Jacobs, *Incidents in the Life of a Slave Girl*

Jen, *Typical American*

M. L. King Jr., *Why We Can't Wait*

Lewis, *Babbitt*

Machiavelli, *The Prince*

Marx, *The Communist Manifesto*

Mill, *On Liberty*

More, *Utopia and Other Essential Writings*

Orwell, *1984*

Paine, *Common Sense*

Plato, *The Republic*

Postman, *Amusing Ourselves to Death*

Rose, *Lives on the Boundary*

Rossiter, *The Federalist Papers*

Rousseau, *The Social Contract*

Shelley, *Frankenstein*

Sinclair, *The Jungle*

Steinbeck, *Of Mice and Men*

Stevenson, *The Strange Case of Dr. Jekyll and Mr. Hyde*

Stoker, *Dracula*

Stowe, *Uncle Tom's Cabin*

Swift, *Gulliver's Travels*

Taulbert, *Once Upon a Time When We Were Colored*

Thoreau, *Walden*

Truth, *The Narrative of Sojourner Truth*

Woolf, *Jacob's Room*

Zola, *Germinal*